Only a Miner

Only a Miner

STUDIES IN RECORDED COAL-MINING SONGS

Archie Green

UNIVERSITY OF ILLINOIS PRESS

Urbana   Chicago   London

To my father
Samuel
for whom the skills of hand and head are one

Acknowledgments

IN GATHERING material for this work, I have incurred the favor of many people — folksingers, singers of folksong, sound-recording company officials, radio- and television-station employees, newspapermen, disc and book collectors, teachers, librarians, archivists, historians, folklorists. Wherever possible I have named those who offered tangible help in chapter texts, notes, checklists, and appendices. However, I am aware that such identification is hardly adequate thanks for all the friends who have shared my interest and excitement in recorded folksong during the past two decades.

Aside from specific aid in obtaining data, a number of persons assisted me in the myriad details involved in readying a book for publication. My wife Louanne typed it initially; in the process we enjoyed talking about many points in regard to both content and style. Jo Ann Hansens of Champaign, Illinois, as well as Anice Duncan and others in the clerical office of the Institute of Labor and Industrial Relations, University of Illinois, typed innumerable "second" drafts. Judith McCulloh transcribed the music.

During past years, early versions of various chapters have circulated among colleagues with whom I have shared the experience of establishing the John Edwards Memorial Foundation at the University of California, Los Angeles. Such friends have not only criticized my work but also have encouraged its completion.

ix

Finally, Lisa Feldman critically read the entire manuscript and helped sharpen the presentation of ideas in this study. While this book was in production I enjoyed working with Elizabeth Dulany and Larry Slanker at the University of Illinois Press.

In addition, my thanks are extended to the following firms for permission to use copyrighted material. Of the nearly three dozen songs and poems included in this work, ten are currently covered by active copyrights.

1. "Only a Miner" by the Kentucky Thorobreds is transcribed from Paramount 3071. It was copyrighted in 1928 by the Chicago Music Publishing Company, Chicago, and renewed in 1956 by John Steiner of the New York Recording Laboratories, Chicago. Used by permission of John Steiner.

2. "Hard-Working Miner" collected from Mary Carr is reprinted from Harvey H. Fuson's *Ballads of the Kentucky Highlands,* copyrighted 1931 by the author. Used by permission of the Mitre Press, London.

3. "Don't Go Down in the Mine, Dad" by Robert Donnelly and Will Geddes is reprinted from original sheet music. It was copyrighted in 1910 by the Lawrence Wright Music Company, London. Used by permission.

4. "The Dream of the Miner's Child" by Andrew Jenkins and Irene Spain is transcribed from Okeh 40498. It was copyrighted in 1925 by P. C. Brockman, Atlanta, and in 1926 by Shapiro, Bernstein & Company, New York. U.S.A. copyright renewed in 1953 and assigned to Shapiro, Bernstein & Company. Used by permission.

5. "Explosion in the Fairmount Mines" by Alfred Reed is transcribed from Victor 21191. It was copyrighted in 1928 by Ralph S. Peer, New York, and renewed in 1955 by Peer International Corporation, New York. Used by permission.

6. "Roll Down the Line" by the Allen Brothers is transcribed from Victor 23551. It was copyrighted in 1931 by the Southern Music Publishing Company, New York, and renewed in 1958 by Peer International Corporation, New York. Used by permission.

7-9. "Dark as a Dungeon," "Sixteen Tons," and "Nine Pound Hammer" by Merle Travis are transcribed from Capitol 48000 and 48001. These songs were copyrighted by American Music, Hollywood, effective 1947. Copyrights transferred in 1968 to Rumbalero Music, New York. Used by permission.

10. "Coal Miner's Blues" by the Carter Family is transcribed from Decca 5596. It was copyrighted in 1938 by the United Publishing Company, New York, and renewed in 1965 by Peer International Corporation, New York. Used by permission.

A Note on the Music

FOR EACH SONG I have transcribed one stanza which seems to me to be reasonably representative of the whole. Variants from the other stanzas are keyed to the transcription by means of lower-case letters above the staff. The three items by Merle Travis ("Dark as a Dungeon," "Nine Pound Hammer," "Sixteen Tons") are so inventive they would certainly repay full, more detailed transcription and study; here I have arbitrarily focused on alternate readings at the first and midway stresses in the measure. In addition to the standard notational devices I have used the following:

↑ ↓   A small arrow pointing upward (or downward) above a note means that the pitch is sung slightly higher (or lower) than written, a quarter tone or less.

A straight line between two note heads indicates a glide from one pitch to the next; the time value of the glide is to be subtracted from that of the first note.

A short diagonal line to (or from) a note head reflects a sliding or scooped attack (or release); its time value is to be subtracted from that of the preceding note or rest.

My thanks go to the library staff at Cecil Sharp House, London, who generously allowed me use of their facilities to complete these transcriptions.

Judith McCulloh

A Note on Sources

THIS WORK is intended as a statement on sound recordings as cultural documents and communicative devices, and is restricted to case studies of a handful of songs which appeared on discs issued between 1925 and 1970 in the United States. These songs portray American coal-mining life and reveal miners' values. This subject limitation permits the presentation of findings within two frames: the study of interaction among sophisticated, popular, and folk societies; the problem of defining and bounding industrial folklore. To the extent of my skills, I shall draw on at least three formal areas within humanistic disciplines: ballad scholarship, labor history, popular-culture studies.

My bibliography is restricted to printed material cited in text, footnotes, checklists, or appendices. For a few items the definition of "print" is stretched to include unpublished theses in libraries, manuscripts in accessible collections, and ephemeral data wherever found. Individual songs which are found in print but not in the context of books or articles are cited only in the checklists and not in the bibliography itself. Following the bibliography is a list of interviews, all in my possession.

This work does not include a full discography of coal-mining songs.[1] Rather, recorded material is itemized in eight detailed checklists of songs, which follow the separate case studies (Chapters 3-10). These checklists are not restricted to aural forms, but also include printed and manuscript data. Commercial and archival as well as public and private material is integrated without distinction in the checklists. The arrangement is chronological by publication or recording date for songs cited. However, when a text or tune is transcribed from a field recording, when a text or tune is reprinted in an anthology, or when a printed or recorded song is reissued (or re-presented by an interpreter) on an LP, all such secondary forms are grouped under the initial dated entry. At times, the distinction between "interpretation" and "original" is arbitrary.

Sample entries are presented at this point as guides to the checklist formats.

Visual Material

BOOK   "Song title." Singer, place of collecting, date of collecting (source or date of song if stated). Author's last name, *initials of book title* (date), page, m if music transcribed.

JOURNAL   Same as above, substituting *initials of academic journal* and volume number for book title. (Other journal titles are presented in full.)

SONGBOOK or SONG FOLIO   "Song title." *Name of book,* compiler or editor, publisher, place (date), page, m if music transcribed. Other data.

BROADSIDE OR NEWSPAPER   "Song title." Singer or author, printer or periodical title, place (date). Other data.

MANUSCRIPT IN ARCHIVAL COLLECTION   "Song title." Singer or contributor, place of collecting or residence, date of collecting or correspondence (source or date of song if stated). Collector, format of item, archive or location, catalog or control number.

SHEET MUSIC   "Song title." Composer's name for either lyrics or music or both, publisher, place (copyright date). Pictorial data.

LEAD SHEET IN COPYRIGHT OFFICE   Same as above with substitution of registration and renewal numbers for pictorial data.

Aural Material

FIELD RECORDING, DISC, OR TAPE   "Song title." Singer, place
of collecting, date (source of song if stated). Collector, archive
or location, catalog or control number. If such an item is issued
for public sale, LP entry added.

DISC, 78 RPM or 45 RPM   "Song title." Singer, label and number
(master number). Recording date, place; release date if substantially separated from recording date. Other data.

LP   Same as above with *LP title* inserted after singer's name.

---

1. Mining-song titles other than those treated in this book can be found in:
Archie Green, "A Discography of American Coal Miners' Songs," *Labor
History*, II (1961), 101; Edwin C. Kirkland, "A Check List of the Titles of
Tennessee Folk Songs," *Journal of American Folklore*, LIX (1946), 423;
Library of Congress, Music Division, *Checklist of Recorded Songs in the
English Language in the Archive of American Folksong to July, 1940* (Wash-
ington, 1942); Bruce Rosenberg, *The Folksongs of Virginia: A Checklist*
(Charlottesville, 1969).

Contents

Only a Miner

WORK TRIP

Folksong and Folk Society 1

OUR HALLOWED flag salute proclaims one nation indivisible, and campaign orators link Maine's rocky coast to California's sunny shore, but zealous rhetoric neither establishes a national community nor delineates its tradition. We are truly a sovereignty but one of many peoples, regions, callings, and values. This diversity, present at the time of earliest colonization, flowed from separate cultures carried to the New World as well as from the brooding space and fantastic loneliness found in Eden. As the United States grew, at least three strands of tradition emerged, at times intertwining but mainly coexisting.

These three, which were all to some degree imposed upon existing American Indian tribal life, are difficult to name. One denominative approach is that of dividing the literary-anthropological term *folklore:* (1) folklore — expressive forms, wisdom, conduct, and implements which are found in enclaved groups within large society; (2) poplore — knowledge, actions, and manners which are conveyed by and accepted from such institutions as commercial entertainment and advertising; (3) patriotic lore — values, legends, and practices, frequently formal and sophisticated, which are sanctioned by government or are semi-mythical and related to culture religion.

It was more than two centuries after Jamestown and Plymouth Rock before collectors reached wide audiences with accounts of characteristic native folklore: Negro spirituals, cowboy songs, northern woods ballads, southern highland tales, frontier humor. When an initial corpus was at hand and a number of genres explored, scholars began to describe objectively the specific groups in which the material was found. Eventually, the folk shared equal attention with the lore. This exploration focused attention on the troubling problem of whether the American folk was a chaotic aggregation of separate peoples or perhaps a unified collectivity. In short, do we perceive the word *folk* as a plural or singular expression today?

In recent years some students have shifted their definitions of the folk from the classic notion of a peasantry — agrarian, semi-literate, hand-skilled — to a relativistic formulation of any unit of two or more persons who produce folklore. This latter fluid definition permits anyone within the total population to don the folk mantle who can find a like-minded companion with whom to swap a joke. Regardless of whether the folk is perceived in classical or contemporary terms, the United States never had and still lacks an indivisible folk. Rather, we are Mormons, Cajuns, mountaineers, sailors, Wobblies, and their cousins by the dozens. We cluster in ethnic, linguistic, geographic, ideational, and occupational groups which to some degree are self-enclaved, inward-looking, continuous, and stable. Such factors enable members of modern society to maintain an identity which is at the same time national and also local or parochial.

To illustrate: Juan Villa, an individual, may label himself as an American, a Latin, a Mexican-American, a Chicano, a Texan, a Catholic, a Democrat, a ranch-hand, a catskinner (tractor driver), a leather craftsman, a corrido singer. The network of associations and activities to which he belongs and by which he lives is unique for Juan Villa, and his many groups are not mutually exclusive. In which group is Juan folk? From which does he draw lore? To which does he contribute lore? Only when one feels the hyphenation or pluralism built into almost every American personality can he begin to cope with the life-style and expressive forms of any particular group. Only by knowing that an individual coal

4

miner may also be Slavic / trade unionist / Pennsylvanian / faith healer, or some or none of these, can one select for examination a mining song from other devices and patterns which compose the network of a single miner's tradition.

Since I am isolating a handful of recorded mining songs for study, it is proper to offer a few introductory definitions of folksong, folk society, and industrial folklore. A threefold paradigm useful in classificatory study is: song, singer, style. A listener can pull any recorded song from a supermarket rack or from an archive shelf and respond to it without being stimulated intellectually. But if one is impelled to place an item in any context beyond pleasure alone, he should start with these queries: What type of song — tribal, folk, pop, art — is at hand? Who sings it? What determines the singer's performing style? It is helpful in any categorization of folk music to view the bins — tribal, folk, pop, art — along an array rather than at unreachable distances from each other.

Admittedly, the problem in folksong definition is thorny, but a core meaning used by some scholars is: a piece received aurally by listeners and singers which is accepted by them and which is also altered in the process of movement over time. Some qualify the place of transmission (folk society) and some add that the song must be performed in a given (folk) style. Such qualifications usually equate the terms *folk* and *traditional* and end with the redundancy: A folksong is a traditional song.

Folklore specialists and enthusiasts alike have long used the word *tradition* in at least three senses: (1) oral transmission as process —"the tale handed down by popular tradition"; (2) a body of forms and behavior that is customary or continuous — "the traditions of a people"; (3) a meliorative standard — "she was more traditional than her sister." When folklorists invoke this tripartite tag to identify "Jack and the Beanstalk" as an international popular tale, or to assert that using firecrackers on the fourth of July is a folkway, or to select a harsh vocal style as a criterion of "authenticity," they illustrate their wide treatment of a vital term. My definition of folksong is keyed to process in its stress on tradition as movement and concomitant variation. Of course, it is devoid of normative standards. A folksong is not better per se than any other literary or musical mate; it has no esoteric virtue.

5

It is relatively easy to compare folksongs having life in tradition with those of no such vitality. Sarah Ogan Gunning, the daughter, sister, and wife of Kentucky coal miners, is a fine exponent of Appalachian folk style. In her repertoire she numbers hundreds of traditional pieces ranging from "The House Carpenter" to "Davy Crockett"; she also composed polemical songs in the nadir of the Big Depression. Although her mining pieces of the 1930's are based on folksong models in structure and rhetoric, and although they are sung in mountain style, I do not choose to label "I Hate the Company Bosses" or "Down on the Picket Line" as folksongs. My definition may be unduly restrictive or irrelevant to social history, but it offers one path into the area of classifying industrial material. Fortunately, an LP of Mrs. Gunning's traditional and topical songs, *Girl of Constant Sorrow* (Folk-Legacy FSA 26), is available for each reader-listener to pursue the problem of definition and classification.

Another example may reveal that the testing process is neither mysterious nor beyond reason. In 1940 two songs were collected from West Virginia miner-composer Orville Jenks, and published by George Korson in *Coal Dust on the Fiddle*. "The Dying Mine Brakeman" is an elegiac ballad for a companion killed in a McDowell County mine accident; "John L. Lewis Blues" is an ode-like piece in blues form. Jenks's ballad entered tradition after it was composed in 1915. It was found in the field by Library of Congress collectors, and had been recorded commercially — once in 1938 under the title "Reckless Motorman" by the Carter Family (Decca 5722), and in 1930 as "The Dying Brakeman" by Jess Johnson (Champion 16255). There is no evidence that the blues piece moved away from its composer Jenks; hence, I state that "John L. Lewis Blues" is not a folksong. It is ruled out neither for political nor esthetic reasons, nor because of title, content, and theme. "John L. Lewis Blues" is not made uninteresting or unimportant because it is outside the folksong canon. The question of why it did not enter tradition is still intriguing, and the study of process is as meaningful as that of status.

After a working definition of folksong is accepted one may ask: Can an industrial song become a folksong? Does not industry connote urban, mass, and technological life — the antithesis of folk-

6

SARAH OGAN GUNNING

life, of earth magic? This has been the precise posture of many British and American antiquarians who have oriented themselves to country life. Their work consisted mainly in rescuing rural lore from the destructive onslaught of the Industrial Revolution or in cataloging it in order to distinguish (good, old) material to be retained from that to be laid aside. The reasons for the choice are complex and may perhaps be found in an ideology of primitivist romanticism, an inability to cope with grime or noise, or just a warm feeling for peasants and mountaineers, linked with a concomitant distrust of their factory progeny.

While some scholars viewed the machine as a monster destroying both sylvan beauty and humanistic culture, the rural folk itself

7

could not view mechanization's thrust in detached intellectual terms. The process may have been brutal but peasants became factory workers. The lash of poverty, coupled with a revolution in farm technology, was the driving force in the climb from worn fields, tenantry, serfdom, sharecropping, and rural unemployment to mill gate or mine mouth. Mountain boys did exchange squirrel rifles for picks and shovels; farm lads did become gandydancers, lintheads, and slatepickers. We know, retrospectively, that much rural lore was lost during the transition but that some was retained or altered.

As early as 1705, a teacher in Germany, Friedrich Friese, began to collect artisans' customs and usages. His example as well as his treatise on twenty trades led others to continuous collecting from German guildsmen and workers. At the opening of the twentieth century, Adolph Strack pointed out specifically that folklore was found in all strata of society, not exclusively among the peasantry. It took three decades for many American folklorists to accept this notion, although songs of cowboys as well as shantymen (maritime) and shantyboys (lumbering) were not overlooked in pioneer collections. It can be generalized that cowboys and clipper-ship sailors were viewed more romantically than miners or steel-mill men, and that early collectors found it extremely difficult to cope with trade-union or radical material when it came to hand. Nevertheless, a significant corpus of work-oriented folklore was gathered in the United States which reflected the three-century task of spanning and filling a continent. Some of the men and women who published books or articles rich in work lore are: Phillips Barry, Mody Boatright, Ben Botkin, Norman Cohen, Joanna Colcord, William Doerflinger, Josh Dunson, Duncan Emrich, Jacob Evanson, Joe Glazer, Roland Gray, John Greenway, Wayland Hand, Freeman Hubbard, Edward Ives, Joyce Kornbluh, George Korson, Alan Lomax, John Lomax, George Milburn, Franz Rickaby. Their findings were paralleled in Canada by Edith Fowke, in England by A. L. Lloyd, in Germany by Gerhard Heilfurth, and in eastern Europe by a host of Marxists concerned with worker and partisan songs.

A core definition emerges from the findings of all these scholars: An industrial folksong describes work itself and portrays the life, diversions, and struggles of men on the job. This extends the

8

meaning of craft lore — basketry, weaving, pottery, wood-carving — to modern industry, which is massive, mechanized, automated, computerized. There is an observable blurring and overlap in the terms *industrial, occupational, labor,* or *worker* when combined with *folklore*. Examples of industrial lore are found at one end of the spectrum in manual crafts, usually studied by folklife specialists. At the other end, examples are found in trade unionism and organized political movements which range from social democracy to nihilism. Hence *industrial lore* may be an umbrella term broad enough to cover all job processes as well as urban living, unionism, radicalism, social reform, civil disobedience, and political action. However, I have found it useful to restrict the term to modern industry, and to employ the narrower tag *labor lore* for specific items denoting trade-union activity, personality, or value. Further, I assume that movements or associations do not compose literary works communally, but rather that gifted individuals within such groups compose hortatory or polemical songs, some of which, in turn, enter tradition.

It is not especially difficult to distinguish a labor piece from a general industrial song; it is sometimes difficult to see why every song about a worker is not an industrial item. The difference can be shown by contrasting the musical sagas of two West Virginians. One, John Hardy, who worked for the Shawnee Coal Company, murdered a fellow coal digger and was executed in 1894. Whatever evil spirit drove him to kill was not the genie in the miner's lamp. His haunting song is a bad-man ballad — a narrative of murder. It reveals nothing of a miner's relationship to his work environment. On the other hand, John Henry, the steel driver and hard-rock driller in the Big Bend Tunnel, completed in 1872, may not have lived in flesh and blood, but he is alive in spirit as a giant symbol of the worker in conflict with the machine. Although the steam drill killed him, John Henry endured in song. His adventure is the most widely loved industrial ballad in the United States. All who work want something of his magic to ease the pain of blasting, drilling, loading, lifting. John Henry has lived for nearly a century because our country is still under construction; his songs and stories mirror our growth.

The most detailed view of American industrial folklore comes from the collected findings of George Gershon Korson, and the best way to test formal definition or conceptual model against a body of work-centered tradition is to know Korson's books and articles. They are either in print or readily found in libraries; also available are two splendid records of anthracite and bituminous miners' songs which he edited for the Library of Congress. When *Minstrels of the Mine Patch* was reissued in 1964, I wrote a foreword which summarized the facts of Korson's life, and offered an appreciation of his role in opening a new seam in Americana — industrial folklore. John Greenway wrote a parallel foreword for the reprinted *Coal Dust on the Fiddle* which stressed Korson's magnificent collecting role against a backdrop of the coal industry's mechanization and decline. After Korson's death on May 23, 1967, Greenway penned a tribute for his friend in the *Journal of American Folklore* that matched in warmth the kinds of obituaries Korson himself had prepared for his beloved miner friends when he was a young reporter in Pennsylvania's hard-coal region.[1]

When Korson was sixty-six years of age, he donated his forty-year collection of manuscripts, correspondence, books, and field recordings to King's College in Wilkes-Barre, Pennsylvania, the "home town" where he sold newspapers as a lad, met young colliers in the Boys Industrial Association, and entered life-work as a cub reporter on the *Record*. On April 4, 1970, the Pennsylvania Folklore Society held a special commemorative meeting at the college during which Wayland Hand from the University of California spoke on the strength of Korson's work as well as his inspiration to others. The measure of Korson's importance to folklorists beyond the United States was stated in a message from Gerhard Heilfurth, author of *Das Bergmannslied,* an exemplary analysis of German mining song.[2] Professor Heilfurth joined Hand in stressing the crucial importance of Korson's findings, in that he had collected at a time when American mining was changing from primitive hand production to semi-automated mechanization — the change process frequently labeled basic to civilization.[3]

In the past decade I have written a number of articles and record notes on the traditions of working people (cited in the bibliography) in which my esteem is expressed for George Korson as a friend and as a folklorist. In many visits with him he expressed the

GEORGE KORSON AT HOME

hope that my research might carry on his work. To the extent that this study selects coal songs as subjects, it is in his field; to the extent that it focuses on sound recordings, I enter an area he did not touch. Korson made his living as a newspaperman and an editor. He sought no higher praise than that of any working journalist proud of his craft; he was pleased when a reader told him that a story was warm or well written. Better yet, he was utterly delighted to receive a song, tale, or yarn from a correspondent. Korson was self-educated as a folklorist and, seemingly, operated more like a compassionate magnet drawn to material than a cataloger or indexer arranging already found data. Like most American folklorists he did not work professionally in his chosen avocation. Korson was called a social historian, a historian-folklorist, and a writer of informal history. He labeled himself neither a scientist nor humanist and stayed out of divisive folkloric battles.

At the time of Korson's presentation of his life collection to King's College, he was interviewed by John Sherwood, a *Washington Evening Star* staff writer. To his fellow reporter Korson equated the end of personal collecting with the mechanization of coal mining and the subsequent employment decline:

> The old-time miners who took up the past 40 years of [Korson's] life
> were all gone now, and in their places have come stripping machines
> and drilling machines and even machines to replace machines. . . .
> George Korson sat down on a Pennsylvania mountain slope — portable
> tape recorder at his side — and watched the giant power shovel at
> work, taking 300-ton bites of coal in single swallows and laying waste
> the Allegheny's surface. There were no ballads being sung around
> there anymore. No mule skinners with braided leather whips scaring
> the kids playing "I Spy the Wolf." No story-tellers. . . . Once, under
> a moonlight sky, by the porch of the Mackin Brothers General Store,
> against a culm bank with a brimstone smell, over an old clay pipe and
> a high-collared beer, the miners and their families gathered to sing
> and dance reels on a sheet of iron . . . and George Korson listened.
> Where once all this happened there are ghost towns now, and a power
> shovel where once there were men. There is no harmonica music in
> rusted iron bones, no Irish brogue in its coughing and sputtering, and
> no folklorist to document the goings-on with a portable tape recorder.
> George Korson has turned his back on such things and has gone on
> home now.[4]

This story, a year and a half before Korson's death, evoked the
dominant theme of his chosen work. In 1958, while working on a
collection of Pennsylvania Dutch mining lore, Korson had explained to a reporter that "folklore is memories and the memories
are growing dim. . . . I came at the eleventh hour."[5] This twilight
mood was present in his very first book, *Songs and Ballads of the
Anthracite Miner,* in which he wrote: "It represents an attempt to
salvage from the past a vein rich in the homespun creations of the
common people before it is lost forever with the passing of that
generation which produced it."[6] Korson's "vein" flourished when
anthracite coal was America's chief metallurgical fuel — from the
Civil War to the decisive strike of 1902 — and hence was "new" as
compared to "old" lore such as the Robin Hood cycle or biblical
legendry. Nevertheless, Korson, like other folklorists, could not resist the bittersweet nostalgia of gathering last leaves. Few folklorists
avoid the trap of the past; it is ironic that Korson, who pioneered
in a new field, was also caught.

STRIP MINING, WHEEL

Korson raced against time to collect, and we are deeply in debt to him for his speed. During the 1920's no one undertook parallel work in metal mining, steel, textiles, printing, or a dozen other callings while old-timers were alive who had themselves helped change the hand trades to massive industries. Korson's monumental achievement is in his collecting and his warmly written books. No other industry holds such a harvest. To have asked more of a man who had already fully integrated his avocation and his profession would have been cruel.

Korson deliberately left to others detailed ballad studies and a theory of industrial folklore which might emerge from such exploration. In a letter to me in response to a query on a song's development, he stated, "My main job was to rescue these ballads before they perished altogether. . . ."[7] Eventually we must go through Korson's books and ephemeral material to formalize his theoretical position — weak or strong — if only to advance industrial folklore as a sub-area within American Studies. The industrial front is crucial to understanding the transition from rural to urban life, from

13

the realm of folk to present-day mass or popular culture. Korson probably never thought of his books' bearing on the discipline of folklore in terms of explaining the deep transformation of folk societies in the United States.

In a personal attempt to cover the expressive forms in modern society which are disseminated by commercial entertainment and related media, but which function traditionally, I have in recent years used a special coinage, *poplore*.[8] I am fully aware that in this term there are found many hidden conceptual difficulties. They hinge on such factors as the status of the individual who accepts an item transmitted by sophisticated communications technology, the functions of the media themselves, and the nature of the society in which these two interact. Korson, as a pioneer student of industrial tradition, was, in my judgment, an early poplorist. This particular ascription might have amused or distressed him. Few scholars in their lifetime are entirely cognizant of the ramifications of their own contribution.

No collector likes to see a single item lost, but surely a paper on the changes in mining songs or styles wrought by machines is as important as a gathered song. Korson was in a singularly good position to test various theoretical formulations concerning stability and change within folksong genres because of the fantastic development in mining technology during his life. Anthracite mining was already a "sick" industry when Korson began to collect. Hand work had given way to simple machines, mules to electric motors, the Anglo-Celtic miners to Slavic immigrants, and isolation in the patch to automobiles, movies, radios, and records. Hulking breakers, where infirm old miners as well as growing boys had cracked coal lumps and picked slate by hand, were mechanized; even some of these modern buildings had metamorphosed into Pennsylvania ghosts before Korson's eyes. In spite of such modernization and decay, he persisted in gathering lore.

The changes commented on to reporter Sherwood in 1965 were of a different magnitude than those of 1925, but there is no evidence that contemporary miners, like building tradesmen who drive to work from distant communities and operate huge machines, lack folklore. One need not assume that industrial lore dies when the work process changes. There simply is no demonstration that power-shovel men in the Alleghenies or the Cumberlands are devoid of traditional expression and action. Their literature, music, and customary behavior may differ radically from that of the Celtic old-timers who performed for Korson, but no judgment or classification can be undertaken unless collecting continues. Badly needed today is intense collecting from miners — north and south, employed and unemployed, union and non-union — by students with a conceptual understanding of the work community refined by current anthropological and sociological theory.

At this juncture I shall touch on a few understated or overlooked problems in Korson's works in addition to the one already noted by the *Washington Evening Star:* "There is no harmonica music in the rusted iron bones [of machines]." Implied in this devolutionary formulation of the Industrial Revolution's corrosive effect is the parallel notion that folksongs touched by print or other technological devices are impure or inauthentic. My treatment of these twin problems at this point is preliminary to observations to be developed in chapters following this introduction.

Korson was aware that not all the songs he gathered were folksongs but he was not impelled to make his distinctions explicit. In his first book he stated: "There are several pieces in this collection that cannot be claimed as folklore. They may be recognized by their artificial ring. . . ."[9] Although Korson identified some pieces as coming from sheet music, songsters, or the vaudeville-variety-circus stage, he did not develop his notion of "artificiality," nor did he indicate clearly whether such material could enter tradition. To collector Robert Winslow Gordon, who had seen his earliest findings serialized in the *United Mine Workers Journal* (November 15, 1926–March 15, 1927), Korson wrote: "I have striven to make my collection one primarily of folk-lore, and my including several 'stage' and 'author' songs was merely incidental."[10] This theme of purity against contamination — constantly prevalent in folkloric thinking — persisted with Korson for decades. To me he wrote: "I was interested in miners' ballads that had been composed by miners and that were in oral circulation among the miners. I wanted these songs in pure form before they had been influenced by radio and corrupted by drug store mineworkers and so-called hillbilly singers. I chose my informants carefully."[11] Korson simply did not concern

15

himself with the process whereby any piece — "artificial" or "hill-billy" — entered or influenced tradition. In fact, he used such pieces on both his Library of Congress discs probably because his affection for the material outweighed his notion of purity.

Seemingly, Wayland Hand and Duncan Emrich were the first scholars to call attention to a blurring of analytic distinctions found in Korson's books. Hand, in an early article on California miners' folklore, defined this lore as "the exclusive property of a comparatively small and homogeneous artisan group," a notion not unlike Korson's. However, while collecting Hand became aware of the link between present-day and past work lore, and called attention to Korson's stress on modernization's negative role. Hand wrote:

> With the changes in mining wrought by industrialization during the last half century and before, much of the "glamour and romance" of mining has been lost, the stirring phrase itself lingering only in promotional literature, and then, usually, with reference only to the entrepreneur. That these changes, economic and social, have had profound effect on the folklore of the miner as well as on his life, is beyond question. Korson, for instance, is chary of the future of miners' folk song, holding industrialization almost alone responsible for the decline of this ancient art. . . . There can be no question that many of the old-time superstitions and beliefs are gradually dying out, yet the common stock itself is being partly replenished from time to time by the addition of new material. As for the future state of events, it is a safe conjecture that an enterprise which makes such great demands on the imagination, resourcefulness, and daring of its workers as does mining will never be wholly without some sort of folklore.[12]

In the context of the parallel issue of whether or not industrialization was causing western metal miners' lore to disappear, Emrich also commented on another problem, in that Korson had glossed over the "distinction between that which is 'folk' and that which is 'popular,' either in creation or adoption."[13]

These moderate statements were not echoed by John Spargo of Northwestern University in his review of Korson's *Coal Dust on the Fiddle*. Spargo's hostility to any workers' songs and his intemperate tone destroyed the grain of wisdom in his piece. In essence, the critic disliked all material of social significance or protest and rejected these quasi-literary, "carelessly-written versicles" as lacking

ANTHRACITE BREAKER

"starry empery." Further, he denigrated Korson as a "feeble Charles Dickens."[14] Spargo's view in no way diminished Korson's contribution, but was representative of academic neglect and rejection of industrial lore.

Korson was the first American folklorist to present any labor lore to the public; nevertheless, he too rejected some data, for he did not include in his books the contributions of communists to union tradition. He knew intimately the internecine conflict which wracked miners' organizations during the 1920's and 1930's, for he had observed the radical movement directly and understood clearly the use by dual unionists of folkloric material.[15] It was not easy to write objectively about Communist party members when they were perceived as union wreckers, aliens, and subversives. Yet Korson's views on a red song or singer would have been most helpful in sketching the little-known relationship of polemical to industrial material.

I am concerned at this point only with the role of such bards as Aunt Molly Jackson — a folksinger, a revolutionary, a prolific mine-song composer, and a real Munchausenian character. Korson chose to overlook her. He wrote to me that in his collecting he distinguished between "the 'folk,' the workers themselves [and] union organizers from the outside. . . . When I found that [a ballad] had been written by an outsider I didn't use it. . . . I had to be especially careful because in the 1920's and 1930's the Communists were making a determined effort to capture the United Mine Workers of America, and some of the songs were composed by their organizers. When I was sure of this source — and I had ways of finding out — I just didn't use the song in my collection."

Obviously, there exists a hierarchy of "the folk": peasant, worker, miner, unionist, radical, communist. Spargo drew the line at one end of the scale and Korson at the other. Korson himself recognized the great difficulty in distinguishing between "organizers from the outside" and those who "were miners first, most of them since they were nine or ten years old, which made them acceptable."[16] Such scholastic hair-splitting breaks down when the life histories of particular miner organizers are pursued. Some UMWA old hands came from a Knights of Labor or Socialist party tradition; some highly conservative Appalachian miners, inheritors of Jeffersonian and Jacksonian values, became Marxists in the Depression. The difference between Knights of Labor songs, which Korson accepted, and Communist party songs, which he rejected, was frequently but a distinction in chronology.

I know of no sure-fire formula for assaying the "folkness" of a singer within a political movement, other than by relating his rhetorical and musical style to his life history. In this sense, the study of a folksinger's status is not unlike the study of how a song enters tradition. Both quests are basic to a viable theory of folklore. Indeed, in a provocative essay on the "folksong revival," Charles Seeger placed a prevailing problem in folklore studies within a dynamic frame which Korson had touched upon intuitively in his

18

MEETING CALL

rejection of "outsiders." Seeger categorized people as "folk" and "non-folk" but indicated that both sets shared "folk" and "non-folk" qualities.[17] Korson accepted rank-and-file miners as "folk," but did not go so far as to label outside organizers "non-folk." Instead, he put aside the latter group's politically centered lore.

The most puzzling lack in all Korson's published works is the absence of any bawdy folklore. Those contemporary students who have the books of Gershon Legman at hand know that some individuals, in many folk groups, include in their repertoires sexual material undifferentiated from other knowledge and expressions. Kenneth S. Goldstein, in the article "Bowdlerization and Expurgation: Academic and Folk," demonstrated that for many years folksingers, field collectors, editors, and publishers all withheld or distorted such data. It is our loss that many excellent anthologies of cowboy, hobo, lumberjack, sailor, and soldier songs were marred by total oversight of any obscenity, however defined. Further, this omission was not discussed by folklorists themselves. Franz Rickaby's *Ballads and Songs of the Shanty-Boy,* published by the Harvard University Press in 1926, is a model collection for its period and extremely useful to present-day students of occupational culture. In a critical review of the book, Ernest Sutherland Bates faulted Rickaby and other "devotees of American folk-lore [who] fight shy of the ribald element" found among woodsmen, westerners, and miners, too.[18]

Although I explored with George Korson his view on communist-inspired lore, I regret that I never quizzed him on the lack of erotica in his books. In one of his last published pieces on the ditty "My Sweetheart's the Mule in the Mines," Korson wrote that he "suspected that the ballad as a whole was essentially ribald." Further, he "reasoned that rollicking young mule drivers who smoked, chewed tobacco and gambled their meagre earnings on cock fights might also use coarse language in a ballad of their own creation."[19] In spite of such insight, Korson seemingly encountered no scatological folklore among miners, or perhaps, accepting academic customs, he chose to overlook what he found.

I raise this point because, as a shipwright and carpenter for many years, I heard my share of sexual on-the-job jokes and metaphoric speech for tools, work processes, and mechanical equipment, as well as stories about job-centered phallic initiation pranks. It is difficult to believe that in this regard coal miners, shipyard riveters, water-front piledrivers, or uptown rodbusters (construction ironworkers who place and tie reinforcing rods in concrete forms) were so different under the skin.

The kind of raw, sexual humor which I took for granted as a young worker, and to which I feel Korson was also exposed, was seldom pressed on sound recordings. The subject of off-color records lies beyond this study; suffice it to say one item, "Cave Man Blues"

GEORGE KORSON: FIELD WORK

(Victor 38605), recorded by the Memphis Jug Band in 1930 and reissued on *The Party Blues* (Melodeon MLP 7324), portrayed a lusty miner with pick and shovel who was "diggin' in every dark hole" but not for coal. Of course, this "cave man" had and has some comrades in every American coal field.

    With the exception of these relatively small bodies of neglected or rejected sexual and political material, Korson was an inclusive and pragmatic field worker. To his great credit he was never a slave to the romantic communal-composition theory held by some of his fellow folklorists. Korson, himself a disciplined writer, knew that chanting diggers did not collectively improvise ballads while turning their auger-drills into the coal seam's face. Nor did bands or marching unionists spontaneously generate labor anthems on the picket line. He knew too many gifted miner-composers who made up songs in deep solitude to believe in singing throngs. Korson liked Henry Mencken's pungent summation well enough to use it in his earliest book: "Folk songs are written, like all other songs, by individuals. All the folk have to do with them is to choose the ones that are to survive."[20]

21

The greatest conceptual issue in all Korson's work, and one to which his contribution was enormous although never stated theoretically, lies in the question: Does the mine patch or camp constitute a folk society? Earlier I noted that defining formulas for the folk range in a field between two poles — the peasantry, and amorphous groups of persons who create forms pleasing to folklorists. Certainly miners were not peasants, although most miners initially entered their occupation from an agrarian background and not from other industries. Because mine sites often were remote from cities, miners were at times perceived as a rural proletariat. Once miners were into their industry, the verbal expressions "my daddy was a miner" or "coal in his blood" helped to separate them from peasants and farmers as well as from other industrial workers. It is likewise apparent that miners had (and have) more cohesion or solidarity than the casual linkage observed, for example, among numismatists. I have found it helpful to use the phrase *folk-like* for miners whether at home, at work, or at a union meeting. The use of a hyphen permits me to place miners between the rigid (peasantry) and relativistic (anyone) lines that bound old and new definitions.

Early scholars in Germany and England had a highly visible and lively model of peasant society, but folklorists in the United States shy away from the word *peasant* as if it were contaminated. Lest anyone think that this class of people is extinct, he might well consult anthropologist Eric R. Wolf's monograph *Peasants*. Wolf reminds us that the majority of mankind is neither primitive nor modern and that this majority still stands between tribal and industrial society. From the perspective of the United States of America, one can use with facility the combinations *underdeveloped people* or *developing nation* instead of the more pejorative *peasantry*. (Our domestic equivalent is, euphemistically, *culturally deprived* or *disadvantaged*.) It is wise to remember that long before Peace Corps volunteers or Viet Nam paratroopers encountered "deprived" or "underdeveloped" people, such persons told folktales to the Grimm Brothers and sang border ballads to Walter Scott. I suggest that the miners who sang to George Korson were in many respects folk-like, whether defined by Scott's romantic or Wolf's sober view of the peasantry.

Contemporary folklorists (or poplorists) who are interested in a wide variety of urban expressive genres — collegiate songs, night-club sick-humor, latrinalia, mnemonic devices, racial slurs — must, understandably, reject classical notions of the folk in favor of the material which they wish to study. In my view, such provocative forms as graffiti, ski songs, and "skin-flicks" are intrinsically interesting, but their creators are not necessarily folk or even folk-like. Does undergraduate sorority singing really bind its members together in the same fashion as toil in the bowels of the earth binds coal diggers? Miners, neither tribal nor rural, are sufficiently linked by the centripetal nature of their work to behave, in part, as the peasantry does.

A reader with only the most casual knowledge of Korson's books knows that he never compared miners either to peasants or to collegians. He assumed that the miners were folk for two basic reasons: (1) Their songs behaved like folksongs. "Their homespun ballads spread in the characteristic way of folklore. . . . The songs and ballads which sprang from the soil of the anthracite coal region have in them the crude strength, the naturalness and the freshness of things that grow out of the earth." (2) Miners were isolated in remote villages, set apart by harsh, dangerous work, and they retained an old life-style. "Hidden from the world by their mountains, these diggers of coal dragged out their years in Biblical simplicity."[21] These passages are drawn from Korson's earliest book, written before he was influenced by the discipline of folklore, to illustrate the conception he held of his chosen field — a view from which he never departed. He was satisfied with this operational definition and did not trouble to extend it to other industrial groups or to sharpen it. Nor did he anticipate that new denominative categories might be required when coal miners in the United States were fully absorbed into mass society.

In my last talks with George Korson, I suggested that he write an account of his own "conversion" to folklore, and of his sense of privilege in having known mining bards. It is our loss that this event and subsequent feeling were never described. During 1965, writing to the *United Mine Workers Journal* on the union's diamond jubilee, he noted that this anniversary also marked his fortieth year as a folksong collector. In the article he tried to remember "the whole

23

shebang," but, characteristically, focused on his miner friends rather than on his own initiation into the discipline. Korson recalled a recent hospital visit to Bill Keating, composer of the humorous "Down, Down, Down." The anthracite old-timer, near death, had joshed: "Take out your pencil, George. I have a dozen ballads swimming around in my head. Take them down."[22] Korson's report to *Journal* readers tells us that he felt the proper stance by folklorist to folksinger to be that of devoted scribe rather than austere analyst. Morally, Korson valued mining society and its members above folklore as a scientific discipline.

When Korson was pressed to talk about his initiation, he would credit Edith Patterson of the Pottsville Free Public Library with encouraging his search for mine balladry after he had asked about books on coal songs similar to cowboy or sailor collections. Not only did she stimulate him to hunt but she also introduced him to the works of ballad scholars such as George Lyman Kittredge. Korson did not have to be directed to anthracite regional or trade-union history; I do not believe he went beyond these fields into sociology or anthropology. In his final letter to me Korson stated: "As I began collecting miners' songs I perceived that I had stumbled upon a folk culture."[23] "Stumbled" is excellent to describe his almost intuitive reach for one of folklore's central disciplinary problems. This guiding perception underlay his first book and grew as Korson's area of investigation both widened (bituminous) and intensified (Pennsylvania Dutch miners). Actually, in Korson's last major book, *Black Rock,* he approached the perspective of folklife scholarship developed in Scandinavia, with its stress on material culture over rhetorical genres. This book, in a revealing sense, complemented Don Yoder's folklife-oriented study of an oral-literary form, the brush-meeting spiritual, known to Pennsylvania Dutch farmer-miners.[24]

Korson's perception of miners as "a folk culture" is important because until now we have lacked ethnographic descriptions of American mining communities by students steeped in the methodology of anthropology. The neglect of the camp or patch by anthropologists is distressing to anyone who knows the immensity of coal's literature. This corpus is seen in Robert F. Munn's bibliography, *The Coal Industry in America* (1965), which contains nearly 2,000

SONGFEST

items, from ephemeral strike pamphlets to extensive governmental reports, excluding technical or geological surveys. To this basic work Munn appended a list of some 700 biographical articles or books on operators, labor leaders, and related figures. Munn did not find for inclusion in his bibliography a single published ethnographic survey comparable to the excellent English book, *Coal Is Our Life: An Analysis of a Yorkshire Mining Community,* by Norman Dennis, Fernando Henriques, and Clifford Slaughter. Their study of Ashton — fictitiously named — told why and how miners formed a cohesive community. It should be required reading for every student of industrial folklore.

Herman R. Lantz, in *People of Coal Town,* a sociological report of a southern Illinois mining town located between the hills and the prairie, focused on an American counterpart of Ashton. Lantz was concerned with the frontier themes of violence, authoritarianism, corruption, and insecurity, as they molded personality for miners and others in a midwestern coal camp. This work is useful as background for one who wishes to go on to a study of the miner as a member of a folk-like group in transition to a different — perhaps more diffused and fragmented, perhaps more urbanized and popular — society. Lantz was not the only social scientist to describe coal miners. Munn cited numerous valuable unpublished academic theses on aspects of mining life as well as articles in learned journals of sociology. However, such dissertations and papers do not compensate for needed ethnographic perspectives.

Fortunately, in the late 1960's two skilled researchers with combined training in sociology and anthropology undertook an intense exploration of the impact of technology on coal miners and their families in the six coal-bearing counties of southwestern Virginia. Professor Helen M. Lewis teaches at Clinch Valley College, Wise — literally over a coal deposit; her co-worker Edward E. Knipe teaches at Virginia Commonwealth College, Richmond. Singly and together they have authored a number of articles (cited in the bibliography) on work and family relationships in a coal community.[25] During 1967, Lewis and Knipe, with a dozen colleagues, participated in an International Seminar on Social Change in the Mining Community sponsored by West Virginia University, and in 1968 the seminar's second session was held in Europe at the

26

University of the Saar.[26] At both meetings the Virginians were able to report on their findings as well as to explore the trans-national and cross-cultural similarities in mining life-style.

The basic principle assumed by many industrial sociologists is that technology affects social patterns and structures. Accordingly, Lewis and Knipe have interviewed and observed various sets of miners in three types of mines: hand loading, mechanical loading, and continuous cutting-loading machines. Apart from the internal differences in work and family relationships found within coal communities stemming from separate work experience, the researchers have also turned to the complex problem of the relationship between the miner and his Appalachian neighbor. At this level, Lewis and Knipe fashioned the provocative phrase "a case of peasantry gained and peasantry lost." They suggested that farm folk gave up agrarian modes to become industrial workers, but returned to a status of political peasantry in the sense that many Appalachian mountaineers, including miners, are colonial dependents within the United States.

The studies by Lewis, Knipe, Lantz, and Dennis are mentioned here as complementary to Korson's books because it is my belief that his "ethnography" will have to substitute for precise technical description until a student in the Redfield tradition turns to a mine town. Today, Robert Redfield's anthropological usage *folk society* is well known. Hence, it is startling to realize that Redfield was doing field work in Tepoztlán, a Mexican village, when Korson was first gathering lore in Pennsylvania's anthracite patches. Redfield's provocative university course on folk society was first given to Chicago students in 1941, when Korson was in southern bituminous fields. Redfield's seminal lecture on "The Folk Society" was not printed in the *American Journal of Sociology* until 1947, when Korson was editing his first Library of Congress recording. These parallels are stressed only to show how recent it is that American collectors have had a workable model of folk society.

Criticism by George Foster and others exists on Redfield's term *folk society*.[27] Nevertheless, Redfield must be honored for a most "useful generalizing concept directing attention toward a constellation of aspects important in primitive or peasant societies and minimized or lacking in urban civilized societies."[28] The language

27

is technical; the meaning is clear for folklorists. George Korson, for one, gravitated toward that "constellation of aspects" which enabled him to name miners *folk* and to write the best popular ethnography of an American industrial group. In 1970 Mike Ross, administrator of the Fairmont (West Virginia) Clinic, read at a health and safety meeting an insightful and challenging paper on the life-style of miners. It complemented Korson's earlier "folk" studies in coal communities.[29]

It is appropriate to close this introduction by noting Korson's discomfort with commercial sound recordings. As early as May, 1924, he reported his awareness that "the music that filled the air in the Schuylkill Valley was largely of the canned variety originating in Tin Pan Alley and not indigenous miners' songs."[30] He held to his view that records were agents corrupting tradition, and was genuinely excited when I sent him a coal-song discography which pointed out the medium's documentary role. However, when I informed him that a specific item ("The Dying Mine Brakeman") which he had collected in 1940 had previously been issued on discs, he was surprised and suggested that he "would have lost interest in the ballad if [he] had known that it had been recorded commercially."[31] Korson did have to his credit two excellent Library of Congress field-recorded anthologies: *Songs and Ballads of the Anthracite Miners* (L 16) and *Songs and Ballads of the Bituminous Miners* (L 60). It is a humorous "family secret" that his wife Rae, head of the Library of Congress Archive of Folk Song, prodded him into the production of these discs.[32]

Essentially, Korson perceived sound recordings as agents of civilization and high culture — the Great Tradition in Redfield's design — and he wanted to preserve and protect folk culture — the Little Tradition — not only against wax and vinyl discs, but also against fearful new tools (record players, television sets, electric power shovels, giant stripping augers) which were, seemingly, destroying mining folklore. His ambivalence in the face of the miners' reach for "blessings" which "blighted the folk imagination" troubled him to the end.[33] To his honor, Korson never deserted his miner friends in their struggle to achieve the same physical comfort their brawn and skill had made possible for others. His final unfinished work, "A History of the United Mine Workers of

MUSIC IN MINE CAMP

America," contained no magic words to weld the benefit of complex technology and the time-tested mystery of folklore.[34]

This search for a formula to blend the best of two realms — folk and sophisticated — faces people throughout the globe today. Can we relate the coal digger's to the atomic engineer's craft, black to white citizens, rural dwellers to urbanites, hardhats to hippies, or folklore to poplore? America is not a simple monolith. It has always been an assemblage of disparate groups in quest of modernity's wisdom. Americans have been and continue to be troubled that they were not and are not an indivisible folk with an encompassing tradition.

1. John Greenway, "George Korson (1900-1967)," *Journal of American Folklore*, LXXX (1967), 343. See also Ben Botkin, "George Korson (1899-1967)," *New York Folklore Quarterly*, XXIII (1967), 237, and "George G. Korson, Folklorist, Dead," *New York Times* (May 25, 1967), 47.
2. Gerhard Heilfurth, *Das Bergmannslied: Wesen, Leben, Funktion* (Kassel, 1954). See also the review by A. L. Lloyd, *Journal of the International Folk Music Council*, IX (1957), 87.

3. Wayland Hand, "George Korson and the Study of American Mining Lore," and Gerhard Heilfurth, "George Korson — An Appreciation," forthcoming in *Keystone Folklore Quarterly* (1971). A useful background article for these memorials is Hand's "American Occupational and Industrial Folklore: The Miner," in *Kontakte und Grenzen: Probleme der Volks-, Kultur- und Sozialforschung*, ed. Hans Foltin (Göttingen, 1969), 453.

4. John Sherwood, "Machines Only Music Left in Mines, Folklorist Finds," *Washington Evening Star* (Oct. 19, 1965), sec. B, 1.

5. Adele Chidakel, "Folklore Smudged with Coal Dust," *Washington Star Magazine* (Feb. 16, 1958), 28.

6. George Korson, *Songs and Ballads of the Anthracite Miner* (New York, 1927), ix.

7. Letter to me, May 24, 1958.

8. At the Berkeley Folk Music Festival (June 30, 1967), I suggested *poplore* as a descriptive key-word. This was noted by Philip Elwood, "Folk Music Goes on a Rock Basis," *San Francisco Examiner* (July 1, 1967), 10. The first prominent usage, to my knowledge, was by Marshall Fishwick, "Folklore, Fakelore, and Poplore," *Saturday Review*, L (Aug. 26, 1967), 20.

9. Korson, *Anthracite Miner*, xix.

10. Letter to Gordon, Mar. 3, 1927.

11. Letter to me, Mar. 2, 1957.

12. Wayland Hand, "California Miners' Folklore: Above Ground," *California Folklore Quarterly*, I (1942), 25.

13. Duncan Emrich, "Songs of the Western Miners," *California Folklore Quarterly*, I (1942), 213.

14. Review by John W. Spargo, *Journal of American Folklore*, LVII (1944), 91. Response by Ben Botkin, "Dust on the Folklorists," *ibid.*, 139.

15. Radical use of folklore is treated in Joyce Kornbluh, *Rebel Voices* (Ann Arbor, 1964), R. Serge Denisoff, *Great Day Coming* (Urbana, 1971), and Richard A. Reuss, "American Folklore and Left-Wing Politics: 1927-1957" (thesis, Indiana University, Bloomington, 1971).

16. Letter to me, May 24, 1958.

17. Charles Seeger, "The Folkness of the Non-Folk vs. the Non-Folkness of the Folk," in *Folklore and Society*, ed. Bruce Jackson (Hatboro, Pa., 1966), 4.

18. Bates review cited in Daniel W. Greene, "'Fiddle and I': The Story of Franz Rickaby," *Journal of American Folklore*, LXXXI (1968), 331.

19. George Korson, "'My Sweetheart's the Mule in the Mines': Memories of Tom and Maggie Hill," in *Two Penny Ballads and Four Dollar Whiskey*, eds. Kenneth S. Goldstein and Robert H. Byington (Hatboro, Pa., 1966), 8.

20. Mencken quotation in Korson, *Anthracite Miner*, xxi.

21. Korson, *Anthracite Miner*, ix, xx, ix.

22. "A Communication from Folklorist George Korson," *United Mine Workers Journal* (Jan. 15, 1965), 18.

23. Letter to me, Sept. 15, 1966.

24. Don Yoder, "Folklife," in *Our Living Traditions,* ed. Tristram P. Coffin (New York, 1968), 47. See also Don Yoder, *Pennsylvania Spirituals* (Lancaster, 1961).

25. Helen M. Lewis and Edward E. Knipe will publish a monograph for Holt, Rinehart and Winston in 1971.

26. The second seminar's papers were edited by H. J. Kornadt, *Social Change in Mining Communities* (Saarbrücken, 1970). The first's are planned for 1971. Letter to me from Ernest A. Vargas, West Virginia University, Aug. 21, 1970.

27. George M. Foster, "What Is Folk Culture?," *American Anthropologist,* L (1953), 159, and "What Is a Peasant?," in *Peasant Society: A Reader,* ed. Jack M. Potter and others (Boston, 1967), 2.

28. Robert Redfield, *Papers,* ed. Margaret Park Redfield, I: *Human Nature and the Study of Society* (Chicago, 1962), 231.

29. Mike Ross, "Life Style of the Coal Miner," *United Mine Workers Journal* (July 1, 1970), 12; reprinted in *Papers and Proceedings of the National Conference on Medicine and the Federal Coal Mine Health and Safety Act of 1969* (Washington, 1970), 243.

30. Korson, *Anthracite Miner,* xxiii.

31. Letter to me, Mar. 2, 1957.

32. In 1956 the Archive of American Folk Song dropped the word "American" from its title.

33. George Korson, *Minstrels of the Mine Patch,* 3rd printing (Hatboro, Pa., 1964), 12.

34. Korson's history appeared serially in fifteen parts in the *United Mine Workers Journal* (May, 1965–July, 1967) and was unfinished at the time of his death.

PLAYBACK

Race and Hillbilly Records 2

DOCUMENTS — aural, visual, tactile — do not alone comprise an ethnography but it is axiomatic that no description of a society can avoid such documentation. George Korson selected historical and folkloric data to frame the coal-mining songs which he collected. These songs were placed in half a dozen books and complemented by two long-playing records. Reading a blues or ballad imprisoned in print may in itself be a fulfilling or draining experience. However, hearing the same piece directly from a folksinger, or indirectly via a disc, imparts a sense of emotional immediacy and tension beyond the feeling evoked in letters. Sound recordings preserve the subtle inflection, unique accent, pulsating rhythm, or irregular tempo of a singer which is inherent in live performance but which is extremely difficult to convey in textual and musical transcription.

Well before the release of Korson's two Library of Congress LPs in 1948 and 1965, several hundred aural documents of miners' life — mournful, banal, humorous, hortatory — were marketed. These discs, intended for sale instead of academic study or archival deposit, proved in time to be a substantial gift from industry to all students of American culture. However, the initial producers and distributors of 78 rpm recordings hardly ever viewed their merchandise as "gifts." Frequently, they failed to perceive the many

levels of significance in their own products. In 1925 a record holding a pair of songs was something that brought 75¢ on a counter;
it was a commodity. But this very object might also carry Celtic or
African memories in its grooves, or fanciful or terrifying narratives
which reinforced and intensified its listeners' experiences. When a
coal miner in a company store purchased a recorded disaster ballad
or blues lament, he expected a story or mood set in a familiar style.
Beyond a given text and tune, he was likely to hear the pick and
shovel's clatter, the hammer's roar, the drill's whine, and even the
heavy underground silence when work stops. In short, miners heard
the ring of truth in discs intended merely to ring coins into cash
registers.

The prime name assigned to this fascinating "gift," so differently viewed by seller and buyer, was not *folksong record;* rather,
such early material was labeled *race* and *hillbilly* by the industry
itself, as well as by the ultimate consumers of folk and folk-like
music of the 1920's. No one has made an accurate count or classificatory analysis of the tens of thousands of such discs which cas-
caded from the stampers between the two world wars. My concern
is with a handful of coal-mining songs from this body. However,
some discussion of the recording industry's treatment of folksong,
along with a consideration of the views of both urban intellectuals
and the folk on race and hillbilly music, will establish background
for the case studies in the chapters to follow.

Although I shall not consider in detail material released before
1925, it is important to note that some folk music was recorded
in America prior to the formal inauguration of the race and hillbilly idiom. Unfortunately, no study of this early corpus is available.
Nevertheless, a potpourri of rural dances, minstrel routines, mono-
logist bits, laughing songs, spirituals, and country fiddling, as well
as concert arrangements of traditional ballads, was found on cylinder and disc from the beginning. In 1897 Emile Berliner released
a seven-inch, single-faced record by George Graham and Billy
Golden, "Virginia Camp Meeting." It hinted at the flood of sacred
song to follow. The 1901 Columbia catalog identified the already
well-known "Arkansas Traveler" as "a native sitting in front of
his hut scraping his fiddle, and answering the interruptions of the
stranger with witty sallies." Music lovers, removed from huts and

34

camp meetings, could (and did) purchase imports of English and Scottish ballads — for example, "The Twa Corbies" by Grainger Kerr or "Bonnie Lezzie Lindsay" by Harry Lauder, both on the HMV Gramophone label. In 1919 Columbia presented a group of ten-inch, double-faced discs sung by Bentley Ball including "Old Dan Tucker," "Go Down Moses," "Jesse James," and "The Dying Cowboy."

Urban audiences, in part, had already been prepared for native material by "folksong revival" literature. Negro spirituals as well as plantation and cabin songs collected from slaves had been presented in book form in 1867; by 1872 the songs of the traveling Fisk University Jubliee Singers were also in print. In 1904 Helen Child Sargent and George Lyman Kittredge offered to the public their one-volume abridgment of Frances James Child's *The English and Scottish Popular Ballads*. In 1910 *Cowboy Songs,* collected by John Lomax and enthusiastically endorsed by Teddy Roosevelt, was published; it helped build a strong case for native folksong.

These few books and recordings are cited as examples of material directed primarily at educated urbanites who had a consciousness of value in folklore. Nevertheless, because of the fluidity in American society coupled with the ready availability of the mass media, some early "folk" recordings reached the folk before race and hillbilly records existed as a special form.

1920 and 1923, respectively, are usually considered the natal years for the race and hillbilly genres. Alternate captions which identify these records as a discrete set are *idiom, tradition,* or *movement*. The best current overview of hillbilly records is found in Bill C. Malone's *Country Music, U.S.A.,* a social history geared to the changes in white rural music and its setting. Some of the performers and songs mentioned in my case studies are also treated in Malone's work, which contains excellent bibliographical data.

An intensive view of the race-record industry is found in Ronald C. Foreman, Jr.'s dissertation, "Jazz and Race Records, 1920-32," and a brief, recent overview is found in Robert M. W. Dixon and John Godrich's paperback, *Recording the Blues*. In a period when many persons are concerned with the propriety of such ethnic names as *Negro, Afro-American,* or *Black,* as well

OKEH RACE-RECORD CATALOGS

as with the color of black culture, it is well to be reminded of the period when the body of popular, folk, and folk-like music aimed at America's black population was named:

> Notwithstanding debates about names proposed for the nation's black minority [1900-1920], the members of that minority responded to the identifying rubric, *the race*. The term implied kinship and fraternity, and its binding signification was assured long before the expression came to be associated with a product controlled by institutions beyond "the race." In the case of General Phonograph and its industry colleagues, the events of 1921 and succeeding years found a ready market eager to have the new, yet responsive to the familiar. The instrumental use of "race" gave phonograph officials a variety of opportunities to provide both for Negro patrons.[1]

Race and hillbilly records were aimed respectively at the huge black and white rural or rural-derived population of the United States. Nevertheless, from the idiom's inception a few critics, academicians, and "serious" music lovers — non-folk by Charles Seeger's standard — turned to and began to appreciate the folkness inherent in commercial sound recordings. The long, complex rejection of hillbilly material by intellectuals will someday be fully

36

portrayed, as well as the subsequent counter-reaction and gradual acceptance of the form. David Riesman in an essay, "Listening to Popular Music," suggested but one clue for the aural blockade: "The very judgment of what is trash may be biased by one's own unsuspected limitations, for instance, by one's class position or academic vested interest."[2] In 1925, when recorded folksongs were few and far between, Josiah Combs, a fine collector born in the Kentucky mountains, wrote:

> It is in the lonely, isolated cabin that the traditional folk-song is much alive; in places that have not yet felt the impact of civilization, education, pianos, organs, phonographs, the "singing-school master," jazz, the turkey-trot, and rag-time music. . . . Musical instruments themselves . . . are aiding in the destruction of the folk-song in the Highlands, and elsewhere over America, in the rural sections. Such are the organ, piano, and especially the phonograph. . . . Whenever an instrument [phonograph] makes all the music itself, "canned music" as the Highlander sometimes calls it, one acquires quickly the habit of listening to it, thus losing personal initiative to learn the art himself.[3]

Combs did not foresee the role of the sound recording in preserving the very music he loved, nor its place in the traditional learning process. Fortunately, some scholars reached out to new techniques and tools, first to jazz and blues on race records and later to ballads and frolic pieces on hillbilly discs. An obvious way to mark this grasp of new materials is to cite the earliest tune and text transcriptions from recordings in folklore studies.[4] Howard Odum and Guy Johnson commented perceptively on race records in *Negro Workaday Songs* (1926), and Ethel Park Richardson in *American Mountain Songs* (1927) transcribed texts and tunes of a few hillbilly discs. During 1932 Alfred Frankenstein used the texts and tunes of Ernest V. Stoneman's "Wreck on the C & O" and Roy Harvey's "The Brave Engineer" to present a detailed case history of "George Alley: A Study in Modern Folk Lore." This process of careful transcriptive usage and commentary continues. Bertrand Bronson's major study, *The Traditional Tunes of the Child Ballads,* is but one example of sophisticated use of once-overlooked recordings.

Can we reconstruct the story of how scholars became aware that race and hillbilly discs were priceless but inexpensive documents, at the time of actual release and sale? To my knowledge, no folklorist has claimed to be the first serious collector of such material. However, Lloyd Lewis, Chicago star reporter and author of *Myths after Lincoln*, left a warm account of his early interest in folksong records. His story involved a colorful Chicago quartet: John Lomax, Carl Sandburg, Tom Peete Cross (a University of Chicago professor of comparative literature), and Alfred Mac-Arthur (a successful publisher). During the early 1920's this group met informally to swap folksongs and stimulate collecting ventures. Lewis vividly remembered some of his friends' favorites: "The Buffalo Skinners," "Hallelujah, I'm a Bum," "Humble Yourself," "Dese Bones Gwine Rise Again."[5]

From that period Lewis also recalled a related event: "Mac-Arthur and I had been making beginnings at the time of collections of cowboy ballads on the phonograph, and you [Lomax] set us off hunting more. There weren't many then, though in succeeding years more came on the market. The Tin Pan Alley boys took it up." We lack Lewis' precise collecting dates but the sense of reaching toward new records without fear of hostility is superb. Lewis, who came from rural Indiana, also supplied an excellent account of the spirit which motivated him and his sophisticated peers to accept race and hillbilly recordings:

> Here were we in a modern metropolis, all farm boys or small-town boys, and all getting a little sick of the efficiency, the mechanism, the culture of the big industrial cities of the 1920's. A lot of people were turning to folk songs, too, at that time. A few years later, and the radio and phonograph began the rage for cowboy songs, rural songs, mountain music, hill-billy ballads, all representing an escape from the complexities of a civilization which was over-scientific, over-capitalized, over-mechanized.[6]

Lewis' motivating drive to recapture something of his rustic past is an important element in folklore collecting; this drive is shown here at its best — harnessed to the ready acceptance of a commercial artifact, the folksong record. If sophisticated disc collectors existed earlier than Lewis and his Chicago friends, who purchased cowboy songs at the very moment when recording firms undertook to merchandise folksongs for the folk, their stories would be welcome today.

38

LEWIS AND SANDBURG

Lewis introduced John Lomax to Carl Sandburg about 1920 and placed his own purchases of cowboy songs in that period. Needless to say, it took decades for this enthusiasm to spread. Actually, it was jazz enthusiasts, not western buffs, who paved the way for wide-scale American folksong-record collecting. Something of this development must be understood to evaluate the role of recordings in scholarship. When European and American intellectuals first turned to jazz, they were faced with a dilemma in placement: Was it folk (like spirituals or work songs)? Was it popular (like musical comedy or light opera)? Was it concert (like Ernst Ansermet's or George Gershwin's compositions)?

As critics struggled to frame answers to these difficult questions, a few emerged who saw with special clarity the relationship of ragtime, jazz, and blues to folk music. Carl Van Vechten, as early as 1917, noted in *Vanity Fair* that Irving Berlin and other ragtime-influenced composers had caught the complicated vigor of American life in their use of folk-derived rhythms and tunes. Further, Van Vechten asserted that this new popular phenomenon was the only American music heard abroad. Commenting on its mode of dissemination, he stated: "It is heard everywhere [for example] in the trenches by way of the record-disc."[7] Two years later, *Current Opinion* identified the blues as "enigmatic folksongs

39

of the southern underworld." Ahead of its time, this magazine —
in a feature on Gilda Gray, famed for provocative shimmying in
the "Gaieties of 1919" — suggested that these "communal chants"
(blues) were worthy of as serious study as Cecil Sharp had given
to Appalachian ballads. Walter Kingsley, the "Broadway ethnolo-
gist," was also drawn to Gilda's art, including "The Dirty Dozen."
Perceptively, he linked the impact of the blues with the quality of
life in folk society: "Just as Henley and Farmer's seven volumes
of slang . . . cover the outlaw vocabulary so do the blues embrace
the outlaw emotions."[8]

During the 1920's composer W. C. Handy and singers such
as Bessie Smith and Ma Rainey gave writers a model closer to
tradition than that furnished by Irving Berlin and Miss Gray.
In this decade Carl Van Vechten began to stress negritude in the
jazz-blues idiom, relating it to African art and centering it in a
black literary renaissance.[9] Also, at the same period Abbe Niles
reviewed race and hillbilly records for *Bookman* readers, taking
pleasure in adding discographical annotations to the material in
Sandburg's then-current *American Songbag*. One example reveals
Niles's standards. He transcribed the full text of Rabbit Brown's
"The Titanic" (Victor 35840) because the bluesman was not easily
understood and Brown's ballad complemented Sandburg's. Niles
can also be credited with introducing the useful combination *folk-
blues* in W. C. Handy's major anthology, *Blues*.[10]

Niles, a Wall Street lawyer, was unusually early in judging
race and hillbilly material as folksong.[11] His peers initially had
been caught up by jazz. About 1927, some Ivy League students
began collecting hot records by junk-shop purchases and by can-
vassing door to door in poor neighborhoods.[12] The Princetonians
burrowed for Bix Beiderbeck and Leon Rappolo; their Yale rivals
for Duke Ellington and Fletcher Henderson. Collecting led to
swapping, to sales by auction lists, and to a mimeographed literature, partially based on performer interviews. Charles Edward
Smith's 1934 *Esquire* article, "Collecting Hot," revealed an esoteric
art to a wide audience. Meanwhile, Hugues Panassie's *Le Jazz Hot*,
solidly grounded in studies of recordings, was published at Paris
during 1934 and translated for a New York edition in 1936. In the
latter year, Charles Delaunay's *Hot Discography* (untranslated)

made the Atlantic jump from France, and American buffs became discographers. The new "science" led to placing performers and material on a continuum: traditional blues to symphonic jazz. How else could the discs of contemporaries such as Blind Lemon Jefferson, Mamie Smith, Fred Waring, and Paul Whiteman be evaluated?

When John Hammond presented a "Spirituals to Swing" evening at Carnegie Hall (December 23, 1938), he brought persons as diverse as Sonny Terry and Sidney Bechet onto the same concert stage. It was appropriate to describe Bechet as a jazz figure; it was imperative to describe Terry as a folk musician. Terry, a blues harmonica player who had recorded initially for the Library of Congress and later for the American Record Corporation, in 1952 made a ten-inch LP for Moe Asch's Folkways label. This firm, geared to culturally sophisticated and politically radical consumers, featured useful descriptive brochures in album jackets. Such inserts as Frederick Ramsey, Jr.'s notes to Terry's Folkways LP served as a bridge between formal folklore scholarship, left-wing journalism, and jazz criticism. Through the 1950's and 1960's early race-record performers were "rediscovered" and presented in second careers on "folksong revival" stages, and late in 1970 a number of such artists sang for black students at a Howard University blues festival in the nation's capital. In these past two decades Mississippi John Hurt, Bukka White, Sleepy John Estes, or Son House, for example, have been labeled *folk* by undergraduates who were born well after the industry had discarded the rubric *race records* originally used to identify Hurt and his fellows.

As has been said, the Chicago folksong enthusiasts described by Lloyd Lewis did not turn to discography as did their peers who collected race records. This lag in critical attention to hillbilly material was great and has never been fully explained. In part, jazz-blues seemed virile and dynamic to intellectuals while comparable white forms seemed mindless and degenerate. It was far easier for *Vanity Fair* and *Esquire* tastemakers to accept Harlem blues than Blue Ridge mountain music. No Ivy League college students admitted to listening to hillbilly music when John Hammond and Wilder Hobson were initiated into the jazz scene.

In a sense, Lewis and other very early cowboy-record collectors were caught up by the urban "folksong revival" of the 1930's and later decades, leaving initial hillbilly-record collecting and discography to persons still in or close to folk society. The disparity between these two groups of enthusiasts stemmed from many differences in social, educational, and economic position. A full analysis of the differences in response between two sets of hobbyists to a parallel series of cultural documents must be reserved for separate study.

A watershed date for widespread intellectual attention to hillbilly material can be cited as August 31, 1941, when Howard Taubman reviewed a reissue album, *Smoky Mountain Ballads* (Victor **P** 79), in the *New York Times*. Previously, the few serious writers on such music had reached small or special audiences. For example, in 1931 Lamar Stringfield, a North Carolina symphonic composer who had drawn considerably upon mountain music, prepared for his state's local music clubs a bulletin-guide which incorporated the use of Brunswick, Columbia, and Victor phonograph records. Not only did Stringfield list more than 100 recorded native songs and instrumental pieces, but the University of North Carolina Extension Division arranged to mail the discs to clubs that assumed responsibility for packing and mailing fees. Stringfield's pioneer article had little circulation beyond North Carolina, and to my knowledge no other university at that period made a similar use of hillbilly discs. By 1936 folklorist and field collector Herbert Halpert had reached a select but national body of music lovers with information that commercial records were excellent sources for traditional song. Halpert spiced his message with textual quotations from mountain performers such as Kelly Harrell and Jilson Setters. In 1940 Alan Lomax, then working at the Library of Congress, compiled a list — published by the State Department — of 350 representative records of "tunes from the South" to help others "explore this unknown body of Americana."[13]

World War II was instrumental in extending the audience for country music — black and white — and serious critics and collectors now linked jazz, folk, and country records for uninitiated readers. In *Vogue*'s Christmas issue for 1946, Alan Lomax presented an appraisal of such material found in New York's stores. The citation of two Tex Ritter albums in a list surrounded by high-

Lay Bros.
Photo

Hear these new southern
fiddle and guitar records

NOT so long ago Gid Tanner with his violin, and Riley Puckett with his guitar came, fresh from the mountains of Georgia, to make records for Columbia.

Gid has walked away with the first prize at some of the Old Time Fiddlers' Conventions in Atlanta. Riley and his guitar are known to thousands in the South who have heard him perform at county fairs.

Hear these Tanner and Puckett records. No Southerner can hear them and go away without them. And it will take a pretty hard-shelled Yankee to leave them. The fact is that these records have got that "something" that everybody wants. So listen to—

"Rock All Our Babies To Sleep"
"Little Old Log Cabin in the Lane"
Record 107 D

"Buckin' Mule"
"Hen Cackle"
Record 110 D

It will pay you to send in your orders at once for these two records. If ever there were a pair of double-barreled hits, these are.

COLUMBIA PHONOGRAPH CO., INC.
1819 Broadway   New York

Write to the Columbia branch or distributor nearest you

Atlanta, Ga., 561 Whitehall Street
Boston, Mass., 1000 Washington Street
Chicago, Ill., 430-440 S. Wabash Avenue
Cleveland, Ohio, 112 East Thirtieth Street
Dallas, Texas, 316-320 North Preston Street
Kansas City, Mo., 2006 Wyandotte Street
Los Angeles, Cal., 809 S. Los Angeles St.
New York City, 121 West Twentieth Street
Philadelphia, Pa., 40 North Sixth Street
Pittsburgh, Pa., 632 Duquesne Way
San Francisco, Cal., 345 Bryant Street

Buffalo, N. Y., 737 Main Street
Cincinnati, Ohio, 222 West Fourth Street
Detroit, Mich., 439 E. Fort Street
Minneapolis, Minn., 18 North Third Street
Montreal, Canada, 246 Craig Street, West
New Orleans, La., 325 North Peters Street
St. Louis, Mo., 1127 Pine Street
Seattle, Wash., 911 Western Avenue

• • • •

COLUMBIA WHOLESALERS, Inc.
205 West Camden Street, Baltimore, Md.

COLUMBIA STORES CO.
1608 Glenarm Avenue, Denver, Colo.
COLUMBIA STORES CO.
221 S. W. Temple, Salt Lake City, Utah
TAMPA HARDWARE CO.
Tampa, Fla.
W. W. KIMBALL
Wabash and W. Jackson Blvd., Chicago, Ill.
COLUMBIA DISTRIBUTORS, Inc.
1127 Pine Street, St. Louis, Mo.

Columbia
New Process RECORDS
Columbia   has   all   the   hits   and   usually   first

COLUMBIA AD

fashion plates was itself a commentary on the new audience. To preface his list, Lomax distinguished four kinds of style:

> By unsophisticated country singers (and these I most strongly recommend as art of lasting interest and value), by commercial hill-billies (and these have value as a new sort of small-town folk music), by the city-billy ballad singers of the big towns (and these present the best repertoires, usually in a singing style that you are probably accustomed to hearing), and finally by art singers (and these are, for me, the least interesting because they lose most of the original earthy essence of country music).[14]

During 1947, a year before the *Journal of American Folklore* accepted for consideration the kinds of discs suggested by Lomax, an Ohio State University graduate student, D. K. Wilgus, completed the first academic study on hillbilly records. Also, in 1947, the *New Republic* aimed at its liberal readers a review which crystallized fresh attitudes:

> If you spent any time in Army PX's during the war, you are unlikely to entertain an overwhelming fondness for the nasal, singsong laments of hillbilly vocalists asserting their fidelity to fair-haired and faithless young things in calico. A powerful indictment of war can be made from the case of several khaki-clad mountaineers weeping into their 3.2 beer and hovering around a juke box to vie for the privilege of playing "No Letter Today" for the five hundredth consecutive time. Therefore, I ask myself why I want to recommend so heartily Columbia's current album of hillbilly music played by Roy Acuff and his Smoky Mountain Boys (C 143). One reason, I believe, is that the tunes selected possess some authenticity as folk music and little of the tedium that identifies most of the chromium-plated ballads today. Songs like "Wreck on the Highway" and "Wabash Cannon Ball" have a forthright, unspoiled vigor. Then too, Acuff and his boys have a way with fiddles, harmonicas and guitars. I think you'll be able to digest this album with little difficulty.[15]

Charles Miller's review also covered Dinah Shore's torch songs and the Golden Gate Quartet's spirituals. His approval of Acuff is particularly interesting when it is known that the *New Republic* in 1947 was edited by former Vice-President Henry Wallace — at that time preparing for his Progressive party presidential campaign. Acuff, the 1948 Republican gubernatorial candidate in Tennessee, was a "people's singer" but not yet accepted by Wallace's radical friends or by folklorists. Further, it is highly unlikely that in that period any academic collector accepted "Wreck on the Highway" as a folksong.

In noting that race and hillbilly records were more than corrosive or malevolent forces, I have chosen not to treat recording history, technology, or discography. Good works on these subjects by Gaisberg, Gelatt, Godrich and Dixon, Mahony, Read and Welch, and Rust are cited in my bibliography. Jazz literature itself — surveyed by bibliographers Merriam, Reisner, and Erskine (also cited) — leads to further data. No sooner does a reader plunge into this corpus than he is surrounded by an unfamiliar talking-machine vocabulary: *master, take, dub, graphophone, gramophone, victrola, Red Seal, A & R, hill and dale, numerical, pirate, 78 rpm, reissue.* Such terms shall be glossed, when appropriate, in chapters to follow. However, readers for whom sound-recording literature is terra incognita must begin with at least three pieces of information: (1) Firms which entered the "folksong" market in the 1920's generally separated race and hillbilly discs into series (blocks designated by continuous release or label numbers). For instance, the General Phonograph Corporation on Okeh issued a race series 8001–8966 (from 1921 to 1935) and an old-time series 45001–45579 (from 1925 to 1934). (2) Collectors commonly equate label names with the corporate titles of parent firms. (3) Discographers present their findings in a wide variety of forms such as numerical series' lists, artists' checklists, thematic discographies, and case studies. This basic information is necessary to illuminate the sound-recording industry's documentary and communicative role.

Before any individual coal-mining piece is selected for detailed examination, a few general queries on the recording firms' treatment of industrial songs are appropriate: How did engineers and talent scouts come to record any coal songs at all? Was there a conscious attempt to fix coal dust in wax? Was the recording and selling of several million copies of "Sixteen Tons" coincidental or peripheral to larger strategies of the industry? When did race and hillbilly talent scouts consciously, if ever, perceive themselves as folksong documentarians?

45

During the initial decade of race and hillbilly recording, the industry viewed itself as in the business of making money, not of gathering folksongs. Two types of evidence support this assertion. *Talking Machine World,* the major phonograph trade journal of the 1920's, gave extensive coverage to the new genre. Expeditions to the South by New York–based firms were covered; full-page advertisements for blues or mountain performers were featured; inside stories on specific campaigns aimed at ethnic or regional audiences were developed. Yet in all this verbiage the generic terms were always *race, jazz, blues, spirituals, sacred, old-time, mountain,* or *southern* but not *folk*. However, when Vocalion advertised a 1924 offering of "Songs of the Homeland" — foreign discs for sale to immigrant groups within the United States — it used the noun *folksong*. Similarly, Columbia in a news release told of recording Bohemian and Italian folksongs in Chicago. On July 15, 1925, the General Phonograph Corporation proudly announced: "The first recording of a 'Cajan' folk song for Okeh records has been made by the Hart Piano House, Southern jobbers for the Okeh line. . . . The initial record is 'Gue Gue Solingail,' or 'Song of the Crocodile.' It is sung for the Okeh by Dr. James F. Roach, a New Orleans non-professional." Curiously, when Gennett's 1926 expedition to record Hopi Indians at the Grand Canyon — in cooperation with the Smithsonian Institution and the Santa Fe Railroad — was announced, the word *folksong* was not employed.[16]

This term was obviously known to music-industry publicists but apparently reserved for exotic material. Were American consumers too close to rural roots to welcome such connotative tags? Inasmuch as the same persons produced and promoted "foreign" records and race and hillbilly discs, it is fair to assume that the industry either failed to see the early connection of the latter genre to folksong, sensed it but felt it of no denominative value, or rejected it. Not until the mid 1930's — parallel to the New Deal's exploration of Americana — did copywriters link *folksong, race,* and *hillbilly* as related terms in album-liner notes, catalogs, and other graphic forms.

A second position to support the assertion that the industry did not emblazon its folksong-collecting role on any banners, figurative or otherwise, emerges from the few available interviews with pio-

FIDDLIN' JOHN CARSON AND FRIENDS

neer Artist and Repertoire men (talent scout–producer–studio fac-
totum–expedition chief) such as Polk Brockman, Art Satherley, and
Frank Walker. I relied heavily on interviews with Brockman to
sketch in an article the "origin" of hillbilly recordings.[17] To the
extent that his views can be accepted as representative, he knew
that Fiddlin' John Carson, the "first" hillbilly artist, was neither
classical nor popular (in a Gene Austin or Vincent Lopez sense),
but Brockman was not impelled to identify Carson as a folk performer. There seems no question today that the Georgia fiddler
would have been so labeled by Lloyd Lewis if he had wandered into
the Sandburg-Lomax Chicago realm instead of an Atlanta 1923
recording session, but such speculation is very much after the fact.

Regardless of the industry's perception of, or nomenclature for,
race and hillbilly discs, it reaped a tremendous folksong harvest in
the 1920's and 1930's. Indeed, the process continues. The documentary role of records could be illustrated by selecting murder ballads
or lonesome love songs as easily as coal-mining pieces. However, the
latter have the virtue of commenting on a specific folk-like community and throwing light on questions which concern folklorists

47

studying industrial society. This is not to suggest, though, that pioneer A & R men directed their expeditions specifically to mining camps or patches or were drawn to the richness of coal folklore.

To my knowledge, the very first coal song recorded in the United States was "Down in a Coal Mine," placed on Edison cylinder 9818 in 1908 by the Edison Concert Band. However, the earliest actual recordings by working miners on home ground were obtained by George Korson and Melvin Le Mon in Pennsylvania's anthracite region during 1935. Some fifty tunes from this search were deposited on acetate discs at Bucknell University as well as at the Eastman School of Music in Rochester, but they were not readily accessible to the public.[18] Previously John Lomax, on his first Library of Congress field trip to Harlan County, Kentucky, in 1933, had recorded Blind James Howard's "The Hard-Working Miner." This was likely the very first field recording of any mining song in the bituminous region, and its Library of Congress accession foreshadowed the many similar recordings of indigenous industrial material that were to come. However, discs such as Howard's are not central to this study; rather, I am concerned with the commercial issues which preceded and paralleled field recordings.

One significant difference between commercial expeditions and folkloric field trips was that the former were much better equipped mechanically. It took academic collectors decades to catch up to the technical standards of Okeh, Columbia, Victor, Edison, and other companies in the 1920's. These firms had the option of setting up portable studios in hotels, lofts, warehouses, and like spots (from Charlotte to Dallas), or of bringing artists to permanent studios. In both settings excellent equipment was used and the industry developed crews with considerable understanding of the habits and styles of folk performers. By contrast, the Library of Congress Archive of American Folk Song was understaffed or underfinanced, and sometimes handicapped by its staff and contributors' special notions of the "folk mind." Many dedicated collectors reached the field infrequently and under trying conditions. One cannot avoid the fact that the industry could finance substantial "collecting" and that scholars could not. Nevertheless, archival holdings proliferated, particularly in New Deal years. But not until 1941 did the Library of Congress issue any recordings for public sale, and then only

48

after subsidies to establish its Recordings Laboratory were provided by the Carnegie Corporation of New York, not by the government itself.

For most scholars and for the music industry alike, coal miners recorded not primarily because they were miners, but because they were talented or had unusual repertoires. It is probably coincidental that some coal diggers did and some did not record mining songs. Not all miners who reached studio or field microphones knew mining pieces; conversely, many with fine industrial items at their command never recorded such material.

The best-known example of a life-long miner who placed no mining songs on wax until the very end of his "second" recording career is Moran Lee (Dock) Boggs from Norton, Virginia. Dock was a trapper boy in the mines at twelve and survived the perils and dangers of his craft to retire on Social Security and his union pension, after serving a stint as financial secretary of UMWA Local 6848, Jackhorn, Kentucky. He was always a compelling singer and banjoist, as well as an active seeker of old and unusual songs. Fortunately, after his retirement he was able to perform at festival and collegiate concerts throughout the United States and to make a number of LPs for Folkways in the 1960's. During 1927 he had recorded eight songs in Brunswick's New York studios and four more in 1930 for a shoestring label, Lonesome Ace. None of the initial dozen pieces stem from mining life yet Boggs was eminently qualified to make such a commentary.

An explanatory note on Boggs's two available coal pieces reveals something of the role of recent "revival" performer-collectors in bringing industrial material to the surface. After an extended search, Mike Seeger located Mr. and Mrs. Boggs in mid-June, 1963, at their home overlooking Norton; two weeks later Mike introduced Dock at a folk festival in Ashville, North Carolina. As Seeger began to record Boggs's repertoire, he also taped much of his life story. In June Boggs had indicated that one of the first "chording pieces" learned by himself was "Coal Creek March." It came to him from two banjoists who had "picked" the tune at a land auction near Mayking, Kentucky, late in 1927. The duo had sung the "March" as well, but Dock was not impelled to learn the words at that time. Responding to Seeger's interest in the piece during 1963, Dock

49

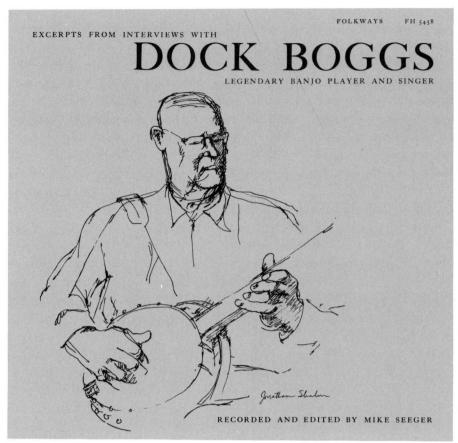

EXCERPTS FROM INTERVIEWS WITH

FOLKWAYS   FH 5458

DOCK BOGGS

LEGENDARY BANJO PLAYER AND SINGER

RECORDED AND EDITED BY MIKE SEEGER

DOCK BOGGS

learned from a relative that the "March" had come out of Tennessee labor troubles, when unionists "tore up" the stockades housing convict coal miners. Apparently the state militia actually had played the stirring bars during the disturbance.

Boggs recorded the strident "Coal Creek March" as an instrumental solo on September 23, 1963; it was released on his first LP (Folkways FA 2351). Subsequently, at concert performances and festival demonstrations coast to coast, Dock played the "Coal Creek March" and told fresh audiences of his work experience, including an account of one function of music: "In the mines we'd be awaiting on cars. Sometimes you'd sit around an hour . . . two hours . . . and you have your coal all prepared and ready to load and nothing to do . . . your timbering up and all . . . and I'd sing some songs I knowed just for my buddies, you know, in the mines. They say: 'Sing us a song or two, Dock, while we're sitting around here.'"[19]

It was in his retirement period, with a new consciousness of educational responsibility to "folksong revivalists," that Dock found a poem, "Prayer of a Miner's Child," in the *United Mine Workers Journal* (November 15, 1963). Writing to author Shirley Hill, a teenager in Dragerton, Utah, Dock secured her permission to set the poem to music, using a tune similar to his traditional "Danville Girl." Dock presented this new song at a Carnegie Hall concert-workshop (June, 1965), and recorded it in 1966 with Seeger backing him on guitar. "Prayer of a Miner's Child" was released in 1970 (Asch AH 3903) with Shirley's *UMWJ* poem reproduced in the LP's brochure. This "new" song — folk in theme, rhetoric, and musical style — was not available until 1970. It could well have sounded "old" on the day when Dock, as a lad, commenced mining coal. Yet I feel we would not have the "Prayer" even now had not Mike Seeger stimulated Dock's interest in coal-song lore. Furthermore, Seeger's careful work with Dock to tape and present four extremely valuable LP documentaries gave us a fine benchmark to measure and judge one miner's relationship to both folk and mass society.[20]

By contrast with Boggs's late recording of a mining song, one of his contemporaries, Frank Hutchison, deserves attention. This West Virginia miner from Logan County, a magnificent guitarist-singer drawing upon black and white traditions, recorded in 1928 a "Miner's Blues" (Okeh 45258). It was composed of stock images held together by a symbol of the highly visible tipple which loomed against the skyline of nearly every patch and camp. Since the tipple was the place where coal cars were unloaded and weighed, it was the site where miners could feel their sweat translated into pay. Hutchison's song sensitively caught the emotion of this scene. Hutchison died in 1958, unreached by any folklorist, but not before an Okeh engineer had inscribed his beautiful "Miner's Blues" in wax.[21]

We know much of Dock Boggs's life story through the attention given to him in recent years by Mike Seeger; we know a little about Frank Hutchison because of Seeger's interviews with the late

TIPPLE

guitarist's friends. In neither case does adequate knowledge of these two folk musicians come from recording companies. If a whole industry can be indicted for neglecting that which it never perceived as its proper function, then the sound-recording industry was derelict in overlooking the story of its folk performers. George Korson's attention to Con Carbon or Bill Keating can be cited in contrast to Brunswick's and Okeh's inattention to Boggs and Hutchison, but this has been only one of the many differences between the roles of the scholarly and commercial worlds.

An obvious difference in these realms which requires exploration is that of the basic purpose behind the physical recording process. Race and hillbilly discs were intended for quick sale; most field recordings were intended for archival deposit. That a few of the latter items were issued for public purchase is secondary. When commercial items sold well they were kept in retail outlets for long periods; when they failed to sell they were deleted from catalogs. Enough is known of the music industry's dependence on smash sales to make further discussion superfluous at this juncture. Suffice it to say that "The Dream of the Miner's Child," released in 1925, was the hillbilly idiom's first substantial coal-song hit, and that it reached an extremely wide audience in a few years' time.

Many other coal pieces of the same period sold almost no copies. To illustrate, "The Burial of the Miner's Child" (Okeh 45422), recorded in 1930 by Jack and Tony, sold so few copies that apparently none have survived. At least no extant copies are known to me, and its singers are also unknown. In this sense Jack and Tony's disc is representative of the tens of thousands of items spewed out by the industry destined to be used immediately, discarded, and overlooked by archives. Scholars lament the gaps in museum and library holdings, but it is my personal view that we are fortunate to have preserved as much of the race and hillbilly corpus as is now found in the hands of private collectors and in such institutions as the John Edwards Memorial Foundation at the University of California, Los Angeles, or the Archives of New Orleans Jazz at Tulane University.

The similarities and differences between field and commercial recordings seem clear today; there is no evidence that such comparisons were drawn either by the industry or the academy in the 1920's. Few were able to ask the proper questions. One was Robert Winslow Gordon, who organized the Library of Congress Archive of American Folk Song in 1928. A measure of his farsightedness is indicated by the fact that he solicited for the archive, in its early period, Victor race and hillbilly recordings. If a single representative business figure can be named who was an unsung folksong collector and archivist in some ways comparable to Gordon, it is

Ralph Sylvester Peer. He was involved in the initial recording sessions for race and hillbilly music and helped name the idiom. Ironically, no folklorist interviewed Peer before his death, but something is known of his views from brief articles, correspondence, and memories of friends. Much more is known of Gordon's position, since he wrote for periodicals as diverse as *Adventure* and the *New York Times Magazine*. Chapters to follow will detail some of the responses by A & R men and academicians alike to folksongs commercially recorded.

A relatively unexplored area is the response of individual folksingers to collectors, whether wearing company or academy badges. This does not mean that performers who made race and hillbilly records were never interviewed or described in articles during the 1920's and 1930's, but rather that reports were not published which commented on artists' perspectives. Early jazz-record collectors talked to celebrities such as Louis Armstrong and Duke Ellington, but cast their findings in the language of popular-music commentary. I do not know when the first enthusiast met a country bluesman who was also a phonograph "star," and felt that a folkloric point of reference, or a sense of the folk esthetic, was needed to frame the interview. Perhaps it was Abbe Niles. In 1926 he had already asserted that blues were folksongs and commented on race records in such a context. Further, he was aware that only a few students previously had "noticed the place of the blues in folksong." Three credited by Niles with understanding this relationship were Dorothy Scarborough, James Weldon Johnson, and Carl Van Vechten.[22] This diversity in viewpoint augured well for the field. Miss Scarborough can be commended for the first article (1923) on the blues in an academic publication.

It took a full decade for folklorists to learn that the wall between jazz-based bluesmen and folksingers was not rigid. By 1934 John Lomax had brought Huddie Ledbetter (Leadbelly) from Texas-Louisiana prison life to northern urban centers for a concert and recording career.[23] Leadbelly, a powerful and inventive artist, was received as the archetypal Negro folksinger and extensively interviewed. Although he made commercial records in 1935, he was perceived in terms of folk- rather than popular-culture values. Huddie had to be identified by the word *folk,* in part because he

54

LEADBELLY

was sponsored by a folklorist rather than a commercial A & R man, and in part because he fell into a role expected of him by many radical intellectuals who admired his dynamic technique in framing message songs. American communists from the 1920's to the present have been drawn especially to black folk expression ("Negro culture is the most genuine workers' culture in America . . ."), despite the fact that much of it was disseminated by race records and related mass-media forms.[24] Lawrence Gellert's early *New Masses* articles and his anthology *Negro Songs of Protest* (1936) helped prepare listeners for Leadbelly's ironic "Bourgeois Blues." During the war, Huddie composed and recorded for home-front and overseas listeners anti-facist songs, enhancing their appeal by setting them always in the rhetoric of his rural folk speech. He died on December 6, 1949, a victim of chronic polio, well before many of his songs emerged as popular and profitable (for others) hits.

Josh White, a Negro folksinger who reached a wider public than Leadbelly, recorded and performed from the 1920's through the 1960's and left several good accounts of his perceptions of folk and mass society.[25] From his home in Greenville, South Carolina,

55

young Joshua took to the road at the age of eight as a lead boy for blind itinerant bluesmen and curbstone evangelists. During 1928 he began a long association with the phonograph industry by playing second guitar behind Blind Joe Taggart at a Paramount session in Chicago. Four years later, Josh started recording blues on his own for the American Record Corporation. During 1936 a particularly effective ARC disc, "No More Ball and Chain" / Silicosis Blues" (released under the pseudynom Pinewood Tom), revealed White's feeling for protest. In 1940, assisted by the Carolinians, he recorded for Columbia an entire album of social material, *Chain Gang,* and in the war years he made many more such topical discs for Keynote and other labor-radical labels. Like Leadbelly, Josh White was caught up in a web of Communist party culture fronts and causes; unlike Huddie, Josh survived the postwar attack on leftists to end his career as a polished concert entertainer.

A critical evaluation of writing on blues from Walter Kingsley's journalistic reports in 1919 to the recent academic studies in Norman Whitten and John Szwed's *Afro-American Anthropology* would be a most helpful tool in black studies and would enlarge our understanding of how race artists saw "their" industry. Perhaps the best present-day view from the perspective of folksingers is found in Paul Oliver's *Conversation with the Blues* (1965), based on transcriptions of tape recordings with some sixty-five musicians. This book, in part, is a popular ethnography and displays a realistic grasp of black folk society in America; it is equally useful to folklorist, historian, and musicologist. Needless to say, there is no work on hillbilly music comparable to Oliver's.

The circulation of the mimeographed *Disc Collector* (official organ of the National Hillbilly Record Collectors Exchange) among fans in 1951 signaled that they had finally reached the point achieved by jazz buffs two decades before. The first two issues featured biographical sketches and discographies of the Carter Family (by Freeman Kitchens) and the Sons of the Pioneers (by Will Roy Hearne); the third introduced D. K. Wilgus reviewing records and using the nom de plume "The Perfesser." Kitchens, Hearne, and Wilgus in the same "fanzine" signified the promising unity of fan, discographer, and folklorist that had finally been achieved in this long-neglected field.[26]

56

The life stories of folksingers who were touched by large society in the shape of the recording industry are as complex and varied as the American dream itself. For some the voice of the talking machine meant wealth and power; for others it meant cruel exploitation. G. B. Grayson, the first man to record "Tom Dooley" — three decades before the Kingston Trio parlayed the ballad into a fortune — lies in an unmarked grave on a hillside near Laurel Bloomery, Tennessee. The name of his place of rest is beautiful, as was his vocal and instrumental music, but "his" industry was not geared to compensate his contribution adequately in life, nor to honor him after death.

In my interviews during the past decade with old-time as well as recent country-music performers (ranging from "Tony" Alderman, a fiddler in the Original Hillbillies band, to John Hartford, a composer-performer of recent soft-rock Nashville hits) I have tried to elicit some notion of the individual's view of the sound-recording industry: What did you think of your A & R man when you met him? How did you learn that you were a "folksinger" and not something else? What is your feeling when your songs appear in books and archives? When did you become aware of the processes of change inherent in commercialization?

No single answer was expected and none was received. The response to large society — beyond the home farm, mill gate, or mine breaker — was as varied as the personalities encountered. A few impressionistic answers to questions are revealing. Dorsey Dixon felt that he had been blessed by God in his song-making skill, and the fact that he was exploited in his lifetime was outweighed for him by the knowledge that his records had cheered and saved others. "Tony" Alderman was initially sensitive to the fact that he helped pin an undignified term, *hillbilly,* on his family's music, but he grew philosophical when be became aware that he had been a participant in the baptismal act for a significant movement. Bill Bolick (of the Blue Sky Boys duo) was distressed that the industry had modernized itself so rapidly within his lifetime that his early records seemed to have no meaning to his present-day peers. John Hartford, in identifying his composition "Gentle on My Mind" as both country and rock, expressed the attractive pull of modernity on rural life. These four examples can only hint at what some country musicians saw when they looked at one of contemporary society's communicative devices.[27]

Much work remains on eliciting folk views on the various roles of the recording industry. I have oversimplified the problem by casting the questions only in terms of a singer's perception. Equally important to any probe of the disc's function is to know what the talking machine meant to the individual listener who had no performing role at stake. No one has counted the tens of millions of phonographs — graphophones, gramophones, victrolas, record players — which have graced American homes for seven decades. It has long been "smart" to note phonographs in poor dwellings as if somehow the folk had no right to high society's toys: "In the delta of the Mississippi it was not unusual to find a ramshackle carpetless darky shanty boasting a bright red mahogany $250 Victrola."[28] This 1932 Depression comment is close to present-day reports on poverty in urban ghettos or Appalachian coves where television sets grace tenement and cabin alike.

For a semi-literate population, or for a people still close to oral tradition, the phonograph was an instrument of compelling importance: relatively inexpensive, easy to play, natural as a source for songs, stories, and instrumental styles. It was ideal for a conservative audience which wanted familiar music, rhetoric, dialect, and values, and it was competitive with many other popular-culture forms and devices. To draw illustrations from the mine community alone, some miners preferred pulp fiction to the phonograph, some preferred movies, some rejected all such "scissorbill" or "bourgeois" forms in favor of trade-union and fraternal life. Some avoided rhetorical expression in favor of pastoral retreat — hunting, fishing, etc. But the hard fact was that many coal miners, whether in boom or hard times, and regardless of "free" pursuits, could and did buy phonographs. In 1919 an ordinary machine cost $75. Translated into real wages it took a miner much time to buy one.

Contrast this home talking machine, controlled by the user himself, with a rival device offered by mass culture — the cinema. In the summer of 1919 the *Dramatic Mirror* carried this note: "The Pittsburgh & West Virginia Coal Mining Company has erected a $25,000 motion picture theater at Colliers, West Virginia, for the benefit of its employees and their families. It was opened

MUSIC IN THE MINE

August 1 and will be free to all in the employ of the Company. The best line of films and current news topics will be shown."[29] The implications in this note for the social use of entertainment media are enormous. No miner could build a $25,000 theater; no miner could select movies for showing. It is not surprising that of all modern technology's aural or visual gifts in this century the sound recording was the easiest assimilated into folk culture.

Perhaps the best metaphor to sum up the plural views of the recording device and process by folksingers themselves as well as by other listeners in folk society is to conjure up a double-vision mirror set into a miner's cottage window. The talking-machine disc or cylinder when spinning or turning is the glass itself. The particular song played by the machine at a given moment enables the listener to see (hear) two ways with a mere glance. When he hears "Yes, We Have No Bananas" he sees as far away as New York's Tin Pan Alley. "Your Cheating Heart" brings Nashville's Tin Pan Valley into view. When he plays "The Trail of the Lonesome Pine" he may see the slope at his back stoop, but through Hollywood's eyes. "Explosion at Eccles, West Virginia" reveals his personal work-world in intimate but somber terms. "Dark as a Dungeon" focuses on his realm again, but in general hues — as it can be felt by a sympathetic outsider. On the whole, folklorists are just such sympathetic outsiders who also use these aural documents as window mirrors to picture coal-mining — and, by extension, other — life.

1. Ronald C. Foreman, Jr., "Jazz and Race Records, 1920-32" (thesis, University of Illinois, Urbana, 1968), 93.
2. David Riesman, *Individualism Reconsidered, and Other Essays* (Glencoe, Ill., 1954), 184.
3. Josiah H. Combs, *Folk-Songs of the Southern United States,* ed. D. K. Wilgus (Austin, Tex., 1967), 48, 102.
4. See Ed Kahn, "Hillbilly Music: Source and Resource," *Journal of American Folklore,* LXXVIII (1965), 257, and Judith McCulloh, "Hillbilly Records and Tune Transcriptions," *Western Folklore,* XXVI (1967), 225.
5. Lewis quotations in John A. Lomax, *Adventures of a Ballad Hunter* (New York, 1947), 86-91. See also Lewis, "Last of the Troubadours," in *It Takes All Kinds* (New York, 1947), 73.
6. Lomax, *Adventures of a Ballad Hunter,* 90.
7. Carl Van Vechten, "The Great American Composer," *Vanity Fair,* VIII (Apr., 1917), 75.
8. Walter Kingsley, "Walter Kingsley writes . . . ," *New York Sun* (Aug. 3, 1919), sec. 4, 2. See also his "Miss Gray's Sad Air Cheers Broadway," *New York Herald* (July 12, 1919), sec. 3, 12. These are supplemented by "Enigmatic Folksongs of the Southern Underworld," *Current Opinion,* LXVII (Sept., 1919), 165.
9. See among Van Vechten's articles from this period "The Black Blues," *Vanity Fair,* XXIV (Aug., 1925), 57, and " 'Moanin' wid a Sword in Ma Han',' " *ibid.,* XXV (Feb., 1926), 61.
10. Abbe Niles, "Ballads, Songs and Snatches," *Bookman,* LXVII (1928), 565, and Introduction, in *Blues: An Anthology,* ed. William C. Handy (New York, 1926), 9.
11. For a retrospective tribute see Samuel Charters, "Abbe Niles: A Pioneer Jazz Critic of the '20s," *Jazz Review* (May, 1959), 25.
12. Stephen W. Smith, "Collecting Hot," in *Jazzmen,* ed. Frederick Ramsey, Jr., and Charles Edward Smith (New York, 1939), 289.
13. Alan Lomax, "List of American Folk Songs on Commercial Records," in *Report . . . on Inter-American Relations in the Field of Music,* ed. William Berrien (Washington, 1940), 126.

14. Alan Lomax, "The Best of the Ballads," *Vogue*, CVIII (Dec. 15, 1946), 208.
15. Charles Miller, "Music: Collection of Folklore," *New Republic*, CXVII (Nov. 17, 1947), 34.
16. For specific usages in Vocalion, Columbia, Okeh, and Gennett publicity see *Talking Machine World*, XX (May, 1924), 57, (Sept., 1924), 126; XXI (July, 1925), 12; XXII (June, 1926), 16.
17. Archie Green, "Hillbilly Music: Source and Symbol," *Journal of American Folklore*, LXXVIII (1965), 204.
18. For Bucknell holdings see George Korson, *Minstrels of the Mine Patch*, 3rd printing (Hatboro, Pa., 1964), 7. For Eastman School of Music holdings see Melvin Le Mon, "Pennsylvania Anthracite Miners' Folk-Songs" (Thesis, University of Rochester, 1941). See also Melvin Le Mon and George Korson, *The Miner Sings* (New York, 1936).
19. Ralph Rinzler in "Some Considerations Regarding the Musical Style of Dock Boggs," supplementary notes to brochure for *Dock Boggs* (Folkways FA 2351).
20. Brochure notes by Mike Seeger to four LPs: *Excerpts from Interviews with Dock Boggs* (Folkways FH 5458), *Dock Boggs* (Folkways FA 2351), *Dock Boggs: Volume 2* (Folkways FA 2392), *Dock Boggs: Volume 3* (Asch AH 3903), supplemented by my interviews and correspondence.
21. For Frank Hutchison see my brochure in Mike Seeger's *Tipple, Loom & Rail* (Folkways FH 5273).
22. Niles, Introduction, in *Blues*, ed. Handy, 32.
23. John A. and Alan Lomax, *Negro Songs as Sung by Leadbelly* (New York, 1936). Early repertoire is available on *Leadbelly: The Library of Congress Recordings* (Elektra EKL 301/2), brochure texts transcribed by Lawrence Cohn.
24. Quotation from Philip Schatz, "Songs of the Negro Worker," *New Masses*, VI (May, 1930), 6.
25. Robert Shelton, *The Josh White Song Book* (Chicago, 1963).
26. *Disc Collector* and other "fanzines" are found in the John Edwards Memorial Foundation at the University of California, Los Angeles, the Library of Congress, and various private collections.
27. Dorsey Dixon interview, Aug. 20, 1961; A. E. "Tony" Alderman interview, Dec. 31, 1962; Bill Bolick interview, Mar. 10, 1963; John Hartford interview, June 16, 1967.
28. Dane Yorke, "The Rise and Fall of the Phonograph," *American Mercury*, XXVII (Sept., 1932), 8.
29. "Theater for Miners," *Dramatic Mirror*, LXXX (Aug. 7, 1919), 1227.

CHEROKEE COUNTY MINER

Only a Miner 3

THE JANUARY, 1928, dealers' list of the New York Recording Laboratories — corporately located at Port Washington, Wisconsin — announced to the trade twenty-seven new releases on its Paramount label, twenty-one in its Race and six in its Old Time Tunes series. Both label and laboratory were subsidiaries of the Wisconsin Chair Company. The company's Paramount operation was based initially twenty miles north of Milwaukee at a Grafton plant which had produced furniture for Sears, Roebuck sales. It was not unusual in the opening decades of this century for furniture manufacturers to become engaged in the sound-recording industry after a stint at producing talking-machine cabinets. Some furniture retailers, similarly, entered the new industry after selling phonographs and records. Because of the Wisconsin Chair Company's proximity to Chicago's large Negro population, it was easy for the firm to enter the race-record market during this genre's formative period as well as to establish a Chicago studio to record artists from the South.

Paramount in 1922 inaugurated a 12000 race series which continued for a decade, ending with label and catalog number 13156. This block included such diverse performers as Blind Lemon Jefferson, Papa Charlie Jackson, Ma Rainey, Blind Blake, Ida Cox, Reverend J. M. Gates, and Charley Patton. Not only were these superb artists well known to record buyers in the 1920's and 1930's, but a few were also known at that time to a second audience of jazz-blues historians as well as to students of popular culture. The first singer in this group widely appreciated by persons beyond entertainment circles was Ma Rainey. A few years before she retired in 1933 she was celebrated by Sterling Brown in a warm poem, "Ma Rainey," addressed to her "second" audience.[1] Of course, most Paramount artists in their lifetime were neglected by intellectuals, but some, like Charley Patton, have been intensely studied in the 1960's.[2]

Many Paramount discs were poorly recorded and cheaply produced, with a low shellac-to-filler ratio in the pressing compounds. Even when "mint" copies issued in the 1920's are found they do not compare aurally to the products of other firms of that era. Not all Paramounts were recorded in Grafton or Chicago; the firm bought or leased from, or exchanged material with, other producers. Consequently the label is an inviting jungle for discographers. When Paramount failed in the early 1930's, much of its stock — masters, stampers, ledgers — vanished. Fortunately, John Steiner, a chemist and jazz enthusiast, purchased what remained of the enterprise about 1948 and began the slow reconstruction of its holdings and history. For some time Max Vreede, a jazz collector in the Netherlands, has been studying Paramount race records intensely, and his to-be-published findings will shed much light in this area.[3] In recent years Chicago discographer Harlan Daniel has made the Paramount Old Time Tunes series (3000-3323) his special province and has managed to interview a number of Paramount performers. Because of the time lag between the undertaking of his and Vreede's study, it is unlikely that Daniel's promised book will reveal data comparable to that already known on the race material.

One of Paramount's January, 1928, releases paired "I've Waited Long for You" / "Only a Miner" (3071). This latter folksong is the American miner's national anthem. It is known from California to Virginia and was collected in coal, gold, silver, copper, and lead areas. It belonged to traditional singers at least from 1888 to 1961, and it seems vital enough to live into the future. Little is known of "Only a Miner's" origin except that it is part of a complex of similar occupational laments: "Only a Cowboy," "Only a

64

3000 Golden Slippers—Vocal—Unaccompanied

Just a Little While
Vocal—Unaccompanied
Edgewater Sabbath Singers

3002 Lord I'm Coming Home
Vocal Chorus—Harry Charles

Almost Persuaded
Vocal Chorus—Samuel Spencer
Hugh Gibbs String Band

Instrumentals

3017 Sailor's Hornpipe
Champion Old Time Fiddler

The Girl I Left Behind
Champion Old Time Fiddler
John Baltzell

3003 Chicken Reel—Instrumental

Double Eagle March—Instrumental
Hugh Gibbs String Band

3009 The Wagoner—Instrumental

Cumberland Blues—Instrumental
The Quadrillers

3015 The Arkansas Traveler
Champion Old Time Fiddler

The Turkey in the Straw
Champion Old Time Fiddler
John Baltzell

3008 Drunk Man's Blues—Instrumental

Rocky Mountain Goat—Instrumental
The Quadrillers

For Sale By

The New York Recording Laboratories,
Port Washington, Wis.

Olde Time Tunes

REG. U.S. PAT. OFF.

Paramount Records

Electrically Recorded

PARAMOUNT RECORDS
Southern Series

3001 I'm Going Crazy
Instrumental with Vocal Refrain

Swinging in the Lane
Instrumental with Vocal Refrain
Gibbs String Band

3004 My Little Girl—Instrumental—Vocal
Chorus—Samuel Spencer

In the Good Old Summer Time
Instrumental
Hugh Gibbs String Band

3005 I'm Going to Leave the Old Home
Vocal—Unaccompanied

Heavenly Sunshine
Vocal—Unaccompanied
Edgewater Sabbath Singers

3006 When the Roses Bloom Again
Singing with Guitar Acc.

The Sporting Cowboy
Singing with Guitar Acc.
Watts and Wilson

3007 The Empty Cradle
Singing with Guitar Acc.

The Night Express
Singing with Guitar Acc.
Watts and Wilson

3010 I Love You Best of All
Vocal—Guitar and Violin Acc.

If I Only Had a Home Sweet Home
Vocal—Guitar and Violin Acc.
Kentucky Thoroughbreds

3011 Mother's Advice
Vocal—Guitar and Violin Acc.

I Left Because I Love You
Vocal—Guitar and Violin Acc.
Kentucky Thoroughbreds

3012 The Death of Floyd Collins
Tenor Solo—Novelty Acc.

The Letter Edged in Black
Tenor Solo—Violin-Guitar-Harmonica Acc.
Vernon Dalhart

3013 My Carolina Home
Vocal Duet—Violin-Cello-Guitar Acc.
Lambert and Hillpot

Zeb Turney's Gal
Tenor Solo—Violin-Guitar-Harmonica Acc.
Vernon Dalhart

3016 Get Away Old Man
Baritone Solo
Arthur Fields

The Wreck of the Royal Palm
Tenor Solo—Violin-Guitar-Harmonica Acc.
Vernon Dalhart

3018 Rovin' Gambler—
Tenor Solo

Wreck of the Old '97—
Tenor Solo
Vernon Dalhart

Sacred Songs

3014 Room for Jesus
Vocal—Guitar and Violin Acc.

This World Is Not My Home
Vocal—Guitar and Violin Acc.
The Kentucky Thoroughbreds

PARAMOUNT BROCHURE

Brakeman," "Only a Tramp." The Paramount "Only a Miner" is possibly the very first "publication" of the mining song. (The word *publication* for the recording process refers to the physical inscription of lyrics and melody in wax, metal, or plastic prior to transcription, notation, and printing of either words or music.) It seems highly unlikely that a mining song known traditionally for three decades was not printed in newspaper, songster, sheet music, or folio, but such an appearance prior to 1931 is unknown to me. Published labor-union and cowboy derivatives of "Only a Miner" were available as early as 1908 and 1910, respectively.[4]

In sketching a folksong's development one can begin with the "earliest" text defined either by initial date of collection, by date of subsequent deposit in archive or presentation in anthology and article, or by the singer's memory of when and from whom he first learned the piece. Such a report may even place the item a few generations back in time. Frequently, manuscript or printed broadside appearances precede documentation of a song's currency in oral tradition. Of course, the actual date of a manuscript or broadside may be at best an educated guess. Regardless of the difficulties in presenting accurately a folksong's chronology, the pursuit is worthwhile if only to bring a body of material into an ordered relationship for comparative study. Checklist One for "Only a Miner" follows this chapter. The list is arranged chronologically by date of publication, recording, or archival deposit. I open my study with the Paramount recording not because it begins the actual chronology, but rather because it is the song's earliest tangible form, aside from "memory" reports. The Paramount 3071 text and tune follow.

Only a Miner

The hard-working miners, their dangers are great,
Many while mining have met their sad fate,
While doing their duties as miners all do,
Shut out from the daylight and their darling ones, too.

He's only a miner been killed in the ground,
Only a miner and one more is found,
Killed by an accident, no one can tell,
His mining's all over, poor miner farewell.

He leaves his dear wife and little ones, too,
To earn them a living as miners all do,
While he was working for those whom he loved,
He met a sad fate from a boulder above.

    Chorus:

With a heart full of sorrow we bid him farewell,
How soon we may follow there's no one can tell,
God pity the miners, protect them as well,
And shield them from danger while down in the ground.

    Chorus: (twice)

ONLY A MINER

stanza 1

The hard-work-ing min-ers, their dang-ers are great,

Man-y while min-ing have met their sad fate, While

do-ing their du-ties as min-ers all do, Shut out—

—from the day-light and their dar-ling ones, too. He's

on-ly a min-er been killed in the ground,

On-ly a min-er and one more is found,

Killed by an ac-ci-dent, no one can tell, His

min-ing's all o-ver, poor min-er fare-well.

Before commenting on the song's content or comparing it with related items, I shall note what was known to consumers in 1928 about this specific Paramount recording. The label as well as various dealers' announcements named the singers: the Kentucky Thorobreds. The record's master number 20052 was pressed into the disc itself at the label's edge. Master numbers mean little, if anything at all, to most listeners but are used by collectors to discover recording dates, sites, and other information. Discography is an esoteric art, but one necessary to all who are concerned with sound recordings for scholarly purposes. However, I shall limit discographical citations to facts which help establish the histories of songs touched in these studies.

Master number 20052 reveals that "Only a Miner" was recorded in Chicago late in September, 1927, and blues discographers Dixon and Godrich indicate a Blind Lemon Jefferson session close to that of the Thorobreds. Much more important than date is artists' identities — someone had to be paid before, during, or after each recording session. How were the Kentucky Thorobreds paid? Who constituted this group? On February 15, 1928, the Chicago Music Publishing Company, Paramount's publishing arm, secured a copyright on the words and melody of "Only a Miner" (E 686013) in the name of the Kentucky Thorobreds rather than the actual singers' names. It was common practice to register music after records were pressed and released. Transcribers prepared musical lead sheets directly from discs and such transcriptions were submitted to the Copyright Office in Washington. The copyright process was generally integrated with each firm's fiscal arrangements with artists for recording fees and record sales. At times, sheet music or folio publication also followed the act of initial recording, but Chicago Music apparently never printed any songs by its hillbilly performers. Whether the Thorobreds drew an initial recording fee, sales royalties, or both for "Only a Miner" is unknown.

The quest for identification of the Kentucky Thorobreds is further complicated when it is known that the Wisconsin Chair Company used various labels to reach different markets, and that it switched artists' names at will. While Paramount records were priced at 75¢ each, many of the firm's masters were also used to

KENTUCKY THOROBREDS

press discs for the 35¢ Broadway label. To illustrate, "Only a Miner" appeared on Broadway 8070 (same master 20052) performed by the Old Smokey Twins. An element of mystery in addition to that of name is the musical accompaniment for the group. A Paramount four-page brochure of Old Time Tunes in the fall of 1927 as well as a dealers' list for November carried a small (2" x 2") cut of the Kentucky Thorobreds, and record purchasers could see a male trio posed with four instruments: fiddle, mandolin, guitar, banjo-ukelele. However, the actual label copy for "Only a Miner" read "guitar and violin acc." Yet the recording itself revealed to the ear a guitar and mandolin duo. If a fiddler was present when this song was recorded he did not perform on "Only a Miner," or was too far from the microphone to be audible. Apart from instrumentation, a solo singer took the lead and he was joined by a second voice on the choruses.

Obviously, in 1927 many persons — A & R men, technicians, music transcribers, bookkeepers — aside from the performers themselves knew the identity of the Kentucky Thorobreds / Old Smokey

69

Twins, and how this set of pseudonyms was selected. Naturally, the trio members knew something of "Only a Miner's" provenience. Songs are not delivered by storks to studios; this particular piece was carried to Chicago during September, 1927, in the mind of a folksinger. But no folklorist interviewed any of the Thorobreds / Twins during their recording careers. It is ironic to note that in the 1960's University of Chicago folksong enthusiasts went to great lengths to rediscover and bring north the same kind of performers who traveled to Paramount's Loop studio quite regularly four decades previously (passing within a stone's throw of the campus when they arrived in Chicago via the Illinois Central Railroad).

Although my study focuses on occupational lore, it can be observed that the Paramount / Broadway issues of the Kentucky Thorobreds / Old Smokey Twins included a good cross section of traditional material: "Shady Grove," "Preacher and the Bear," "This World Is Not My Home," "Wagoner," "I'll Not Marry at All." In the 1920's such numbers were more interesting to folklorists than mining songs and might have caught their ears. Nevertheless, I do not mean to suggest that these specific performers deserved special attention from the academy while their discs were being marketed. Paramount cloaked dozens of equally overlooked artists under picturesque names: Golden Melody Boys, Blue Ridge Highballers, Fruit Jar Guzzlers, Lookout Mountain Revelers, Red Brush Rowdies, Highlanders, Meridian Hustlers, Lonely Eagles, Gunboat Billy and the Sparrows. (Is it necessary to mention that bizarre nomenclature preceded post-Beatles rock bands?)

My attempt to identify the Kentucky Thorobreds / Old Smokey Twins did not begin until a decade after obtaining the Paramount "Only a Miner." In the summer of 1968, when I actually transcribed the piece, I was impelled to learn who sang it. The text attracted me because of its esthetic integrity, and the unknown lead singer's style appealed in that it seemed especially appropriate to a mining folksong. After transcription, I compared the text to that preserved on this song's second recording, "He's Only a Miner Killed in the Ground" by Ted Chestnut (Gennett 6603). The two texts proved to be virtually identical except that Chestnut changed a last-stanza phrase; "protect them as well" became "protect them from harm" on Gennett. Chestnut's number, recorded on August

23, 1928, could have been copied from the then-available Paramount disc; such "covers" were not uncommon. It was also possible that Chestnut and the Paramount group had both learned "Only a Miner" from the same source, or that Chestnut himself was a member of the Thorobreds. I favored the last assumption, and fortunately evidence came to the surface to demonstrate that Chestnut indeed was a member of the Paramount unit.

The clue to the relationship was found in Copyright Office entry catalogs.[5] My findings follow this chapter (Appendix One), but briefly, the Chicago Music Publishing Company registered "Phil Roberts Blues" by Phil Roberts on July 19, 1927. On this same date three additional items were registered by Roberts and Parman, and on February 15, 1928, one other by them as well as three by Roberts, Parman, and Chestnut (no first names given). Significantly, on the February date, twelve items were also copyrighted in the name of the Kentucky Thorobreds, including "Only a Miner." Of the twenty registered pieces, some numbers composed by Roberts, Parman, and Chestnut (alone or in combination) were released pseudonymously as by the Kentucky Thorobreds on Paramount and Old Smokey Twins on Broadway. To complicate matters, other pieces by the same trio were released on Paramount as by the Quadrillers and on Broadway as by the Lone Star Fiddlers. Although Paramount publicity carefully kept the group members' real names hidden, it was easy to follow the copyright data lead to full identification.

When I became certain that Roberts, Parman, and Chestnut comprised the Kentucky Thorobreds, I asked fellow collectors if anything was known of this trio's background. Doc Roberts was best known as a country fiddler who had absorbed blues style. He had begun to record for the Gennett label in the mid-1920's with Welby Toomey and Ed Boaz. Over a period of time, Roberts' group shifted to include his son James Roberts as well as Asa Martin, Green Bailey, and others. Early in 1969, Norman Cohen of the John Edwards Memorial Foundation, also curious about the aggregation's history, learned "Acey" Martin's whereabouts, and during May, Cohen and I were able to visit Martin at his Estill County, Kentucky, home in the foothills close to the Daniel Boone National Forest. Subsequently, Harlan Daniel and I saw "Acey" in September. Martin, in turn, led me to Doc Roberts, James Roberts, Green Bailey, Welby Toomey, Dick Parman, and Ted Chestnut.[6] A full report of these visits lies beyond this work; I touch on the matter here only to document how curiosity about a given pair of forty-year-old recordings led to valuable studies.

Phil "Fiddlin' Doc" Roberts was born April 26, 1897, on a hill farm between Richmond and Kirksville, Kentucky. To this day he lives "under the hill." Following his Gennett recording debut, he took to Chicago for two Paramount sessions Charles Richard "Dick" Parman (born September 17, 1895), an L & N railroad switchman and guitarist from Corbin, Kentucky, and Charles Roy "Ted" Chestnut (born December 3, 1906), a young mountain singer from London, Kentucky. Apparently the trio was named the Kentucky Thorobreds by A. C. Laibly, Paramount's sales manager (and A & R man) in Chicago.

To this trio, Roberts contributed chiefly the fiddle tunes; Parman and Chestnut brought the songs and ballads. "Only a Miner" was Chestnut's piece, learned in his Laurel County boyhood. In mountain string bands, even when all members held a song in common, there was consensus on who knew it "first" or who knew it "best," and Doc and "Acey" were eager to credit Ted with the lament. On the Chicago recording of "Only a Miner," Doc played the mandolin and Parman the guitar; Parman, who was later identified in Paramount publicity as the "Mountain Poet," also joined Chestnut as the second voice on the chorus. On the Gennett disc, however, Chestnut sang solo accompanied by Doc Roberts on fiddle and Asa Martin on guitar.

The Gennett label, owned by the Starr Piano Company of Richmond, Indiana, close to the prosperous bluegrass region of Kentucky, was able to draw on a sizable body of traditional performers already involved in some aspects of commercial music: radio, lodge affairs, formal entertainments. For example, before Doc Roberts and Asa Martin recorded for Gennett the former had won prizes at Kentucky fiddlers' contests and the latter had made a living in vaudeville. Roberts did not find his arrangement during 1927-28 with Paramount as satisfactory as that with Gennett for a number of reasons. The former firm stressed race-music sales over old-time sales; it was a longer trip from Richmond, Kentucky, to

ASA MARTIN

Chicago than to Richmond, Indiana; Paramount did not seem as prompt or generous in royalty payments as Gennett.[7]

It is understood in ballad scholarship that no case study is ever complete. The right questions are not asked until decades or even centuries after a song has entered tradition. Scholars themselves do not always agree on the nature of the "right" question. I consider myself fortunate that a series of names in 1927-28 copyright catalogs led me to visits in 1969 and 1970 with Asa Martin, Doc Roberts, Dick Parman, and Ted Chestnut, as well as to the opportunity to play for them a tape of their own performance on a mine-song recording, unheard by them for four decades.

When Gennett announced the release for November, 1928, of "He's Only a Miner Killed in the Ground" coupled with "Bring Back My Boy," a company publicist wrote: "Ted Chestnut brings

73

us two vivid pictures in song of the every-day life of the people far back in the mountains of Southern Kentucky — first the life and finally the accidental death of a miner and second a mother's plea for the return of her wandering boy."[8] The pairing on Gennett 6603 may have been coincidential or dictated by the notion that heart songs belonged together. Did a Starr Piano executive in 1928 understand the coal industry's force in breaking up hill families and sending Appalachian boys wandering?

My 1970 visit with Ted Chestnut was not within the shadow of any Kentucky tipple; rather, it took place in his comfortable Chicago home, not too far from the earth-moving equipment manufacturing plant where he is employed as a stationary engineer. His memory of recording "Only a Miner" for Paramount and for Gennett was vivid and complemented by a sophisticated awareness of his brief role in the song's dissemination. Ted's father, Charles Farris Chestnut, had been a Methodist preacher in his native Kentucky county, Laurel, but had also established new churches in the raw camps of Harlan County, where he had buried many miners and shared the sorrows of their loved ones. Ted remembered from the age of six that his father frequently had sung "Only a Miner," accompanying himself on the family parlor organ, thus making the song sound like a familiar hymn. While young Chestnut was still in high school, he had worked for several summers in the "Hardburly" (Harding-Burlington Company) mine in Laurel County. He recalls having taught his father's piece to fellow miner Kelly Nichols, who irreverently parodied the chorus: "His mining's all over, he's done gone to hell."

A few years after Chestnut's "Hardburly" experience, he was able to travel to Chicago and record the lament as he had originally learned it. "Only a Miner" was but one of many folksongs which Ted had obtained from his parents; his consciousness of folk music had been made articulate during Laurel County school days when he studied voice culture. In Paramount's studio he reverted to a "natural" pre-school manner.

I close Chestnut's account of "Only a Miner" with an anecdote which dates the Paramount session and reveals one type of association frequently cherished by the folk. On the Roberts-Parman-Chestnut first trek to Chicago in April, 1927, the trio had stayed at the modest Hotel Lorraine, near the Marsh Recording Laboratory in the Lyon & Healy Music Building. But on the second trip Chicago was full of visitors, attracted to the Dempsey-Tunney prize fight (September 22, 1927), and the musicians had to select the more expensive Sherman Hotel. The scene and time remain fresh with Ted, for Doc Roberts had warned his team not to mingle with strangers — possibly gangsters. But Chestnut broke Doc's rule long enough to engage screen star Tom Mix in a hotel lobby conversation. The cowboy thought it strange that the Kentuckians were in town but unable to attend the Soldiers' Field fight. Ted, in turn, was excited that the Mix encounter could be added as a bonus to an already heady and profitable expedition.

In this book I shall frequently use the interrelated terms *family, cycle, cluster,* and *complex* (as well as the allied figure *family tree*) to signify all the versions and variants in a chain of linked pieces. Ted Chestnut's "Only a Miner" text is very close to many of the items noted in Checklist One and can be taken as a starting point in characterizing the family. "Only a Miner" usually consists of three four-line stanzas and a similar chorus. The stanza and chorus generally rhyme a a b b. The core incident, which holds the song in focus even when the piece is lengthened or shortened, is death from an overhead boulder. The overall emotional tone is resignation to accidents. Bituminous coal miners became so familiar with loose forms in the overhead "roof" that they named them by shape and size: *horseback, niggerhead, kettlebottom, spider, bellmound* (a fossil tree trunk embedded in coal).[9] Regardless of familiarity, such rocks were treacherous and whispered constant danger.

It is a truism that some trades — mining, deep-sea diving, steel erecting — are highly dangerous. Certain calamities such as gas explosions or shipwrecks are fully vivid and present to the public mind, even though sunken ships or seared mines are completely out of ordinary sight. This "visibility," before electronic communication, was partly developed by storytellers and singers. After any modern industrial accident — an elevator-shaft fall, a wall collapse, a crane boom's touching a power line — workers still engage in functionally therapeutic talk. Creative individuals for centuries fashioned such talk into patterned accounts of bravery, lucky escapes, or resignation to death. Listeners dissolved their fears or

A MINE FALL

borrowed courage from such anecdotes. When craftsmen were together in stable communities over long periods of time, their job yarns assumed the character of local legend or folktale. In particular areas — sometimes called "singing communities" — narratives of job danger were frequently cast in ballad form, which might hold the alternative emotions of sorrow or hope.

No industry in the United States produced more disaster songs than coal mining. Tragedies as far apart in time as Avondale, Pennsylvania, 1869, and Centralia, Illinois, 1947, to cite but two prominent events, were memorialized in songs (which in turn were made available on discs). John Quinn recorded the anthracite "Avondale Mine Disaster" for the Library of Congress (L 16), and Larry Godsey recorded "New Made Graves in Centralia" for an obscure country label (Rich-R-Tone 411). Nearly all mine-disaster compositions are ballads — timely, graphic, localized, specific. Ballads, more sharply than other folksongs, are seen while heard; the singer becomes a camera eye. It is not the duty of the Bureau of Mines to issue sound recordings, but on its fiftieth anniversay it published a *Historical Summary of Coal-Mine Explosions in the United States, 1810-1958* with nearly 200 diagrams of underground explosion areas or photographs of wreckage and destruction. Some of these very pictures were cast into comparable aural documents (ballads) by miner-bards. There is no better way to grasp immediately a worker's response to the luck of the mine than to hear a disaster piece sung by a miner who toils daily within death's shadow.

"Only a Miner" is such a response to danger, but not to a particular rock-fall in an identified mine. It is a ballad only to the extent that a few essential facts are presented: all miners work in danger, a boulder crushes one miner, he leaves a wife and little ones, God is asked to shield other miners from a similar fate. Malcolm Laws, long concerned with problems in ballad scholarship, wisely stated that "Only a Miner" is "as much a lament [lyric folksong] as a ballad."[10] I feel it to be mainly a lyric folksong, intended to evoke an emotional tone of resignation rather than to narrate a specific tragedy. It is significant that of the many variants considered in this chapter, only two forms — Aunt Molly Jackson's and the Colorado "Only a Miner Killed in the Mine" — are particularized to some degree.

Folksong students who wish to illustrate the interrelationships within either ballad families or lyric folksong clusters frequently construct an idealized archetype or model poem — one never really known by living singers. Such constructs are useful for pieces of ancient lineage, considerable variation, or complicated pedigree, but hardly necessary for relatively stable material. Hence, instead of fashioning a model I shall contrast the typical, generalized Kentucky Thorobreds' song with three others which can be characterized simply as: personalized, hymn-like, literary.

The year 1931 was one of much suffering throughout the United States; many of the bituminous coal fields which had been stricken in the mid-1920's were particularly hard hit by industrial and political conflict at the nadir of the Depression. In this period some southern mountaineers under the aegis of the National Miners Union, a Communist party–led rival of the United Mine Workers of America, made the transition from either religious fundamentalism or Jacksonian democracy to Marxism. One of a group of miners and mine-family members whose lives were changed by new revolutionary creeds when NMU organizers appeared on the scene was Aunt Molly Jackson, then about fifty years old and living in Clay County, Kentucky. Something of the fervor generated in the dual-union movement at that time is documented in Theodore Dreiser's *Harlan Miners Speak* (1932). The terror and pathos of blood on the coal and of brother fighting brother in feud-like strikes is also preserved in Aunt Molly's songs, deposited on Library of Congress field discs and also available by Pete Seeger, John Greenway, and other interpreters of her work.[11]

During October, 1932, the Workers Library Publishers of New York issued a thirty-two-page *Red Song Book* which sold for 15¢ a copy. It was compiled by the Workers Music League (which included such persons as Charles Seeger and Elie Siegmeister) to express the aims and aspirations of the revolutionary working-class movement. The booklet included stirring European classics — "Bandiera Rossa" (Italy), "Whirlwinds of Danger" (Poland), "Internationale" (France), "Red Army March" (USSR) — as well as American trade-union songs set to familiar melodies — "Preacher and the Slave" (to the tune of "Sweet Bye and Bye"), "On the Picket Line" ("Polly Wolly Doodle"). The booklet also contained a few new numbers modeled in text and tune on American folksongs.

The first critic to appreciate the significance of *Red Song Book* material stemming from native tradition was Margaret Larkin. Having learned folksongs as a girl in New Mexico, she brought her songbag and guitar to New York in the late 1920's. There she arranged several numbers for Lynn Riggs's Theatre Guild production of "Green Grow the Lilacs," an Indian Territory (Oklahoma) "folk play" which opened in January, 1931. Also in that year her fine anthology *Singing Cowboy* was published. Attracted to radicalism, she spoke up for worker poets such as Ella May Wiggins and Aunt Molly Jackson. Perceptively, Miss Larkin championed new voices on the left. Also, she deflated the polemics of doctrinaire Marxists like the *Worker Musician* critic who had attacked American folk melodies as "immature" and "arrested" by attributing their debased state in culture to the "exploitation of the coal barons."[12] Miss Larkin, well ahead of her peers, was armed with an esthetic which valued the unadorned Appalachian idiom, and which avoided placing Aunt Molly either in a "folk cellar" or on a revolutionary pedestal.

78

Here to Aid Kentucky Miners

Herald Tribune photo—Steffen
"Aunt Molly" Jackson

Mine 'Aunt' Here To Help Dreiser By 'Blues' Song

Mrs. Molly Jackson Brings 'Powerful' Thanks of Kentuckians for 'Foreign Aid'

Put Harlan Plaint in Verse

Mountain Woman to Take Part in Meeting Sunday

By Ben Robertson Jr.

Mrs. Molly Jackson, wife of a soft coal miner, a woman known in southeastern Kentucky in the fold between Pine Mountain and the Cumberlands as "Aunt Molly" Jackson, midwife and general nurse, arrived in New York yesterday "to be on hand in case" Theodore Dreiser, John Dos Passos and the sev-

descent." Her father belong Garland family. Aunt Mol am almost ashamed to tell old I am—I look so old. I six years old the 30th d month. I know I look tough not tough. Wait until I g sleep."

Allegory Enriches Sp

Mrs. Jackson's conversatio riched with allegory, with idiom and colloquialisms o tion. She drew many simile woods and mines and from She spoke bitterly of the miners. She did not, howe the employers. She even the lot of the people there w of grim humor.

"The Red Cross fellow about biscuits. Biscuits? haven't seen a biscuit in so I wouldn't recognize one no it. I'd probably think a t a terrapin and would lay coal on it to keep it fro away."

Her manner was gentle. when Mr. Dos Pessos entered his hand, she said, "Howdy, to see you again, sir." She with Mrs. Adelaide Walke Avenue and Ninety-sixth S calls Mrs. Walker "Miss A old-fashioned Southern style startling thing to Aunt M that she is visiting on Park She told of children starv

AUNT MOLLY IN NEW YORK

Upon Aunt Molly's arrival in New York from Kentucky in December, 1931, to agitate for her miner friends, she gravitated toward intellectuals, for she was acutely conscious that her song lore could be used in the cause. Her earliest composition to impress listeners in the radical movement was "Miners' Hungry Ragged Blues," but the first to be transcribed for any songbook was "Poor Miner's Farewell." This printing in the *Red Song Book* held five stanzas and included music but did not name collector or transcriber.[13] The item was identified by a footnote: " 'Aunt Mollie' Jackson is the wife of a miner of the Kentucky coal fields. This is one of the songs which she wrote at the time of the miners' strike in Kentucky early this year."

The *Red Song Book* was out of print by 1933, superseded by different compilations reflecting shifts in radical positions. To my knowledge, "Poor Miner's Farewell" was not printed again for two decades, nor did Alan Lomax or Mary Elizabeth Barnicle record it for Library of Congress deposit. However, during July, 1952, Aunt Molly sang a truncated version for John Greenway in Sacramento, California, which he used, prefaced by a short explanatory note, in *American Folksongs of Protest*. During 1961 Greenway

himself recorded the song for Folkways. A year later Hedy West
placed "Miner's Farewell" on a Vanguard LP, but in a form
learned from her father. Subsequently, Miss West included the
song's text and tune under the title "Poor Hardworking Miners" in
the *Hedy West Songbook,* published in Germany. Aunt Molly
Jackson's 1932 text, when compared to Greenway's, illustrates
either her memory lapses or her pruning of superfluous stanzas
after the passage of time. The *Red Song Book* text follows.

POOR MINER'S FAREWELL

Poor hard working miners, their troubles are great,
So often while mining they meet their sad fate.
Killed by some accident, there's no one can tell,
Their mining's all over, poor miners farewell!

> Only a miner, killed under the ground,
> Only a miner but one more is gone.
> Only a miner but one more is gone,
> Leaving his wife and dear children alone.

They leave their dear wives and littles ones, too,
To earn them a living as miners all do.
Killed by some accident, there's no one can tell,
Their mining's all over, poor miners farewell!

> Chorus:

Leaving his children thrown out on the street,
Barefooted and ragged and nothing to eat,
Mother is jobless, my father is dead,
I am a poor orphan, begging for bread.

> Chorus:

When I am in Kentucky so often I meet,
Poor coal miners' children out on the street.
"What are you doing?" to them I have said,
"We are hungry, Aunt Molly, and we're begging for bread."

> Chorus:

"Will you please help us to get something to eat?
We are ragged and hungry, thrown out on the street."
"Yes, I will help you," to them I have said,
"To beg food and clothing, I will help you to get bread."

> Chorus:

Aunt Molly's first two stanzas and chorus are traditional, for every line is found elsewhere. The only surprising element is that a boulder is not specified as the accident's cause. Her last three stanzas are unique. They depart from the tone of resignation normal in "Only a Miner" to a depiction of Aunt Molly's then-recent radical role in Kentucky. Whereas all the song's previous variants counseled fortitude in the face of death, Aunt Molly spoke up for action to succor bereft children. In a sense she substituted herself for the song's God of pity. Whether her changes are to be judged blasphemous or naive depends on each listener-reader's reaction to Molly Jackson in the context of her time and place.

Greenway's publication of Aunt Molly's prefatory anecdote to "Poor Miner's Farewell" ("I composed this song one day while I was walking along thinking of how soon a coal miner is forgotten after he is dead . . .") filled in some background on the nature of her creative techniques. In my California visits with Aunt Molly (1958), I attempted to elicit her views on original composition and recomposition. This was difficult because she did not like to be told that she operated within fixed parameters of rhetoric, musical style, and ideology. She was driven to absurd lengths of self-aggrandizement and self-deception to establish her priorities and to certify her originality. My present-day observations come more easily at a distance (and after her death) than in Aunt Molly's home.

Her full preface to "Poor Miner's Farewell" — twice told to me, each time with different embellishments — comes as close to a true picture of her method in composition as we are likely to get from any folk poet who "works up" songs or "just naturally" finds them in the heart. Her anecdote goes back to Pineville, Bell County, three weeks after her brother's death:

> That's a awful sad thing. Three weeks after my brother, Richard Garland, was mashed up in the coal mines — it took fifteen men to raise a piece of slate off of him — 'til they could get his body out — it caught him just in his shoulders here, and every bone in him was just mashed — they'as nothing that you could tell that was him, only just from his face and head. Three weeks after he was killed I — my brother's widow and the children lived right in the suburbs of Pineville, there. Every year I'd get 25 cents for every birth certificate I'd send in to Louisville, to the Statistics Board [midwife's fee]. Once a year they

sent me a check and I took it down to Pineville and got it cashed. I think it was a check for 35 or 40 dollars I had, and I had to get the check cashed.

My brother's — these three little children they'as a-comin' out of Pineville — and hit was a-drizzlin' rain. I says, "What in the world is you children a-doin' out here in this rain?" And little Vernon, the little boy, he says, "We've been over," he says, "to W. T. Slusher's" — that 'as a grocery store — "to try to get some groceries on the credit." He says, "We don't have nothin' to eat at our house, but they wouldn't let us have no groceries, Aunt Molly." He says, "But you'll get us something to eat." I says, "You're doggone right I'll get you something to eat." I went and got my check cashed and got all the groceries that we could carry.

The train just run once — it come down of a mornin' — then hit was four o'clock in the evenin' before it went back up to Straight Creek. It was about three mile and a half to where I lived. So I stopped at my sister-in-law's house, and I decided that ruther than I'd have to stay 'til four-thirty and wait for the train that I'd just walk back. In walking along — going back — I was a-studyin' about how soon a man was forgot — and their little children — and about Sade didn't have no work, or nothin' — and I just found myself a-walkin' along there a-singin' "Poor hardworkin' miners their troubles are great / So often when mining, they meet their sad fate / Killed by some accident, there's no one can tell / Their mining's all over, poor miner, farewell." And then there comes the chorus — meaning my brother, you know — I says, "He's only a miner killed under the ground / He was only a miner and one more is gone / Only a miner and one more is gone / Leaving his wife and little children alone."

I think, you know, that my whole life is just a poet by nature. I was just born like that.

A.G.: That's certainly true . . . can you sing us a little part of the verse and chorus? [Aunt Molly sings verse and chorus.]

A.G.: Was that an old Kentucky mining song, Aunt Molly?

A.M.J.: No, no! I never heared — since I composed this song I've heard different versions of that — pretending that somebody else wrote it, but, you see, I know how these things is done for I've done 'em myself, and that's what makes me so mad when I find my honest, true things — songs and stories and everything else — messed up.[14]

On the second telling of this anecdote, Aunt Molly interjected by pointing to a picture of her brother Richard's children, Vernon

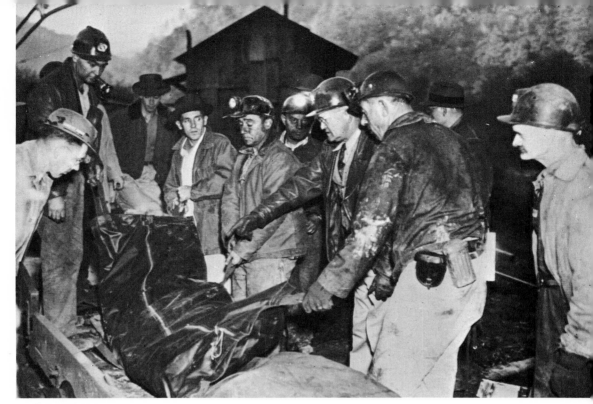

STRAIGHT CREEK, KY.

and his three sisters. Also, she underscored Mr. Slusher's refusal to grant credit by noting that he was a preacher. More important, she told me not only that she composed ("a-singin' and a-studyin' ") the song while walking up Straight Creek, but that she composed the "beggin' for bread" stanza "when I came out on tour for the miners."[15] I interpret this distinction to mean that the traditional verses came to mind shortly after Richard's death, but that the personalized or polemical stanzas were added in New York when the awareness of her new political role became acute.

Molly Jackson's preface is as good as her song — perhaps better. It tells us that she could not stand to be a passive tradition-bearer. She reviled others who "messed up" her songs and professed a most conservative loyalty to old forms. Nevertheless, she was driven to build new pieces out of the material obtained from family and friends. When she could synthesize bonds to the past with her compelling need to innovate, she became a powerful composer. It did not unduly bother Aunt Molly that none of her personal compositions apparently entered tradition (in the sense that one of her peers' numbers, "Which Side Are You On," traveled widely from its radical point of origin in the sectarian National Miners

83

Union to the labor movement far beyond Harlan County). That is, she was not concerned about her songs moving away from her to become folksongs; she assumed by virtue of her act of composition that they were folksongs. In short, she did not stress a number's status as much as its intent. She wanted passionately that "Poor Miner's Farewell" and her hortatory numbers be useful to working people. She equated bread and justice; this creed propelled her to move from old to new verses literally as she recalled a traditional lament appropriate to her brother's death.

One obvious purpose of a case study is to permit the testing of folkloric concepts. As part of my definition of folksong I have suggested the notion that an item must be passed along from one singer to another and that it must be assimilated into the latter's repertoire. Normally we infer this process after we collect (record, publish) variants. Generally, the world *folksong* is not used to label a piece that has been incorporated only into the repertoire of an academic collector-singer or professional singer of folksongs not a member of folk society. Professor Edward Ives of the University of Maine, a spirited folksong interpreter and a collector of considerable woods lore in the Northeast, has indicated to me a difficulty in my narrow definition. Ives has suggested that Aunt Molly may well have been the only one who sang her own compositions but that other people in her community could have called upon her to sing them. Hence, a Jackson "original" could be "in the consciousness of that community." Specifically, people could "know *of*" a given song but "not know *it*."[16] The pragmatic limitation in testing community consciousness, of course, is in finding and interviewing a folk composer's peers to ask about the process of song movement and meaning.

My personal awareness of Aunt Molly's "Poor Miner's Farewell" as a discrete song came about 1954 while reading John Greenway's book, and curiosity to explore her variant was stimulated by visits to her during 1958. Hedy West's Vanguard liner notes in 1963 explaining her source for "Farewell" ("I learned [it] from my father, who first heard it in Bell County, Kentucky, when he was still a student at Lincoln Memorial University around 1930") puzzled me in that the date was too early and Mr. West's precise source was unstated. It took me until the summer of 1970 to learn

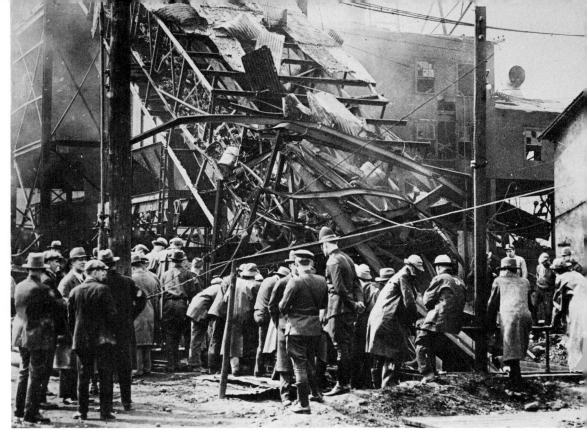

COMMUNITY

Don West's source for the lament; I detail this time sequence partly to show how long it takes to "complete" a case study, and partly to indicate that at least one member of Aunt Molly's community learned a song from her.

Don West, poet, educator, and churchman, came out of a poor white family in Georgia's hill country. Following his university days he became an organizer for the Communist party, striving always to break down northern misconceptions concerning poor people in the South. Late in October, 1935, during a "Blue Eagle" mine union strike, West was arrested and jailed in Pineville, Kentucky, on a criminal syndicalism charge. While in jail he wrote briefly to Michael Gold of the *Daily Worker* about meeting a fellow prisoner, Gilford, who was not a political radical but as an outlaw was hostile to the rich and powerful in society.[17] Gilford hated coal operators because they had forced his mother to sell the family farm, and during the 1931 mine strike he had refused to work as a "gun thug" (company private guard). Gilford taught West something of a murderer's "politics" as well as three songs: "Maple on

85

the Hill," "Shut Up in the Mines at Coal Creek," "Poor Miner's Farewell." Apparently Gilford retained the secret of his source for Aunt Molly's piece, for to my knowledge he talked to no one about his song lore other than Don West.

As a youngster, Hedy West had learned many songs from her father, uncle, and grandmother. Upon completing graduate study in music and drama at Columbia University, Hedy began to represent in traditional style her family's song heritage at concerts and on discs. After recording "Shut Up in the Mines at Coal Creek" for the Topic label in England (1967), she noted in its brochure that Norman Gilford had written down this ballad in the Pineville jail for Don West, who had passed the text and tune on to Hedy.[18] During August, 1970, on a visit to West's school-farm at Pipestem, West Virginia, Don told me something of Gilford's powerful impact on him in 1935. Also, West sang for me the Pineville prisoner's mournful version of "Poor Miner's Farewell."

It is possible, of course, to use this recollection — so long hidden in Don West's memory — to demonstrate that at least one person, Gilford, in Aunt Molly's own community had learned one of her songs, either directly from her, from another person, or even from the *Red Song Book*. I am aware that this anecdote does not support Professor Ives's contention that Aunt Molly's compositions were folksongs by virtue of the fact that they were known to her contemporaries but unsung by them. Just as important as our attempt to test conceptual formulation is the knowledge that an Aunt Molly song entered tradition, if only fleetingly, and that one of her personal folksong recompositions itself came to life in the mind and heart of Norman Gilford, a fellow mountaineer, an underdog, and an outlaw.

When Aunt Molly composed "Poor Miner's Farewell" she turned it away from its normal tone of lamentation in the face of accident to a polemical statement on hunger. Also, in it she departed from the accepted religious beliefs of her society by deleting the song's reference to God. Obviously, other singers of "Only a Miner" could not and did not make such changes. In fact, some persons who knew this piece thought of it as a hymn rather than an occupational ballad, and some sang it in a Moody-Sankey spirit. We do not know which "Only a Miner" form — work or sacred —

came first, but the generalized variant and the hymn-like variant seem equally old. Perhaps an early singer recast the "original" into a hymn-like piece; however, it is equally valid to say that the generalized variant (Kentucky Thorobreds') may have been recast from the hymn-like piece. There is not enough evidence today to suggest priority.

Harvey Fuson, a Harlan County mine owner, local historian, poet, and private collector, can be credited with obtaining from Mary Carr an excellent hymn-like variant of "The Hard-Working Miner." Fuson was probably the first academic collector to discover this song and write out the words from a traditional singer's rendition. He identified Miss Carr by name but not by residence and he neglected to date his meeting. Fuson's first volume of poetry was published in 1921 and he was an officer of the Kentucky Folklore Society from 1926 to 1931. He encountered Miss Carr's song sometime before August 21, 1930, for on this date he finished the introduction to *Ballads of the Kentucky Highlands*. The book has been long out of print.

I reprint the Carr text because it is the best example of "Only a Miner's" hymn-like branch. The chorus and final stanza which carry the sacred message invoke both God and Jesus. Miss Carr's variant is one stanza longer than Ted Chestnut's, but her third stanza is frequently used as a chorus by other singers. Possibly in the song's development two choruses were composed independently and then incorporated into a single number. A full "Carr" text was collected in 1939 by Herbert Halpert from Goldie Hamilton (Wise County, Virginia) for Library of Congress deposit. This Virginia "Hard-Working Miner" differs from the Harlan County song only in stanza arrangement and a few internal word shifts. Miss Hamilton's piece is excellently sung with a keen balance in style between calm narration and devotional mourning. At least one hint at the age of the Carr-Hamilton variant is available. During 1940 George Korson recorded at Braeholm, West Virginia, G. C. Gartin's "The Hard-Working Miner." Gartin, the president of UMWA Local 5850, dated the piece back thirty years (1910). The Carr and Gartin pieces are parallel (with minor word changes) except that the West Virginian left out Miss Carr's "extra" third-stanza chorus. Mary Carr's text follows.

The Hard-Working Miner

The hard-working miners, their dangers are great,
And many while working have met their sad fate.
They are doing their duty, as all miners do,
Shut out from the daylight and darling ones too.

> The miner is gone, we see him no more;
> God be with the miner wherever he may roam;
> And may he be ready Thy calls to obey,
> Looking to Jesus, the only true way.

He leaves a companion and little ones too,
To earn them a living as all miners do;
But while he was working for those whom he loved
The great stone that crushed him fell down from above.

He's only a miner killed under the ground;
He's only a miner and one more is gone.
Just where he was taken there's no one can tell,
His mining's all over, poor miner, farewell.

God be with the miner; protect him from harm;
And shield him from danger with Thy dear strong arm;
And bless his dear children wherever they be,
And take them at last up to Heaven with Thee.

An important technique in folksong study is to illustrate variation and to offer explanatory hypotheses for differentiation. An alternative is to stress commonality of development of meaning despite variation. In the Kentucky examples selected in this chapter — Chestnut, Jackson, Carr — the differences and similarities seem obvious on reading and require little explication. There is no question that all three performers dealt with the "same" song. By definition, their variation helps determine "Only a Miner's" folksong status. The family member furthest removed from these three numbers is the Colorado piece, "Only a Miner Killed in the Mine," a song-poem in the Bret Harte manner. I shall discuss this item in some detail as it is one of the rarest in the "Only" cluster — one apparently known to but a few metal miners in the West.

The two leading collectors of western mining lore, Duncan Emrich and Wayland Hand, both commented on the movement of songs and other traditional material from coal to hard-rock mining (of precious metals in deep quartz veins). Hand tended

88

to see and explain more interaction between coal and other extractive industries than did Emrich; however, a detailed comparative study of all American mining lore awaits a new scholar in the field.

In February, 1942, Duncan Emrich heard brothers "Dinger" and "Doughbelly" Williams sing an unusual "Only a Miner Killed in the Breast." The title alone to one unfamiliar with mining technology might suggest death by shooting — the fate of the unfortunate cowboy in the many variants of "Streets of Laredo" and "Tom Sherman's Barroom." However, miners understood the word *breast* to mean the actual place in an underground chamber where coal or ore was exposed and worked. Specifically, the breast was "the face of a working."[19]

During 1942, Emrich, a Denver University English professor, was devoting much time to intense collecting of nonferrous-mining lore. In his commentary he stressed the use by western miners of parody and he suggested at least one source for models: "the relatively exciting life of the camp with its saloons, poker and panguinge tables, honkeytonks, and social drinking."[20] Interestingly enough, he met the Williams brothers in Mrs. Hein's bar at Georgetown in Clear Creek County, forty miles west of Denver. The brothers recalled hearing their piece about 1897 in nearby Silver Plume, and "Dinger" attested to its rarity by stating, "The song ain't known by more than six people anywhere." Of course many singers tell folklorists that certain numbers are unique, but, uncannily, "Dinger" was right. Emrich included "Only a Miner Killed in the Breast," with music transcribed by Margaret Grubb, in the *California Folklore Quarterly*'s first volume; it was subsequently made available to a second audience by inclusion in *Songs of the American West.*

In 1942 Emrich observed that the Georgetown–Silver Plume piece was related thematically as well as in its chorus's opening line to the familiar "Hard-Working Miner," which he had encountered from California to Colorado. He guessed that the widely recovered song was probably older than the Williams item. During October, 1945, Wayland Hand added a second "Only a Miner (Killed in the Breast)" variant to the family complex. He recorded it in Los Angeles from Willard Peck, a former Coloradan who had also learned it as a young miner in Clear Creek County (Idaho Springs) about 1890, thus bringing it very close in time and place to the Williams brothers' variant. Peck told Hand that the song came to him from his uncle George Dory, a "real hard rocker," who had been born in Idaho Springs, and who had worked there all his life, including a stint as a "shifter" (shift boss) in the Topeka mine at Russell Gulch. Peck added that "Only" was commonly sung in saloons by entertainers.[21]

It is not my intent to reprint texts readily available in scholarly journals or anthologies. Rather, I wish to bring to the surface newly transcribed variants from recordings, long out-of-print items, or previously unpublished forms. The most complete example of this Colorado cluster is a typescript copy of "Only a Miner Killed in the Mine" mailed to Robert Winslow Gordon in 1923 by C. W. Beauchamp, whose letterhead announced his skill: "Practical Ore-Dressing / Concentration Flotation / Mill Flow Sheets."

From 1923 to 1927 Gordon had edited the column "Old Songs That Men Have Sung" for the pulp fiction magazine *Adventure*. In this period he received nearly 4,000 letters containing texts, requests, and comments on song history by friendly readers. This correspondence, his field recordings, and some twenty manuscript collections given to Gordon by others are now at the Library of Congress and at the University of Oregon (donated by his daughter after her father's death).[22] Beauchamp, writing to Gordon from Idaho Springs, indicated that his miners' song "used to be quite a favorite with the old time rock busters" and that its "author's name [was] among the missing."[23]

Gordon's rapport with correspondents who had busted rock and dressed ore was rare among collectors. The multiplicity of American folk and folk-like groups, coupled with the United States' continental expanse, has made it extremely difficult for a single folklorist to know all our folk or lore. Robert Winslow Gordon, during the 1920's, came closer than most of his peers in gathering a national folksong garland. Although he organized the Archive of American Folk Song at the Library of Congress in 1928, he did not receive the kind of attention that was to come to the archive under John and Alan Lomax in the New Deal era. Nor did Gordon publish a single popular anthology comparable to Sandburg's *American Songbag*, to which he contributed material. Gordon's interest in

ROBERT W. GORDON

folksong stemmed from his Harvard education under George Lyman Kittredge, and led to many intense years of field collecting as well as library study. Gordon's life story, not entirely happy, deserves a contemporary telling in terms of America's slow and often painful accommodation to its traditions.

Beauchamp's typescript, from the Gordon collection, reads:

ONLY A MINER KILLED IN THE MINE

Softly the moon-light rose over the hill,
Where the good Miners cabins lay peaceful and still,
Built on the hill-side above the deep mines,
The wind whispered softly through the dark pines,

> Only a Miner, Killed in the Breast,
> Just a poor working-man gone to his rest,
> You can read oe'r his grave, Neath the whispering Pines,
> Our Joe, Age just Twenty; Was killed in the mines,

Down in the earth, In a dark dismal drift,
Two Miners were working their long Mid-night shift,
With muscles of steel and a heart of good-will,
Their song was in tune, With their hammer and drill,

> Chorus:

Unconscious of danger the night hours fled,
They heard not the crash of a rock over head,
Till it fell like a bolt to the death blow of one,
At the feet of his comrade he sank with a moan,

> Chorus:

91

> Oh Comrade; Goodbye and he sank in the clay,
> The candles weird light on his pale features lay,
> His comrade bent oe'r him, His life had all gone,
> Death ended his shift; And his misery was done,
>
> Chorus:
>
> Oh! Mother, Joes dead! He was killed in the mine,
> The Telegram trembled along oe'r the line,
> The fate that she feared had oe'r taken her boy,
> Struck down in his manhood, Her pride and her joy.

Without reprinting the two similar songs gathered by Emrich or Hand at this juncture, it can be noted that there are some interesting differences between these items and the one sent to Gordon in 1923. Peck and the Williams brothers both sang four stanzas and a chorus but not all the same stanzas or in the same order. Seemingly, they had heard a longer song which they compressed in memory. Beauchamp's form was the longest of the three and almost certainly closest to the original of this special Idaho Springs reworking. It seems unlikely that additional variants of "Only a Miner Killed in the Mine" will be recovered in the future. The chances are slim; there has been no significant hard-rock folklore collecting since Emrich's and Hand's last field trips in 1942 and 1948 respectively.

The contrast between Beauchamp's Colorado piece and the three Kentucky variants previously used in this chapter is dramatic. None of the bituminous-area singers directly mentioned coal mining; such specificity would have been redundant in Kentucky. But Peck, singing for Wayland Hand, identified his ballad hero by craft — gold miner. Beauchamp wrote "good miner," and it is difficult today to guess whether the word *gold* or *good* came first. Whereas the coal singers all plunged directly into the accident scene, Beauchamp, in his first stanza, set a pastoral stage with moonlight and whispering pine. This tone was echoed by the singing miners themselves: "Their song was in tune, With their hammer and drill." Regardless of these rhetorical differences, death lurking in the overhead strata was constant from Colorado to Kentucky.

"Only a Miner Killed in the Mine" has the lilt and color of a Bret Harte ballad. Another reader may relate it to Robert Service or to any other western local colorist of his choice. Folklorists are no longer surprised to find printed sources for folksong. Much cowboy balladry began life in the formal poetry of known authors: Jack Thorp, D. J. O'Malley, Henry Herbert Knibbs, Charles Badger Clark, Joseph Mills Hanson. We now have enough studies by John White and Austin Fife to indicate how journalistic poetry became cowboy folksong; we lack comparable studies for the hard-rock mining tradition. I am in Harlan Daniel's debt for suggesting to me that "Captain Jack" Crawford's poem, "Only a Miner Killed," is a likely model for the "Only a Miner" complex. Neither Daniel nor I know exactly how Crawford's work was metamorphosed into a folksong.

It is difficult to speculate about any song's lineage until enough variants are found to support a hypothesis. When American folksong collecting began, few industrial items were sought or found in numbers sufficient to demand background data. "Only a Miner" was first recorded commercially in 1927 on a disc which apparently reached no scholars at that time. Fuson first printed "The Hard-Working Miner" in 1931 in a book of limited circulation. The 1932 *Red Song Book* tune transcription probably reached a few scholars, but apparently none who were interested in the pedigree of "Poor Miner's Farewell." For their finds, Duncan Emrich and Wayland Hand wrote good headnotes in the *California Folklore Quarterly*. Hand's was particularly useful for its attempt to shed light on the ancestry of "Only a Miner"; Professor Frank Goodwyn had suggested to him its relationship to "Only a Brakeman" and "Only a Hogger," a notion also utilized by Vance Randolph. (See Checklist One for bibliographical citations.)

The main difficulty in interrelating the entire "Only" occupational complex is that some family members are clearly built on the same structural model and others on quite different ones. In short, there are more than two poetic patterns found in these songs. To bring all the "Only" numbers together would demand a tome. Here it can be asserted briefly that "Stand By Your Union," "Only a Cowboy," and "Only a Brakeman" very likely stemmed directly from "Only a Miner." However, the various "Only a Tramp" numbers were derived from several other models. This assertion is evident upon comparing "Captain Jack's" poem (below) with "The Tramp's Lament" in M. C. Dean's *Flying*

Cloud or with "The Tramp" in Vance Randolph's *Ozark Folksongs*. "Only a Tramp's" history must wait for an extensive study of America's hobo tradition.[24]

"Captain Jack," John Wallace Crawford (1847-1917), did not enjoy being likened to his rival "Buffalo Bill," William F. Cody, yet both these Indian fighters helped open the West and establish its traditions. Recently Paul Nolan edited three melodramas by "Captain Jack" and added to them a fine biographical sketch of "The Poet Scout."[25] Crawford, like other frontier heroes, led a kaleidoscopic life: Scottish child immigrant, boy laborer in America's anthracite industry, young Civil War volunteer in a Pennsylvania "Miner's Regiment," Black Hills scout in the Sioux Wars, U.S. Army Chief of Scouts in New Mexico and Arizona, Alaska gold seeker, Wild West Show actor, minor poet and playwright, Chautauqua lecturer, myth-maker. To these exploits can we now add that one of his poems was the progenitor of the American miners' anthem?

Seemingly, Crawford never drew on his childhood experiences as a coal-mine slatepicker, but a number of his poems were set in western mine locales, and some were both read and dedicated to the men in the powerful Butte Miners Union at the turn of the century. From the fall of 1876 through the following spring, "Captain Jack" had been with "Buffalo Bill's" company in a national tour of two shows — "Scouts of the Prairie" and "Life on the Border." On June 29, 1877, Crawford was wounded on the stage in Virginia City, Nevada, and abandoned by Cody. After recovery, Crawford tried to ready his own play, "Fonda or The Trapper's Dream," for an Australian visit (including an Indian troupe never yet seen on that continent) but failed for lack of money. Then Crawford returned to Army scouting and writing.

His first book, *The Poet Scout,* was published in San Francisco in 1879. Included was "Only a Miner Killed," written after Commodore Vanderbilt's death on January 4, 1877, and perhaps inspired by juxtaposition of a newspaper account of the capitalist's ostentatious life and the paltry funeral procession of an unknown miner. It was written presumably while the poet was acting with "Buffalo Bill." In its first printing, the poem was headed by a few lines which hinted at a Nevada (Comstock silver mine) setting:

94

"CAPTAIN JACK" CRAWFORD

"Although everything that science, skill, and money can devise is done to avert accidents, the average of fatal ones in the Comstock is three a week. 'Three men a week.' " This was retained in subsequent reprintings of *The Poet Scout*.[26] However, for *Lariattes,* published in 1904, "Captain Jack," possibly expanding the poem's oral introduction developed in frequent recitations while on tour, altered the headnote:

ONLY A MINER KILLED

While in Virginia City, in 1877, a wagon passed up Main Street, with a soiled canvas thrown over it. Some curbstone brokers rushed out to

95

investigate, and when they returned were asked what was the matter. "O," replied one, "It's only a miner killed." Old Commodore Vanderbilt died on the same day and the papers were full of accounts concerning this multi-millionaire. A paragraph in the Virginia City Chronicle, referring to the above incident, suggested the following verses:

> Only a miner killed — oh! is that all?
> One of the timbers caved, great was the fall,
> Crushing another one shaped like his God.
> Only a miner lad — under the sod.
>
> Only a miner killed, just one more dead.
> Who will provide for them — who earn their bread? —
> Wife and the little ones: pity them, God,
> Their earthly father is under the sod.
>
> Only a miner killed, dead on the spot,
> Poor hearts are breaking in yonder lone cot.
> He died at his post, a hero as brave
> As any who sleeps in a marble top grave.
>
> Only a miner killed! God, if thou wilt,
> Just introduce him to Vanderbilt,
> Who, with his millions, if he is there,
> Can't buy one interest — even one share.
>
> Only a miner, bury him quick;
> Just write his name on a piece of a stick.
> Though humble and plain be the poor miner's grave
> Beyond, all are equal, the master and slave.[27]

Had "Captain Jack's" poem been set directly to music by himself or by an unknown singer and started on its path in tradition, this chapter would have ended neatly. But folksong case studies infrequently tie up all loose ends. Crawford did sing old songs while on Chautauqua lecture tours, at Grand Army of the Republic veterans' encampments, and to temperance audiences. But there is no evidence to suggest that "Only a Miner Killed" was itself sung by "Captain Jack" or anyone else. More likely, it served as a pattern for either the standard or hymn-like "Only a Miner." This postulates that between 1879 and 1888 someone read or heard "Captain Jack's" poem and refashioned it into a new song. The relationship between the folksong and the poem is too close to be coincidental.

If, indeed, this recomposition happened, "Captain Jack's" theme and rhetoric were retained but the topical Vanderbilt reference was discarded.

It is assumed that Crawford's poem preceded the song by a decade, but there is an outside chance that the mining song was in tradition before Vanderbilt's death and was heard by Crawford. He did use time-tested material. For example, his long poem "Rattlin' Joe's Prayer" is a retelling of the centuries-old folktale, "A Deck of Cards."[28] However, until an "Only a Miner" item can be dated before 1877, "Captain Jack's" poem "Only a Miner Killed" has priority over the folksong. I am not optimistic about finding such an early mining song in the "Only" family. However, it is important to note that in 1879 a Cincinnati publisher issued sheet music for "Only an Emigrant" by Charlie Baker.[29] Nothing is known to me about Baker, or his song's source and circulation. In structure and rhetoric but not in music it is close to the standard "Only a Miner" considered in this chapter.

The decade of the 1880's seems the likely time for the transformation of Crawford's poem or possibly Baker's music into a folksong. Vance Randolph was told that "Only a Miner" was sung in 1888; Duncan Emrich obtained the dates 1890 and 1897; Wayland Hand was given 1900, 1904, and 1908. Significantly, on May 14, 1908, the *Miners Magazine* (Western Federation of Miners) included a poem sent in from Douglas, Alaska, by a parodist who clearly knew a member of the "Only a Miner" song complex. The Alaskan's offering, "Stand By Your Union," opened its chorus with the line, "Only a workingman, dressed out in jeans," and was built on the meter and rhyme scheme of the mining lament. The *workingman* tag appears solely in the three "Killed in the (Breast) Mine" variants, and not in its more widely dispersed relatives, but we do not know which song served as the model for "Stand By Your Union." Apart from the labor poem's hortatory message, it is interesting as the earliest printing known to me of any "Only a Miner" family member after "Captain Jack's" example.

The question of place of origin for "Only a Miner" is also open. Anthracite coal miners carried lore to the West at least as early as the 1849 gold rush. Conversely, stage songs heard in California by Argonauts were carried "home" to enter tradition in New England

and the Appalachian South. It is precisely because "Only a Miner" was called an "old" song in Kentucky, West Virginia, Colorado, and Montana that it is impossible today to guess its birthplace. Conveniently, the "earliest" variants, according to singers' reports to collectors, placed it in mid-America: Zinc (Boone County), Arkansas, and the nearby Joplin, Missouri, area. It would be facile to assert that a lead miner in the tri-state region (the adjoining corners of Arkansas, Missouri, and Oklahoma) first transformed "Captain Jack's" poem and sent it on its way east and west, north and south. Such speculation is fanciful until additional facts surface.

Apart from our concern with problems in origin and movement, "Only a Miner" is an excellent demonstration of song as reflector of a community's varied response to industrial death. One expects the shock of an accident to lead to grief. There is some evidence that "Only a Miner" helped workers and their loved ones turn grief to resignation and eventually to a fatalistic belief in the "luck of the mine." During 1948, Dolph Shaner of Joplin published a local history of his town. Shaner, in noting the apprehension caused by lead-mine accidents, wrote:

> There were no mortuaries, ambulances, or hospitals until the first unit of St. John's in 1900 [was built]. When a man was mangled or killed in the mines, the nearest vehicle, usually a delivery wagon, was commandeered. The miner was loaded in and hauled, bleeding, mangled or dead, to his own home, often to a shrieking wife and crying children. On some occasions when there was a very bad accident, whistles blew to draw quick help. This always threw a community into a feverish excitement. Mine accidents were due principally to cave-ins, falling rocks, mine explosions, "bad air" and tub drops. Operations on injured men were performed in the home and on the dining room table. The dead also were dressed there for burial. The author remembers as a boy peeking through a window and watching a physician amputate a miner's arm. The odor of iodoform still lingers in memory. . . . A song of those days by some unknown author was many times repeated after a fatal mine accident. The words of one verse are remembered:

> > "Only a miner killed in the ground,
> > Only a miner and one more is gone,
> > Killed by an accident,
> > How, no one can tell,
> > Goodbye poor miner, poor miner farewell."[30]

98

DEATH PERSONIFIED

The vividness in memory of iodoform and the song is significant. Shaner did not make the point explicitly, but is it not too much to assume that "Only" helped miners expunge the smell of death?

During 1949 "Captain" Thomas J. Nicholas, a retired mine supervisor who had migrated from his native Cornwall to the Ishpeming area (Marquette County) of Michigan's Upper Peninsula, recalled that "Only a Miner" had been sung in bars freely and frequently after a man was killed in the mines. Nicholas had heard it about 1891 at the Sheridan Tunnel mine, Telluride, San Miguel County, Colorado.[31] Similarly, William Travenna told Wayland Hand that about 1904 the Park City, Utah, silver miners "would get around and have a drink" while singing "Only a Miner." These reports of group drinking and singing suggest that communal catharsis was one of the functions of this piece.

Nevertheless, some miners objected strongly to such public treatment of tragedy. James J. Gleason, a Butte copper miner,

99

reported to collector Hand that when "a little Cousin Jack" had sung "Only a Miner," his comrades, objecting to the term *accident,* "got sore at him" and "bawled him out" in order to silence him.[32] This negative note was also heard by Duncan Emrich in Grass Valley, California, when Israel James, a Cornish gold miner, refused to sing the full "Hard-Working Miner" known to him. This rejection of the sympathetic emotion implied in the piece was expressed in James's phrase: "A man has to be half naked to sing that."[33]

Obviously, some workers dissolved gloom in singing or hearing "Only a Miner." For others, the number intensified painful associations. When this lament was sung in a saloon it became part of the open ritual surrounding a fellow worker's departure, and when superstitious miners refused to hear "Only a Miner" it became a symbol of the necessity to cope privately with imminent death.

An understanding of "Only a Miner's" therapeutic function touching a worker's death helps return a reader-listener to an aspect of its first recording by the Kentucky Thorobreds. Ted Chestnut's father, a Methodist pastor, had associated the piece with ministerial duties in Harlan and Laurel counties. No man of God in a coal community could avoid some symbolic expression — whether in song or sermon — in response to ever-present mine accidents. In 1928 when Paramount Records placed "Only a Miner" on sale, the lament was still a private item known largely to miners and their friends in particular folk societies. In a sense, the many field and commercial recordings pressed since the Kentucky Thorobreds entered a Chicago Loop studio have converted this song into a public document.

Two LPs of the 1960's containing "Only a Miner" make a good commentary on the sound-recording industry's recent documentary role. During 1961, the A. L. Phipps Family, a Barbourville, Kentucky, hillbilly and gospel-singing group, recorded "The Miner's Fate" for Starday Records in Madison, Tennessee. This variant was fully traditional in text, tune, and stylistic presentation, yet the record's jacket liner told nothing of the source and little about the Family itself. Fortunately, I learned directly from A. L. Phipps that his wife Kathleen had obtained the song from her mother, who had it on "an old ballad . . . faded and partly decayed."[34] Not only was it traditional to Mrs. Phipps, but A. L. and Kathleen had lost friends and relatives in Kentucky mine slate-falls. Witnessing disaster firsthand made it "a true song" for them.

It can be seen that Paramount's and Starday's operations in 1927 and 1961, respectively, were much alike despite the passage of time. Neither firm was particularly interested in song lore or generous in supplying cultural data. Yet it is not too far physically from Barbourville to Richmond, the starting place for Doc Roberts, Dick Parman, and Ted Chestnut on their Chicago recording trips. Likewise, it is not far in spirit or tone from Paramount's "Only a Miner" to Starday's "Miner's Fate." Such affinity demonstrates considerable continuity over a four-decade span.

Discontinuity and change in the music industry's practice is demonstrated by Mike Seeger's Folkways recording, *Tipple, Loom & Rail,* an LP delineating southern industrialization. Seeger presented sixteen songs from textiles, railroading, and coal mining, including "The Hard-Working Miner." His source was Blind James Howard's 1933 Library of Congress field disc from Kentucky. This was clearly stated in the LP's brochure, which also offered notes on Seeger's background. In a Folkways recording, listeners not only hear miners' laments but understand something of the artist's strategies and values.

I am drawn to the Phipps Family as well as to Mike Seeger, accepting the former as folksingers and the latter as an excellent folksong interpreter. I decry Starday's lack of documentation for the Phipps numbers but welcome eagerly the firm's products. Equally, I applaud Folkways' scholarly contribution, but am aware of the limited utility inherent in recorded folksong interpretation, no matter how faithful.

Actually, the two sets of performers cited appear mainly before differing audiences and serve separate functions. The Phipps Family continues to reach via radio and records what still can be called a folk community, including Kentucky miners. Mike Seeger, in the past decade, has addressed himself primarily to conscious folksong enthusiasts from Cambridge to Berkeley. These contrasts must be understood in any serious appraisal of fluid American folk and popular culture, but contrasting symbols are often overstressed. Occasionally in the 1960's, Seeger and the Phipps Family reached

MIKE SEEGER

the same festival audiences; such happy meetings were exceptional, and perhaps pointed to one contour of future poplore. I find little difference in stylistic tone between Seeger and A. L. Phipps, or, for that matter, between both and Ted Chestnut, who carried "Only a Miner" to Paramount and Gennett studies so long ago.

A word here on melody draws together the remaining strands in the song's history. Judith McCulloh's musical transcription of

"Only a Miner" in this book is taken from the Kentucky Thorobreds' 1927 disc. When it is compared to the "earliest" (1888) musical form, published by Vance Randolph in a folksong collection,
or to the most recent (1961) traditional performance on a Phipps
Family LP, one discerns a remarkably constant melody. The assertion of similarity for various "Only a Miner" tunes follows my
listening to the nearly twenty field or commercial recordings cited
at this chapter's end. Yet any such assertion of melodic constancy
or sameness is subjective even when supported by a musicological
comparison of contours demonstrated in actual transcriptions.
(Checklist One indicates the transcribed music in published forms
for "Only a Miner.")

Considerable work lies ahead for musical analysis in the area
of hillbilly and gospel material.[35] Although tune-family analysis is
beyond my scope, I can indicate that to date no one has placed
"Only a Miner" in a given musical family or categorized it beyond
likening one treatment to that of a revival hymn — an observation
by Wayland Hand. Previously, D. K. Wilgus had suggested "Only
a Miner's" melodic similarity to "Young Jamie Foyers," sung by
Sheila Stewart of Berrybank, Scotland, on *The Stewarts of Blair*
(Topic 12T 138).[36] The Stewarts are a family of "travelers" (Scots
migratory laborers) with a wide selection of "bothy" (farm workers' quarters) songs. Whether or not Sheila's melody in a ballad
commemorating a Peninsular War (1808-14) casualty has any
specific association with "Only a Miner," I do not know.

In opening this case study I suggested that "Only a Miner"
was the American miner's national anthem, known wherever coal
or metal ore was found in our land. To demonstrate that this lament was indeed a folksong, four texts and a background poem
were presented as well as comments on origin and movement. Additionally, the function of the piece in helping workers cope with
accidental death was noted. Folkloric analysis of given songs frequently touches more bases than those treated here. Hopefully,
some readers will desire to seek further data specifically on "Only
a Miner" or, more widely, on the entire occupational family cluster
of which the mining item is but a part. In this book, my special
attention to sound recordings (from cylinder to film track) will be
revealed.

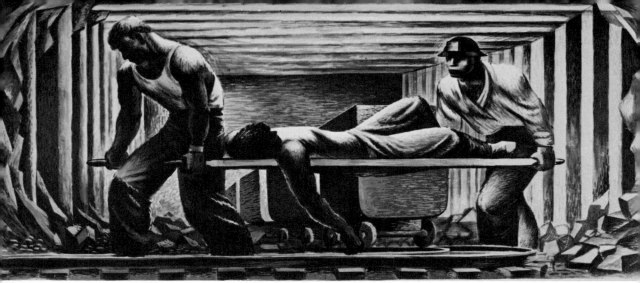

MINE RESCUE

As I turn away from "Only a Miner," it strikes me that the Kentucky Thorobreds, the Phipps Family, Blind James Howard, Aunt Molly Jackson, Hedy West, Mike Seeger, and others recorded it appropriately as a ballad-lament and as a sign of proper acceptance of industrial death. It is in the polarities as well as similarities between these singers — separated in time and status — that the present-day documentary and communications role of America's sound-recording industry is displayed in its manifold forms.

1. Sterling A. Brown, *Southern Road* (New York, 1932), 62.
2. John A. Fahey, "A Textual and Musicological Analysis of the Repertoire of Charley Patton" (master's thesis, University of California, Los Angeles, 1966). See also Derrick Stewart-Baxter, *Ma Rainey and the Classic Blues Singers* (London, 1970).
3. Max Vreede, *The Paramount 12/13000 Series,* forthcoming. See also Ronald C. Foreman, Jr., "Jazz and Race Records, 1920-32" (thesis, University of Illinois, Urbana, 1968). For hillbilly series see Doug Jydstrup and others, "The Paramount 3000 Numerical Listing," *Blue Yodeler,* nos. 7-15 (1967-68).
4. "Stand By Your Union" in Richard E. Lingenfelter and others, *Songs of the American West* (Berkeley, 1968), 165; "Only a Cowboy" in John A. Lomax, *Cowboy Songs and Other Frontier Ballads* (New York, 1910), 124.
5. *Catalogue of Copyright Entries. Part 3, Musical Compositions for the Year 1927* (Washington, 1928), 1427. See also 1928 *Catalogue.*
6. All interviews with Martin, Roberts, Bailey, Parman, and Chestnut are dated in my "List of Interviews." A published account of one is Norman Cohen, "Tapescript Interview with Welby Toomey," *JEMF Quarterly,* V (Summer, 1969), 63. Additional data on these men can be found in the *JEMF Quarterly* throughout 1971.

7. For Gennett history in the 1920's see George W. Kay, "Those Fabulous Gennetts," *Record Changer* (June, 1953), 4.

8. "Gennett Records Advance Release: October 15, 1928," a single-sheet printed announcement.

9. George Korson, *Coal Dust on the Fiddle*, 2nd printing (Hatboro, Pa., 1965), 222.

10. G. Malcolm Laws, Jr., *Native American Balladry*, rev. ed. (Philadelphia, 1964), 228.

11. For Aunt Molly's life history and discography see Archie Green, spec. ed., "Aunt Molly Jackson Memorial Issue," *Kentucky Folklore Record*, VII (Oct., 1961).

12. Margaret Larkin, "Revolutionary Music," *New Masses*, VIII (Feb., 1933), 27; Nathan Nevins, "Reviews: *Red Song Book*," *Worker Musician*, I (Dec., 1932), 13.

13. The collector-transcriber was likely Lan Adomian. Letter to me, Sept. 15, 1968.

14. Interview, Jan. 12, 1958.

15. Interview, Apr. 5, 1958.

16. Ives letter to me, Dec. 9, 1969. Ives's views on a community song are developed in his *Lawrence Doyle: Farmer-Poet of Prince Edward Island* (Orono, Me., 1971).

17. West's letter on Gilford appeared in Michael Gold, "Change the World," *Daily Worker* (Nov. 8, 1935), 7. Earlier reports in this paper were "Two Miners Held on Frameup in Kentucky" (Oct. 29, 1935), 1, and "A Communist Organizer in Court" (Nov. 1, 1935), 5. See also "John Hart Is Held under Bond of $5000," *Pineville* [Ky.] *Sun* (Oct. 31, 1935), 1. Don West's background article for this Kentucky experience is "Georgia Wants Me — Dead or Alive," *New Masses*, XI (June, 1934), 15.

18. Brochure notes to Hedy West's *Old Times and Hard Times* (Folk-Legacy FSA 32).

19. Albert H. Fay, *A Glossary of the Mining and Mineral Industry* (Washington, 1920). The current expanded revision of this work is Paul W. Thrush, *A Dictionary of Mining, Mineral, and Related Terms* (Washington, 1968).

20. Duncan Emrich, "Songs of the Western Miners," *California Folklore Quarterly*, I (1942), 214.

21. I am indebted to Wayland Hand not only for Willard Peck's "Only" text but for continuous encouragement in my studies.

22. Karen Grimm, "Prolegomenon to a Catalog for the Robert W. Gordon Collection of American Folksong," *Northwest Folklore*, II, no. 1 (1967), 8. See also Arthur G. Brodeur, "The Robert Winslow Gordon Collection of American Folksong," *Oregon Folklore Bulletin*, I, no. 4 (1962), 1. Mrs. Rae Korson and Joseph C. Hickerson at the Library of Congress and Mrs. Karen Grimm and Barre Toelken at the University of Oregon have extended me many courtesies in my use of Gordon material.

23. Beauchamp letter to Gordon, Sept. 15, 1923.

24. There are at least four distinct forms titled "Only a Tramp": (1) the type printed by Dean and Randolph which was also found on hillbilly records; (2) a sheet-music piece by Addison D. Crabtre copyright in 1880; (3) a poem printed in *Railroad Man's Magazine* (Dec., 1911); (4) a secularization of the gospel song "Tramp on the Street" by Nevada Slim on *Old Time Favorites* (Rural Rhythm 186).

25. Paul T. Nolan, *Three Plays by J. W. (Capt. Jack) Crawford* (The Hague, 1966).

26. Captain Jack Crawford, *The Poet Scout* (San Francisco, 1879), 63. This first edition, published by H. Keller & Co., was subsequently reprinted in 1886 by Funk & Wagnalls, New York, and Price-McGill, St. Paul. "Only a Miner" appears on page 74 in these reprints.

27. Captain Jack Crawford, *Lariattes* (Sigourney, Iowa, 1904), 25.

28. The poem appears in Austin Fife, "The Prayer Book in Cards," *Western Folklore*, XXVII (1968), 208, without credit to Crawford.

29. Reproduced in Lester S. Levy, *Grace Notes in American History* (Norman, Okla., 1967), 57.

30. Dolph Shaner, *The Story of Joplin* (New York, 1948), 65.

31. Data on Nicholas from Harry B. Welliver, Jr., interview sheet in Library of Congress for field disc AFS 9715.

32. Travenna and Gleason data from Wayland Hand and others, "Songs of the Butte Miners," *Western Folklore*, IX (1950), 15, supplemented by Hand letter to me, Oct. 23, 1968.

33. Emrich, "Songs of the Western Miners," 221.

34. Letter to me, Dec. 29, 1969.

35. For tune-family study problems see Bertrand H. Bronson, *The Ballad as Song* (Berkeley, 1969). For additional material and references see Roger Abrahams and George Foss, *Anglo-American Folksong Style* (Englewood Cliffs, N.J., 1968).

36. See review by D. K. Wilgus, *Journal of American Folklore*, LXXXI (1968), 178.

CHECKLIST ONE

A guide to checklist format is found in the preliminary "Note on Sources."

"Only a Miner Killed in the Mine." C. W. Beauchamp, Idaho Springs, Colo., Sept. 13, 1923 ("favorite with old time rock busters"). Robert W. Gordon, typescript, Gordon mss, AFS 177.

"Only a Miner." Kentucky Thorobreds, Paramount 3071 (20052). Sept., 1927, Chicago. Guitar and mandolin. Parallel issue: Old Smokey Twins, Broadway 8070.

———. Kentucky Thorobreds, Chicago Music Publishing Company, Chicago (Feb. 15, 1928), E 686013. Copyright renewed: John Steiner, Chicago (Feb. 13, 1956), R 164762.

"He's Only a Miner Killed in the Ground." Ted Chestnut, Gennett 6603 (GE 14168). Aug. 23, 1928, Richmond, Ind. Guitar and fiddle. Parallel issues: Cal Turner, Champion 15587; Alvin Bunch, Supertone 9180.

"The Hard-Working Miner." Mary Carr. Fuson, *B K H* (1931), 141.

"Only a Miner." Walter Seacrist, Brookwood Labor College, Kotonah, N.Y., 1931 (from Holly Grove, W.Va.). Josephine "Polly" Colby, typescript, Helen Norton Starr files, Long Island City, N.Y.

———. Walter Seacrist, Mims, Fla., Aug. 22, 1965. Self-recorded. Green tape files.

"The Miner." Flora Havens, Binfield, Tenn. Anderson, *C B S E T* (1932), 221.

"Poor Miner's Farewell." *Red Song Book,* Workers Music League, Workers Library Publishers, New York (1932), 24, m. From Aunt Molly Jackson, Ky.

———. Aunt Molly Jackson, Sacramento, Calif., July, 1952. Greenway, *A F P* (1953), 263.

Reprinted: *Sing Out,* III (June, 1953), 11, m. Also in *Reprints from Sing Out,* 4 (1964), 34, m. Source unstated for music adapted by Jerry Silverman.

———. John Greenway, *The Songs and Stories of Aunt Molly Jackson,* Folkways FH 5457. ca. Feb., 1961, New York. Brochure includes text and headnote.

———. Aunt Molly Jackson, Sacramento, Calif., Jan. 12, 1958. Archie Green and Barry Olivier, Green tape files.

———. Aunt Molly Jackson, Sacramento, Calif., Apr. 5, 1958. Archie Green and Billy Faier, Green tape files.

"Miner's Farewell." Hedy West, *Hedy West,* Vanguard VRS 9124. ca. Nov., 1962, New York. Liner notes state source is Don West, singer's father.

Transcribed: *Sing Out,* XV (Jan., 1967), 24, m.

Transcribed: West, *H W S* (1969), 69, m.

"The Hard-Working Miner." Blind James Howard, Harlan, Ky., Aug., 1933. John and Alan Lomax, AFS 76.

Transcribed: Lomax, *A B F S* (1934), 437, m.

Reprinted: Lomax, *H H S H H P* (1967), 136, m.

———. Mike Seeger, *Tipple, Loom & Rail,* Folkways FH 5273. Apr., 1965, New York. Brochure includes text and headnote.

"The Hard Working Miner." *Hearth and Home Songs,* Asher Sizemore, A. Sizemore, Louisville, Ky. (1935), 34, m.

Reprinted: *Fireside Treasures* (1936), 33, m.

"The Miner." *Choice Selections,* E. W. Anderson, Holiness Church Evangel Office, Cleveland, Tenn. (ca. 1936). A small hymn-book.

"The Hard-Working Miner." Tilman Cadle, Middlesboro, Ky., Sept. 15, 1937. Alan and Elizabeth Lomax, AFS 1401.

"The Miner's Death." Susan Shepherd, Cumberland, Ky., Sept., 1937. Alan and Elizabeth Lomax, AFS 1435.

"The Miner's Farewell." Findley Donaldson, Pineville, Ky., Jan., 1938. Mary Elizabeth Barnicle, AFS 1985.

"The Miner." Goldie Hamilton, Wise, Va., Oct. 12, 1938. Emory Hamilton, typescript, WPA mss, AFS 11702.

"The Hard-Working Miner." Goldie Hamilton, Hamiltontown, Va., Apr. 8, 1939. Herbert Halpert, AFS 2828.

"The Hard-Working Miner." Joe Glancey, Harlan, Ky., Mar. 23, 1940. George Korson, AFS 12010.

"The Hard-Working Miner." G. C. Gartin, Braeholm, W.Va., May 28, 1940 (known for thirty years). George Korson, AFS 12011. *Songs and Ballads of the Bituminous Miners,* Library of Congress AFS L 60; released Dec. 15, 1965. Brochure includes text.

Transcribed: Korson, *C D F* (1943), 237.

"Only a Miner Killed in the Breast." "Dinger" and "Doughbelly" Williams, Georgetown, Colo., 1942 (learned forty-five years ago in Silver Plume). Emrich, *C F Q,* I (1942), 220, m.

Previously printed: *Mines Magazine,* XXXII (Mar., 1942), 118.

Reprinted: Lingenfelter, *S A W* (1968), 160, m.

"The Hard-Working Miner." Mrs. Walter Mosch, Central City, Colo., 1942 (mother heard song at Joplin, Mo., 1890). Emrich, *C F Q,* I (1942), 221, m.

Previously printed: *Mines Magazine,* XXXII (Mar., 1942), 118.

"Only a Miner." Willard Peck, Los Angeles, Oct., 1945. Wayland Hand, AFS 8892.

———. Willard Peck, Los Angeles, Aug. 11, 1951. Sidney Robertson Cowell and Wayland Hand, AFS 11309.

"Only a Miner." Shaner, *S J* (1948), 67. One stanza but in context of mining-town life.

"Only a Miner." Lulu Lough and Selma Barker, Butte, Mont., July 23, 1948 (from southern Idaho about 1900). Charles Cutts and Robert Wylder, AFS 9724.
Transcribed: Hand, *W F,* IX (1950), 15, m.

"Only a Miner." Thomas J. Nicholas, Palmer, Mich., Feb. 8, 1949. Harry B. Welliver, Jr., AFS 9715.

"Only a Miner." Coral Almy Wilson, Zinc, Ark., Nov. 10, 1929 (heard song in 1888). Randolph, *O F,* IV (1950), 127, m.

"The Miner's Fate." A. L. Phipps Family, *Old Time Mountain Pickin' and Singin',* Starday SLP 195. Apr. 11, 1961, Madison, Tenn.

"The Miner." Howard Vokes, *Tragedy and Disaster in Country Songs,* Starday SLP 258. Aug. 12, 1963, Madison, Tenn. Learned from Phipps LP: letter to Green. Parallel issue: Sparton LP 258 (Canada).

APPENDIX ONE

KENTUCKY THOROBREDS COPYRIGHTS

Songs copyrighted in the names of Roberts, Parman, and Chestnut as well as the Kentucky Thorobreds by the Chicago Music Publishing Company. The entry arrangement is: Copyright Office registration number; song title; composer credit for words or melody; (Paramount master number); Paramount and Broadway label numbers under following pseudonyms: KT — Kentucky Thorobreds, OST — Old Smokey Twins, Q — Quadrillers, LSF — Lone Star Fiddlers.

July 19, 1927

E 670383   Phil Roberts Blues: m by R
E 670384   Mother's Advice: w & m by R & P (4463) Pa 3011, KT
E 679385   Durkin Blues: m by R & P
E 670386   Rocky Mountain Goat: m by R & P (4456) Pa 3008, Q
                    Bw 8046, LSF

Feb. 15, 1928

E 681974   Wagoner: m by R, P, & C (4457) Pa 3009, Q
                    Bw 8045, LSF
E 681975   Drunk Man's Blues: m by R, P, & C (4454) Pa 3008, Q
                    Bw 8046, LSF
E 681976   I Love You Best of All: w & m by R & P (?) Pa 3010, KT
                    Bw 8047, OST
E 686004   Shady Grove: w & m by KT (20059) Pa 3080, KT
                    Bw 8184, OST
E 686005   Old Man Brown: w & m by KT
E 686006   I'll Not Marry at All: w & m by KT (20056) Pa 3080, KT
                    Bw 8184, OST
E 686007   New Money: m by KT
E 686008   My Baby Don't Love Me: m by KT
E 686009   Jim and Me: w & m by KT
E 686010   He Cometh: w & m by KT (20054) Pa 3049, KT
                    Bw 8064, OST
E 686011   Wouldn't Take Nothing for My Journey: w & m by KT
E 686012   Bring Back My Wandering Boy: w & m by KT
E 686013   Only a Miner: w & m by KT (20052) Pa 3071, KT
                    Bw 8070, OST
E 686014   Hallelujah Side: w & m by KT
E 686015   I've Waited Long for You: w & m by KT (20051) Pa 3071, KT
                    Bw 8070, OST
E 686026   Cumberland Blues: m by R, P, & C (4455) Pa 3009, Q
                    Bw 8045, LSF

These twenty songs were all recorded at Chicago sessions in April and September, 1927. It can be assumed that copyright lead sheets were transcribed directly from test pressings. However, apparently only eleven of the songs were publicly released by Paramount on records. In addition to the copyrighted songs above, Roberts, Parman, and Chestnut recorded other material for Paramount. Below are listed all their known Paramount and Broadway discs, released under four pseudonyms: Quadrillers, Lone Star Fiddlers, Kentucky Thorobreds, Old Smokey Twins. Paramount 3008 and 3009 are by Q and LSF; the rest are by KT and OST.

Pa	Bw		
3008	8046	Drunk Man's Blues	(4454)
		Rocky Mountain Goat	(4456)
3009	8045	Wagoner	(4457)
		Cumberland Blues	(4455)
3010	8047	I Love You Best of All	(?)
	8048	If I Only Had a Home Sweet Home	(4459)
3011	?	Mother's Advice	(4463)
		I Left Because I Loved You	(4467)
3014	?	Room for Jesus	(4465)
		This World Is Not My Home	(4466)
3036	8128	In the Shade of the Old Apple Tree	(4461)
		Preacher and the Bear	(4464)
3059	8064	He Cometh	(20054)
	8065	Till We Meet Again	(20055)
3071	8070	I've Waited Long for You	(20051)
		Only a Miner	(20052)
3080	8184	I'll Not Marry at All	(20056)
		Shady Grove	(20059)

RESCUE TEAM

The Dream of the Miner's Child 4

CRAFTSMEN CONVEYED much cultural baggage from Europe to America in the centuries after Jamestown and Plymouth Rock. At times it was difficult, or even criminal, to carry tools, patterns, molds, templates, or models. However, it was always possible to secrete trade customs, job beliefs, craft argot, guild rituals, and union loyalties in the mind. All immigrants brought some lore to the New World; English-language tradition, of course, is best known. Americans but dimly aware of folklore transmission as a process perceive on hearing "Sir Patrick Spens" or "Brennan on the Moor" that these are Old World heroes.

Relatively unknown is the fact that folksingers carried alongside classic and broadside ballads some industrial songs in tradition "back home." To cite but one example, during 1943 Samuel Bayard collected an elegiac ballad, "The High Blanter Explosion," from Jennie Craven in Pennsylvania's Westmoreland County. The disaster about which she sang dated to 1877 at Dixon's Colliery, High Blantyre, near Glasgow, Scotland; no one knows how early the piece entered tradition. Although Mrs. Craven's text and tune vary from a related item collected in 1951 by A. L. Lloyd at Midlothian, Scotland, she is still clearly singing the same song.[1]

More than industrial-song lore was carried across the Atlantic. Cornish miners, frequently called "Cousin Jacks" in America, retained old stories about Tommy Knockers — dwarf-like creatures who lived underground. Sometimes these wee people were said to be spirits of dead miners. Whether dwarfs or ghosts, these creatures were talked about in Cornish tin mines long before America was discovered; possibly Caesar's legionnaires heard such tales when they came in search of Britain's precious metal. Tommy Knockers engaged in pranks against men but also saved them from danger or led them to rich lodes. Tommy Knocker stories, which embodied parallel beliefs in good or bad luck, also implied related underground work practices to humor or placate these spirits.[2]

No collector, to my knowledge, ever questioned that "The High Blanter Explosion" was a folksong or that Tommy Knocker anecdotes were folkloric to the core. If all industrial songs and stories encountered in the field were comparable to these items, scholars would remain untroubled. Some songs, however, seem destined to trouble folklorists (but, happily, not the folk). One such item, based on the belief in prescient children, "The Dream of the Miner's Child," was spread almost entirely by commercial records in the mid-1920's. Not only were these discs widely sold, thereby precluding anonymity or obscurity, but the "Dream's" leading singer, Vernon Dalhart, met no scholar's criterion for a folksinger — then or now. Further, when the oracular song itself was studied, it led back to a music-hall piece flatly rejected as a folksong in England. In the spring of 1951, A. L. Lloyd undertook considerable collecting as part of the mining industry's contribution to the Festival of Britain. Lloyd had asked workers to submit material to *Coal* but the collector reported that not all entries were folksongs. "Some were parodies, literary recitations, parlour ballads of the type of 'Don't Go Down in the Mine, Daddy.' "[3]

This maudlin piece may not have entered tradition in Britain but its hillbilly offspring, "The Dream of the Miner's Child," became a widespread American folksong. Perhaps the fence between folk and popular culture is lower in the United States than in England; perhaps there were special elements in the American number which endeared it to folksingers. The two pieces are best studied as a unit, not only because of their close relationship but also because of the contrast in reception on either side of the Atlantic. In historical case studies there are many possible points from which to begin: a song's initial time of composition, its probable period of entrance into tradition, the era of scholarly attention to the item. In this chapter I shall pursue all three openings.

The origin of "Don't Go Down in the Mine, Dad" is not shrouded in mystery. It was composed by Robert Donnelly and Will Geddes and published in 1910 by the Lawrence Wright Music Company of London. It proved popular enough to be kept in print, and during 1957 I obtained the sheet music directly from the publisher. Not finding any story on the song's background in standard accounts of twentieth-century English popular music, I enlisted the aid of Lionel McColvin of London's Central Music Library. He, in turn, ascertained that the song was apparently suggested by the great 1907 mining disaster at St. Genaed in South Wales. "Will Geddes was a Lancashire man who was inspired to write the song, so the story goes, by the tale of a young boy who supposedly dreamt that the disaster would occur and warned his father not to go, thus saving his life, as over a hundred people were blown to pieces in the accident."[4]

The relationship between the Donnelly-Geddes song and the St. Genaed disaster may or may not be factual; the tale of the boy's dream is almost surely apocryphal. The impulse to relate saving dreams to danger is both worldwide and time-tested. Songs which employ this motif usually dissolve in a happy wish-fulfillment, but not in all cases. From the Welsh "Miner's Doom" we learn that "So true was her dream to that poor woman's sorrow / The rope broke while ascending and her dear husband died." Similarly, "The Trapper Boy's Dream" (originally printed in a leaflet, "The Dreadful Explosion at Westmoor Colliery") is a nine-stanza broadside graphically portraying a boy's dream of death from a coal-fall. The pressure of poverty overcame the nocturnal warning and drove him to work, where he was killed.[5]

Whether or not the author or composer of "Don't Go Down in the Mine, Dad" ever wrote out an explanation of the song's composition, or reported it to another person, is unknown. During 1957 I was tempted to pursue Donnelly and Geddes via correspondence, but was overwhelmed by the difficulty in reaching composers closer to home. When Mr. McColvin relayed the St. Genaed anecdote to me, I had already sensed that it would take years to explore

115

the music-hall number's offspring in the United States. In spite of my focus on the secondary item, curiosity kept pulling me back to the parent piece. What follows is the Donnelly-Geddes text as published in 1910 in London by the Lawrence Wright Music Company.

Don't Go Down in the Mine, Dad

A miner was leaving his home for his work,
When he heard his little child scream;
He went to his bedside, his little white face,
"Oh, Daddy, I've had such a dream;
I dreamt that I saw the pit all afire,
And men struggled hard for their lives;
The scene it then changed, and the top of the mine
Was surrounded by sweethearts and wives."

> Don't go down in the mine, Dad,
> Dreams very often come true;
> Daddy, you know it would break my heart
> If anything happened to you;
> Just go and tell my dream to your mates,
> And as true as the stars that shine,
> Something is going to happen today,
> Dear Daddy, don't go down the mine!

The miner, a man with a heart good and kind,
Stood by the side of his son;
He said, "It's my living, I can't stay away,
For duty, my lad, must be done."
The little one look'd up, and sadly he said,
"Oh, please stay today with me, Dad!"
But as the brave miner went forth, to his work,
He heard this appeal from his lad:

Chorus:

Whilst waiting his turn with his mates to descend,
He could not banish his fears,
He return'd home again to his wife and his child,
Those words seem'd to ring through his ears,
And, ere the day ended, the pit was on fire,
When a score of brave men lost their lives;
He thank'd God above for the dream his child had,
As once more the little one cries:

Chorus:

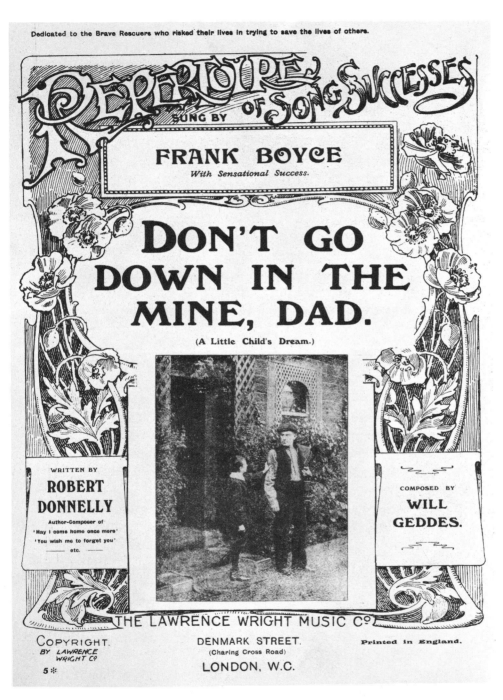

"DON'T GO DOWN IN THE MINE, DAD"

The song was immediately popular in places of entertainment, on sheet music, and on cylinder and disc recordings. (See Checklist Two for details.) In fact, Geddes followed it with a sequel, "A Collier's Child, or Why Have I No Daddy?," which did not achieve success. Presumably, the popularity of "Don't Go Down in the Mine, Dad" stemmed from the happy ending, which acted out the wishes of multitudes who experienced actual danger in their work or felt it vicariously. The present sheet-music printing carries the note, "Sung by Frank Boyce with Sensational Success." Also, baritone Stanley Kirkby made a popular recording of the song in 1910. "Don't Go Down in the Mine, Dad," in cockney rendition, is currently available on an English LP by John Foreman, *The 'Ouses in Between.*

A recent Australian recording, *The Tex Morton Story,* treats the piece in an unusual manner. Morton, an Australian country-western performer influenced by Jimmie Rodgers and Goebel Reeves, sings only the first verse and chorus but adds to it a recited description of the boy's dream: "I saw the sad faces of those praying there. Dear Mommy, so brave, and so still. Said one ghostly miner, 'My kid is like you, he lives far away in Springhill.' There was Hank from Kentucky, and Taffy from Wales. All urgently whispered, 'Don't wait.' Then a big draegerman said, 'Aye, laddie, wake up now. Go back. Warn them. Hurry, before it's too late.' "[6] This recitation, accompanied by a funeral organ, may seem banal to a sophisticated audience, but it is an accepted part of hillbilly fare.

Morton's invocation of four archetypal miners in the dream scene is effective — particularly the ghost from Springhill, Nova Scotia, the site of two tragic disasters in 1956 and 1958. His usage *draegerman* refers to specially trained rescue-squad miners. The contrast between the Foreman and Morton treatments is significant for a piece not considered to be a folksong. Foreman, who stays close to the sheet-music text, probably learned the song for recording purposes. Morton not only substitutes the imaginative dream sequence for the final two stanzas, but departs from the standard text for his opening stanza, as if he recalled the song after Springhill's news reached Australia.

The only folklorist to explore "Don't Go Down in the Mine, Dad" in U.S. tradition was Wayland Hand.[7] During 1948 he found

WAYLAND HAND

many Butte, Montana, residents who partly remembered it. Hand was intrigued to learn that two "Cousin Jacks," Harry Broad and Jim Bennetts, dated the song back to the old country, Cornwall, about 1908. (Unless Donnelly and Geddes sang their composition before publication, which seems unlikely, the Cornishmen simply erred by a few years.) Both recalled that "Don't" was sung in theaters and pubs while stereopticon slides were flashed upon the screen to accompany each verse. In fact, Broad brought a set to Butte from which Hand learned that the slides were copyrighted by the Lawrence Wright firm, though undated. The current sheet music is illustrated by a picture of a lad in front of a trellised cottage imploring his father not to venture to work. Possibly this photo comes from the 1910 slide set.

Hand unearthed an additional clue worth exploring. Annie Matthews (Santa Monica, California) remembered that the song was parodied by colliers coming to London for Christmastime football matches: "Don't go down in the mine, Dad / Wait 'till it comes up to you." She placed this couplet back to 1898, which indicates either that her memory was faulty or that Donnelly and Geddes built their song on an early model, presently unknown.

On February 9, 1911, the *United Mine Workers Journal* printed "Don't Go Down in the Mine" by J. R. Lincoln without listing his residence. Presumably he was a UMWA member at that time; hardly a *Journal* appeared without a poem submitted by a correspondent. It can be assumed that Lincoln had a copy of the original sheet music, the text alone, or had committed the words to memory. He changed but three terms: *white face* to *face white, sadly* to *faintly, pit* to *mine* (twice). This last switch represents differences between British and American on-the-job terms. None of Lincoln's changes are significant.

It is difficult to gauge how widespread was "Don't Go Down in the Mine, Dad" outside Butte. In an autobiographical study, Woody Guthrie wrote of his Oklahoma childhood: "The soft coal mines, the lead and zinc mines around Henryetta, were only seventeen miles from my home town, Okema, and I heard their songs. . . . I sold newspapers, sang all of the songs I picked up. I learned to jig dance along the sidewalks to things called portable phonographs and sung for my first cancered pennies the 'Dream of the Miner's Child,' 'Sinking of the Titanic'. . . ."[8] We lack a precise date for this "cancered pennies" episode; perhaps Guthrie himself could not have placed it in a given year. He was born on July 14, 1912. Vernon Dalhart's records of "Dream" were available in Okema stores by Christmastime, 1925, when Guthrie was thirteen. Richard Reuss, who has studied the Oklahoma bard extensively, suggests that this jigging period took place sometime before 1925.[9] Guthrie's imprecise recollection may well indicate that he heard Henryetta miners sing the English music-hall song when he was a young boy, but that he substituted the secondary title in his 1947 memoir.

This guess about the substitution by Woody Guthrie of "Dream" for "Don't" is supported by the fact that the typescript copy of his "song notebook," duplicated at the Library of Congress, holds a "Miner's Child" which is very close to Dalhart's text.[10] Seemingly, for Guthrie and other listeners, the American song drove the English one into the background everywhere except in Butte, where "Don't" retained a hold on "Cousin Jack" affection.

The close thematic and rhetorical relationship between the parent and child songs is displayed upon a comparison of the two. "The Dream of the Miner's Child" exists in a number of early texts: the copy sent by Polk Brockman of Atlanta, Georgia, to the Library of Congress Copyright Office for registration purposes; the verbal texts on several phonograph recordings made by Vernon Dalhart, some showing slight differences from each other; the sheet music published by Shapiro, Bernstein & Company (New York) early in 1926. Normally we expect a copyrighted, published song to be granite-like with words constant in form through time. The slight differences in the early texts of "The Dream of the Miner's Child" are not significant, but they demonstrate that transcribers, printers, publishers, and singers find it extremely difficult to accept any given words as correct or final. The text and tune here are transcribed from Okeh 40498, the first of many "Dream" recordings by Dalhart.

THE DREAM OF THE MINER'S CHILD

A miner was leaving his home for his work,
He heard his little child scream,
He went to the side of the little girl's bed —
"Oh! Daddy, I've had such a dream."

"Oh! Daddy, don't work in the mines today,
For dreams have so often come true,
Oh! Daddy, my Daddy, please don't go away,
I never could live without you.

"I dreamed that the mines were all seething with fire,
The men all fought for their lives.
Just then the scene changed, and the mouth of the mines
Were covered with sweethearts and wives."

Chorus:

Her daddy, then smiling and stroking her face,
Was turning away from her side.
But throwing her small arms around Daddy's neck,
She gave him a kiss and then cried:

"Go down to the village and tell your dear friends,
As sure as the bright stars do shine,
There's something that's going to happen today,
Oh! Daddy don't go to the mine."

Chorus:

THE DREAM OF THE MINER'S CHILD

stanza 1

A min-er was leav-ing his home for his work, He heard his lit-tle child scream, He went to the side of the lit-tle girl's bed— "Oh! Dad-dy, I've had such a

chorus

dream." "Oh! Dad-dy, don't work in the mines to-day, For dreams have so of-ten come true, Oh! Dad-dy, my Dad-dy, please don't go a-way, I nev-er could live with-out you.

This first recording of "The Dream of the Miner's Child" was made by Vernon Dalhart on October 9, 1925, in New York for the General Phonograph Corporation. It was paired with "Mother's Grave" and released on Okeh's popular (rather than old-time) series. In the next three months he recorded the song for at least eight more companies, which in turn issued it on various labels or leased it to others. At times it is extremely difficult to reconstruct the discographical pattern for a single Dalhart song. Not only did he use many pseudonyms, but most of the firms for which he worked are defunct and their ledgers are destroyed or inaccessible. I am in debt to Marion Hoffman of Valley Center, Kansas, who provided me with a tape of Dalhart's "Dream" renditions on various label groups. (Known discographical details for Dalhart's "Dream" are provided in Appendix Two.) For all firms Dalhart sang alone, usually accompanying himself on the harmonica. At all sessions he was also backed by two or three musicians. For example, on his last Vocalion recording of "Dream" he was accompanied by Carson Robison, guitar, Murray Kellner, violin, and Del Staigners, cornet. The music notation above transcribes the voice alone.

It must have been obvious to Dalhart's listeners who knew the English song that "Dream" derived from "Don't," although the melodies differed. During 1926 the Lawrence Wright firm became aware of the relationship of the parent song to its American offspring and took action to assert priority rights. Apparently when the Dalhart disc reached London, the Wright directors questioned Shapiro, Bernstein & Company in New York about "Dream's" authorship. At that point the American publisher got in touch with the song's composer, Andrew Jenkins, who demonstrated the propriety of his claim to original composition for the number. My knowledge of this challenge is sketchy and does not come from legal or business files.[11] Rather, it derives from correspondence and interviews with Irene Spain, Jenkins' stepdaughter.

Both father and daughter richly deserve a full biographical study; here I can but outline their lives and touch on their role in placing a few ballads in American tradition.[12] Andrew Jenkins was born on November 26, 1885, at Jenkinsburg, Georgia, on Atlanta's outskirts. As an infant he was made almost sightless by a faulty medication; in adult life (1939) he lost even this partial vision. The two main sustaining forces in Jenkins' life were religion and music, which seemed to compensate for poverty. Converted to Methodism in his ninth year, he preached to playmates from tree stumps and porches. From an early age he could play almost any instrument placed in his hands; also during childhood, he began to compose songs effortlessly. He apparently had no regular trade except selling newspapers, but after accepting the call to the pulpit in his early twenties, he was addressed as Reverend. His denominational values were strongly shaped by the Holiness revival, so influential in the South at the opening of the century. In 1910 he married Mattie Chandler, who died two years later. On August 5, 1919, he married Frances Jane Walden Eskew, a young widow with three children — Irene, Mary Lee, and a son, "T.P."

All three youngsters were musical, and with "Daddy," in time, formed the Jenkins Family, one of the first folk and gospel groups to appear on WSB. The *Atlanta Journal*'s radio station "Covered Dixie Like the Dew" and brought considerable attention but, sadly,

123

THE JENKINS FAMILY

never any pay to "Doctor" Jenkins, who obtained this fancy title from WSB's pioneer manager, Lambdin Kay. Throughout the 1920's the Family received fan letters from coast-to-coast listeners as well as from radio friends in Canada and Mexico. The air waves were uncrowded; WSB was a powerful station. One listener who fully understood the Family's appeal and potential sales value was Polk Brockman, Atlanta's Okeh distributor and local talent scout, who helped the group begin its recording career in 1924. The Family's first issue was "Church in the Wildwood" / "If I Could Hear My Mother Pray Again" (Okeh 40214). Members of the Jenkins Family continued to record, in various combinations, for some years under different names: Jenkins Sacred Singers, the Irene Spain Family, Blind Andy, Gooby Jenkins, Andrew Jenkins and Carson Robison.

Unlike many hillbilly artists, Jenkins was not unknown in his time. Because he performed on a powerful radio outlet which belonged to an influential newspaper, he was accorded good features in the *Atlanta Journal*. On September 19, 1924, a picture of Jenkins and his daughters (Irene at the melodeon) announced that the Family had recorded for Okeh. A decade later a reporter

124

described Jenkins' composing speed: "His most popular number, 'The Death of Floyd Collins,' was completed in forty-five minutes." A 1951 story detailed evangelist Jenkins' volunteer work singing in Fulton County prison camps, and his receiving a gift recorder to enable him to "make a comeback as a ballad singer."[13] But no comeback in terms of the postwar music industry was possible; instead Andrew Jenkins spent his final years preaching at local revivals. Additionally, he was engaged in radio evangelism on Mexican border stations, recording these songs and sermons in his Atlanta home. However, it was as a composer rather than as a performer or an evangelist that Jenkins left his mark.

In February, 1925, Floyd Collins died in a sandstone wormhole while attempting to return to the surface from a limestone cave (Edmonson County, Kentucky).[14] The public was galvanized as the dramatic attempt to rescue the spelunker was covered by national press and radio; his death struggle was excruciatingly slow. Many symbolic elements were sensed in Collins' story long before Robert Penn Warren took it in hand for *The Cave*. Although the death scene was near Mammoth Cave, in a non-coal-producing area, coal miners participated in the rescue. Photographs of miners digging (and praying) appeared in the national press, and helped establish the belief in some minds that Collins was a victim of a Kentucky mine disaster rather than a "cave bug" trapped when exploring. While in Florida in mid-February, Brockman telegraphed to Jenkins to compose a Collins ballad. Until this time hillbilly performers brought traditional material to recording studios; now a new ballad was composed on demand for a music-industry executive. This method of quickly creating the Floyd Collins song remained vivid in Irene Spain's mind (as well as the $25 fee received). Her father composed "this tragedy song" accompanying himself on guitar or piano while Irene took down words and music. Also, it was her task to score the music and to send the text-tune to Brockman. She recalled wistfully that if she had anticipated that "The Death of Floyd Collins" was destined to become both a national hit and an American folksong, she would have added a few grace notes to color its melodic simplicity.

The history of "The Death of Floyd Collins" is intimately associated with "The Dream of the Miner's Child." Okeh's first

125

issue of the former piece (sung by Fiddlin' John Carson on Okeh 40363) was recorded on April 14, 1925, within two months of Collins' death. The Carson rendition made slow progress, but Brockman was confident of the song's appeal and sent it to Frank Walker, Columbia's A & R man in New York. Vernon Dalhart recorded it on May 27 (Columbia 15031-D, under the pseudonym Al Craver), and again for Victor in September. The latter firm coupled the Floyd Collins song with another journalistic item, "The Wreck of the Shenandoah," and released the pair (19779). When the widow of Commodore Lansdowne objected to the dirigible hero's elegy, Victor obligingly withdrew the disc. At this juncture, the producers paired "The Death of Floyd Collins" with a new Jenkins piece, "The Dream of a Miner's Child" (19821). The December *Victor Records Supplement*, which reached the public usually via music-store counters, commented on this fresh pairing: "The first describes, in epic fashion, the death of Floyd Collins in his new-discovered cave in the Kentucky mountains. The companion number is like it dealing with a disaster of mine-life. These are stern transcriptions of things which add to the weight of all humanity's tragic experience."[15]

This sequence — composition, recording, publicity — is presented in detail because it is important to know that by 1925 the sound-recording industry was able to release topical records while the events portrayed were vivid in memory. Also, it illustrates the phonograph record's broadside function. Printed broadsides normally carried words only. When notes were present they had meaning to music readers alone. A disc was a broadside in which one heard rather than saw text and tune. It was awkward to learn words from a disc but this practice had the virtue of not separating lyrics and melody. Recordings fused sounds and ideas in a manner beyond the limits of print. To complete the analogy sketched here, it can be said that commentary on new records in advertising supplements was comparable to a ballad monger's cries when hawking fresh material. We have, then, in "The Death of Floyd Collins" and "The Dream of the Miner's Child," two broadsides of known authorship (by a composer in folk society) sold by a popular culture–oriented industry to a wide range of buyers at all levels of society.[16]

126

There are many facets to any song's story and each is worth some exposure. I have been primarily interested in learning how Andrew Jenkins heard enough of "Don't Go Down in the Mine, Dad" to recompose it, and secondarily in delineating "The Dream of the Miner's Child's" life as a folksong. It is important in commenting on the folk process to distinguish recomposition from plagiarism. Some folk composers were fully conscious of their use of old material and specific in acknowledging sources; many were not. Those who were prolific creators hardly felt it necessary to use the material of others. Jenkins, who was both prolific and a Christian, drew on "inspiration" but was generous with credits when he was conscious of sources. Fortunately, he described his writing methods in an unpublished autobiographical manuscript. Also his daughter, in numerous interviews with and correspondence to folklorists, complemented "Daddy's" accounts. She told me frequently of his pleasure in composing. "I used to tell him to stay away from the piano or guitar for a while for I knew that if he sat down and started playing, he would be calling for me soon to take down a song." Religious material was composed well before the topical ballads. "He never tried to make any tragedies [songs] until Floyd Collins was trapped in the Sand Cave." After this "Daddy made tragedy songs of almost every kind." Jenkins was fully aware of the value in his homiletic formula. "His trade mark was always in the last verse or two last verses, warnings."[17]

Before Jenkins lost all his sight he had read by holding books up to his face, but when this proved too difficult he learned Braille. After his second marriage, Jenkins' wife and daughters read to him; of course, from 1922 until his death he listened to the radio. His mind retained hundreds of brief narrative plots, as well as a full stock of ballad clichés to flesh out the abundant material which came to him from the mass media. For example, his "Billy the Kid" was based on information in a 1926 Book-of-the-Month Club brochure for Walter Noble Burns's *The Saga of Billy the Kid*. At year's end, Polk Brockman, thinking that Billy's adventures had commercial-song potential, sent the advertisement to Jenkins, who composed the number in January, 1927; soon it was recorded by Dalhart on Victor 20966, paired with "Jesse James." In 1934 "Billy the Kid" appeared in the Lomaxes' *American Ballads and*

Folk Songs (transcribed from the disc), and in 1962 it moved from this anthology to Burl Ives's *Song in America.* (Neither collection credited Jenkins for this "western folksong.")[18]

Irene Spain helped her father compose many songs, based directly on then-current newspaper and broadcast reports. She recalled that "The Tragedy on Daytona Beach" was written "when we read of it or heard it over radio. We gathered all the information we could get from the press and from radio reports and made the song when it happened." The ballad's facts concerned driver Lee Bible's death on March 13, 1929, when he attempted to capture the day's speed trophy. In 1929 Jenkins himself recorded the song (Okeh 45343); in 1950 Alton Morris printed its text and tune, gathered from a Daytona Beach resident, in *Folksongs of Florida.*[19] A final example of this process concerns "The Wreck of the Royal Palm," which Irene indicated "was written by Daddy when it happened" (December 23, 1926). Nearly three decades later it was collected at Berea, Kentucky, for the Library of Congress.[20]

It is obvious that "The Dream of the Miner's Child" event did not happen in the same manner in which the Southern Railway fliers, Ponce de Leon and the Royal Palm, collided near Rockmart, Georgia. Nor was the tragedy in "Dream" as actual as the death of "that brave young mechanic," Lee Bible, on a Florida racing course. It is easy for us to correlate Jenkins' hearing news of train or auto wrecks with his subsequent compositions. It is impossible to establish such a facile correlation for "The Dream of the Miner's Child." I feel certain that Andrew Jenkins could have explained his inspiration for his dream-motif number; I do not know whether he was conscious of the Donnelly-Geddes predecessor. My letter attempting to query Jenkins about "Dream" reached Atlanta a few days before his death at Thomaston on April 25, 1956. However, it led to a rewarding friendship with his daughter.

In response to my questions, Mrs. Spain stated that "Daddy" had no firsthand knowledge of mining other than through reading. His travel was limited to revivals and tent meetings in Georgia and neighboring states, with a few recording trips after 1925 to New York. She wrote that "there didn't have to be anything special to cause him to make such songs."[21] Since I was conscious of the English music-hall piece which lay behind "Dream," I jogged

Irene's memory. I was sensitive to the fact that she might consider my query as an accusation of plagiarism. However, in her fourth letter to me she summed up her memories of the song's origin. In fairness, it must be said that Irene had some association (tune composition, transcription from discs, lead-sheet preparation) with at least a thousand songs, and there was no special reason for her to retain each history. Her recollection is presented, at this point, in great detail not only for the light it sheds on "The Dream of the Miner's Child," but, far more important, because it is a statement on composition more explicitly made than one usually obtained from folksingers.

I have a copy of the words ["Dream"] but up to now, through looking over the music [in Irene's files], I find no copy of that particular song. I can rightly give you an answer to that though. I remember the tune very well. I also remember the part you called a mystery about it. Daddy made the song. At that time Mr. Brockman had the Okeh to do a good bit of recording as he was connected with that Company. . . . That tune is VERY original and so are the words. Soon after the releasing of the record, we were informed that this song ["Don't"] had possibly come from this English someone. So in order to vouchsafe our own authenticity of the song, I dug up the original copy of the music, with its erasures and changes of notes, etc., that always go with any original copy — before the final copy is made — and I sent that to Mr. Brockman. I think he in turn sent it to Mr. Ralph S. Peer of Peer International. At that time Mr. Peer was with Okeh company in some capacity or other. I am not too sure that it was Mr. Peer, but it seems that it was. I know there was quite a bit of confusion about it at the time, but our copy was really and truly our own original one and it was proven so by my authentic copy. This music script was not returned to me. I imagine it ["Dream"] was completely cleared as we never heard about it any more.

Daddy actually made the song, I arranged the music and at that time we never knew there was ever any song that existed even kin to it. However, all songs are kin in some way or other. . . . I'm sure that WE never heard that special song ["Don't"] over here. Our own original theme and tune could well be an honor to us for being so near that of the English version, if it had not been attacked by them. You can rest assured that The Dream of the Miner's Child is an original product of Daddy's and it was proven so to our and the Record Company's satisfaction. Of course WE KNEW that it was. Daddy was very honest for he was a real God-sent composer and a Christian. His every song was truly his own. If we had anyone's lyrics or aria from anyone's song to rearrange for them, we always put their name on it and gave them their due credit. Daddy was too prolific in his own right in composing to even wish to intrude on other's songs. I know for I was half of the team in the making of his wonderful songs.[22]

In subsequent letters and interviews, Mrs. Spain could not add to this account, but she did offer a happy parallel which involved proof of authorship to another Jenkins composition. One of his obscure sacred songs, "God Put a Rainbow in the Cloud," somehow entered Negro tradition and eventually was recorded by Mahalia Jackson. Fortunately it had been registered in 1931, but when it became a gospel standard (with the patina of an old spiritual) Jenkins' rights were overlooked. In "the nick-of-time" Irene mailed her "original music" to Sesac (a music-licensing organization in New York) to establish the fact that she and "Daddy" had really authored this song, as well as to renew its copyright. It is characteristic of Irene Spain's faith that she now attributes the royalties from "God Put a Rainbow in the Cloud" jointly to Miss Jackson and the Lord.[23]

When I endeavored to corroborate A & R man Ralph Peer's possible role in the "Don't"-"Dream" relationship, he replied: "I do not recall ever supplying information which 'proved authenticity of the Jenkins version.' "[24] Similarly, "The Dream of the Miner's Child" did not make much of an impression on Polk Brockman. Although he held the original copyright (October 28, 1925), he had assigned it to Shapiro, Bernstein & Company (February 17, 1926). In that period Brockman was more interested in recording royalties ("mechanicals") than in sheet-music and song-folio publication profits.[25] Naturally, in 1926 some Lawrence Wright official or barrister had to reach one of Dalhart's many recording firms or Shapiro, Bernstein to protest that "Dream" was too close for comfort to the Donnelly-Geddes song, but the name of such a person has eluded me. Presumably the American publisher had established the fact of Jenkins' "originality" based on sufficient textual differences between the two pieces to meet copyright standards.

We can only assume at this point that Jenkins in some way

reworked the English music-hall song in 1925. We know that the American folk accepted the offspring, and in time collectors gathered it unaware of Jenkins' role. In the 1920's and 1930's quite a few of his pieces (recorded by Dalhart) became "instant" folksongs, in part because Jenkins adhered to folk conventions in his poetry, in part because Dalhart employed down-home style, and in part because the total resources of the music industry made Dalhart's discs available to the folk.

I am fully aware that neither Dalhart as a singer nor Jenkins as a singer-composer is a well-known figure in American Studies today. Nevertheless, the attention by scholars to such "folk" composers as Woody Guthrie, A. P. Carter, or Jimmie Rodgers bestows the mantle upon figures no more rustic, natural, or unsophisticated than the Atlanta newsboy-evangelist. One does not have to be an isolated mountaineer retaining "Elizabethan" speech, or a Delta sharecropper clinging to "African" customs, to compose songs destined for life in tradition. No view of the American folk is useful which restricts it to one class, region, minority, or esthetic. Andrew Jenkins was in some respects quite unlike other commercial performers accepted by folklorists — Uncle Dave Macon, Riley Puckett, Clayton McMichen, G. B. Grayson, Henry Whitter — yet Jenkins had features in common with them, and along with these peers helped establish the earliest boundaries of recorded hillbilly music.

I am convinced that it is only a matter of time before Jenkins' role as a composer of songs which entered tradition will be appreciated; I am far less certain that folklorists will ever evaluate Vernon Dalhart's complex role. During 1960 Jim Walsh published in *Hobbies* a fine series of biographical articles on Dalhart as a popular recording star.[26] Ideally this series should be supplemented by a folkloric study which traces the material both gained from and given to tradition by Dalhart. My capsule sketch at this point is intended only to illustrate his position before he recorded "The Dream of the Miner's Child." He was born Marion Try Slaughter at Jefferson, Texas, on April 6, 1883, and took the pseudonym Vernon Dalhart from two Texas towns quite far removed from his bayou-region home. By 1912 he was a successful light-opera tenor on the New York stage, and in 1916 he made his recording debut

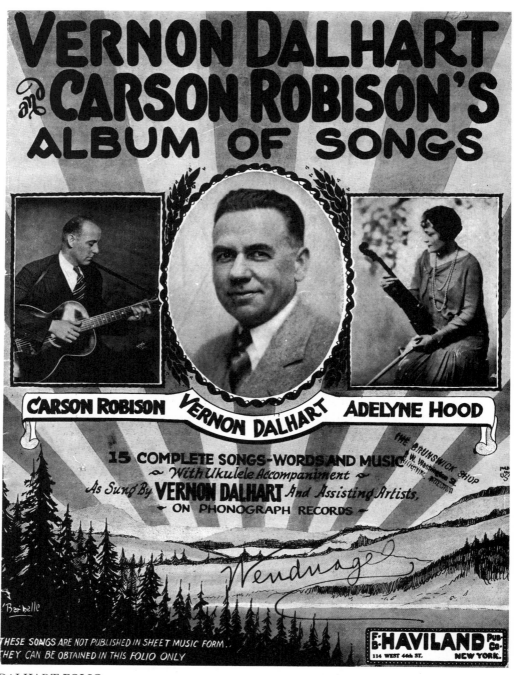

DALHART FOLIO

featuring pseudo-Negro plantation and coon songs. His switch to hillbilly music came in the summer of 1924 when he "covered" for Edison a railroad ballad previously recorded by Henry Whitter for Okeh, "The Wreck on the Southern Old 97." Edison 51316 sold well and Dalhart recorded the ballad once more for Victor. "The Wreck" was now coupled with "The Prisoner's Song" (Victor 19427); the phenomenal success of this particular pairing helped nationalize hillbilly music.

My brief portrait overlooks the troublesome question of Vernon Dalhart's style. After 1924 Victor exploited him as a country singer. In the 1920-23 catalogs he had been identified as a Century Theater light-opera star, but after 1924 he was described as a singer of mountain ballads. No sophisticated artist becomes a folksinger by fiat; actually, Dalhart had heard enough traditional material — Anglo and Afro — to be able to discard Victor Herbert or Stephen Foster in favor of Andrew Jenkins. It is interesting to note, as discographer Will Roy Hearne has observed, that Dalhart's boyhood home (Harrison County, Texas) was across the state line from Huddie "Leadbelly" Ledbetter's (Caddo Parish, Louisiana).[27] The field hands who followed the crops, and laborers who worked in the east Texas lumber and turpentine camps, were heard by Leadbelly and Dalhart as youngsters. Something of the tremendous polarity in American life is seen in the contrasting careers of these two singers. We can only speculate on what Dalhart would have sung for a folklorist if one had queried him about his sources or style. Recently, Walter Haden of the University of Tennessee, Martin, has published an account of Dalhart's life in folk society before his musical fame in New York. Haden's forthcoming biography of Dalhart promises to answer some of the questions raised in this study.[28]

In adulthood Dalhart was the first "citybilly" to reach a wide folk audience. His rendition of "The Prisoner's Song" alone was known in nearly every American home that boasted a phonograph between 1924 and 1929. Dalhart's reception can only be likened to the subsequent appeal of Bing Crosby or Frank Sinatra. Yet in spite of an initial audience, both folk and popular, numbering in the millions, Dalhart's career ended with the Great Depression. This watershed in American life marked profound changes in country- as well as popular-music tastes. Only a few folk-based recording artists such as the Carter Family remained active throughout the difficult early 1930's. At that time Dalhart lost his hold on rural and urban audiences as well as his utility to the commercial music industry.

This assertion is demonstrated in the near-total neglect of Dalhart by both the industry and private collectors in the record-reissue program of the 1960's. To illustrate, Jimmie Rodgers' full recording output of 1927-33 is currently available; likewise, more than half of the Carter Family's output of 1927-41 is on the market. By contrast, of the some thousand songs recorded by Dalhart, only two are found on present-day reissues. Despite this minuscule sample, the esthetic response of self-styled, country-music "moldy figs" has been harsh. A recent reviewer, on finding a Dalhart item reissued on an LP, stated: "A disastrous triumph of folk valuability, *per se*, over musical enjoyability or worth," and "Dalhart is certainly out of place in an authentic country LP of any kind."[29] Time may bring a more temperate judgment of Dalhart's worth; possibly this case study will focus some attention on one of his most popular songs.

"The Dream of the Miner's Child" is an excellent example of a "new" song with a known life history which became a hillbilly hit and an American folksong almost simultaneously. Appendix Two, which follows this chapter, illustrates the range of Dalhart's "Dream" recordings as well as the song's availability in the 1920's. During 1927 the text-tune, perhaps from the same source, was presented in two contrasting books: Sigmund Spaeth, *Weep Some More, My Lady*, and Ethel Park Richardson, *American Mountain Songs*. Neither editor gave any provenience for "Dream" or indicated that it could be found in every record store in the land. The two titles reveal the spirit in which "Dream" was presented; Spaeth treated it as a quaint parlor piece and Richardson as a folksong. If the two authors did not take the song directly from sheet music or discs they must have encountered singers who learned the piece from a Dalhart record shortly before the books were published.

Twenty-three years elapsed after the Spaeth and Richardson anthologies before the song was printed in any standard folksong collection. However, during 1932 it had appeared at two other levels: an unpublished academic collection and a hillbilly songster. Geneva Anderson obtained a text in Blount County, Tennessee; the text-tune also was found in Bradley Kincaid's *My Favorite Mountain Ballads and Old Time Songs*, sold by Pittsburgh station KDKA. There is no point in commenting on every subsequent printing of the song, scholarly or popular. Through the 1930's it was widely issued in radio stations' booklets and music publishers' folios. All such appearances demonstrate that it was performed by singers whose versions derived in one way or another from the Dalhart rendition. The main phrase that caused difficulty to singers was "mines all seething with fire," which became "steaming," "streaming," or "blazing" in subsequent texts.

A good question in folklore studies is: How much variation over what time period is looked for before a song is said to be in tradition? Was "The Dream of the Miner's Child" more a folksong in Geneva Anderson's thesis than in Bradley Kincaid's KDKA booklet because the former text was more garbled than the latter? Was the piece automatically judged to be a folksong when Mary Elizabeth Barnicle deposited two versions on Kentucky field discs at the Library of Congress in 1938? In my view the field recordings, the thesis texts, and the folio printings all stem ultimately from Dalhart. The judgment of whether any particular item has circulated from singer to singer and has been altered in the process should be based on reading and hearing a number of text-tunes, as well as studying the context in which any given item is found. By this standard I can say that "The Dream of the Miner's Child" is an American folksong despite limited textual variation.

Actually the one "Dream" text which shows considerable variation from the Jenkins-Dalhart mold is the unique "Explosion in the Fairmount Mines" by Blind Alfred Reed, recorded on December 19, 1927 (Victor 21191), and offered below. This song title, with its special spelling of *Fairmount*, points back to one of the greatest industrial holocausts in the United States, the Monongah (Marion County, West Virginia) disaster of December 6, 1907.[30] It took place in the Fairmont Coal Company's mines; the official death count was 362 men and boys, largely Italian and Polish immigrants. Few miners survived the cyclonic underground blast. Investigators attributed the carnage to gas ignited by open

135

MONONGAH MORGUE, 1907

lights or to coal-dust clouds ignited by electric arcs. Some notion of the tragedy's scope is seen in the note that by New Year's Day (1908) "the Catholic Sisters had placed most of the one thousand children in orphan asylums."[31] A month after the blast, the *United Mine Workers Journal* carried a long narrative poem contributed from Illinois, "The Monongah Disaster."[32] If anyone at the site made up a song when the event was vivid, it has not been found. It is possible, of course, that non-English-language ballads did circulate which failed to reach print or George Korson's attention.

The press of constant wrecks, blasts, cave-ins, and fires in West Virginia mines insured short life for many traditional items born in disaster. During 1930 union organizer Tom Tippett visited the Monongah mine cemetery. Uniform stones marked the known victims, but their unnamed companions lay in a weedy hillside plot with only a fallen wooden marker to note their final place. Not far from this lonely spot, Tippett found a personal memorial to the unidentified dead, a pile of hundreds of tons of coal in a back yard. The ten-foot pile had been laboriously gathered — one sack at a time for twenty-three years — by an insane widow seeking her

136

husband lost in 1907 and never properly buried. Mrs. Daves, symbolically, memorialized not only her husband but all his fellows in Monongah and beyond. Something of her intensity can still be heard in Blind Alfred Reed's "Explosion in the Fairmount Mines." Although his text reveals an alteration of "The Dream of the Miner's Child" rather than a Fairmont narrative ballad, Reed was impelled to name his song after the great explosion.

I have long wanted to learn the precise circumstances of Reed's recomposition but this story has eluded me, except for the fact that Ralph Peer copyrighted the song in Reed's name on April 7, 1928 (E 687574). Reed was an excellent exponent of Appalachian ballad style who accompanied himself on the fiddle. He made some superb recordings for Victor in 1927-30 and then fell out of sight. The content of several of his recorded local ballads such as "The Wreck of the Virginian" or "The Fate of Chris Lively and Wife" indicated that Reed lived in one of three West Virginia counties — Mercer, Raleigh, Fayette — quite far removed from Fairmont. Perhaps, when the Jenkins-Dalhart song reached him, he altered it to suit his memory of a two-decade-old disaster without having the specific facts at hand.

My curiosity about Reed's residence and occupation, coupled with my pleasure in his vinegary style, led me in 1969 to correspondence with one of his friends, Bernice Coleman, a retired Norfolk & Western railroader in Princeton, West Virginia. During the early 1930's, Coleman, an old-time fiddler, had recorded with Ernest Branch, Roy Harvey, and Jess Johnson for the Okeh and Gennett firms. One of Coleman's personal compositions, "The Wreck of the C & O Sportsman," sung by Harvey, a railroad engineer, was released under the pseudonym John Martin (Superior 2701). Coleman fiddled on this disc; the ballad itself commemorated a 1930 accident on the C & O "just west of the station called Hawk's Nest," not far from the juncture of the New and Kanawha rivers.

When he learned of my interest, Coleman kindly interviewed Reed's son, Arville, who had accompanied his father on the guitar at some of their Victor sessions. In time, I was able to supplement Coleman's interview with a long visit to him as well as to Arville and his wife.[33] They reported that Alfred Reed had been born on June 15, 1880, in Floyd County, Virginia, and during his childhood

137

his family had moved to Mercer County, West Virginia. Musical from an early age, Reed played fiddle, banjo, mandolin, and guitar at county fairs and church socials. His major calling, however, was as a Methodist minister; his last pastorate was Kegley in Mercer County. Reed died on January 17, 1956, at Cool Ridge (Raleigh County) but was buried at Elgood (Mercer County) beside his wife, Nettie Sheard Reed.

Arville knew of no specific source for his father's "Explosion in the Fairmount Mines." Unless some facts come to the surface on the specific impulse for Reed's localizing "Dream" to Fairmount, the recorded text must stand alone:

Explosion in the Fairmount Mines

One bright morning, the miner just about to leave,
Heard his dear child screaming in all fright.
He went to her bed, then she looked up and said:
"I have had such a dream, turn on the light."

"Daddy please don't go down in that hole today,
For my dreams do come true some time, you know.
Oh don't leave me daddy, please don't go away,
Something bad sure will happen, do not go."

"Oh I dreamed that the mines were burning out with fire,
Every man was fighting for his life.
And some had companions and they prayed out loud,
'Oh God, please protect my darling wife.' "

Chorus:

Then her daddy bent down and kissed her dear sweet face,
Turned again to travel on his way,
But she threw her small arms around her daddy's neck,
She kissed him again, and he heard her say:

Chorus:

Then the miner was touched, and said he would not go:
"Hush my child, I'm with you, do not cry."
There came an explosion and two-hundred men
Were shut in the mines and left to die.

Chorus:

Blind Alfred Reed's alteration in "The Dream of the Miner's Child" was slight. He retained most of its language but departed

138

NEW ORTHOPHONIC VICTOR RECORDS	Number	Size	List prc.
Rainy Weather—Fox Trot *with Vocal Refrain*　Kyser's Orchestra *Juat a Haven (Is Heaven With You)—Fox Trot　Kay Kyser and His Orch.*	V– 40222	10	.75
Reapers Be True　*with Piano*　F. Stamps and His All Star Quartet *I'm Only Here On a Visit　Frank Stamps and His All Star Quartet*	V– 40228	10	.75
Red and Green Signal Lights *with String Band* Grayson-Whitter *Dark Road is a Hard Road to Travel*　Grayson-Whitter	V– 40063	10	.75
Red-Headed Widow Was the Cause of It All　Willard Hodgin *Don't Get One Woman On Your Mind*　(Banjo Joe)	21485	10	.75
Red River Valley "Mac" (Harry McClintock) and His Haywire Orch. *Old Chisholm Trail　"Mac" (McClintock) and His Haywire Orchestra*	21421	10	.75
Red Rose Rag *Guitar Duet*　Fletcher and Foster *Charlotte Hot Step　Guitar Duet with Harmonica　Fletcher and Foster*	V– 40232	10	.75

REED, BLIND ALFRED—Violin Accompaniment

Always Lift Him Up	21360	
Explosion in Fairmount Mines	21191	
Fate of Chris Liveley and Wife	21533	
How Can a Man Stand Such Times	V-40236	
I Mean to Live for Jesus	20939	
Money Cravin' Folks	V-40196	
Prayer of Drunkard's Girl	21191	
Why Don't You Bob Your Hair, Girls—No. 2	V-40196	
Why Do You Bob Your Hair, Girls	21360	
Woman's Been After Man Ever Since	V-40196	
Blind Alfred Reed　You Must Unload	20939	

REED, ORVILLE—Telephone Girl　21190

REEVE, PHIL-ERNEST MOODY

Down Where the Watermelon　20540　　Sweet Evelina　　21188

	Number	Size	List prc.
Rejoicing On the Way　Avondale Mills Quartet *Stilling the Tempest　Male Voices—Unacc.　Avondale Mills Quartet*	V– 40211	10	.75
Rescue the Perishing　*with Piano*　The Stamps Quartet *Bringing in the Sheaves*　The Stamps Quartet	21035	10	.75

REVELERS, THE—Male Quartet

Dinah　　　19796　　Oh, Miss Hannah　　19796

	Number	Size	List prc.
Revive Us Again　Turney Brothers *At the Cross　with Violin, Piano and Cornet　Turney Brothers*	V– 40027	10	.75
Ring Them Heavenly Bells　McCravy Brothers *Dip Me in the Golden Sea　with Violin, Harmonica, Banjo　McCravy Bros.*	V– 40026	10	.75
Rippling Waves Waltz　Mellie Dunham's Orchestra *Boston Fancy　with Calls*　Mellie Dunham's Orchestra	20001	10	.75
River of Jordan *with Guitar and Autoharp*　Carter Family *Keep on the Sunny Side*　Carter Family	21434	10	.75

ROARK, SHORTBUCKLE, AND FAMILY

I Truly Understand　　V-40023　　My Mother's Hands　　V-40023

	Number	Size	List prc.
Robertson County　Paul Warmack and His Gully Jumpers *Stone Rag　String Band*　Paul Warmack and His Gully Jumpers	V– 40009	10	.75

ROBERTSON, ECK—Violin

Texas Wagoner　　V-40145　　There's a Brown Skin Girl　V-40145

PAGE FROM VICTOR CATALOG, 1931

entirely from its melody in favor of a doleful fiddle tune appropriate to a memorial song. By contrast, Henry Whitter, one of his contemporaries who also recomposed the Jenkins-Dalhart piece, retained its music but changed its plot setting. Whitter, a Fries, Virginia, textile-mill worker and self-trained guitar and harmonica player, is remembered for his pioneering trip to New York in the spring of 1923 to persuade Okeh executives that he could do better as an entertainer than as a cotton spooler. His "Wreck on the Southern Old 97" (Okeh 40015) proved to be an influential disc. Whitter is also remembered for some excellent numbers recorded with G. B. Grayson for Victor and Gennett, for example "Tom Dooley," "Handsome Molly," "Train 45," "Little Maggie."

During 1927 Whitter recorded a group of now-overlooked songs for Paramount and some affiliated labels. One piece, "The Snow Storm," was "The Dream of the Miner's Child" literally transposed from a mine village to a snow storm. Thematically and musically it was clearly the familiar Jenkins-Dalhart piece. "The thunder is roaring, the lighting is flashing, / And the snow is falling thick and fast . . . Oh, Daddy, don't go out in the storm tonight / For I fear you are going to die." In order to underscore "The Snow Storm's" dependence on a coal-mining model it was shrewdly coupled with "The Explosion at Eccles, West Virginia" (released on Paramount 33183, Broadway 8023, and Herwin 75537).[34] The Eccles (Raleigh County) explosion on March 8, 1926, killed nineteen men as a consequence of failure to rock-dust the mine after gas was detected. Either Whitter wrote the ballad himself or it was sent to him by an Eccles resident — possibly a relative. Presumably Whitter wrote "The Snow Storm." Neither of these songs was registered in the Copyright Office.

There is no need to transcribe "The Snow Storm" to demonstrate its complete dependence on "The Dream of the Miner's Child." It is fair to assume that Henry Whitter and Blind Alfred Reed were not the only folksingers to accept the Dalhart recording and to particularize it in some manner. I cite the recompositions "The Snow Storm" and "The Explosion in the Fairmount Mines" because these two recorded songs are available in archives. However, we lack complementary accounts by Whitter and Reed of their motives and methods in transforming "The Dream of the

Miner's Child." Only a few collectors sought to elicit a reaction to this piece from folksingers. Lillian Crabtree indicated that in Tennessee "the song is said to be the result of a real happening." James Taylor Adams wrote: "Rev. George Wesley Blevins of Wise, Viriginia, says that the song, 'The Dream of a Miner's Child' is factual and that it is of one of the explosions at Coal Creek, Tennessee."[35] We know that Blevins erred; however, his mistake is less significant than his need to certify the "truth" of the song. It is likely that other collectors would have heard such testimony stressing reality, had they but asked.

Generally, folksong collectors are so involved in the actual search for material or subsequent editing that they seldom comment on either their own modes of discovery or treatment of classes of song. Folklorists are not even-handed in their attention to song lore. Some items are surrounded by considerable commentary; others — secretly disapproved — are punished by inattention or the withholding of bibliographical detail in notes. "The Dream of the Miner's Child" illustrates this contention. Mrs. Richardson can be credited with the very first suggestion that "Dream" might be a folksong, but her *American Mountain Songs* (1927) was marred by its neglect of basic data on sources. The minimum apparatus expected in a serious folksong anthology is an indication of who sang a song as well as where and when.

The first collector to print a "Dream" text properly identified was Vance Randolph in *Ozark Folksongs*. His headnote read: "Sung by Robert Eddy, Joplin, Mo., May 1, 1922." Inasmuch as Eddy's text was straight Jenkins-Dalhart, the seeming error in the date intrigued me. Was it a typographical error, or, possibly, did someone in the tri-state lead- and zinc-mining area actually recompose the English song three years before Jenkins? My interest led me to a warm visit with Randolph and one of the most enjoyable interviews — collector interviews collector — I have ever experienced. Well before meeting Randolph, I wrote to inquire whether 1922 might be a mistaken date. He responded: "Robert Eddy was just one of the 'overall boys' who frequented a certain bar in Joplin. I'm sure I was in Joplin in May, 1922, as I never missed the May Day celebrations in those days. It is possible, of course, that I was mistaken in the date."[36]

Randolph's letter stimulated me to seek a point of transition from "Don't" to "Dream" in the Ozarks rather than Atlanta. I toyed with the hypothesis that an Ozark resident was responsible for the recomposition. On New Year's day, 1962, Doyle Moore and I interviewed Lloyd Richardson in Jimmie Driftwood's home at Timbo, Arkansas. Richardson, a Stone County resident, was a fountainhead of folklore and folk locutions. He had been a singing-school teacher and retained many Christian Harmony shape-note hymns along with traditional ballads and song "ballets" learned from young friends. I was delighted that he knew both "The Dream of the Miner's Child" and "The Death of Floyd Collins," and curious to know whether he had learned them at the same time or associated them in any way. He recalled learning "Dream" about 1920, certifying the time by mentioning that he was married in that year and hadn't kept up his interest in songs "of that kind" after marriage. Yet he clearly remembered learning "Floyd Collins" after 1925 from a phonograph record at his sister's home in Mountain View. Richardson had never worked in a mine, and had never talked to Ozarkers who returned home after working in mines. Although he had no idea of his source for "Dream," he liked it because it was a "true song."[37]

If one wishes, it is possible to speculate, on the basis of Randolph's book and Richardson's memory, that "The Dream of the Miner's Child" was composed about 1920. This notion seems highly unlikely to say the least. I was convinced after obtaining Richardson's version that he learned the song when Dalhart's disc reached the Ozarks. This led me to repoen the question of Vance Randolph's date.

In the fall of 1963, I visited the folklorist to ascertain whether his date might be challenged, and I was regaled with a fascinating glimpse into a great collector's life.[38] Randolph's childhood home at Pittsburg (Crawford County), Kansas, was in a coal region, and just across the state line was Joplin (Jasper County), Missouri, a great lead and zinc area. The elder Randolph, an attorney, was partial to the many overseas miners from Ireland, Italy, the old Austro-Hungarian Empire, Cornwall, and Wales, who had sought work in Kansas and Missouri. Young Vance, made sensitive to social issues by his father's compassion, equated foreign birth and

VANCE RANDOLPH AT HOME

terrible working conditions. His first newspaper job on the radical *Appeal to Reason*, at Girard, Kansas, was close to home, and it brought him in touch with populists, unionists, socialists, and syndicalists. He dramatized this telling by singing a rousing Industrial Workers of the World (Wobbly) classic, "Conditions They Are Bad," and by casually mentioning that he knew such figures as Eugene Victor Debs, Emma Goldman, Jack Reed, and Alexander Howatt, the Kansas coal digger who led a factional fight within the UMWA in the 1920's. Randolph "graduated" from journalism to free-lance work for E. Haldeman-Julius, publisher in Girard of the phenomenally popular "Little Blue Books" during the 1920's. When Randolph wrote pamphlets for this series on the Ozarks — his real interest — he signed his own name, but he also wrote about a hundred booklets under various pseudonyms. He was amused to recollect that his bestseller, *The Autobiography of a Pimp,* sold a half-million copies at $1 each. For this spicy treasure chest, banned from the mails, Randolph received only $500. Upon complaint to Haldeman-Julius he netted $200 more.

It was difficult for me to turn from anecdotes about the *Appeal to Reason* and "Little Blue Book" days back to "The Dream of the Miner's Child." Randolph told me that from about 1918 to 1926 he had attended May Day — "a kind of Labor Day" — celebrations at Joplin, Missouri. (Consequently, he might have collected "Dream" after Dalhart's disc reached Joplin.) After parades and oratory the men had gathered in bars. Eddy was a workingman, probably a lead miner. Randolph had him go over "Dream" several times to get the words, and then wrote them down on the back of an old envelope or a scrap of paper. Such manuscript scraps were thrown away after *Ozark Folksongs* was published. Randolph concluded his comments on Eddy, Joplin, and "The Dream of the Miner's Child" by saying: "I thought at the time the song was common and well known, so I just wrote it down. I wasn't particularly hot about it, didn't think it amounted to much."[39]

Few folklorists are as candid as Randolph or carry their achievements as lightly as he. It meant much to me to hear him report that he had collected in bars, written songs out on scraps of paper (which he subsequently discarded), and wasn't "hot" about a song. Anyone who has used any of his books knows that he was "red-hot" about a mass of important songs, jokes, and tales.

Another collector, George Korson, gave me quite a different "Dream" anecdote which has considerable bearing on some problems in contemporary folklore studies.[40] Korson had encountered "The Dream of the Miner's Child" during his anthracite collecting years, 1925-35. When he readied *Minstrels of the Mine Patch* for publication (1938), he learned from Copyright Office files that the song belonged to Shapiro, Bernstein & Company. He requested permission to use it and the firm asked for a fee of $100. Korson considered this sum to be excessive; although he had collected "Dream" in tradition he left the song out of his anthracite book. When Korson turned to the bituminous fields in 1940, he encountered "Dream" again in Pittsburgh, Pennsylvania, and Welch, West Virginia. By coincidence, at this time he also found the *United Mine Workers Journal*'s early printing of "Don't Go Down in the

Mine." Recognizing the relationship of the two songs, he assumed that the earlier one was composed by the contributor, and hence was in the public domain. He reprinted the *UMWJ* item in *Coal Dust on the Fiddle* with the careful note: "This was the first printed version of a ballad that has gained wide popularity since another, a copyright version, came on the market some years ago."[41]

There are several ironies in this note. "Dream" had already been printed twice in 1927 (Spaeth, Richardson) and in dozens of folios during the 1930's without copyright credits to anyone. Korson could well have contended that he had found a folksong. Instead, he boycotted the Jenkins-Dalhart number and refrained from naming it in his books. Consequently, he put the folk variants which he had collected aside in favor of a printed text that subsequently turned out to be an English music-hall item fully covered by copyright. What would he have done if he had learned before 1943 that "Don't" was protected by Lawrence Wright? At least two ethical questions are involved in Korson's experience: Should a folklorist reject folksongs touched by the copyright process? What fee is appropriate for a publisher to ask when one of his properties is transcribed from a folksinger for publication in an anthology? Not only are there no easy answers to these queries but there are apparently no clear legal cases where folklorists have confronted copyright owners. It is certain that this reluctance to use "commercial" songs will deny full understanding of the processes of oral tradition to scholars, as the walls between folklore and poplore are breached.

My approach to "The Dream of the Miner's Child" has touched three areas: the transformation of a music-hall piece into a hillbilly classic, the role of a sound recording as a folksong source, and the recomposition of a folksong into a mine-disaster memorial. As wide as is the scope of this study, I am aware that unexplored fields remain. For example, one problem is that of the length of time a song lives in tradition. When Wayland Hand collected "Don't Go Down in the Mine, Dad" in Montana (1945), he speculated that the sentimental song had run its course in a thirty-five-year period. It is now more than four decades since Polk Brockman mailed Andrew Jenkins' "Dream" to New York for Vernon Dalhart's recording purposes. The song is still in tradition.

Pennsylvania folklorist Henry Glassie recorded an excellent version in 1965 from Doc and Eva Owens Girvin near Mt. Nebo, Lancaster County. Mrs. Girvin had come as a youngster with her parents from the Blue Ridge Mountains in North Carolina to the Susquehanna River area. Mr. Girvin, a dairy-farmer teamster, is of Pennsylvania Dutch background. Eva told Glassie that "she never learned songs from records" but her "Dream of the Miner's Daughter" is pure Dalhart. She might easily have learned it from parents or peers but collector Glassie observed that many of her songs were "only a short step from wax," including a Kingston Trio–inspired "Tom Dooley."[42] The Girvins sang at MacEdward Leach's retirement concert in Philadelphia (March 13, 1966) and included the "Dream." I was in the audience and was a little surprised at this particular selection, knowing something of Dr. Leach's austere taste. His own response was to note that folksong definitions had changed in his lifetime to include the sentimental and gospel pieces favored by Doc and Eva Girvin.[43] In a sense, the offering of a Jenkins-Dalhart number at a gathering for one of America's outstanding ballad scholars is but a symbol of the continued influence of Dalhart recordings on the folk. Ironically, folk-loric attention to him may not begin until after the death of most traditional singers who learned songs directly from his discs.

I do not believe that Dalhart's name was mentioned in any learned journal until 1950, a few years after his death in Bridgeport, Connecticut (September 15, 1948). At the height of his career his records had been reviewed by Abbe Niles for a sophisticated readership in the *Bookman;* the critic tagged Dalhart "the official hired mourner to the nation."[44] Fittingly, when Dalhart's name finally appeared in a folklore journal, it was in connection with a Jenkins' composition rather than with an "old" or "true" folksong.

After Wayland Hand had been told by several singers that "Don't Go Down in the Mine, Dad" was found on phonograph recordings, he searched American record catalogs but found no "Don't" entries. At this point D. K. Wilgus, a scholar with a keen interest in hillbilly music, called attention in *Western Folklore* to the fact that Dalhart's "The Dream of the Miner's Child" was indeed listed in American record catalogs of the 1920's. (Hand also could have found its predecessor in English catalogs.) Further, Wilgus identified "Dream" as an Andrew Jenkins song — the first mention of the folk composer in an academic context.[45] But it was not until 1965 that any folk variant of "Dream" was actually represented as coming directly from Dalhart. Ralph Rinzler wrote in liner notes for a Doc Watson LP: "Vernon Dalhart crooned the newly copyrighted version into thousands of homes (including the Watson's) on a Victor record."[46] The acknowledgment was both refreshing and overdue. It was followed by A. L. Lloyd's comment that the English music-hall "Don't" became an effective object of transatlantic cultural exchange in 1925 when the Donnelly-Geddes tearjerker reached Andrew Jenkins and Vernon Dalhart.[47]

A rich commentary on the continuous process of Anglo-American cultural exchange is represented in recent recordings of "The Dream of the Miner's Child" (see Checklist Two). Doc Watson's "Dream" recorded in 1965 for Vanguard in New York was also released in England on the Fontana label. This rendition is very close to Dalhart's and preserves the tone and style intended by Andrew Jenkins. (Comparable to Watson's example is that of Arnold Keith Storm.) A treatment removed a step or two from Watson and Storm is Bill Clifton's "Dream" done in bluegrass style for Starday of Nashville. (Comparable is the Stanley Brothers recording.) Clifton's LP, interestingly named *Code of the Mountains,* was released in the British Isles during 1964 on the London label. One can only wonder how these renditions — hillbilly and bluegrass — have been received by English folksong enthusiasts who have neither accepted nor rejected, much less heard, the Donnelly-Geddes 1910 music-hall hit still available to them in London.

1. Samuel Preston Bayard, "The British Folk Tradition," in *Pennsylvania Songs and Legends,* ed. George Korson (Philadelphia, 1949), 44; A. L. Lloyd, *Come All Ye Bold Miners* (London, 1952), 78.

2. A. K. Hamilton Jenkin, *The Cornish Miner* (London, 1927), 294. See also Arthur Cecil Todd, *The Cornish Miner in America* (Truro, Cornwall, 1967).

3. Lloyd, *Come All Ye Bold Miners,* 9.

4. Letter to me, Oct. 25, 1957.

5. Lloyd, *Come All Ye Bold Miners,* 71, 75.

6. Transcribed from Festival FL 7093.

7. Wayland Hand and others, "Songs of the Butte Miners," *Western Folklore,* IX (1950), 12.

8. Woody Guthrie, *American Folksong* (New York, 1961), 2.

9. Letter to me, Oct. 21, 1968. See also Richard A. Reuss, "Woody Guthrie and His Folk Tradition," *Journal of American Folklore,* LXXXIII (1970), 273.

10. "Songs of Woody Guthrie," typescript from author's notebook (ca. 1941), 154.

11. Inquiries to Lawrence Wright Music Company and to Shapiro, Bernstein & Company led to negative results. Letters to me, Oct. 29, 1968, and Sept. 11, 1968, respectively.

12. The former Irene Spain is now Mrs. John Futrelle of Mableton, Ga. Our correspondence dates from July 12, 1957, and is supplemented by interviews. See also Judith McCulloh, "Hillbilly Records and Tune Transcriptions," *Western Folklore,* XXVI (1967), 225.

13. Willard Neal, "Writing Songs at Five Points," *Atlanta Journal Magazine* (Apr. 8, 1934), 7; Betty Wilkison, "Gift of Recorder Made to Blind Ballad Writer," *Atlanta Constitution* (Dec. 17, 1951), 18.

14. Oland Russell, "Floyd Collins in the Sand Cave," *American Mercury,* XLII (Nov., 1937), 289; *The Frank C. Brown Collection of North Carolina Folklore,* II (Durham, 1952), 498.

15. James Edward Richardson wrote much of the publicity for Victor in this period.

16. For a concise statement of Jenkins' role in tradition see D. K. Wilgus, "Folksong and Folksong Scholarship, Part IV," in *A Good Tale and a Bonnie Tune,* Publications of the Texas Folklore Society, no. XXXII, ed. Mody C. Boatright and others (Dallas, 1964), 229. See also Wilgus, *Anglo-American Folksong Scholarship since 1898* (New Brunswick, N.J., 1959), 283.

17. Letter to me, July 30, 1957.

18. "Billy the Kid" composition data from Irene Spain letters to me, Nov. 29, 1957, and May 5, 1969; letter to Judith McCulloh, Dec. 28, 1967. See also a forthcoming article by D. K. Wilgus in *Western Folklore* (1971).

19. Letter to me, Nov. 29, 1957, and Alton C. Morris, *Folksongs of Florida* (Gainesville, 1950), 106.

20. Letter to me, Nov. 29, 1957. See also my brochure notes to *Railroad Songs and Ballads* (Library of Congress AFS L 61).

21. Letter to me, Aug. 8, 1957.

22. Letter to me, Sept. 10, 1957.

23. Interview, Aug. 22, 1963.

24. Letter to me, Nov. 4, 1957.

25. Letter to me, Nov. 29, 1957.

26. Jim Walsh, "Vernon Dalhart," *Hobbies,* LXV (May, 1960), 33; continued in seven following issues.

27. Will Roy Hearne first suggested to me a study of Dalhart's early environment. Interview, Dec. 31, 1956.

28. Walter D. Haden, "If I Had Wings Like an Angel: The Life of Vernon Dalhart," in *Country Music Who's Who, 1970,* ed. Thurston Moore (New York, 1970). Haden's continuing Dalhart research is to be published by the Vanderbilt University Press.

29. Bill Vernon, "Country Music News from the U.S.A.," *Country News and Views,* VI (Jan., 1968), 4.

30. H. B. Humphrey, *Historical Summary of Coal-Mine Explosions in the United States, 1810-1958* (Washington, 1960), 27. See also Alden Todd, "The Horror at Monongah," *United Mine Workers Journal* (Dec. 1, 1957), 14.

31. Tom Tippett, "Black Star Mothers," *Labor Age,* XIX (Sept., 1930), 14.

32. George Korson, *Coal Dust on the Fiddle,* 2nd printing (Hatboro, Pa., 1965), 264.

33. Data on Alfred Reed from correspondence in 1969 and interviews with Bernice Coleman and Arville Reed, July 31, 1970, and Aug. 2, 1970. (The latter's name on Victor disc labels was spelled Orville.)

34. John MacKenzie, "Herwin: Part One," *78 Quarterly,* I (1967), 18; continued in following issues.

35. Lillian G. Crabtree, "Songs and Ballads Sung in Overton County, Tennessee" (master's thesis, George Peabody College, Nashville, 1936), 120; James Taylor Adams, *Death in the Dark* (Big Laurel, Va., 1941), 120.

36. Letter to me, Sept. 8, 1957.

37. Interview, Jan. 1, 1962.

38. Interview, Oct. 26, 1963.

39. From typescript by Judith McCulloh after Randolph interview.

40. Interview, July 29, 1962.

41. Korson, *Coal Dust on the Fiddle,* 213.

42. Letter to me, Sept. 18, 1968.

43. See Henry Glassie, "MacEdward Leach, 1892-1967," *Journal of American Folklore,* LXXXI (1968), 107.

44. Abbe Niles, "Ballads, Songs and Snatches," *Bookman,* LXVII (1928), 689.

45. D. K. Wilgus, " 'Don't Go Down in the Mine Dad,' " *Western Folklore,* IX (1950), 266.

46. Liner notes to *Doc Watson and Son* (Vanguard VRS 9170).

47. A. L. Lloyd, *Folk Song in England* (New York, 1967), 387.

CHECKLIST TWO

PART I: "DON'T GO DOWN IN THE MINE, DAD"

Song titles are constant except that *UMWJ* deletes "Dad."

―――. Robert Donnelly l, Will Geddes m, Lawrence Wright Music Company, London (1910). Cover photo of a boy entreating father.

―――. Stanley Kirkby, Regal G 6460 (12593 E). Oct., 1910, England.

―――. J. R. Lincoln, *United Mine Workers Journal*, Columbus, Ohio (Feb. 9, 1911).
Reprinted: Korson, *C D F* (1943), 213.

―――. Robert Howe, Zonophone 342 (WA 5923). Aug., 1927, England.

―――. R. J. Stodden, Butte, Mont., June 16, 1948. Wayland Hand, AFS 9724.
Transcribed: Hand, *W F*, IX (1950), 13, m.

―――. Tex Morton, *The Tex Morton Story*, Festival FL 7093. ca. 1959, Australia.

―――. John Foreman, *The 'Ouses in Between*, Reality RY 1004. ca. 1966, England.

PART II: "DREAM OF THE MINER'S CHILD"

All song titles are "Dream of the (or "a") Miner's Child" unless otherwise specified.

Entries from country-music songbooks and song folios below are restricted to the earliest one known to me (Kincaid, 1932) and a current folio (*Prison and Mountain Songs*, 1959) by the song's publisher.

―――. Andrew Jenkins, arranged by Irene Spain, P. C. Brockman (publisher), Atlanta (Oct. 28, 1925), E 628110. Brockman copyright assigned to Shapiro, Bernstein & Company, New York (Feb. 17, 1926), E 636039. Copyright renewed: Shapiro, Bernstein (Oct. 29, 1952), R 101984 and (Mar. 16, 1953) R 109415.

For all Vernon Dalhart discs see Appendix Two.

―――. Richardson, *A M S* (1927), 40, m.

―――. Spaeth, *W S M M L* (1927), 142, m.

"A Miner Child." Fronie May Parker, New Concord, Ky., June 6, 1927. Robert W. Gordon, holograph "ballet," Gordon mss, AFS 3256.

―――. Harry Bradley, Grey Gull 4148 and Radiex 4148 (2640). ca. 1928.

―――. Liston Chandler, Seymour, Tenn. Anderson, *C B S E T* (1932), 251.

—————. *My Favorite Mountain Ballads and Old Time Songs, Book 5,* Bradley Kincaid, KDKA, Pittsburgh (1932), 37, m.

—————. Overton County, Tenn. Crabtree, *S B S O C T* (1936), 120.

—————. Lina Melton, Galax, Va., 1937. John Lomax, AFS 1340. Dulcimore solo.

"Miner's Child." Fanny Begley, Middlefork, Ky., 1937. Alan and Elizabeth Lomax, AFS 1453.

"Miner's Child's Dream." Bill Atkins, Pineville, Ky., 1938. Mary Elizabeth Barnicle, AFS 1991.

"Dream of the Miner's Girl." George Roark, Pineville, Ky., 1938. Mary Elizabeth Barnicle, AFS 2015.

—————. Morris Brothers, Bluebird 8841. Feb. 5, 1939, Rock Hill, S.C. Guitar and mandolin.

—————. Dema Bowen, Geedville, Tenn. Mason, *F S F T C C T* (1939), 29.

—————. Mrs. Ralph Thompson, Pittsburgh, May 25, 1940. George Korson, Green tape files.

—————. Jimmy Ratliff, Welch, W.Va., May 30, 1940. George Korson, AFS 12012.

"Miner's Child." Woody Guthrie, ca. 1941. Typescript in Guthrie notebook, Washington, D.C., AFS.

—————. Robert Eddy, Joplin, Mo., May 1, 1922. Randolph, *O F,* IV (1950), 387.

—————. Jack Kingston, Quality 1596. ca. 1949, Canada.

—————. Marty Robbins, Columbia B 2153. ca. 1959, Nashville.

—————. *Prison and Mountain Songs,* Shapiro, Bernstein & Company, New York (1959), 40, m.

—————. Lloyd Richardson, Timbo, Ark., Jan. 1, 1962. Archie Green and Doyle Moore, Green tape files.

—————. Bill Clifton, *Code of the Mountains,* Starday SLP 271. Aug., 1963, Washington, D.C. Bluegrass band. Parallel issue: London HAB 8193 (England).

—————. Arnold Keith Storm, *Take the News to Mother,* Folk-Legacy FSA 18. ca. Apr., 1964, Indianapolis.

"Dream of the Miner's Daughter." Doc and Eva Girvin, Mt. Nebo, Pa., Jan. 11, 1965. Henry Glassie, Glassie tape files, Harrisburg.

—————. Doc Watson, *Doc Watson and Son,* Vanguard VRS 9170. Nov. 4, 1965, New York. Parallel issue: Fontana TFL 6055 (England).

"Miner's Child." Grace Goforth, Dec., 1965. Burton and Manning, *C F F* (1967), 21, m.

————. Jack Casey, *Jack Casey*, Rural Rhythm RRJC 206. ca. Apr., 1968. Blue-grass band.

"Miner's Child's Dream." Ruby Vass, Fancy Gap, Va., June 20, 1959. Shellans, *F S B R M* (1968), 64, m.

————. Ralph and Carter Stanley, *The Legendary Stanley Brothers,* Rebel SLP 1487. Disc from undated tape released in 1970.

APPENDIX TWO

VERNON DALHART'S "DREAM OF THE MINER'S CHILD"

This list is in order by recording dates for separate companies or related label groups. Dalhart's name appears on all labels unless a pseudonym is specified. Abbreviation: b/w = backed with.

1. Okeh 40498 (73696) rec. Oct. 9, 1925. b/w Mother's Grave.
2. Columbia 15046 (141152) rec. Oct. 17, 1925. b/w Convict and the Rose (Al Craver).
3. Victor 19821 (33587) rec. Oct. 20, 1925. b/w Death of Floyd Collins.
4. Cameo 812 (1675) rec. ca. Oct. 22, 1925. b/w Mother's Grave.
   Romeo 332   b/w Little Mary Phagan.
   Lincoln 2429   b/w Mother's Grave.
5. Pathe 32150, 032150 (106334) rec. ca. Oct. 25, 1925. b/w Convict and the Rose.

   Perfect 12229   b/w Convict and the Rose.
6. Edison 51649 (10667) rec. Nov. 6, 1925. b/w Letter Edged in Black.
   Edison 5085 — cylinder.
7. Gennett 3197 (9853) rec. Nov. 21, 1925. b/w Death of Floyd Collins.
   Challenge 505   b/w Life of Tom Watson.
   Herwin 75502   b/w Death of Floyd Collins.
8. Banner 1672 (6308) rec. Nov. 25, 1925. b/w Sydney Allen.
   Domino 3642   b/w Sydney Allen.
   Oriole 545   b/w Mother's Grave (Frank Evans).
   Paramount 33176   b/w Mother's Grave.
   Regal 9978   b/w Stone Mountain Memorial.
9. Vocalion 5086, 15217 (2133) rec. Jan. 14, 1926. b/w Convict and the Rose.

ATTACKING THE STOCKADE

Coal Creek Troubles 5

AMERICA'S FOLKLORE map is marked with names on the land remembered in song: Big Bend Tunnel, Chisholm Trail, Springfield Mountain, Sierra Peaks, Birmingham Jail, the Banks of the Ohio, the Lake of Pontchartrain, the Streets of Laredo. Each of these locales is a place of contour and substance, an intersection of latitude and longitude. Coal Creek, one such specific community in Tennessee, is also the setting for a folksong cluster — but this designation no longer appears on current maps. After a lake was impounded behind the Tennessee Valley Authority's Norris Dam in 1936, Coal Creek renamed itself Lake City. The new appellation is apt, for TVA hydroelectric power and atomic energy are giants in the region and a prominent Lake City neighbor is Oak Ridge. Coal Creek was also an apt name: Tennessee's coal-bearing counties lie on the Cumberland Plateau, which forms a mountainous corridor bisecting the state from northeast to southwest. This belt (some forty to fifty-five miles wide) lies directly east of a Cumberland Gap–Chattanooga diagonal. The plateau's eastern edge — Cumberland Mountain, Walden Ridge (North), Walden Ridge (South) — forms a belt prominent in history and folklore.

Coal Creek's original settlers built their cabins on the banks of a mountain stream bearing the same name, below the point where the stream broke through Walden Ridge in Anderson County. The early frontier economy of hunting and fishing, small-scale farming, and livestock raising prevailed until the Civil War, but it was severely disrupted by that conflict. East Tennessee was divided in its loyalty between Jeff Davis and Abe Lincoln, and Coal Creek was but one of many border communities devastated by virtue of its geography. Until 1805 Walden Ridge had been a legal boundary line between settlers and Cherokees in the Indian Territory; during the Civil War it became an unofficial boundary between Unionists and Confederates and the site of considerable guerrilla warfare. But Walden Ridge was more than a forested dividing line: its flanks were rich in coal. Desultory mining on the Cumberland Plateau began in 1814 in Roane County. The extension to commercial use of east Tennessee coal occurred in the 1830's, when it was shipped by river as far away as New Orleans. When railroads pushed their lines into the mountains during the 1850's, coal mining became a major Tennessee industry.[1]

Prior to the Civil War, Anderson County coal was floated down Poplar Creek and the Clinch River for southern sales, and some was carted by oxen to nearby Knoxville for local sales. By 1871 the Knoxville & Kentucky Railroad reached Coal Creek, and the Knoxville Iron Company opened a mine which employed fifty men and shipped, in its first year, 2,000 tons of coal to Knoxville for rolling-mill and related processes. Like many isolated Appalachian towns, Coal Creek became an industrial boomtown after mining began, although it was physically set in a verdant area of hills and streams, and never really escaped the aura of being "in the woods."

The earliest residents of the area came largely from the Carolinas and Virginia. In the decades 1880-1900, Anderson County led Tennessee in coal production, and therefore it attracted some Negro as well as European immigrant miners. A few years after the Knoxville Iron Company's initial operation, four additional mines were opened. During 1875 more than 60,000 tons of coal were shipped from the district. Coal Creek was never immune from the problems which plagued bituminous mining throughout the United States. The Coal Creek miners called their first strike in 1876 to protest against a company wage cut from 5¢ to 2½¢ per bushel. In the

COAL CREEK MINERS

following year, one response of the Knoxville Iron Company to its workers' action was to bring in convicts to replace them. The miners showed their concern by exploding three powder kegs under the convicts' quarters, but the intruders remained. This powder smoke lingered in Coal Creek's air for decades.[2]

Organized labor's fight against the convict-lease system is one of the most dramatic episodes in trade-union history. It was largely a political campaign mounted in legislative halls and from convention or journalistic platforms, but the Coal Creek encounters became shooting battles between miners and militia in Anderson and neighboring Morgan counties, as well as in Grundy and Marion more than a hundred miles to the southwest. Parallel to this political and physical encounter was the long fight by a handful of southern reformers against the post–Civil War retention of slavery.[3]

The arrival of a group of prisoners in Coal Creek during 1877 was not an isolated phenomenon. Throughout the defeated South a surreptitious re-enslavement of the Negro had occurred under the convict-lease system instituted by post-Reconstruction, white-supremacy state governments. Heavy penalties for petty crime were enforced rigidly against black men; consequently large numbers of ex-slaves were available for lease to railways, turpentine and logging operators, mining corporations, or individual planters. The system eliminated penal expenses, provided state revenues, and perpetuated prewar patterns of labor relations. Some intellectuals opposed

157

the system from its inception. John Berrien Lindsley — Tennessee physician, educator, and minister — was one of the earliest public critics of convict leasing; in 1874 he published a pamphlet, *On Prison Discipline and Penal Legislation,* which showed fellow southerners the road to reform. Other tireless social critics such as Mrs. Rebecca Felton of Georgia and Miss Julia Tutwiler of Alabama joined Lindsley in the uphill fight against the mores of their region. They linked their attack on the convict-lease system with their fight for woman suffrage and temperance.

The most effective fighter in this cause was George Washington Cable, the Louisiana writer on Creole life. While a member of the New Orleans grand jury, Cable discovered that blacks arrested on charges of hog stealing or fistfighting were subsequently leased out by penal authorities to private contractors for long periods of heavy and forced labor, which in turn led to appalling death rates. When he learned that the system extended far beyond New Orleans, he assembled data from twelve states and took to the lecture platform to rally southerners against the evil which he characterized as "murder for money." On September 26, 1883, Cable addressed the National Conference of Charities and Correction at Louisville on the subject; his paper was subsequently printed as "The Convict Lease System in the Southern States." This lucid essay was followed by "The Freedman's Case in Equity," in which Cable enlarged his subject to cover Negro civil rights.

While describing an Alabama train trip, Cable penned a few lines pertinent to understanding the response of coal miners to convict labor: "At the next station there came aboard a most melancholy and revolting company. In filthy rags, with vile odors and the clanking of shackles and chains, nine penitentiary convicts chained to one chain, and ten more chained to another, dragged laboriously into the compartment. . . . The keeper of the convicts told me he should take them in that car two hundred miles that night. They were going to the mines."[4]

Cable's revelations brought him credit as a social critic, but at the price of renunciation as a traitor to his native South. Notwithstanding the esteem in which he was held as a novelist, Cable was exiled to Massachusetts and withdrew from public controversy. But the attack on the prison-labor system continued. J. C. Powell, a

Florida prison guard, published *The American Siberia* (1891), a matter-of-fact narrative exposing the barbarism inherent in the convict-lease system: medieval tortures of prisoners, cruel guards, primitive living conditions, lack of state inspection. Among other vivid details, Powell revealed that many ordinary citizens displayed their opposition to the system by aiding prisoners to escape. In the very year of *The American Siberia*'s appearance, great numbers of convicts were helped to flee the Coal Creek mines.

In a multi-level view of literature — sophisticated, popular, folk — one can place Cable's and Powell's writings, respectively, in the first two categories, and then look for folk parallels. The ballad to be discussed in this chapter, "Coal Creek Troubles," commented specifically on local happenings which occurred when miners themselves challenged the pernicious convict-labor system. Although the history of the war (*insurrection* and *rebellion* are alternate designations) is well documented, no ballad scholar has brought together its songs. Before turning to such material (in this and the next chapter) I shall summarize the war's events and comment on its treatment in subsequent historical and folkloric studies.[5]

The Coal Creek miners had revealed their hostility to convict workers as soon as they appeared in the community (1877), but no major demonstration recurred until July 14, 1891. On this anniversary of the French Bastille Day, more than 300 miners, some active in the Knights of Labor, stormed the Briceville stockade of the Tennessee Coal Mining Company intent upon eliminating "slave" labor — predominately black — from the area. The prison guards were no match for the aroused workers, many of whom were Union or Confederate veterans newly united in a common cause. After a bloodless victory, the guards and convicts were marched to Coal Creek and loaded on a convenient freight train to Knoxville. This action brought Governor Buchanan to the scene for a confrontation with miner leader Eugene Merrell at Thistle Switch (between Coal Creek and Briceville).

The contrast between the workers' and the state's spokesmen reveals something of the polarization which industrialism forced upon agrarian America. Merrell, whose name is hardly mentioned in historical annals, had been born Jean Rousseau in France on October 8, 1849. During his childhood his parents brought him to

159

New Orleans, where his father died. Upon his mother's remarriage, Jean took his stepfather's name. When still a young man, Merrell became a coal miner near Paris, Illinois. About 1880 he joined the Danville, Illinois, local assembly of the Knights of Labor, and he organized for them in Indiana and Tennessee. While working at Briceville, he was discharged and blacklisted. Eugene opened a small grocery store, but during the troubles distributed his entire stock of goods to the miners, going heavily into debt for this contribution. Merrell's devotion to his fellows never wavered. Long after he had been driven out of Tennessee with a price on his head, he returned to Knoxville, where he spent his last years organizing wool-mill and other workers; he died about 1923.[6]

John P. Buchanan (1847-1930), a coalition Democrat as well as the president of the Tennessee Farmers' Alliance, had been elected in 1890 with labor and populist support.[7] The decade of the 1890's marked the high point of the "wool hat" revolt which brought to power such figures as "Pitchfork" Ben Tillman in South Carolina and Tom Watson in Georgia. Not all the radicals were able to cope with the pressures of a modern South caught between the rival forces of finance capitalism and agrarian tradition.[8] Buchanan, less militant than his peers, turned on the Coal Creek "insurrectionists," returning the Tennessee Coal Mining Company convicts and augmenting their guards with state troopers. The first physical encounter between the militia and the "Free Men of the Mountains" took place on July 20, resulting in a defeat for Colonel Granville Sevier's soldiers at the Tennessee mine. After entraining both prisoners and militiamen for Knoxville, the miners set their own guards around company property to prevent employers from planting dynamite to turn the community against the union. The rebels also captured the Knoxville Iron Company's stockades (near Coal Creek), where, years before, convicts had been introduced to the area. Following these twin victories, the men returned to work by accepting the Governor's promise that, through the General Assembly, he would seek to end the convict-lease system. The legislators, in a special session (August 31–September 21), refused to act on behalf of the miners; instead, they gave Buchanan more funds and troops and made it a felony to interfere with working convicts.

160

The miners' response to legislative intransigence, as well as to the militia in their midst, was renewed direct action, which they styled as their personal "extra session." On October 31 they burned the Tennessee mine's Briceville stockade — the first violence to property in the war. Nearby, they liberated the Knoxville mine's prisoners, without a fire because the warden's wife was ill. This time there was no train trip for the released convicts. Instead, the captives were told to scatter over Walden Ridge; some formed a "colony" in Harlan County, Kentucky. Governor Buchanan posted a $5,000 reward for the arrest of the unionists' leader, $250 for each man who had attacked a stockade, and $25 for the return of a convict. However, Anderson County residents supported the miners' cause. The Briceville mines reopened with free workers and the small operators began dealing with newly organized United Mine Workers of America committees. On November 2 the rebels launched their toughest battle at Oliver Springs (Morgan County), where the Cumberland mine (Big Mountain Coal Company) prisoners were released and their stockade set ablaze. No shots were fired and no miners were identified. It seemed that the war was over, with the mountain region free of convicts.

In the face of normalized labor relations, the Governor, spurred by the powerful Tennessee Coal, Iron & Railroad Company, stepped up action against the miners. On New Year's Day, 1892, Colonel Keller Anderson, a cavalryman, arrived in Coal Creek with 200 convicts consigned for the Knoxville Iron Company. The Colonel built "Fort Anderson" on a hill overlooking Coal Creek and instituted Gatling-gun law. To this day his encampment is called Militia Hill. The occupation dragged on all year with continuous harassment by the outside troopers. After the hanging by the militia of a young miner named Drummond — giving rise to several local legends about the ghost at "Drummond's Trestle" — open hostility resurfaced.

During the summer slack period, men in the "free" mines were only partially employed, but the convicts, protected by a standing army, worked full time. The volcanic situation exploded in mid-August when the miners burned the Tracy City (Grundy County) stockade of the Tennessee Coal, Iron & Railroad Company, entraining the convicts for Nashville. The operation was repeated at

161

TENNESSEE NATIONAL GUARD

Inman (Marion County), except that the stockade (under a railroad bridge) was dismantled rather than burned. On October 16 the miners suffered their first setback in a pitched battle at Oliver Springs, when the guards refused to surrender their charges and opened fire on the miners. After the wounded men received reinforcements, they set the torch to the stockade. This intensified action led Governor Buchanan to call unsuccessfully for U.S. War Department troops.

The rebellion had now touched base in widely separated points on the Cumberland Plateau, and had involved free miners from Kentucky and other states. By late August, General Samuel Carnes had more than 5,000 Tennessee troops in the region as well as considerable field artillery. Ironically it was his forces — cloaked under such flamboyant names as the Rosier Zouaves, the Memphis Chicksaw Guards, the Maurelain Cadets, the Hibernian Rifles, and the Tullahoma Light Infantry — who instituted a reign of terror. Supported by 40,000 rounds of ammunition from the federal arsenal at Indianapolis, Carnes hunted down rebel miners and also guarded convicts, who continued to dig coal during the turbulence. In the face of massive arrests of miners and their citizen friends, who were imprisoned in temporary jails in Coal Creek's schoolhouse and Methodist church, and of indictments for conspiracy and murder, the rebellion ended. However, troops remained at Militia Hill for a year, and at faraway Tracy City the rebels staged a defiant last battle on April 19, 1893.

162

Although the miners felt their cause to be just, they could not win a military war against Tennessee. Consequently they transferred their battles to the political and legislative arena. As a result, Governor Buchanan, stripped of the labor element of his previous coalition, was soundly defeated in August, 1892. His successor, Peter Turney, a Bourban Democrat, visited Coal Creek in September, 1893, and called for order in the district; in the next month he finally removed the state troops. Meanwhile, legislators, reading the election returns, reopened their debate on the convict-lease system. Nevertheless, it was not actually ended until 1896. One of the aftermaths was the construction of Brushy Mountain State Prison at Petros, near Oliver Springs, in which convicts dug coal for Tennessee itself until World War II. This locale is remembered in the hillbilly and bluegrass ballad variously titled "In the Hills of Roane County" or "Roane County Prison."

No historian has ventured to say precisely why the Tennessee miners were more militant than their fellow workers elsewhere, who also opposed the convict-lease system. Miners in all fields — before and after the Coal Creek war — had been and continued to be extremely active in labor disputes. The Coal Creekers, in addition, were engaged against a complex political ring (governor, legislators, lobbyists, penal officials) as well as a major corporate power. Tennessee's convict-lease system dated to 1866. An early lessee was the Tennessee Coal, Iron & Railroad Company (popularly known as the TCI), which began to use prisoners in Tracy City mines early in 1871. In 1889 the TCI took over for a six-year term all the state's leased convicts — about 1,600 men at $100,000 per year. The company used some directly but leased others to subcontractors at Coal Creek and elsewhere. In its *Annual Report* for this period the TCI president prided himself that this firm had "obtained the [convict] labor for $1000 per annum less than the amount required under the previous lease." The *Report* added: "The prisons owned by the company, both in Tennessee and Alabama, are in excellent condition, and the entire management . . . is satisfactory to the authorities of the respective States. The health of the prisoners has been better than in any previous year, and the death rate is lower." Complementing this presidential statement, the general manager for the Alabama division wrote:

163

The convict department [Pratt mines] is in first-rate condition, the men
are well treated, are in good health, and cheerful and contented. Their
tasks are easily performed and nearly all of them earn extra money every
day. . . . The new prisons are large, well ventilated and lighted, and
arranged with strict regard to proper sanitary precautions. They [con-
victs] do their work well and regularly, and in case of strikes they can
furnish us enough coal to keep at least three of the Ensley Furnaces
running and possibly all four of them.[9]

The use of prisoners as potential strikebreakers was important
to American entrepreneurs after the Civil War, as craftsmen became fully aware of industry's power. In a *New York Times* interview a TCI official stated: "One of the chief reasons which induced
the company to take up the system was the great chance it offered
for overcoming strikes. For some years after we began the convict-
lease system, we proved that we were right in calculating that the
free miners would be loath to enter upon strikes, when they saw that
the company was amply provided with convict labor."[10] The scene
of the TCI's largest use of convicts, the Pratt mines (on the outskirts of Birmingham), was far from Coal Creek, but Pratt events
frequently appeared in the labor newspapers read by all coal
miners. In April, 1891, the *United Mine Workers Journal* carried a
long report by a correspondent on the Pratt use of specially trained
small, dull red foxhounds — not bloodhounds — who ran down the
convict-miner escapees. Two months later the *Journal* reported a
horrible accident at Pratt, naming the white and colored convict
miners killed by fire and suffocation.[11] These reports on foxhounds
and fires were read in Coal Creek and Briceville at the time when
local miners were displaced by TCI-leased prisoners. The accounts
belied the company's position that its convicts were "cheerful and
contented."

While the TCI established basic mine-labor conditions for
much of Tennessee and Alabama, it was actually a "captive corporation draining profits northward."[12] The TCI president at the
time of the Coal Creek conflict was Thomas C. Platt, New York's
powerful Republican party boss; in 1907 the TCI, largely based in
the Birmingham area, became a U.S. Steel Corporation subsidiary.
In 1945 the TCI relinquished its Tennessee charter in favor of one
from Alabama, and in 1952 it was reorganized as a division within

CONVICTS AT PITT COUNTY, N.C.

U.S. Steel. By 1964, in a further streamlining of the parent structure, the TCI division was phased directly into the U.S. Steel Corporation. Metaphorically, the old TCI ghost still lingers at U.S.
Steel's Fairfield Works — the South's largest steel-making operation — in the Opossum Valley to the west of Birmingham. For
many decades Fairfield employees have been organized by the
United Steelworkers of America, but it is doubtful that these
present-day unionists are aware of Coal Creek history or folklore.
It can be observed, however, that in a spirit of editorial justice, the
United Mine Workers Journal noted in an article on the Coal Creek
rebellion that the TCI was at that time (1938) under contract with
the UMWA (CIO) and "our relations with the company are
satisfactory."[13]

The specific event which had precipitated the Coal Creek
turmoil was a labor dispute during the spring of 1891 between the
Tennessee Coal Mining Company at Briceville and its employees,
members of a Knights of Labor local assembly. The issues at stake
were typical of bituminous-mine industrial relations in the 1880's
and 1890's. The men objected to payment in scrip tokens instead
of legal tender. Such tokens were redeemable at par in the company
store but discounted elsewhere; naturally company-store prices
were higher than elsewhere. The second grievance was directed

against the demand that men sign iron-clad agreements with the company certifying their "implicit confidence in the integrity" of their employers and pledging not to join unions of their choice. (In later years the synonymous term *yellowdog contract* took the place of *iron-clad agreement*.)

Additionally, the company insisted that the men dismiss their checkweighman, A. H. Bradley. Before miners were organized it was customary to cheat them when loaded coal was weighed at the tipple. Hence, an early organizational demand was for the men themselves to elect a checkweighman, paid out of their wages, to give them honest weight. The job demanded strong character and considerable intelligence. This right to representation at the point of economic payment had been guaranteed by Tennessee law in 1887.

Because the Coal Creek miners were adamant in defense of their demands, the Tennessee Coal Mining Company shut down its Briceville operation in April, 1891, transforming the strike into a lockout. On July 4, violating the spirit of Independence Day, the company announced that it would reopen the mine with prisoners leased from the TCI. It was this specific importation of convicts from Tracy City during an unsettled labor dispute that led to the Bastille Day uprising. Since miners in east Tennessee were sensitive to political and economic strategies, national as well as local, this Briceville incident in turn sparked a widespread rebellion.

During January, 1890, at Columbus, Ohio, a number of rival groups — industrial and craft, secret and open, radical and conservative — had formed the United Mine Workers of America. In its formative years this new international union competed with the older semi-secret Knights of Labor, which had previously organized a large coal-digger membership in its National Trades Assembly 135. In spite of rivalry at the top, many rank-and-filers maintained two affiliations: at times covertly in KL local assemblies and openly in newly chartered UMWA local unions, and sometimes openly in both. Normally, American laborites, with strong beliefs in exclusive jurisdiction, viewed dual unionism as anathema, but for a few years after 1890 some miners accepted an "undercover dualism" with the same staff serving the dual national bodies.[14] This situation prevailed during the Coal Creek war, which opened with Knights storming a Briceville stockade, and ended with UMWA leaders convincing state legislators to abolish the convict-lease system.

The Coal Creek miners were supported in their rebellion by their friends and neighbors, many of whom were populist in their views, as well as by local merchants with whom they traded. James Lee, a Farmers' Alliance spokesman, stated early in the struggle: "Our fathers years ago took guns and fought for liberty, and shall we, their sons, at the sanctions of Mr. Morrow [TCI agent], be made to acquiesce . . . ?" In addition to bringing together farmers and miners, Knights of Labor and UMWA members, as well as Civil War veterans from North and South, the Coal Creek rebels also included black and white workers in their ranks. An early observer noted of the disciplined miners: "The captains of the different companies are all Grand Army [of the Republic] men. Whites and Negroes are standing shoulder to shoulder." Late in the war a Negro leader, Jake Witsen, was shot to death by the militia. "His body was carried to his home at Clinton and a funeral was held which was attended by several thousand white fellow-workers and neighbors."[15]

In the century of American engagements between trade unionists and troopers or police, the issues have always been the same: law and order versus anarchy, syndicalism, insurrection, and violence. The *Nashville American*'s formulation was vivid and typical: "Shall Tennessee allow a gang of thieves, robbers, ruffians, and outlaws to trample with impunity upon the law?"[16] During 1890-92 Governor Buchanan clearly represented the prevailing notions of property rights in contracts. The TCI contract to lease Tennessee convict labor was fully sanctioned by law and upheld by the courts. Against this notion, Eugene Merrell, the Coal Creek Knights of Labor leader, invoked a Jeffersonian belief in personal liberties and human rights which seemed perfectly natural to the descendants of Tennessee's mountain pioneers. Merrell's dialogue with Buchanan began early in the war and continued long after the unionist fled the state because of his role as miners' spokesman. The rebel position was stated very early in the conflict when the workers informed the Governor that they had "come together to defend [their] families from starvation, [their] property from depreciation, and [their] people from contamination from the hands of the convict labor."[17]

Needless to say, it was many decades after Coal Creek before legislators and courts fleshed out these notions of workers' rights to their jobs.

Even while miners and politicians expressed intransigent positions, a few figures emerged who sought a path away from conflict. Perhaps the most farsighted participant in the Coal Creek event was George W. Ford, Tennessee's first commissioner of labor and inspector of mines and factories. Ford, born in Boston in 1855, had followed his father's trade of shoemaking, joining the Knights of St. Crispin at the age of twelve. He became active in the Knights of Labor after his affiliation in 1876, and was sent to Knoxville as an organizer a decade later. Working equally with city artisans in then-new AFL craft unions and outlying coal miners in Knights' assemblies, Ford was influential in establishing the state's Bureau of Labor. Through the bureau he became actively involved in the legislative fight against the convict-lease system. On Labor Day, 1894, he founded the *Knoxville Independent,* a newspaper "devoted to the interests of the common people." He continued to publish this crusading journal until his death in 1945.[18]

Ford's detailed reports on the Coal Creek war are found in two official Tennessee documents: *Special Report of the Commissioner of Labor and the Inspector of Mines to His Excellency John P. Buchanan,* and *Second Annual Report of the Commissioner of Labor.* These reveal his compassion for the miners as well as his attempt to find equitable means to resolve the conflict. Upon inspecting the convict mines, he wrote: "A sickening stench is met with, showing the air to be so contaminated that it is a wonder human beings can exist therein; and in passing through some of the entries a person has to pass through so much mud, slush, and stagnant water that any man with a proper regard for his cattle would hesitate to keep them in such filthy quarters. . . . It is shameful to think that any class of men, whether free or convicts, are compelled or allowed to work therein."[19]

The initial accounts of the Coal Creek war appeared in Tennessee newspapers, trade-union journals of the period, state documents, and even souvenir books of militia units assigned to fight the miners.[20] It was not until 1931 that Andrew C. Hutson, Jr., reviewed these contemporary accounts and supplemented them by interviews with participants for an excellent University of Tennessee thesis on the "Insurrection." Two published articles were drawn from this study. Interestingly, Hutson used the name for the event that was current in the 1890's. For instance, *Harper's Weekly* featured several drawings of Buchanan, Merrell, and Anderson (the hero of Coal Creek) under the caption "The Insurrection in Tennessee."[21]

During 1938 Walter Wilson wrote a long account of the "Rebellion" for the *United Mine Workers Journal,* which was followed in 1958 by Alvin Toffler's "Convict Miners in Tennessee: Briceville Saw Them 67 Years Ago." Wilson had not encountered Hutson's articles but shared his conclusions. A parenthetical point in Wilson's *Journal* article forms a valuable guide for students who delve into industrial folklore. Wilson noted that labor historians had neglected Coal Creek in favor of contemporaneous struggles — the Homestead steel strike, the Coeur D'Alene silver and lead miners' strike, and the Buffalo switchmen's strike. However, Frederick Sorge, the friend of Marx and Engels, had written several dispatches in German on Coal Creek for European socialist newspapers. Wilson did not stress the point, but it is important to indicate that much labor lore was initially noted by radical intellectuals attached to trade unions.

Hutson, Wilson, and Toffler all drew on some traditional material but none had an orientation toward folklore. To the best of my knowledge, the first writer on Coal Creek with some consciousness of folklore as a discipline was James Dombrowski, a staff member of the Highlander Folk School at Monteagle, Tennessee. While there in the 1930's, he became interested in the stories told by Tracy City veterans of the convict-lease war, and wrote an informal history on the war, "Fire in the Hole."[22] George Korson collected a Briceville ballad in 1940, but confined his remarks on the rebellion, which appeared in *Coal Dust on the Fiddle,* to a historical overview drawn from Hutson and Wilson. The most recent historian to approach Coal Creek events, Philip Foner, added fresh details not available to Hutson, but Foner's contribution was chiefly that of his radical perspective. He prefaced his study with a stanza transcribed from a hillbilly song, but beyond this token he made no use of Coal Creek folklore.

169

Many scholars place no importance on the intimate relationship of the disciplines of folklore and history.[23] But even folklorists (like Korson) and historians (like Foner) who clearly understand the relationship find it difficult to blend disciplinary skills. I do not believe that an isolated ballad text per se preceding or following a historical study adds any real dimension beyond emotional illumination. Nor does factual data surrounding a collected song necessarily explicate all its meaning. Some songs which describe past events are so diffuse or lyrical as to seem unreal or ahistorical. Other songs, fully historical, demand extremely close analysis because their stories are so tied to local or topical events as to render them incomprehensible to listeners beyond the specific community in which they originated. Some ballad texts in themselves reflect or preserve hidden facts, otherwise undocumented. In this sense these latter ballads, if discovered by an academician, may become valuable historical documents. However, this and the following chapter treat material which in my judgment calls for an integrated historical-folkloric technique — one that assumes, as I do, that folk composers and formal historians both cope with narrative art. In short, not only do I feel that the folk ballad is a historical document but that the historian is also a special kind of singer of tales.

In the opening pages of this book I alluded to the difficulty of labeling the mine patch or camp as wholly a folk or folk-like society. It cannot be overstressed that America's industrial work force included immigrants directly out of conservative and custom-bound peasant communities throughout the world as well as radical, sophisticated political refugees from various lands. Native-born workers also represented such extremes, often posed in terms of the dialogue between fundamentalist religious sectarians and free-thinkers or libertarians. Coal Creek reportage and anecdotes reveal these polarities in American folk society. In an early message to Governor Buchanan, a miners' committee stated: "We are neither of the school of the commune nor nihilist."[24] Obviously, such topical references to Parisian and Russian revolutionary positions were understood by Coal Creek miners, even though the formulation was not cast in the normal modes of east Tennessee folk speech.

I suspect that rank-and-file, self-educated union leaders born on the Cumberland Plateau used mountain dialect in oral presen-

FIRST UMWA BOARD

tations at local meetings, while at national gatherings they switched to a polished, political rhetoric deemed appropriate for labor journalism or convention proceedings. This implies considerable mobility for the individual member in an American folk group. An illustration of such conflicting rhetorical forms is found in the reports of W. C. "Billy" Webb, the president of UMWA District 19 (Jellico, Tennessee) during the Coal Creek troubles.

Webb, a mountain miner from Pittsburg, Laurel County, Kentucky, had gone over from the Knights of Labor to the new UMWA, and became one of the best spokesmen for Tennessee coal diggers in their struggles. As early as 1877, Webb had organized Kentucky miners in Knights' assemblies, kept secret to protect the men against discrimination and discharge. During 1888 he extended his activity across the state line by organizing the Woolridge mine, three miles from Newcomb. Previously, the Tracy City miners had already formed a KL assembly in 1884; perhaps this was the first Knights coal union in Tennessee. Before 1890 Webb had emerged as leader of the Kentucky-Tennessee mountain miners' Knights District 5, which in time gave way to UMWA District 19.[25]

Because Anderson County, Tennessee, was in "Billy" Webb's area, he sent some Coal Creek dispatches to the then-new *United Mine Workers Journal* during 1891. On May 28 Webb mentioned that the Briceville slate and stone (coal) miners were "still idle, resisting the signing of the worst iron-clad in the history of the South." On the eve of the Bastille Day uprising, he noted that the Tennessee Coal Mining Company had discharged its blacklegs in favor of convicts. "What a pity, for the blacklegs cried when convicts arrived. Better for them to have sympathized with the miners instead of operators." *Blackleg,* the British term for the better-known American epithet *scab,* was widely used in the United States by English, Scottish, and Welsh immigrants.

Webb had a good ear for labor lingo and an excellent eye for the kinds of vignettes out of which local legends are formed. While at Coal Creek in August, he saw a group of trapper lads in action. It was their job to open and shut the heavy ventilation doors in the mine passageways to permit the mule drivers through. Such lonely work in total darkness, frequently in muck and water, also served an apprenticeship purpose. Many trappers went on to heavier and more skilled labor as their strength developed. Webb reported:

> About one dozen boy trappers at Coal Creek mine received notice of 10 cents reduction per day (they were getting 50 cents per day). The result was the boys stopped at once and the mine stood idle one day after the boy trappers ceased to work. A young man went and took one of the doors to trap. At that juncture the whole crowd of striking trappers seized the scab and took him to the creek nearby and ducked him in the hole of water prepared to wash mules. They told him if he would not blackleg any more they (the boys) would take him to the company "pluck me" and treat him. The scab agreed not to blackleg any more and went on his way terribly dilapidated. "Rah" for the boys of Coal Creek.[26]

The promise to treat the young blackleg was a wise gesture on the part of the strikers. Their choice usage "pluck me" was a euphemism for the company store.

Not only did "Billy" Webb have an open eye and ear for

TRAPPER BOY

folkloric detail, but he also, in the report on the ducking episode, provided an American example of the old British practice of "rough music." The social historian E. P. Thompson has defined this term succinctly: " 'Rough music' is the generic term applied to a widespread and variegated group of customs, all of them ritualised, all of them expressive of controlled community hostility towards individuals who have in some way offended against community practices and sanctions. . . . In the eighteenth century striking weavers in the West Country rode blacklegs out of town on a pole, to the duckpond ('cool-staffing')."[27] Today we can only speculate whether or not any of the Coal Creek trapper boys sense that their treatment of the scab was part of a time-honored ritual.

In November Webb described another vivid scene, one which resulted from the act of giving citizens' attire to the "zebras" in exchange for their convict stripes, upon liberation. "Nothing is left to mark the once convict camp, save the clothes scattered for miles along the Coal Creek valley. One amusing scene, near the Hamrock switch was a dead hog dressed in a convict garb and an empty jug lying beside the dressed hog and an old pipe lying on the hog."[28] Can there be a better statement of the miners' views toward scabs or convicts than these portraits of a mule-washed trapper boy or a dead hog in stripes? It is not too difficult, even today, to hear "Billy" Webb telling these anecdotes in mountain locution to his peers.

Webb also knew the language expected of a trade-union leader. This elocutionary style is well preserved in the prose of Terrence Powderly, John Mitchell, and John L. Lewis — all champions. Webb's vigorous letter from Pittsburg, Kentucky, following his visit to Coal Creek at the rebellion's start, asserted the unity of Kentucky and Tennessee mountain miners in UMWA District 19. Webb asked:

> If the thirst for money is to make a craze among the people; if it is to put poison in the blood; if it is to divert the currents of healthy life and thought away from their natural channels into a dark and turbulent river of unfathomable depth, bearing upon its surface the Babylonian splendors of a shameful prosperity, whilst carrying beneath the degradation and suffering of thousands of men, women, and children, condemned like galley-slaves to hopeless penury, then why not the workingmen of both states arise from their slumber, the miners being in one district (No. 19), and thoroughly concentrate their forces for the betterment of their condition and the amelioration of their craft? Why should men, such men as William Morrow [TCI agent] live in a grand mansion and humble miners be deprived of life's comfort? No wonder they would rise up like the morning sun or evening star and assert their rights so bravely and nobly. The miners of the South for several years have been but little better treated in the convict camps than the colored man before the late war. Emancipation must come legally or the people will take the law in their own hands. And why not?[29]

Ideally, a folklorist today should ascertain how many Anderson County residents, generations removed from the Coal Creek war, perceive its events in terms of "Billy" Webb's partisan rhetoric, and how many in terms of his vignettes steeped in folk imagery. Mrs. Della Tuttle, a coal miner's daughter, informed me that she "was reared in the big old house, with 9 big rooms, that Captain John Chumbley [Knoxville Iron Company warden] lived in when the convicts were brought to Coal Creek to break the Miners Strike. I have played around the rock walls which used to be stockades — and seen many convicts graves near the old house, and heard the history from my parents many times."[30] What a marvelous place to play war games this ruin must have been after a child heard the old folks talk of miners bushwacking the militia, or saw a gun or bit of a uniform retained as a mine-family trophy.

Any expressive practice or physical object can become the

cluster point for tradition when it is infused with particular association or meaning. In contrast to Mrs. Tuttle's pleasant impressions of childhood activity, I obtained a grim recollection from a pensioned ex-miner in La Follette, Tennessee, which is fifteen miles north of Coal Creek. Bob Forrester was the son of an Italian miner named Forrestino who married a "hillbilly girl." Bob was about four years old at the time of the local troubles and recalls running to his grandfather's bed when militiamen were shooting in the vicinity. But his most vivid memories were of guards whipping the convicts with great leather straps dipped in oil to "break their ass."[31]

Folklore includes more than the major genres in oral literature (such as ballads or myths). It is also the repeated telling of very simple anecdotes which concomitantly retain frozen values. Obviously, any activity or material thing — games at stockades, boys dipped in mule-wash, dead hogs in stripes, straps dipped in oil — has the potential to embody and convey considerable lore. One example of a hand-crafted artifact holding an association beyond its intrinsic esthetic worth underscores this point. In the late 1930's Mollie Scoggins of Coal Creek recalled: "When the convicts were turned loose their convict clothes were thrown all over the streets when they changed into clothes given them by the people. The women picked them up and made quilts out of them. I still have mine."[32]

The chief piece of trade-union tradition which emerged from the assault by Tennessee miners on the convict-lease system is a ballad variously titled "Coal Creek Troubles," "Coal Creek War," "Coal Creek Rebellion." (All versions known to me are identified in Checklist Three.) The text below is from Jilson Setters' singing on a field disc (1017) recorded in 1937 by Jean Thomas and John Lomax at Ashland, Kentucky, for Library of Congress deposit. Although the disc was poorly recorded, the words are understandable. The musical notation of Setters' ballad presented below is from Mike Seeger's rendition on *Tipple, Loom & Rail* (Folkways FH 5273). All other melodies transcribed in this book are drawn from the same source as texts. The exception here stems from the fact that Seeger's LP is more accessible than the field disc, that the former is better recorded than the latter, and that Seeger's music is faithful to Setters' original. The tune and text follow.

175

COAL CREEK TROUBLES

My song is founded on the truth,
In poverty we stand.
How hard the millionaire will crush
Upon the laboring man.
The miner's toiling under ground
To earn his daily bread;
To clothe his wife and children
And see that they are fed.

Some are from Kentucky,
The place known as my birth;
As true and honest-hearted man
As ever trod this earth.
The Governor sent the convicts here
And works them in the bank;
The captain and his soldiers
Are leading by in rank.

Although the mines are guarded,
The miners true and fair,
They mean to deal out justice,
A living they declare.
The corruption of Buchanan
Brought the convicts here,
Just to please the rich man
And take the miner's share.

The miners acted manly
When they turned the convicts loose;
You see, they did not kill them
And gave them no abuse.
But when they brought the convicts here
They boldly marched them forward;
The miners soon were gathered
And placed them under guard.

Soon the miners did agree
To let them take their place;
And wait the legislature
To act upon the case.
The law has made no effort
To lend a helping hand;
To help the struggling miner
Or move the convict band.

Buchanan acted cruelly
To put them out to toil.
He says he has not room enough
For the convicts in the wall.
He has no law to work them
Only in the pen.
Why should they be on public work,
To rob the laboring man?

I am in sympathy with the miners,
As every one should be.
In other states they work free labor,
And why not Tennessee?
The miners true and generous
In many works and ways,
We all should treat them kindly,
Their platform we should praise.

The Lord in all His wisdom
Will lend a helping hand,
And if we hold out faithful,
God will strive with man.
He gives us happy sunshine,
A great and glorious light.
He'll give us food and raiment,
If we'll only serve Him right.

COAL CREEK TROUBLES

stanza 1

My song is found-ed on the truth, in pov-er-ty we stand. How hard the mil-lion-aire will crush up-on the la-bor-ing man. The min-er's toil-ing un-der ground to earn his dai-ly bread; To clothe his wife and chil-dren and see that they are fed.

Before detailing the life of "Coal Creek Troubles" in tradition, I shall comment on it as a poem. Students of Anglo-American balladry frequently begin stylistic and structural analysis by dividing the subject into three categories. Priority is assigned to a model "Child ballad" — austere, impersonal, compressed. Against this standard are judged pieces of "lesser" worth, such as broadsides — turgid, mechanical, trite; or parlor ballads — florid, homiletic, bathetic.

It is difficult to place this song recorded by Setters in any of these neat compartments. Although the piece is camera-like in its description of the troubles, it is far from impersonal, for the composer tells us plainly that he is "in sympathy with the miners." Not only is it strongly didactic; it is also an excellent and tightly wound statement of the politics of mountain miners "true and fair," who were responding to the New South's industrialization by invoking populist and libertarian creeds. It is in this combination of straightforward historical description and ideological message that the poem's stress moves from classical ballad to broadside mode. It is in the homiletic ending, which takes the struggle out of the militant workers' hands and places it with the Lord, that the piece is related to the parlor genre. It might be argued that the composer felt no contradiction between his support of the miners' cause and the Lord's purpose, just as he probably saw no scholastic distinction in ballad types.

For a "moral" report inveighing against injustice, Setters' song is remarkably free from concern for the brutalized convicts. The statement that they were turned loose, which implied their freedom, is calm and factual in proper ballad fashion; one wonders what would have been composed had the piece been written from the perspective of an exploited or liberated convict rather than that of an aroused miner. (My next chapter is concerned with "Roll Down the Line," sung by convict miners and delineating the anguish of their lives.)

A closing question on the status of "Coal Creek Troubles" as a ballad is that of incident. We expect a mining ballad to focus sharply on a specific disaster or labor disturbance. Instead of narrating an actual fight at a burning stockade or the death of a brave miner, the composer substitutes a "position paper" against Bu-

UP IN FLAMES

chanan. Probably Setters, while singing, knew that his audience understood fully the details of the skirmishes and needed a rallying song more than a journalistic report. We can assume that the message expressed in the song made full sense to Knights of Labor and United Mine Workers members. Both sets of unionists could accept the ballad's opening assertion that millionaires did indeed crush the laboring man, as well as the pointed query, "In other states they work free labor / And why not Tennessee?" The stereotype of unlettered mountain folk unaware of outside political forces does not hold for the Coal Creek miners, whose position on the convict-lease system was identical with that stated in the writings of George Washington Cable and in Knights of Labor resolutions. We can only speculate whether Cable's articles were known in Coal Creek, but we are certain that labor journals were read in the region.

179

Finally, to close this look at Setters' song, comments on its time setting and a few technical terms are in order. The period described in the ballad follows the initial freeing of the convicts, when Eugene Merrell, W. C. Webb, and their fellow miners visited the General Assembly in Nashville to plead for justice against the demands of the corporation lobby. The ballad noted that the miners agreed to wait for the legislature to act, but it did not specify any of the dramatic events which ended the war badly for the rebels. Two unfamiliar phrases need to be glossed: convicts working "in the bank" is a reference to the mine itself; work "in the wall" is a reference to the penitentiary at Nashville.

During 1939 Jean Thomas published *Ballad Makin' in the Mountains of Kentucky* and included the text of Jilson Setters' "Coal Creek Troubles." Her headnote — "when 'trouble' came up in the Coal Creek mines, the valiant old minstrel of the Kentucky mountains promptly declared himself 'in sympathy with the miner' " — did not indicate whether the singer composed the number or learned it in his travels. About 1940 a valuable but little-circulated Works Progress Administration compilation of east Kentucky folksongs appeared, including the text (one stanza) and tune of a "Coal Creek Troubles" version from Rowan County. This obscure publication held the only transcription of the ballad's music. Unfortunately neither singer, collector, transcriber, nor editor was named. In *Coal Dust on the Fiddle*, George Korson published an additional fragment; during 1940 he had met a retired Briceville miner, "Old Charlie," who sang a bit of the ballad (six couplets) after draining a pint of "toddy." This fragment was the first printed evidence that an Anderson County miner knew the song.

My personal curiosity about Coal Creek's song lore began in 1956 when I became aware that this Tennessee place name appeared in a full cycle of ballads, lyric folksongs, and banjo instrumentals which linked the war-insurrection-rebellion itself to two mine disasters: the Fraterville explosion, May 19, 1902, and the Cross Mountain explosion, December 9, 1911.

Upon listening to Setters' field disc of "Coal Creek Troubles," I was surprised to learn that the recording also contained Jean Thomas' voice prompting the singer. Further, her printed text

JILSON SETTERS

(1939) did not follow the stanza sequence of the field recording (1937). It is entirely possible that Setters' memory of the ballad was weak late in his life and that Miss Thomas assisted him for this Library of Congress session. Regardless of Thomas' function or the relationship of disc to book, it is unfortunate that we know so little about Setters' role in the song's composition.

Jean Thomas wrote extensively on Setters but she flawed her portrait, in my judgment, by needlessly investing him after her "discovery" with a romantic pseudonym, Jilson Setters, in lieu of his real name, James William Day. Also, she continually placed Setters in a frame of "sixth century Gregorian chants" and "Chaucerian and Elizabethan" language survivals in the Kentucky highlands.[33] My main interest in Setters, however, is not in Miss Thomas' cloying portrait, but rather in his importance as an identifiable performer, composer, and disseminator of folksong comparable to other artists discussed in this study.

James William Day was born at Thomas Branch, Rowan

County, about 1860. Blinded during infancy in a cholera epidemic, he turned to balladry and fiddle music. It can be inferred from "The Rowan County Crew," one of his best-known feud narratives, that he was composing and singing lengthy broadsides on local events by 1884. Mountain folk knew him as "Blind Bill" Day, an itinerant fiddler and singer. "The Rowan County (Crew) Feud" was recorded commercially in 1928 (Gennett 6513) by Ted Chestnut, who had learned it from Asa Martin. As a lad, "Acey" heard Day sing it at the Clark County courthouse in Winchester, Kentucky. Martin had also learned from Day the well-known murder ballad, "The Death of J. B. Marcum," and Martin's own rendition was coupled by Gennett with the feud song.

In the interaction of folksingers and representatives of popular culture, many alternative roles are possible for the various participants. Under Jean Thomas' guidance, Day "began to play the part of Jilson Setters. . . . Miss Thomas dressed him in home-spun, took him to New York and introduced him as a representative Kentucky mountaineer."[34] Through Jean Thomas' books and her American Folk Song Festival ("The Singin' Gatherin' ") at Ashland, Day reached a large "revival" audience. He died at Ashland on May 6, 1942, remembered partly as Miss Thomas had portrayed him and partly in terms of his commercial discs. In 1928 he had recorded for Victor nine excellent fiddle tunes and a lyric folksong, but ironically none of his ballads. (Day's Victor output is listed in Appendix Three.)

Sharing my desire to relate the recording fiddler with "the Singin' Fiddler of Lost Hope Hollow," Fred Hoeptner queried Miss Thomas about the composition of "Coal Creek Troubles." She replied: Setters "was blind at the time of the 'trouble' at the mines but being a roving minstrel he made his way with a 'pilot' to various county seats in Kentucky and Tennessee and 'heard the talk' of mountain folk who congregated in the courtyard on court days. So he learned as he listened and then put together a song-ballet."[35] This is a fine general description of Setters' techniques, but leaves open the problem of whether he made up, learned, or recomposed the Coal Creek narrative.

Fortunately there is another clue to the ballad's origin and life in tradition. During 1937 Alan Lomax collected from G. D.

Vowell at Harlan, Kentucky, two stanzas of the "Coal Creek War," melodically similar to Setters' version, as well as a good spoken account of the happenings. The field-disc text follows.

COAL CREEK WAR

The miners working underground
To earn their daily bread;
To clothe their wives and children
And see that they are fed.

Buchanan sent the convicts here
To work them in the bank.
The captain and his army
Was standing by in rank.

The Harlan coal fields, which were opened later than those in Tennessee, attracted new men from the old district. Vowell identified himself to Lomax as a Coal Creek native, born in 1872. He was a young man when he learned the "Coal Creek War" after hearing an "old gentleman, a fiddler named Day," singing and playing it at a union picnic during the rebellion. Vowell recalled that the fiddler "came around at our picnics where we'd hear this agitation about the convicts being in competition with us."[36] Vowell's matter-of-fact statement is an excellent corroboration of James William Day's (Setters') composition of the ballad.

The information on the scene of the ballad's performance makes full sense in terms of knowledge of the audience, for celebrating miners would have been quick to accept a hortatory, topical song which sharpened their experiences. A brief note on a union fete rounds out Vowell's remembrance. "Billy" Webb in a report to fellow miners described the first anniversary (July 20, 1892) of the convict liberation at Briceville. After opening addresses by Eugene Merrell (spelled Marrel) and Webb, there was dancing all afternoon and evening on a platform built of convict-stockade timber. "It was a fine celebration, no trouble in any way, all sober and quiet throughout the day."[37] Did Webb hear any ballads sung between the dance sets or after the speeches? Could fiddler Day have been on the platform?

Vowell made a secondary point pertinent to labor-lore study. He noted that the Coal Creek operators opposed the use of penal

183

UNION MEETING

labor — "Doing all they could to get the convicts out of the coal mines." While this was true of some of the small firms after the men won a series of victories, it was not true before the troubles. Nor did Vowell account for the position of the dominant Tennessee Coal, Iron & Railroad Company. This detail is stressed to underscore the point that all industrial lore does not come from labor partisans. Indeed, Vowell's defense of the employers was indicative of his political views in the 1930's. During the critical Harlan mine-war year of 1932, Vowell submitted a poem to his local paper labeling "visiting meddlers" (National Miners Union organizers) as traitors to Kentucky.[38] In hindsight one can phrase an obvious question: Did Vowell perceive the 1891 miners as patriots or insurrectionists?

During 1961 Ed Kahn and I visited Alvin H. Vowell, a Briceville house painter and paper hanger. He had been a coal miner until 1942 at the Slatestone mine, scene of the Cross Mountain explosion, as well as in various Harlan fields. The Vowells are Coal

Creek pioneers originally from North Carolina. A. H.'s great-great-grandfather "Son" had settled and named Vowell Mountain, which overlooks Militia Hill. A. H.'s father, William Royal Vowell, had worked at Fraterville, scene of the Fraterville explosion, and at other Anderson County mines from about 1901 to 1932, including a long stint as a mine-company bookkeeper. W. R. told his children many firsthand stories about the troubles and the explosions. For Kahn and me, A. H. could only recall three stray couplets of the "Coal Creek Song," also using Setters' melody:

Coal Creek Song

A place known as Kentucky,
A place known as my birth.

The true and honest-hearted men
That ever trod the earth.

Buchanan sent the convicts here
And placed them under guard.

Vowell stated that he had never heard anyone sing it except his father, and added that W. R. believed it had been written by a Middlesboro, Kentucky, coal miner. In response to my comment that the song was also known to G. D. Vowell, of Harlan, A. H. stated that G. D. or "Doc" was a distant cousin of William Royal Vowell.[39] Previous to meeting Alvin H. Vowell, I had known the Coal Creek ballad only from print and field recordings. Vowell's singing in his cottage on Briceville's outskirts — literally between Vowell Mountain and Walden Ridge — was both exciting and rewarding to me far beyond the brevity of the text.

A constant problem in folksong scholarship is the haunted feeling imposed on a student by the knowledge that he can never have "all" the versions of a given item. How many singers hold pieces in memory beyond the reach of an investigator? In the fall of 1968, while working on the problems posed by the long Day and fragmentary Vowell texts, I asked a friend from Tennessee, Richard Hulan, if he could help. Hulan, at that time director of the Belle Meade Mansion near Nashville, queried his wife Kathleen's great-aunt, Mrs. Lonnie Davis (born Betty Litton) of Robbins, Scott County, Tennessee. "Aunt Betty" responded by sending her niece and nephew a handwritten song "ballet":

185

Coal Creek Trouble

My song is founded on the truth,
in poverty we stand
how hard the millinar will crush
upon the Laboring man
the miners working under ground
to Earn thir Dayly Bread
to cloth thir wife and children
and see that they are fed.

god Bless the Kgnights of Labor
with all thir wit and skill
thir Eforts to Acomplish
Ententions to fullfill.
I am in simphy with the miner.
as Every one should be
other states they work free labor,
and why not Tennessee

Upon receiving the text from the Hulans, I was elated both by its relative fullness and, more important, by its unique reference to the Knights of Labor. Not even the ballad's composer, James William Day, had specifically labeled the unionists who stormed the Briceville stockade on Bastille Day, 1891. On June 8, 1969, the Hulans attended the Litton Family Historical Society meeting at Oneida, Tennessee, where "Aunt Betty" sang her "Coal Creek Trouble"; a week later she made a tape of the ballad for Dick and Kathy. Her melody and stylistic presentation resemble closely those of Day; behind her unaccompanied singing one can almost hear his archaic fiddling.

Mrs. Davis, born on the Big South Fork of the Cumberland River on April 26, 1880, had moved to Oneida as a young child. She learned this song "during the troubles . . . from hearing an old man sing it."[40] Is it possible that fiddler Day himself had wandered from Briceville to Oneida — some thirty miles away — and that the eleven-year-old Betty heard the blind composer sing his own ballad? Mrs. Davis capped her account by mentioning to the Hulans that the song had appeared in a Huntsville (Scott County) newspaper. If such a version is located, we will be rewarded by the earliest known printing of any composition by James William

eod creek Trueble

my song is founded on the truth.
in poverty wet stand
how hard the milling will crush
upon the Laboring man
the miners working under ground
to Earn this Dayly Bread
to cloth this wife and children
and see that they are fed.
2

god Bless the Knights of Labor
with all this wit and skill
this Efforts to Acomplish
Ententions to fullfill.
I am in simplify with the miners.
as Every one should be
other states they work free Labor,
and why not Tennessee

"AUNT BETTY'S" BALLET

Day, and will be afforded an opportunity to compare his original "Coal Creek Troubles" with subsequent forms.

A glance at Checklist Three will summarize the available versions of "Coal Creek Troubles": a full text-tune by Jilson Setters (Day) in print and on field disc; a re-presentation of Setters' number by Mike Seeger; an unidentified Rowan County, Kentucky, stanza (probably directly from Setters); three fragments by "Old Charlie," G. D. Vowell, and A. H. Vowell; a handwritten "ballet" and tape from "Aunt Betty" Davis. All singers employed the same melody, one also commonly used for the ballad "Charles Guiteau,"

concerning President Garfield's assassin, as well as for the sentimental hillbilly and bluegrass standard, "Jimmie Brown the News-
boy." Jean Thomas suggested that Setters used a tune for his "Coal
Creek Troubles" which was familiar in campaign songs of the
1890's. Heretofore, in American folk-music studies, tune-family
analysis by such scholars as Samuel Bayard, Bertrand Bronson, and
George Pullen Jackson has largely covered fiddle pieces, English-
Scottish classical ballads, and white spirituals. There is no major
study of the dominant tune families used in hillbilly tradition, but
it is only a matter of time before such an investigation will be
undertaken. This chapter's musical transcription of "Coal Creek
Troubles" from Mike Seeger's *Tipple, Loom & Rail* hopefully may
contribute to an analysis of the Charles Guiteau–Jimmie Brown
tune family.

During 1891 and 1892 a group of miners — insurrectionists
in the eyes of the state, but "true and honest-hearted" in the view
of an itinerant blind fiddler — helped rid Tennessee by direct action
of a brutal convict-lease system. The Coal Creek ballad, "founded
on the truth," lives on largely by virtue of two sound recordings —
a documentary field disc and a spirited LP. This latter recording
by Mike Seeger is an excellent communicative tool; it is also a
warm tribute to the "Free Men of the Mountains" and their folk
balladeer, James William Day. Further, the 1965 LP helps perpetuate Lake City's first name, Coal Creek. It is useful in a time of
national turmoil and discontinuity to be reminded of former names
on the land as the nation itself is remolded by new energy sources,
new modes of production, new conflicts between established powers
and "colonial" dependents, as well as new life-styles.

1. L. C. Glenn, *The Northern Tennessee Coal Field* (Nashville, 1925); Edward
   T. Luther, *The Coal Reserves of Tennessee* (Nashville, 1959).
2. R. Clifford Seeber, "A History of Anderson County, Tennessee" (master's
   thesis, University of Tennessee, Knoxville, 1928).
3. Herbert J. Doherty, Jr., "Voices of Protest from the New South, 1875-1910,"
   Mississippi Valley Historical Review, XLII (1955), 49. See also Jane Zimmerman, "The Penal Reform Movement in the South during the Progressive
   Era, 1890-1917," *Journal of Southern History*, XVII (1951), 462.
4. George Washington Cable, "The Freedman's Case in Equity," *Century
   Magazine*, XXIX (Jan., 1885), 416, reprinted in *The Silent South* (New

York, 1885), 1. For a recent analysis of Cable's position see Arlin Turner's introductory essay, "George W. Cable as a Social Reformer," in the Patterson Smith reprint of *The Silent South* (1969).

5. Overviews of the war are: Andrew C. Hutson, Jr., "The Coal Miners' Insurrections of 1891 in Anderson County, Tennessee," *East Tennessee Historical Society's Publications*, VII (1935), 103, and "The Overthrow of the Convict Lease System in Tennessee," *ibid.*, VIII (1936), 82; George Korson, *Coal Dust on the Fiddle*, 2nd printing (Hatboro, Pa., 1965), 353; Philip S. Foner, *History of the Labor Movement in the United States*, II (New York, 1955), 219. An excellent example of a recent newspaper feature is Willard Yarborough, "Miners' Guns Finally Helped End Convict Lease Law," *Knoxville News-Sentinel* (Oct. 30, 1966), sec. F, 3.

6. Data on Merrell from Mrs. Grace Roberts, Clinton, Ind., in James Dombrowski, original field notes and interviews for "Fire in the Hole."

7. James A. Sharp, "The Entrance of the Farmers' Alliance into Tennessee Politics," *East Tennessee Historical Society's Publications*, IX (1937), 77, and "The Farmers' Alliance and the People's Party in Tennessee," *ibid.*, X (1938), 91.

8. For a bibliographic summary see Allen J. Going, "The Agrarian Revolt," in *Writing Southern History*, ed. Arthur S. Link and Rembert W. Patrick (Baton Rouge, La., 1965), 362.

9. *Annual Report of the Tennessee Coal, Iron & Railroad Company for the Fiscal Year Ending January 31, 1890* (Nashville, 1890), 7, 13.

10. Quoted in Walter Wilson, "Historical Coal Creek Rebellion Brought an End to Convict Miners in Tennessee," *United Mine Workers Journal* (Nov. 1, 1938), 10.

11. "Catching Convicts," *United Mine Workers Journal* (Apr. 23, 1891), 7; "Pratt Mines Accident," *ibid.* (June 4, 1891), 4. For background see Robert Ward and William Rogers, *Labor Revolt in Alabama: The Great Strike of 1894* (University, Ala., 1965).

12. For early TCI history see Ethel Armes, *The Story of Coal and Iron in Alabama* (Birmingham, 1910). For brief accounts by former presidents see Robert Gregg, *Origin and Development of the Tennessee Coal, Iron & Railroad Company* (New York, 1948), and Arthur V. Wiebel, *Biography of a Business* (Fairfield, Ala., 1960). For a recent comprehensive thesis see Justin Fuller, "History of the Tennessee Coal, Iron and Railroad Company, 1852-1907" (University of North Carolina, Chapel Hill, 1966). For early illustrations see the 64-page prospectus, *Tennessee Coal, Iron & Railroad Company* (Birmingham, 1897).

13. Wilson, "Historical Coal Creek Rebellion," 10.

14. For Knights of Labor see Norman J. Ware, *The Labor Movement in the United States 1860-1895* (New York, 1929). For "undercover dualism" see Charles F. Anson, "A History of the Labor Movement in West Virginia" (thesis, University of North Carolina, Chapel Hill, 1940), 85, 97.

15. James Lee quote in Hutson, "Coal Miners' Insurrections," 110; comment on Jake Witsen in Wilson, "Historical Coal Creek Rebellion," 11, 13.

16. Hutson, "Overthrow of the Convict Lease System," 90.

17. Hutson, "Coal Miners' Insurrections," 108.

18. Data on Ford from interview with Ford in Knoxville, Tenn., July 16-17, 1938, in Dombrowski, original field notes. . . . See also Morris Simon, "Labor Leader 70 Years, Founder of CLU, George Ford Still Alive at 82," *Knoxville News-Sentinel* (Sept. 6, 1937).

19. George W. Ford, *Special Report of the Commissioner of Labor . . .* (Nashville, 1891), 45, 47.

20. I am indebted to Herb Peck of Vanderbilt University for reproducing for me several photos from his copy of *Souvenir of Company C, First Regiment of National Guard, State of Tennessee* (St. Louis, 1893). The booklet includes a historical sketch by Leonard Rankin of the *Nashville Banner* and photographs by W. E. Singleton of Knoxville.

21. "The Insurrection in Tennessee," *Harper's Weekly*, XXXVI (Aug. 27, 1892), 834.

22. "Fire in the Hole" and Dombrowski's original field notes are deposited at Tuskegee Institute, Tuskegee, Ala. Material cited in this and the following chapter is duplicated in my files.

23. An overview on the relationships of folklore to history is found in the Preface to William Lynwood Montell, *The Saga of Coe Ridge* (Knoxville, 1970). Two recent history anthologies which touch on "inarticulate" members in society are Barton J. Bernstein, *Towards a New Past* (New York, 1968) and Tamara K. Hareven, *Anonymous Americans* (Englewood Cliffs, N.J., 1971).

24. Hutson, "Coal Miners' Insurrections," 116.

25. Data on Webb from interview with Ford in Dombrowski, original field notes. . . . See also details on Webb in S. L. Bastin and S. A. Morey, *History of Coal Mining in Laurel County, Kentucky, 1750-1944* (London, Ky., 1944), 11. A useful background article is Frederick Meyers, "The Knights of Labor in the South," *Southern Economic Journal*, VI (1940), 479.

26. W. C. Webb, "District 19," *United Mine Workers Journal* (May 28, 1891), 5, "Kentucky and Tennessee," *ibid.* (July 16, 1891), 5, and "Strike of Boy Trappers at Coal Creek," *ibid.* (Sept. 3, 1891), 4.

27. E. P. Thompson, "English Trade Unionism and Other Labour Movements before 1790," *Bulletin of the Society for the Study of Labour History*, no. 17 (Autumn, 1968), 21.

28. W. C. Webb, ". . . Scene of the Late Convict Limbo," *United Mine Workers Journal* (Nov. 19, 1891), 6.

29. W. C. Webb, "From the Districts," *United Mine Workers Journal* (July 30, 1891), 1.

30. Letter to me, Aug. 4, 1958.

31. Interview, Aug. 28, 1961.

32. "The woman's side of the labor trouble in Coal Creek by Mollie Scoggins as told to Grace Roberts," in Dombrowski, original field notes. . . .

33. Jean Thomas, "The American Folk Song Festival," *Register of the Kentucky Historical Society,* LXV (1967), 25, 27. See also Jean Thomas, *The Singin' Fiddler of Lost Hope Hollow* (New York, 1938).

34. "Death Takes Bill Day, Fiction's Singin' Fiddler," *Louisville Courier Journal* (May 8, 1942). See also "Entertainer Succumbs," *Ashland Daily Independent* (May 7, 1942), and Jim Dawkins, "Poster Depicts 'Old Time Kentucky Fiddler,'" *Ashland Daily Independent* (Jan. 22, 1969).

35. Thomas letter to Hoeptner, Mar. 25, 1959.

36. My transcription from Library of Congress Archive of American Folk Song disc 1381.

37. W. C. Webb, "Celebration of Convicts' Departure at Briceville," *United Mine Workers Journal* (July 28, 1892), 5.

38. Malcolm Ross, *Machine Age in the Hills* (New York, 1933), 167.

39. Interview, Aug. 28, 1961.

40. Hulan letters to me, Dec. 26, 1968, and June 12 and 20, 1969.

CHECKLIST THREE

"Coal Creek Troubles." Jilson Setters, Ashland, Ky., 1937. John Lomax, AFS 1017.

————. Jilson Setters. Thomas, *B M M K* (1939), 192.

————. Mike Seeger, *Tipple, Loom & Rail,* Folkways FH 5273. Apr., 1965, New York. Brochure includes text and headnote.

"Coal Creek War." G. D. Vowell, Harlan, Ky., 1937 (learned in Coal Creek, Tenn., about 1891). Alan and Elizabeth Lomax, AFS 1381.

"Coal Creek Trouble." *Folk Songs from East Kentucky,* Federal Music Project, WPA (ca. 1939), 5, m. Song from Rowan County.

"Coal Creek Rebellion." "Old Charlie," Briceville, Tenn., Mar. 20, 1940. George Korson, AFS 12012.

Transcribed: Korson, *C D F* (1943), 370.

"Coal Creek Song." Alvin H. Vowell, Briceville, Tenn., Aug. 28, 1961. Archie Green and Ed Kahn, Green tape files.

"Coal Creek Trouble." Betty Davis, Robbins, Tenn., Dec. 20, 1968. Richard Hulan, holograph ballet, Hulan files, Nashville.

————. Betty Davis, Clinton, Tenn., June 16, 1969. Richard Hulan, Hulan tape files.

APPENDIX THREE

JILSON SETTERS (JAMES WILLIAM DAY) DISCOGRAPHY

All items were recorded for Victor in New York City on February 27, 1928. Jean Thomas, acting as Day's agent, accompanied him to New York and supplied information on his music. The data below is drawn from the session's ledger sheet (copy in my files) and the *Victor Records of Old Familiar Tunes and Novelties*, a 62-page catalog issued about 1931.

Song and instrumental titles are drawn from the catalog and are supplemented by titles in brackets from the ledger sheet. All numbers were identified as "frolic tunes" except the last two, which included singing or talking. The guitar accompanist was Carson Robison.

Matrix No.	Title [alternate title]	Catalog No.
BVE-42483-1	Forked Deer	21407
BVE-42484-1	Marthie Campbell	21353
BVE-42485-1	Wild Wagoner	21353
	Note: reissued on *American Folk Music* (Folkways FA 2952)	
BVE-42486-2	Billy in the Lowland	21407
BVE-42487-1	Wild Horse of Stoney Point	40025
	[The Wild Horse or Stoney Point]	
BVE-42488-1	Black-Eyed Susie	40127
BVE-42489-1	Grand Hornpipe	40127
BVE-42490-1	Little Boy Working	40025
	[Little Boy Working on the Road]	
BVE-42491-2	Way Up on Clinch Mountain (singing by Day)	21635
	[Drunken Hiccup Song or . . .]	
BVE-42492-2	Arkansaw Traveler (talking by Day)	21635
	Note: Miss Thomas identified number as "imitation of Scottish 'Flyting' (Scolding)"	

BEEHIVE COKE OVENS

Roll Down the Line 6

IN THE YEARS 1912-17, William C. Handy composed a number of songs which were widely performed by vaudeville stars and dance-band vocalists. "St. Louis Blues," "Memphis Blues," "Hesitating Blues," "Joe Turner Blues," and "Beale Street Blues" have been available on sheet music and phonograph records for half a century; they are still alive as popular-music standards. Folklorists are fortunate that the "Father of the Blues" was highly conscious of his use of traditional material and eager to share his secrets with ballad scholars. When Texas collector Dorothy Scarborough perceived the relationship of Negro folksong and popular blues of the World War I period, she sought out "the man who had put the bluing in the blues," and questioned him about the then-novel form.[1]

Handy asserted that the blues were indeed traditional. To illustrate he told Miss Scarborough that his "Joe Turner Blues" stemmed from a folksong he had known for more than thirty years. Joe Turney (also called Turner), the brother of Tennessee governor Peter Turney (1892-96), was a penal officer who transported convicts from courts to prisons and various work sites. A perfunctory comment on the officer's action was noted in a local newspaper: "Capt. Joe Turney the agent of the lessees of the State Prison was in town Wednesday and took John Daugherty to the

195

penitentiary on a charge of felonious assault."[2] Handy had composed his blues about Joe Turney "around an old Negro song," retaining the melody but resetting the plot to change Turney from a dreaded official — the long-chain man — to an absent masculine lover. This explanation made comprehensible a fragment Miss Scarborough had heard years before but never understood:

> Dey tell me Joe Turner's come to town.
> He's brought along one thousand links of chain,
> He's gwine to have one nigger for each link.
> He's gwine to have dis nigger for one link!

Handy's "Joe Turner Blues" has been sung in concert and recorded by such performers as Louis Armstrong, Lena Horne, and Nat Cole. It is unlikely that many members of the recent audience for these popular artists could have placed the real Joe Turney in the context of Tennessee history, when the state's convict-lease system was formally ended. The "Coal Creek Troubles" has been discussed as a mountain narrative revealing the attitudes of free miners toward Governor Buchanan, the defender of the convict-lease system. There is, of course, an association in time between the ballad about Buchanan and the folk blues about his successor's brother. In 1926 Abbe Niles called for a study of all versions of the Joe Turner folksong; sadly, no one responded to the challenge.[3] If the story is ever written, we may or may not learn that this blues was sung by miners on the Cumberland Plateau in the 1890's. Without such a specific connection to coal or to Tennessee's convict wars, the "Joe Turner Blues" is but an intriguing prologue to a less-known song, "Roll Down the Line," clearly sung by black prison miners in the turbulent years of Buchanan and Turney. My study of this latter "Roll" complex concerns a blues ballad distant from the Anglo-American rhetoric and structure of the "Coal Creek Troubles," but nonetheless an equally significant commentary on the convict-lease system.

Earlier in these studies I have touched on Robert Winslow Gordon's contributions as a folksong collector. Gordon was one of the first field workers in the United States to use extensively a cylinder recording machine for English-language folksong, as distinct from American Indian song. He acquired such equipment after accepting a teaching appointment at the University of Cali-

GORDON'S "CONVICT SONG"

fornia in 1918, and made more than a hundred recordings in Berkeley and elsewhere in the early 1920's. Subsequently he used cylinders on field trips in Georgia and North Carolina.

Previously I have noted a few differences between the recording expeditions of commercial firms and of folklorists. This contrast is highlighted in the separate journeys of Gordon and Ralph Sylvester Peer of Okeh Records to Asheville, North Carolina. At the end of August, 1925, the General Phonograph Corporation engineers set up a portable laboratory on the roof of Asheville's George Vanderbilt Hotel.[4] Okeh old-time records were already known in the Blue Ridge region, and hundreds of performers flocked to the session, which was combined with a qualifying fiddlers' convention. At least three artists who recorded at the Vanderbilt — Ernest Stoneman, Kelly Harrell, Henry Whitter — are still known to contemporary listeners by virtue of reissues of their early discs. While the Asheville session records were released in October, Gordon undertook a three-month field trip in North Carolina. He netted some 200 cylinders, but to my knowledge none has been publicly released by the Library of Congress or any other archive. Such an issue of Gordon's material is long overdue, not only to illuminate his role, but also to afford comparison of commercial and scholarly expedition standards.

One particular item, the "Convict Song," sung for Gordon by William H. Stevens at Biltmore (an Asheville suburb), is the first collected member of the "Roll Down the Line" family. Gordon's typescript from the recording does not identify Stevens or comment on the song itself. In 1927 Gordon wrote an excellent series of articles for the *New York Times Magazine* and he included this "purely local song from Asheville" in his feature on jail ballads. Gordon carefully noted that he "changed the names originally used" in the song by substituting fictional names. Presumably he did not wish to embarrass Stevens or the Buncombe County judiciary. Gordon's comment "purely local" indicates that he had not encountered the "Convict Song" elsewhere. The text below was recorded on November 16, 1925.

CONVICT SONG

Soon a-Monday mornin',
See them convicts comin',
Guards all on behind.

Guns on their shoulders,
The bullets made of lead;
All them guards is a-guardin' fer
Is that ole fat grease an' bread.

O buddy, won't yer roll down the line,
Hop down, skip down,
Well, yonder comes my darlin'
Rollin' down the line.

Walk around old Asheville,
You'll think you are a sport;
Fifteen minutes an' you're arrested,
An' Judge Brown got yer bound over to court.

They'll take yer over before ole Judge Shaw,
A mighty cruel man, he'll try yer mighty well.
He'll try his best ter send
Yer poor soul down to Hell.

Take yer to the chain gang,
Shove yer in a hole,
Very first words you hear ole Cap'n Britton say is,
"Now, nigger, God bless yer soul."[5]

198

Stevens' "Convict Song" stands in stylistic contrast to James William Day's "Coal Creek Troubles," as the former derives from Afro-American blues and the latter from Anglo-American balladry. In recent years D. K. Wilgus, Marina Bokelman, and others have explored the interaction of these traditions and have employed the term *blues ballad* to cover songs characterized by slight story lines, by flexible temporal sequence, and by fluid verse order.[6] In spite of such impressionistic patterns, blues ballads are still expository in nature, with their elliptical narratives partially hidden or assumed to be known by singer and audience. Because the tag *blues ballad* is recent in folksong studies, it is treated differently by each user. Hopefully this case study of "Roll Down the Line" will add to the concept's utility.

The "Convict Song's" main event depicts a stroller in town who is arrested and quickly sentenced to the chain gang. This detail contains the potential of being fleshed out into a full ballad with realized characters, but it is not. Instead, the piece reports sardonically on guards concerned with "grease an' bread" and ironically on Cap'n Britton's profane greeting to his new prisoner. The problem of the singer's perspective is meaningful. Gordon did not identify Stevens' race or his status in Asheville. Presumably the song's "original" singer was a vagrant aware that court procedures were imperfect but unable to fight cruel judges in any significant way. Can we assume that his listeners — fellow convicts — took wry pleasure in hearing a confirmation of their view of the judiciary's actual function: to provide free labor for the community? Long after the convict-lease system was eliminated, local authorities used prisoners on road construction and maintenance. Fletcher Melvin Green, the distinguished historian, has noted that this local practice retains "vestigial evidence of a system that left a trail of dishonor and death" across the South.[7] During 1932 national attention was drawn to this practice in a vivid film starring Paul Muni, "I Am a Fugitive from a Georgia Chain Gang." Figuratively, William Stevens' "Convict Song" is a soundtrack for these stark scenes of chain gangs on red-clay and piney-wood roads.

Robert Gordon's *New York Times Magazine* printing of the "Convict Song" appeared on Sunday, June 19, 1927. The *Times'* readership was wide, but I doubt that anyone wrote to Gordon

GEORGIA CHAIN GANG

about this particular item. Nor do I know whether any reader was aware that a then-available Paramount disc by Watts and Wilson, the "Chain Gang Special," held a spirited parallel to the Asheville number. My study of the "Roll Down the Line" complex began in San Francisco in 1956, but I did not suspect the existence of the Paramount version until David Freeman played it for me in New York at year's end, 1964. This circumstance illustrates how contingent is much scholarship upon recorded folksong.

Freeman, the proprietor of County Records, has reissued on LP considerable southern mountain music from his personal collection. Additionally, he has corresponded with most serious students of race and hillbilly discography. Freeman, Harlan Daniel, Malcolm Blackard, and a handful of friends have tried for some years to locate all the exceedingly rare Paramount discs by the string band known as Watts and Wilson and Wilmer Watts and the Lonely Eagles. The duo recorded at least six numbers in Chicago during March, 1927; the Lonely Eagles recorded more than ten pieces in New York during October, 1929. Not only did the group know some excellent versions of unusual folksongs but its performing style was striking.

Like other Paramount old-time performers, Wilmer Watts

was overlooked by scholars during his life, despite the fact that his records offered tantalizing clues to his locale. Watts's "Walk Right in Belmont" was the familiar Texas "Midnight Special" localized to North Carolina. His "Cotton Mill Blues," containing the line "Belmont is a lousy town," further suggested that Watts was a Gaston County textile worker in 1929. Actually, one Watts and Wilson disc, "The Sporting Cowboy," was transcribed by Ruth Crawford Seeger for *Our Singing Country* (1941), but unfortunately it led no one to seek out the singers for permission to use their ballad. Such a quest might have brought Watts and Wilson, while they were still alive, to the attention of folklorists. It was not until 1966 that any biographical data on Watts became available. On a visit to Belmont, Malcolm Blackard located Carl Lee Freshour, the son of Charles Freshour, a member of the Lonely Eagles band. The elder Freshour had died in May, 1959; Watts had died previously.[8] The full story of the Lonely Eagles must be told by Blackard; here I can offer only the transcribed text of the "Chain Gang Special" and the note that this 1927 recording presented the first publicly available melody for "Roll Down the Line."[9] In this sense, Watts's record functioned similarly to the Kentucky Thorobreds' "Only a Miner" in that both discs were early musical publications of native folksong. The text from Paramount 3019 follows.

CHAIN GANG SPECIAL

Wish I was in Mobile
At some swell hotel,
With a New York paper in my hand
Just sporting to my dear.
I'd march around to Cuba,
I'd take a trip to Spain,
I'd drive back down to Belmont,
And . . . I'd sleep again.

> Hey, nigger won't you roll down the line,
> Roll down the line.
> Yonder comes my darling, roll down the line,
> Keep a-rolling — won't you roll down the line,
> Roll on — won't you roll down the line.
> Yonder comes my darling, roll down the line.

You lay around ol' Belmont,
Call yourself a sport.
In fifteen minutes they'll arrest you
And bind you over to court.
You get up in the courthouse
And listen to the lawyers fight.
First captain say, "Big black nigger,
"I need you on my gang."

    Chorus:

Every morning 'fore day
They loose you off the chain.
They come right through to the white folks
And treat them just the same.
And then, it's when they feed you,
They feed you out of a bucket and pan.
And when you get through eating,
It's get to shovelin' sand.

The points of similarity and difference between the Belmont and the Asheville songs are obvious. Watts deleted or did not know Stevens' opening stanza descriptive of the guards. Also, Watts added a stanza on the treatment of white and black prisoners in jail. What is intriguing in the "Chain Gang Special," however, is the fantasy stanza by Watts on travel to Mobile, Cuba, and Spain. It is not always easy to transcribe worn copies of old records and I am uncertain that I fully understand the "sporting" action in the "swell hotel." Is *sporting* merely a garbled *strolling* or *sparking* or is it a substitute for a more pungent figure of speech? Does this escape wish mainly symbolize the prisoner's longing to leave Belmont's chain gang, or does it also personify his longing for a woman? These rhetorical queries probably can never be adequately answered. Apparently Gordon did not ask Stevens about the "Convict Song's" background; certainly no folklorist talked to Watts.

Fortunately, a partial answer to this query about the fantasy opening as well as about the song's history is possible, based on other available versions. At Memphis in November, 1930, Lee and Austin Allen recorded "Roll Down the Line," which was released on Victor 23551 and subsequently on Bluebird 6148. This piece was copyrighted in 1931 by the Southern Music Publishing Company,

VICTOR AND VOCALION LABELS

a Ralph Peer firm. During 1934 the Allen Brothers recorded this number for a second time under the title "Hey Buddy, Won't You Roll Down the Line" (Vocalion 02818). Although the Victor and Vocalion pieces are extremely close in text they are sung at quite different tempos; the second is more relaxed than the first. The Victor 23551 text and tune are transcribed at this point.

ROLL DOWN THE LINE

I wish I was in Mobile,
Sitting in a big arm chair,
A newspaper in my hand,
Strolling to my dear.
Oh, I'm a-goin' around by London,
Oh, I'm a-goin' around by Chi,
Gonna stop awhile in New Orleans
To see that gal of mine.

 Hey Buddy, won't you roll down the line,
 Roll down the line.
 Hey, yonder comes my darling, roll down the line,
 Oh, roll down the line,
 Roll down the line.
 Hey, yonder comes my darling, roll down the line.

(Humming with scat interjection in lieu of a stanza)

 Chorus:

203

I spy my captain coming,
He's coming over the hill.
He puts me in the mind of a country gal
Just getting home from the mill.
It's over the hills and valleys
'Till he gets to the mouth of the hole,
And the last words I heard him say,
Was, "Nigger doggone yo' soul."

Chorus:

ROLL DOWN THE LINE

In comparison to previous versions, the Allen Brothers' "Roll Down the Line" is not only the shortest but the furthest removed from ballad norms. The Allens share an opening "wish I was in Mobile" stanza with Watts, but substitute for Cuba, Spain, and Belmont the equally unlike combinations of London, Chicago, and New Orleans. They also share a blasphemous closing couplet with Stevens, but fail to retain the key story element from either Tar Heel song. Normally the three minutes available on a ten-inch 78 rpm disc permitted at least three eight-line stanzas and two choruses. The fact that the Allen Brothers hummed their middle stanza to fill out their time suggests to me that they knew but a fragment of an older or longer song.

In 1958 I attempted to reach the Allens to ask about their source, but all leads failed. I learned only that Austin Allen had lived at 3804 Rossville Boulevard, Chattanooga, from 1928 to 1932, and that his employment in 1930 was at the American National Insurance Company. During 1959 Fred Hoeptner and Bob Pinson, while on a summer field trip, visited Chattanooga to seek out the Allens. A former neighbor recalled that Austin had left Chattanooga for New York during the Depression and that Lee had dropped out of sight at this time. Another neighbor suggested that the boys had attended the University of the South at Sewanee, Tennessee.[10] This clue was intriguing, because not many hillbilly performers were college graduates. However, the university alumni office had no files on the Allens.

A few discographical details round out this meager account. The Allen Brothers made their debut for Columbia in Atlanta on April 7, 1927, returned on November 4, and followed with a third session in the same city on April 20, 1928. They also recorded twice for Victor: Atlanta on October 15, 1928, and Memphis on November 22, 1930. They concluded their recording careers in an extended session, October 3-8, 1934, for the American Record Corporation in New York. Material from this last appearance was issued on the Vocalion label. Collectors aware of the interaction of Afro and Anglo styles prize Allen Brothers discs for their treatment of "mountain blues." Their personal synthesis of these two forms was so successful that in 1927 Columbia mistakenly released two

Allen items, "Chattanooga Blues" and "Laughin' and Cryin' Blues," in its race-record series (Columbia 14266-D) instead of its hillbilly 15000-D series. Their A & R man Frank Walker recalled that this error distressed the Allens to the extent that they sued Columbia.[11] Perhaps the suit was settled privately; I have found no written reference to it. Such a legal account might fill in some important details in the Allen Brothers' biography, as well as document an actual instance of musical interaction between the races in the late 1920's.

Whereas the "Convict Song" and the "Chain Gang Special" were localized to Asheville and to Belmont, North Carolina, respectively, "Roll Down the Line" was not set in any area. Fortunately, a previously unpublished Tennessee "Lone Rock Song" is available which helps establish a time and place setting for the Allen Brothers' piece. The "Lone Rock Song" was found at Palmer, Grundy County, by James Dombrowski while he was on the staff of the Highlander Folk School at Monteagle, in the same county. Because this version was not limited to a disc's length, it presents a relatively full narrative as well as a basis for relating all the "Roll Down the Line" members in a common cluster.

Dombrowski's achievements are told elsewhere; a word is in order in this study to explain how he became a collector. A Florida native, he was educated at Emory and Columbia as well as the Union Theological Seminary. His Columbia dissertation was published as *The Early Days of Christian Socialism in America* (1936). Along with other idealistic students of his era, he left both academy and cloister for a life of social action: in 1929 he participated in the great textile strikes at Elizabethton, Tennessee, and Gastonia, North Carolina. (It is tempting to speculate that his path crossed that of Wilmer Watts.) Between 1934 and 1941, Dombrowski worked with Myles and Zilphia Horton at Highlander, and from 1941 until his retirement at sixty-nine in 1966 he was a leader in the civil-rights movement, for the Southern Conference Education Fund.[12]

It was during the Highlander years that Dombrowski completed his unpublished manuscript, "Fire in the Hole," an informal social history of one section of the Cumberland Plateau. While interviewing grizzled miners who had joined the Knights of Labor

"UNCLE JESSE" JAMES

in the 1880's and had survived the hazards of their calling to welcome the CIO (Congress of Industrial Organizations) in the 1930's, Jim and a fellow Highlander, Ralph Tefferteller, met William Ely "Uncle Jesse" James at Palmer in the miners' union hall on March 27, 1937. James had been a charter member of UMWA Local 510, formed in 1898 after the convicts were eliminated from Grundy County, and he was still a miner when Dombrowski met him. For the collector, "Uncle Jesse," a sixty-six-year-old militant, sang the "Lone Rock Song," which he had learned as a young miner directly from black convicts at Tracy City.[13]

Dombrowski noted James's full text and also made a personal transcript of his melody in a numerical code. The miner recalled that he had learned songs from Negroes at Sunday night "preachings," when they would play and sing outside the church. At this chapter's end, I have appended Dombrowski's field notes of his meeting with "Uncle Jesse" because they reveal the veteran miner's deep loyalty to unionism, and also because they are a fine example of field work in industrial folklore. James's text from Dombrowski's original typescript follows.

LONE ROCK SONG

See a man a' going
Across the little hill,
Made me think of a little boy
Goin' to a mill.

> Buddy won't you roll down the mountain
> Buddy won't you roll down the line,
> Yonder come my darlin'
> Comin' down the line.

He'll come down to the mine,
He'll poke his head in the hole,
The very first word you'll hear him say,
Nigger gimme that coal.

See them guards a clustering
Pulling for the shore,
Their shotguns on their shoulders,
The convicts on before.

Roving 'round the mountain,
Their guns loaded with lead,
All the guards was a-guardin' fo'
Was his fat meat and his bread.

There was a cross entry in Lone Rock.
Charlie Medlick drove it through,
News came that Charlie was dead,
And his friends was grievin' too.

They took him to the stockade,
And there three hours lay,
Walker a' takin' him in his cart,
And they hauled him to his grave.

I can't go back to Georgia,
I can't go back to France,
I'll go back to New Orleans,
To give my girl a chance.

I wish I was in Ireland,
Seated in my chair,
Mornin' paper in my hand
And by my side my dear.

The foreman he was bank boss,
And he knows the rule,
If you don't get your task,
He's sure to report you.

And when he does report you,
The warden with a squall,
Bend your knees
Across that door piece fall.

And after you are counted
Then they'll ring the bell,
And from that to eight o'clock
The Nigger catches hell.

"Uncle Jesse's" song contained some elements of the three pieces already presented, but it was far more elaborate. In common with the Allen Brothers, he included a sketch of the captain at the hole (mine mouth), but, significantly, the captain was after coal. In none of the other versions was the work site presented so clearly. Both James and the Allens employed a curious and probably uncomplimentary simile in which the captain, an authority figure, was likened to a little boy (or country girl) going to (or coming home from) a mill. This must be understood in the context of industrial workers demeaning farm folk new to the complex technology of mining life. Workers, ever conscious of their antecedents, have used terms such as *hayseed, turdkicker,* and *appleknocker* to ridicule new recruits in industry. Implying that a mining superintendent was capable of no more than trailing to a country grain mill was the lowest pejorative available to black convicts who had to cloak their hostility in oblique comment.

"Uncle Jesse's" version paralleled Stevens' "Convict Song" in the portrait of the guards concerned only with their sustenance. With both Watts and the Allens, he shared the wishful escape or fantasy stanza but the scene was transferred to Georgia, France, New Orleans, and Ireland. Whereas the ballad plot of the two North Carolina songs focused on a vagrant arrested in town, the main narrative element in James's piece was the death and burial of Charlie Medlick, a convict miner. True to blues-ballad tradition, this dramatic detail was not developed to its full potential. Rather, it was set in a framework of descriptive and lyrical commentary on convict life. Presumably the Lone Rock prisoners knew Medlick well and did not require the elaborate circumstances of his death. Apparently the convict laborers were as interested in remarks on the habits of their foreman (bank boss) and warden as on the death of a peer, for James's three ending stanzas concerned working conditions in which "the Nigger catches hell."

In the previous chapter, George Washington Cable's response to the brutality of the convict-lease system was noted, along with Bob Forrester's childhood memory of the sounds of miners being strapped. The best reports of such cruelty I have encountered in folk memory are found in James Dombrowski's unpublished Highlander field notes:

MRS. SARAH L. CLEEK

Me and a widow woman used to carry pies to the stockade and sell them to the convicts. They were treated cruelly. With my own eyes I saw where they were buried. Their thighs or shank bones were not buried deep enough or somethin! They used to dig there for clay to daub the coke ovens with. The bones stuck out on the ground. I could see where the coffins was buried. Nigger hill, the convict burial ground was called. They sent them out to work, sick or not. My daddy said the warden and the doctor sent one man out to work one morning. He lay around the ovens during the day. A white man found him dead. They used to cry out to my daddy to let 'em out. The lice and chinch bugs were eatin' 'em up.

MR. THOMPSON

When the convict trouble came we was only gettin' one day work a week. And the convicts was workin' full time. My brother was a guard. I used to visit him no tellin' how many a Sunday. I heard 'em beatin' the convicts. You could hear the strap from clear over as far as that cabin a half mile away. I heard 'em holler. Yes, Lord! It was a sight to behold. I saw 'em killed in the mines. By the mine boss, that is, for not getting their tasks. And maybe they was sick. It was shameful.

I. H. CANNON

Convicts would be punished for not getting their tasks. The warden and deputy warden would do the whippin'. . . . The whipping was done with a two ply strap as wide as your three fingers, tied to a staff. The convicts were face down with their pants off. They were whipped on the hips and legs five to twelve lashes. Ordinary offences were punished with a few lashes. If they tried to kill a man they were whipped more.[14]

I have found the "Lone Rock Song" particularly interesting because it offers clear evidence that Negro convict miners made up or modified older songs to lighten the burden of prison time. We have "Uncle Jesse's" word that it was sung by the prisoners themselves. Also, there exists some "folk" corroboration for his assertion. No detailed formal account of the convict wars in Grundy County exists comparable to Andrew Hutson, Jr.'s writings on the major Coal Creek events.[15] During 1934 Allen McCormick, a Tracy City teacher, completed a George Peabody College thesis, "Development of the Coal Industry in Grundy County, Tennessee." Although McCormick had interviewed convict-war partisans he did not follow his study with any articles, technical or historical.

Despite the lack of publications on this dramatic scene, I have found a few references to Lone Rock, a prison mine operated at Tracy City by the Tennessee Coal, Iron & Railroad Company. The full story of the TCI's rise from a "foxhole" Cumberland Plateau venture to its affiliation with the U.S. Steel Corporation was well told by Ethel Armes in *The Story of Coal and Iron in Alabama* (1910). An exemplary thesis, "History of the Tennessee Coal, Iron and Railroad Company, 1852-1907," completed in 1966 at the University of North Carolina by Justin Fuller, supplements Armes's work with a wealth of original and recent material. The TCI's use of convict labor was described in the preceding chapter; here I shall quote only an early rationale for the convict-lease system, as well as a later company self-appraisal printed at the time when "Uncle Jesse's" number began to circulate. These two statements can be viewed as the ideological framework for the "Lone Rock Song."

In 1876 Arthur St. Clair Colyar, a flamboyant Nashville promoter, argued that the TCI's use of prisoners would result in "cheap coal, lower taxes, and protection of city mechanics." This last-named benefit would flow from the concentration of convicts in mining, which "would eliminate their competition with free labor in the cities."[16] Actually, a number of complex forces — geographic, economic, entrepreneurial — rather than the specific use of convicts, accounted for the TCI's prosperity. During 1893 Thomas C. Platt, TCI president, reported: "This Company [is] the largest producer of bituminous coal and pig iron for the open market of any company in America . . . not withstanding this fact, we are not working and have not worked, over five percent of our property. This vast mineral domain represents in area more than thirty percent of all the available and accessible mineral lands of the States of Tennessee and Alabama. . . ."[17]

The TCI's progenitor was the Sewanee Mining Company, chartered in 1852 to develop Grundy County's fabulous deposits and named after Tennessee's principal bituminous seam, the Sewanee. Between the Civil War and the turn of the century, more than six million tons of coal were mined from this vein below Tracy City. This town, which came to life as a pine-board commissary centered in a bleak coal camp, was named after New York capitalist Samuel F. Tracy, the first president of the Sewanee Mining Company. Coincidentally, this firm was instrumental in establishing the University of the South at Sewanee. It was near the university in the Sequatchie Valley area, late in 1870, that convict labor was first used in any southern coal mine. Because Tracy City was only eighty-four miles from Chattanooga and because of the richness of the Sewanee seam, Tracy City coal mines emerged as the most extensive in Tennessee in the 1880's. Well before its mines were electrified, Tracy City achieved a daily output above 1,200 tons. A large part of this sulphur-free coal was converted to coke for use in TCI iron and steel furnaces at Cowan, Tennessee, and elsewhere. Hence, Tracy City was a key link in TCI's corporate development.[18]

For the year 1890, James L. Gaines, the general manager of TCI's Tennesse department, noted that he was operating three Tracy City mines: Old Mines Numbers One and Two, East Fork, Lone Rock. He reported: "In the 'Lone Rock' mine convict labor is worked entirely, and this class of labor cannot be worked in the mine to advantage for more than another year." In January, 1892, Gaines elaborated: "The mine (Lone Rock) in which convicts have been worked for the past five years being well-nigh worked out, the necessity of preparing another mine for the accommodation of this labor was forced upon us." Gaines further described the relationship of the various Tracy City entries to tipples, coke ovens, and railroad tracks, as well as steam plants and rope-haulage (early conveyor) plants. He concluded that the Lone Rock operation should be shifted to Bryant's Ridge, anticipating that it "would give

"THE FIERY GIZZARD": TRACY CITY FURNACE

employment for five years to the force required to be moved from the exhausted Lone Rock Mine." Gaines, of course, did not antici-pate that the free miners of Grundy County were shortly to rebel against his well-operated system. Accordingly, he spent $2,851.05 to open the new convict mine.[19]

These details constitute the only primary accounts I have found of Lone Rock and they suggest that "Uncle Jesse's" song dates to 1887-92. The first burning of a Grundy City stockade by free miners occurred on August 13, 1892; presumably the unionists assaulted the Bryant's Ridge mine rather than the already worked-out Lone Rock site. One can speculate on the fates of thousands of American mines — decayed, abandoned, forgotten. Yet Lone Rock with its "clusterin' guards" and "grievin' friends" (convicts) is still vivid, thanks to James's memory. In my desire to visualize Lone Rock as it originally existed, I inquired of the State of Tennessee Division of Geology for photographs, but none are found in its files. Nor is the mine named on any of the division's current maps.[20]

213

A host of questions are hidden in the "Lone Rock Song." For example, can Charlie Medlick's death be documented? The fact that he drove a cross entry (an entry running at an angle with the main entry) suggests that he was a worker of skill or perhaps a supervisor. Previously, I speculated that he was a convict miner. Yet a search of the Tennessee Department of Correction files as far back as 1864 reveals no prison inmate by this name.[21] Two possible explanations are that the name in the song was garbled during transmission from person to person, or that Medlick was a TCI free employee rather than a prisoner. There is a chance that information on his death exists in Tracy City newspapers or in TCI archive records, although such data have not come to hand.[22] Hypothetically, there may even have been a separate song on Medlick's death. It is my feeling that in ballad scholarship the known song itself is but the visible portion of a largely hidden iceberg. If this analogy is apt, we are always in danger of losing even the visible peak to the sun and sea.

During the fall of 1970 I met two of "Uncle Jesse's" children, Albert M. James at Palmer and Mrs. Oda Roberts at nearby Laager, and I attempted to add to my knowledge of their father's song.[23] Both recalled his singing of the convict piece but neither could sing it for me. Each was fully aware of its setting in the convict wars, and eager to relate to me the same kind of anecdotes about brutality and violence that Dombrowski had gathered in Grundy County thirty years ago. Al James is as loyal a unionist as was his father and fully conscious that "Uncle Jesse" had helped bring the "organization onto the mountain." Al is currently a retired member of UMWA Local 5881 in Palmer as is his sister's husband, Henry Roberts. In listening to Al and Oda's childhood memories of hearing their father sing "miles away" while coming home from lodge meetings, as well as their early memories of strikers and union soup kitchens, I asked myself these difficult questions: Was "Uncle Jesse" the last folksinger to know the "Lone Rock Song"? If his children, Al and Oda, recall its setting but not its text and tune are we in a position to date the end of this song's life in tradition with the death in 1963 of William Ely James? Is there a chance, however remote, that some of "Uncle Jesse's" grandchildren, growing up in the 1960's and 1970's, may turn in a conscious

SAM McGEE AND UNCLE DAVE MACON

manner to "Grandpa's" former use of labor lore and folksong as
tools for coping with life? Such rhetorical queries need not be answered explicitly if it is understood that they stand behind technical
folksong analysis.

My correspondence with James Dombrowski (beginning in
1957) and delight in receiving his Lone Rock prize had actually
followed my earlier exploration of "Roll Down the Line's" most
visible as well as most widely heard version — Uncle Dave Macon's
"Buddy Won't You Roll Down the Line." It was recorded in Chicago (Brunswick 292) on July 25, 1928, with Sam McGee assisting
Macon. Sam used a banjo-guitar (six-string banjo) and Uncle
Dave used his regular five-string banjo, making a highly unusual

combination. In Checklist Four following this chapter I have outlined the chronology of Macon's disc and its derivatives. Like most hillbilly records, "Buddy" circulated briefly and went out of stock during the Depression. Fortunately it was reissued in 1952 on Harry Smith's influential Folkways set, *American Folk Music;* consequently, the song reached a "revival" audience including Pete Seeger, the Gateway Singers, and the Kingston Trio.

Seeger was particularly drawn to the piece, in part because of Macon's banjo artistry, but also because Seeger was aware of the events of the Coal Creek rebellion. In a *Sing Out* headnote for Macon's number, Seeger suggested that the Tennessee star "probably learned the song first hand."[24] Uncle Dave was born October 7, 1870, near Smartt, Warren County (immediately north of Grundy), but spent part of his growing years in his father's Nashville theatrical hotel. We can only speculate just where, when, and from whom Macon first heard a song about the convict-lease system and its turbulent ending. When my correspondence and interviews with Macon's children and colleagues failed to provide any specific links of "Buddy" to the miners' wars, I wrote to Pete Seeger, who generously mailed to me Dombrowski's "Lone Rock Song." There is, of course, an obvious but still-puzzling relationship between the James and Macon songs. The latter is transcribed here to point up this relationship.

BUDDY WON'T YOU ROLL DOWN THE LINE

Way back yonder in Tennessee,
They leased the convicts out.
They worked them in the coal mines
Against free labor stout.
Free labor rebelled against it;
To win it took some time.
But while the lease was in effect,
They made 'em rise and shine.

Oh, Buddy, won't you roll down the line?
Buddy, won't you roll down the line?
Yonder come my darling, coming down the line.
Buddy, won't you roll down the line?
Buddy, won't you roll down the line?
Yonder come my darling, coming down the line.

Every Monday morning
They've got 'em out on time.
Marched them down to Lone Rock,
Said to look into that hole;
March you down to Lone Rock,
Said to look into that mine;
Very last word the captain say:
"You better get your coal."

Chorus:

The beans they are half done,
The bread is not so well;
The meat it is burnt up
And the coffee's black as heck!
But when you get you task done,
You're glad to come at all.
For anything you'd get to eat
It'd taste good, done or raw.

Chorus:

The bank boss is a hard man,
A man you all know well;
And if you don't get your task done
He's gonna give you — hallelujah!
Carry you to the stockade,
That's on the floor you'll fall,
Very next time they call on you
You'll bet you'll have your coal.

Chorus:

Separate performances by Pete Seeger (cited in Checklist Four) of this number are available; Macon's original is also reissued on LP. Anyone who has heard these discs will not have to be told that Macon turned his "ballad" into a humorous narration quite different in spirit from the "Lone Rock Song." Macon clearly related his version to Tennessee history and described what actually happened to the prison miners at Lone Rock. It is my personal belief that Macon heard some form of the "Lone Rock Song," perhaps as fragmentary as the one heard by the Allen Brothers, and used this fragment as a basis for a "new" composition. Macon was not one to retain in a ballad a dimly understood or non-narrative lyrical element such as "wish I was in Ireland." He was a superb commentator who prized clarity and intelligibility.

Macon's recompositional skill has never been studied. All Grand Ole Opry histories pay perfunctory tribute to him, but only the recent monograph by Ralph Rinzler and Norman Cohen is commensurate with the "Dixie Dew Drop's" extraordinary talent.[25] Even these notes by Rinzler and Cohen are but a prelude to a needed study of Uncle Dave. Particularly welcome would be an analysis of his total recorded repertoire with attention paid to the degree to which he altered traditional material. "Buddy Won't You Roll Down the Line" is set at Lone Rock and employs the chorus common to all in this song cluster, but in other respects it does not resemble Stevens, Watts, the Allen Brothers, or James. Thus, I submit that it is a creation of Macon's, something he heard after 1892 but possibly did not fully "compose" until 1928, when it was actually recorded in Chicago. Interestingly, Macon also departed from the standard "Roll Down the Line" tune. I label the Allen Brothers' tune as standard because it is very close to Watts as well as to the two Library of Congress field recordings for "Roll Down the Line." The extent of Macon's melodic deviation can be demonstrated in a comparison of Hally Wood's tune transcription in *The New Lost City Ramblers Song Book* and Judith McCulloh's notation of the Allen Brothers' item in this study.

I have stated my view of Macon's recompositional techniques in strong terms and welcome any evidence that his "Buddy" was known to other traditional singers. Also, I would like data which might reveal his specific attitudes toward the convict wars. Macon, a life-long, articulate, and opinionated agrarian, was hostile to industrialism and urbanization in the South; nevertheless, as a pioneer hillbilly recording artist he helped nationalize and commercialize country music. He came of voting age during the terms of Governor Buchanan, a populist leader who ended his stewardship supporting the TCI against the free miners. Yet Macon did not criticize Buchanan as did balladeer Day in the "Coal Creek Troubles." Nor did Macon grieve for Charlie Medlick or any other individual prisoner. Instead, he fashioned an objective commentary on one aspect of the convict-lease system, leaving undeclared his political and moral position or else masking it by a tone of humor.

Macon died on March 22, 1952, before I had made any field trip to Tennessee. My interviews with his son Dorris and his recording partners Kirk and Sam McGee failed to elicit any data on "Buddy."[26] However, the McGees suggested a visit to Luther Watson, Kirk's father-in-law. On August 30, 1961, Ed Kahn and I met Mr. Watson at his home in one of Nashville's south-side housing projects, and we were rewarded with a highly important link in the "Roll Down the Line" complex. Watson was born on October 16, 1884, at Monroe's Campground, Rutherford County, Tennessee. While still a boy in grade school, perhaps at the age of nine or ten, he witnessed a pageant presented by his playmates. Its theme was the then-current Tracy City turmoil, an incident in the Coal Creek insurrection. Some youngsters acted as guards; others blacked their faces to personify the convicts. At this time Jess Walden, a Murfreesboro-area man who had been employed in Tracy City as a guard, taught the children a convict song for use in the entertainment. He had learned the song from convicts while on duty at the mines. Watson recalled that "Old" Sam Walden, Jess's father, had also worked as a TCI guard and that Sam had been saved from death (miraculously as in much legendry) during an encounter with the free miners, when a shot hit his breast-pocket silver watch.

Watson's recollection in 1961 of hearing his playmates sing a Tracy City convict song nearly seventy years previously was electrifying for me. During the interview, Watson was pressed to sing Jess Walden's piece, but it was obvious that it had not been in his conscious memory for many decades. At this point Ed Kahn sang the first stanza of Uncle Dave Macon's ballad, and Watson responded with the fragment "I wish I was in Tracy City / Sitting in my rocking chair." Not only was this the Allen Brothers' opening localized to Grundy County rather than to far-off Mobile, but Watson clearly sang it to the Allen Brothers' melody. Watson's memory supported my guess that the Allens had learned their version in the Sewanee-Sequatchie area, no great distance from their Chattanooga home. Watson regretted his failure to remember more except the phrase "courting to my dear," but he was explicit about the song's context and time — free miners fought against convict labor when the song was fresh.

Monroe's Campground is nine miles from Murfreesboro. From about 1900 to 1920 Uncle Dave hauled freight in this area as proprietor of the Macon Midway Mule and Wagon Transportation Company. Possibly Macon learned the Tracy City song from Jess Walden or a former Monroe's Campground schoolchild. This is as good a guess as any for Macon's source. Although Luther Watson had known Uncle Dave, he could not account for his mine-war ballad. He liked Macon as a good neighbor and a comical entertainer. Watson, in a nice comment on folk creativity, stated that "Dave may have added or dropped a little from songs to suit himself."[27]

This study of five "Roll Down the Line" texts — two from North Carolina and three from Tennessee — demonstrates considerable adding and dropping, normal in blues balladry. By definition a blues ballad links black and white expressive forms, yet all the singers named to this point were white. A new series of questions thrusts itself to the surface at this juncture: Was "Roll Down the Line" in Negro tradition before the Coal Creek events? Did the specific "Lone Rock Song" stay in such tradition after its composition? Are the Asheville and Belmont chain-gang songs older or younger than 1892? No conclusive response to any of these queries can be offered at this time except to report that two field recordings by black singers exist which extend the geographic spread of the complex. During July, 1933, on one of their first Library of Congress trips, John and Alan Lomax collected "Rollin' Down the Line" from a group of unnamed "young" prisoners at Memphis. It is impossible today to reconstruct who brought this number to Memphis and from where. The song was poorly recorded and the transcribed text is marred by some guesswork on my part.

ROLLIN' DOWN THE LINE

Oh, Buddy, won't you roll down the line,
Roll down the line,
Yonda come my darlin' rollin' down the line.
Roll down the line,
Roll down the line,
Yonda come my darlin' rollin' down the line.

"Oh captain, captain, captain,
Oh, will you tell me true?
Is my darlin' Willy boy
On this ship with you?"
"It's no, no my dear,
No, Willy boy's not here.
Yo' Willy boy got drownded
In that deep blue sea."

Chorus:

When you see Cap'n Armour sweatin'
With his pick up under his chin,
He set upon that old boxcar rig
Just like a sitting hen.
And any time of day you'll come
You will find him settin',
And every now and then you'll hear him say,

. . . .

Chorus:

It's when the cap'n left Memphis;
He had a hundred men.
But when he got to Nashville
The number was down to ten.
You ought to heard him holler,
You ought to heard him squall:
"Oh, once I had a hundred men,
But now I've lost them all."

Chorus:

This number's chorus matches the refrain in the songs already
noted. Its opening stanza is also familiar, for it is related to a well-
known British broadside, "The Sailor Boy," found in American lyric
tradition under various titles, such as "Deep Blue Sea" or "My
Willie's on the Dark Blue Sea." However, "Rollin's" two remaining
stanzas approach a story about a strong character, Cap'n Armour,
who is presented in mocking terms. His stated actions are portrayed
in the loss of ninety out of a hundred prisoners, presumably through
death caused by mistreatment. This staggering loss, over a distance
of less than 200 miles, is itself an oblique commentary on the cruel

convict-lease system. In my listening to the field disc, I placed Captain Armour on a boxcar, perhaps in transit with his wards. However, after this song was recorded in 1933, either John Lomax or one of his assistants transcribed it and heard a somewhat different portrait of Cap Thomas:

> You see Cap Thomas a settin'
> With his feet up under his chin
> He set in dat ole rocker there
> Jus like a settin' hen
> An' any time day you come
> You will find him settin'
> In the cane back rocker
> Oh, gawd ought you to let him?[28]

It is this reaching for a developed character — Cap Thomas or Cap'n Armour — within a narrative structure, however slight, by "Roll Down the Line's" composers and singers which places it in the blues-ballad category. If one sees blues ballads as syncretic forms drawing strength from separate and older traditions, one can range the six texts already presented along an array from fluid or weak to strong or developed stories: Allen Brothers, Memphis prisoners, Stevens, Watts, James. Macon's descriptive commentary on prison-camp life is neither ballad, blues, nor blues ballad; "Buddy" challenges students concerned with structure and genre in folksong.

The theme of convict transportation, found in the Joe Turner folksong, must have been one that gnawed at the emotions and sensibilities of prisoners, white and black, in the post–Civil War decades; it is implicit in all the versions of "Roll Down the Line." On the last day of 1968, I was fortunate to receive from Homer Layne (principal of Tracy City High School), to whom I had written for help, a holograph manuscript by Ned Arbuckle on this same theme. It read:

LONE ROCK MINE SONG

Sung to me by my father, Jasper W. Arbuckle, who actually visited the Lone Rock area on a day-to-day basis. His father [William E.] operated steam engines which drove washers, etc. and the endless cable through the hill to Pryor Ridge mines.

According to my father, the song was sung by convicts who were sent on contract from the state to the stockade at Tracy City. These convicts were, for the most part, Negroes and had the task of "pulling coke" from the beehive ovens which were located below Lone Rock.

The song was about "Humpy" Hargis, an official of the coal company [TCI] who was in charge of convict labor and was sung to the traditional tune of "Roll on buddy, why you roll so slow."

> Ole Humpy went to Nashville
>> He went up to the pen
> And there he told the warden
>> I want fifty of your men.
>
> Give me fifty of them healthy,
>> And fifty in their prime
>> (or, And fifty all in line)
> I'm going to take them down to Tracy
>> To work in the Lone Rock Mine.
>
> Roll on buddy, why you roll so slow
>> How can you roll, when the wheel won't go.

This song must date to around 1895-1900. My father heard it as a boy and he was born in 1889.[29]

Metrically and rhythmically the "Old Humpy" verses are related to the Memphis prison song collected by Lomax and not to the hillbilly-bluegrass standards "Nine Pound Hammer" / "Roll On Buddy" (treated in Chapter Nine) identified by Arbuckle's chorus. Curious about this association and eager to tape the "Lone Rock Mine Song," I visited Tracy City on Mountaineer's Day, October 10, 1970. Not only did I secure a fine tape, but Ned Arbuckle was good enough to guide me and my companion Richard Hulan to the now-verdant site of the former Lone Rock convict stockade as well as the still-standing, vine-clad beehive coke ovens under the old mine hill. Only to say that fifteen years elapsed from first hearing the Allen Brothers' Bluebird recording in San Francisco to the actual touching of the fire-contorted stones in a Lone Rock oven does not convey my sense of excitement as well as pleasure in this long journey.

William E. Arbuckle had come from a frontier farm in Rutherford County about 1880 to seek employment in the TCI mines near Tracy City. In time he became a coal-mine stationary engineer. His son Jasper William Arbuckle (1889-1968) worked most of his adult life either as a miner or as a brakeman, hauling coal,

ABANDONED COKE OVENS

on the Nashville, Chattanooga & St. Louis line. Jasper's son Ned, born in 1933, came of age when Tracy City was no longer an active mining center; he currently works as a real-estate salesman in Murfreesboro. Ned is particularly interested in Grundy County history — much of it learned orally from his parents and early neighbors — and is intrigued by the possibility of developing a pioneer mining / railroad museum in now-depressed Tracy City.

In my visit with Ned Arbuckle, I ascertained that he had heard his father "recite" the "Lone Rock Mine Song" about 1956 or 1957, while telling his son stories of the old days. Jasper had not been a singer (Ned stated, "I had never heard him sing the National Anthem") and his son was surprised to hear this fragment.[30] On singing it for us, Ned switched the number of Captain Hargis' charges from fifty to a hundred. Ned was unsure of his father's "tune" for the two recited stanzas, but after he sang it from memory Hulan identified it as close to "It Ain't Gonna Rain No More." The tune for the chorus was that used in "Nine Pound Hammer" by Tennessee Ernie Ford, and it was so tagged by Ned.

It is possible that the word *roll*, which appeared in both "Roll Down the Line" and "Nine Pound Hammer," triggered Ned Arbuckle's association of the melody for his father's "Lone Rock Mine Song." It is my belief that Ned's chorus tune was somehow grafted onto the older music used by the Allen Brothers and previous con-

224

vict singers of "Roll Down the Line." However, I feel that this musical uncertainty is far less important than a consideration of the strong thematic association which ties the Grundy County fragment to the Library of Congress Memphis field recording previously treated. One key difference, of course, between the relatively full Memphis and fragmentary Lone Rock items is that the Hargis route was directly from the state penitentiary at Nashville to Tracy City. Further, the call for "healthy" men reemphasized the toll taken by the convict-lease system on life and limb. A dramatic footnote to Ned Arbuckle's recollection is that A. D. Hargis' son Joe "was a strong union man . . . who set off the fuse to the charge of dynamite that destroyed the [Tracy City] convict stockade" at the time of the troubles.[31] Throughout the southern highlands, when trade unionism reached the area, close-knit families divided in their loyalties and actions.

In my commenting on my visit with "Uncle Jesse" James's children I posed the question as to whether their father was the last singer to retain the "Lone Rock Song." A parallel question lies in the relationship of his piece to Arbuckle's "Ole Humpy" fragment. Intrigued by these problems, Dick and Kathy Hulan returned to Grundy County on October 23, 1970, where they were rewarded with an important "Humpy Hargis" bit recited by Mrs. Ethel Brown:

HUMPY HARGIS

See ol' Humpy Hargis,
Comin' 'cross the hill,
Put you in mind of a little boy
Goin' to the mill.

Aside: That was because of the hump on his back, you know, it looked like he was bent over carrying a sack of meal.

Goin' to the mill, boys,
Goin' to the mouth of the hole,
The very first words you hear him say,
"Boys, you better hit that coal."[32]

Mrs. Brown had been born at Tracy City in 1890 and had been married to a coal miner. One of her earliest memories was the excitement at the burning of the prison stockade (presumably the

225

```
┌─────────────────────────────────────────────┐
│                                             │
│              BY-LAWS                        │
│              ──OF──                         │
│                                             │
│         LOCAL UNION, 510,                   │
│                                             │
│       United Mine Workers                   │
│                                             │
│           of America.                       │
│                                             │
│         ────────                            │
│                                             │
│   TOGETHER WITH CONTRACT OF TENN. COAL,     │
│       IRON & RAILROAD COMPANY.              │
│                                             │
│         ────────                            │
│                                             │
│        Tracy City, Tenn.                    │
│                                             │
│         ────────                            │
│                                             │
│          Tracy City, Tenn.                  │
│          I. B. Woodward's Print.            │
│             —1901.—                         │
│                                             │
└─────────────────────────────────────────────┘
```

TITLE PAGE, LOCAL 510 BYLAWS

last one: April, 1893). For the Hulans she was unable to sing or chant the "Humpy Hargis" tune but suggested that she might play it on a piano.

The importance of this item, I feel, is in its close tie to "Uncle Jesse's" piece. Whereas Jasper Arbuckle's fragment echoes the Memphis prison song of 1933, Mrs. Brown's parallels closely the two opening stanzas of the "Lone Rock Song." The man in "Uncle Jesse's" song and Mrs. Brown's Hargis are both pejoratively likened to a little boy en route to a mill, and each makes a similar demand

226

to "gimme" or "hit" that coal. No one knows how many different themes were touched in all the Lone Rock convict songs, but it is remarkable that at least one citizen, born before the revolt of the Tracy City miners, still can recite in 1970 a stockade comment about a TCI official — "a hard master," universally disliked.

In her desire to help the Hulans, Mrs. Brown sent them to meet a retired Church of Christ preacher, Brother Bailey Brooks, at Palmer. Brooks, born in 1886, had started working in the Ramsey mines as a trapper boy. He knew Hargis ("Humpy had a long beard") and remembered that the convicts sang about him, but could not recollect the song. However, he did recall a particularly striking incident from the troubles — one that I had not encountered previously. When the Knights of Labor or free laborers turned out the convicts, the newly freed men had no trouble escaping "because the hollers were so wild they would get lost out there." To counter such escapes, the company had provided the convicts with heavy brogans "with tacks in the bottom that spelled TCI, TCI, TCI, every step they took. After the convicts were eliminated, the company store sold those shoes to the [free] miners and they wore them for years — they were good shoes."[33]

Conscious that folksong study is boundless, I nevertheless conclude my discussion of Lone Rock material with a portion of a letter forwarded to me by Herman Baggenstoss, publisher of the *Grundy County Herald*. In response to his printing of my letter of inquiry, Mrs. Charles (Ada Sewell) Hampton of Southgate, Michigan, generously offered an explanation of the phrase "roll down the line":

> My husband drove a mule in Lone Rock Mine at one time as he was growing up through the years you have mentioned [1890's]. He was a favorite driver with the convicts because he delivered the cars for their coal. So that they could get their number loaded. He was experienced in handling mules and also a born lover of horses and mules. He did not have the trouble that some of the other boys had with their mules that balked and kicked and reared and sometimes broke out of harness. Consequently the drivers could not deliver the number of cars the diggers had to load to escape punishment. My husband used to sing some of their songs for me but I have forgotten all of them but some lines of one. It went something like this. ("Roll on down the line boys.

DARLING ON THE LINE

Buddy won't you roll down the line, Yonder comes my darling a rolling down the line.") The line referred to the track through the entry and tunnels from which the rooms opened and my "darling" was the driver who delivered promptly. And was a favorite. Of course I can't give the tune but it was a simple easy going one. Just an expression of the convict who wanted to do as he was bidden. And didn't want to be known as a "slacker" and be punished.[34]

One is tempted to pursue these recollections of the TCI's Captain Hargis, TCI footprints made so long ago in Grundy County's "hollers," and favorite mule drivers, but the task of exploring the background of the Lone Rock's blues ballad still remains. During 1939 Charles Seeger had also collected a "Roll Down the Line," at Brevard Plantation, Adams Mill, near Columbia, South Carolina. The singers, Thaddeus Goodson and Belton Reese, used bones and banjo. I find their text impossible to transcribe; it sounds to me as if a whole minstrel troupe were turned loose in front of Seeger's microphone. Of course, just two men are droning the familiar chorus, with some interpolation of calls to each other or perhaps some interjection of nonsense syllables.

Peter Tamony has suggested that *scat* and *bop* are terms in the field of jazz to cover the verbalizations of such artists as Louis

Armstrong and John Birks "Dizzy" Gillespie on songs in which they distort actual words or sing vocables for the notes of musical scales.[35] I find the Goodson-Reese field recording close in spirit to Armstrong's "Heebie Jeebies" or Gillespie's "Salt Peanuts," but this may be a subjective response not shared by other listeners. Seeger himself never attempted a transcription nor could he recall hearing any facts about the song's background. All we know is that one of the singers closed the field recording by commenting that Tad and Belton had played "to the old country dances at the B'ard Plantation." Seeger had been taken to Brevard by E. C. Adams, a prominent Columbia resident, who encouraged Goodson and Reese with a jug of fine bourbon.[36] Perhaps the genii in the jug destroyed any coherent text, but, providentially, it may have offered a stylistic clue to the source of "Roll Down the Line's" melody and chorus: the minstrel stage.

I do not know under what circumstances this "roll" chorus and tune became attached to a Negro prison song in the Carolinas or Tennessee. Of the versions cited, only "Uncle Jesse's" and the two fragments about Hargis can be dated clearly to the era 1887-92; this does not necessarily mean that these are the oldest. If any data surfaces concerning the age of this song, it will probably stem from a study of the usage of the lyric commonplace, "I wish I was in Tracy City–Mobile–Ireland."

Patrick Weston Joyce's classic *Old Irish Folk Music and Songs* includes "The Irish Girl," sung by old people of Limerick when Joyce was a child. Almost all the many variants of this haunting song find a rejected lover wishing he were transformed into a flower, a bird, a butterfly; at times he consoles himself with the desire to drink, and at times he combines the transformation and the liquor motifs. A Missouri text reads:

> I wish I was in Ireland,
> A-sitting in a chair,
> In my hand a glass of wine,
> And by my side my love.
>
> I'd call for rum, for brandy and wine,
> And pay it as I'd go;
> I'd sail the deepest ocean,
> Let the wind blow high or low.[37]

Newfoundland and Nova Scotia versions place the wish in Dublin. However, a Tennessee version collected by Ruby Duncan transfers the fantasy site from the Emerald Isle to the mouth of the Mississippi:

THE IRISH GIRL

I stepped out one morning
Down by the riverside;
I cast my eyes all around me,
That blue-eyed girl I spied.

So red and rosy were her cheeks,
And yellow was her hair,
How costly was the jewelry
That blue-eyed girl did wear.

Tears came rolling down her cheeks,
How mournful she did cry:
"My love has gone and left me,
And surely I will die."

Love, it is a killing thing
Did you ever feel the pang?
How hard it is to be in love
And can't be loved again.

I wish I were in New Orleans,
A-sitting in my chair,
A glass of brandy in my hand,
My arms around my dear.

I'd wish for whisky, Roman wine,
I'd drink before I'd go;
I'd sail through the deepest ocean,
Let the wind blow high or low.[38]

This New World localization of "The Irish Girl" seemingly contributed to a very widespread American lyric and frolic complex, known as "Bowling Green" or "Shady Grove," to name but two titles. A North Carolina example is:

I wish I was in Tennessee
A sittin' in my chair,
One arm round a whisky keg
"Tother round my dear.

> If I had a scolding wife
> I'd beat her shore's you're born;
> I'd take her down to New Orleans
> And trade her off for corn.[39]

It is these latter stanzas, with their frontier switch from a wine glass to a whiskey keg, and the brag of wife beating and trading, which probably provide the key to the movement of the lover's wish from "The Irish Girl" into black-face minstrel repertoires. The North Carolina stanzas were contributed to Frank C. Brown as part of an antebellum minstrel song, "The Gal from the South," popularly called "Massa Had a Yaller Gal." The "Gal" appeared in printed songsters of the 1850's, and for a century was found in Afro and Anglo tradition, mixed with old forms of "The Derby Ram" as well as coon-song stereotypes such as "Who Broke the Lock on the Henhouse Door."

I do not know exactly how the "wish I was in Ireland" commonplace was mixed into the "Yaller Gal" conglomerate, but I suspect that the stanza made its shift when the rollicking roll-down-the-line chorus also appeared on the minstrel stage. This hunch is unsupported by a textual or melodic example of the chorus in a printed minstrel songster. However, I feel it wiser to advance a hypothesis at this stage than to offer no alternative account of "Roll Down the Line's" development. Certainly, the "wish" stanza and "roll" chorus must have been united before the TCI leased convicts for its Lone Rock mine. Specifically, I suggest that the given melody and chorus transcribed for this case study were available to a black miner around 1890 who desired to sing about his condition and, particularly, to memorialize a respected fellow worker, Charlie Medlick.

"Uncle Jesse" preserved in the "Lone Rock Song" one form of the blues ballad which marked Medlick's death. The Allen Brothers apparently retained only a fragment of his song, but Uncle Dave Macon used its outline to fashion a humorous commentary on Tennessee's convict-lease system. Chance circumstance gave Macon's number a far longer lease on life than the Allens'. The precise reason for the selection of the Macon item for inclusion in *American Folk Music,* a Folkways anthology of race and hillbilly reissued discs, is unknown to me. Curiously, editor Harry Smith

231

MINSTREL SONGBOOK

identified "Buddy" as a work song or one "structurally adapted to responsive chanting by gang workers."[40] Pete Seeger must be credited with correctly relating Macon's ballad to George Korson's story of the Coal Creek rebellion as well as to James Dombrowski's unpublished research in "Fire in the Hole." Seeger also offered the ballad to a new and wide audience to whom Macon was, at best, a droll ancestor figure of totemistic import.

From Lou Gottlieb, a member of two successful "folksong revival" groups, the Gateway Singers and the Limeliters, I obtained a specific illustration of the entrance path of a hillbilly song into the popular-music idiom of the 1950's and 1960's.[41] Gottlieb, while working toward an advanced degree in musicology at the University of California, had listened to the Folkways anthology shortly after its 1952 release. "Buddy Won't You Roll Down the Line" made no conscious impression on a first listening, but when Seeger transcribed the Macon song for *Sing Out* (1955), Gottlieb picked out its melody on the piano. Finding it provocative, he returned to the Folkways set and transcribed Macon's number for possible use by the Gateway Singers at the Hungry I, a San Francisco nightclub. This "folk" quartet used Macon's ballad frequently at the "I," and recorded the song for Decca during 1957 in Hollywood.

In its formative years, the Kingston Trio played at San Francisco's Purple Onion, literally across the street from the Hungry I, and picked up songs and stylistic pointers from the Gateway Singers. During 1960 the Trio recorded for Capitol in Hollywood its own "Buddy Better Get on Down the Line," but departed considerably from the Macon piece, to which Seeger and Gottlieb had been faithful. Even though the Kingston Trio's rendition of "Buddy" did not become a hit, as did its hillbilly-derived "Tom Dooley," the inclusion of "Buddy" on a popular LP automatically meant that it reached a wider audience than all the other discs mentioned in this case study. I place no special virtue in mass-circulation figures, and detail these events only as an account of how one coal-mining song became grist in the popular-culture mill.[42]

Perhaps the simplest conclusion to draw from this sequence is that of the audience message inherent in "Roll Down the Line." We can assume that the Lone Rock convict who first sang about Charlie Medlick's death was fully understood by his peers. Likewise, "Uncle Jesse" James, singing about black convicts, was comprehended by his family and neighbors. Stevens' and Watts's numbers were true or powerful songs to Asheville and Belmont vagrants on chain gangs. Pete Seeger, reaching urban audiences in the 1950's, always prefaced "Buddy" with a good historical introduction, which was fortuitously recorded at Carnegie Hall. The Gateway Singers, even for nightclub listeners, featured Macon's ballad as "a protest from the coal mines in the South." The Kingston Trio's LP con-

233

taining "Buddy" offered no formulaic tag whatsoever to frame its diffuse reworking of Macon's text and tune.

During the 1960's only a few folksong buffs in the Kingston Trio's audience recognized that "Buddy" derived from a convict-lease blues ballad fashioned on the Cumberland Plateau about 1890. Similarly, only a few jazz buffs after 1915 had recognized that W. C. Handy's "Joe Turner Blues" derived from a folk blues about Tennessee convict transportation in the 1890's. Handy was able to explain his shifts to folklorist Dorothy Scarborough. We do not know whether a poplorist will emerge to question the Kingston Trio's Dave Guard on his reworking of "Roll Down the Line." It may well be that in a few decades the Kingston Trio will fade into the kind of obscurity which now surrounds Watts and Wilson and the Allen Brothers. Possibly we shall never learn what "Roll" meant to Dave Guard or the Trio's extremely large audience. Regardless of whether or not we obtain this knowledge, regardless of how society treats folk and popular entertainers, and regardless of the self-perception of such figures, their recordings retain an impersonal objectivity as cultural and historical benchmarks. "Roll Down the Line," on any listener's turntable, remains both a document of an oppressive form of labor and a specific response by some convicts to the human condition.

1. Dorothy Scarborough, "The 'Blues' as Folk-Songs," in *Publications of the Texas Folk-Lore Society*, no. II, ed. J. Frank Dobie (Austin, 1923), 52. Revised in Scarborough, *On the Trail of Negro Folk-Songs* (Cambridge, Mass., 1925). For William C. Handy on "Joe Turner Blues" see his *Blues: An Anthology* (New York, 1926), 40, 79, and *Father of the Blues* (New York, 1941), 145.
2. *Cumberland Chronicle* [Huntsville, Scott County, Tenn.] (Apr. 5, 1890).
3. Abbe Niles, Introduction, in *Blues: An Anthology*, ed. William C. Handy (New York, 1926), 41. A Mississippi localization of "Joe Turner Blues," with commentary, is found in William Broonzy, *Big Bill Blues* (New York, 1964), 53.
4. "Old Time Tune Artists Given Test Recordings," *Talking Machine World*, XXI (Oct., 1925), 71.
5. This text is collated from both Gordon's 1925 typescript and his printing of Stevens' song in "Folksongs of America: Jail Ballads," *New York Times Magazine* (June 19, 1927), 15. There are slight differences in the two texts. See also the mimeographed book compiled from Gordon's *Times* articles, *Folk-Songs of America* (New York, 1938), 50.

6. Marina Bokelman, "The Coon Can Game: A Blues Ballad Tradition" (master's thesis, University of California, Los Angeles, 1968).

7. Fletcher Melvin Green, "Some Aspects of the Convict Lease System in the United States," in *Essays in Southern History,* ed. F. M. Green (Chapel Hill, N.C., 1949), 122.

8. Carl Lee Freshour interview with Malcolm Blackard, Belmont, N.C., June, 1966. Data in Blackard letter to me, July 18, 1966.

9. Malcolm Blackard has transcribed fourteen song texts in "Wilmer Watts and the Lonely Eagles," *JEMF Quarterly,* V (Winter, 1969), 126.

10. Hoeptner letter to me, July 21, 1959. Recently Lee Allen was located. See Donald Lee Nelson, "The Great Allen Brothers Search," *JEMF Quarterly,* VII (Autumn, 1971), 126.

11. Frank Walker interview with Mike Seeger and John Cohen, June 19, 1962, tape copy in my files. See also John Cohen and Mike Seeger, *The New Lost City Ramblers Song Book* (New York, 1964), 29.

12. "A Man with Staying Power," *The Southern Patriot,* XXI (Nov., 1963), and "Dombrowski Retires as SCEF Executive," *ibid.,* XXIV (Feb., 1966). See also H. Glyn Thomas, "The Highlander Folk School," *Tennessee Historical Quarterly,* XXIII (1964), 358.

13. "Lone Rock Song" in its first form is found in James Dombrowski, original field notes and interviews for "Fire in the Hole." A retyped copy is deposited in the "Zilphia Horton Folk Music Collection," Tennessee State Library and Archives, Nashville. Still another copy is used in the "Fire in the Hole" manuscript, 64.

14. Interview with Mrs. Sarah L. Cleek, Laager, Tenn., July 28, 1938, with Mr. Thompson, Tracy City, Tenn., July 5, 1938, with I. H. Cannon, Tracy City, Mar. 28, 1937, all three in Dombrowski, original field notes. . . .

15. In lieu of a Grundy County local history I have used Gilbert E. Govan and James W. Livingood, *The Chattanooga Country: 1540-1951* (New York, 1952), supplemented by typescript prepared by Mrs. Marean Crabtree, Tracy City (Jan., 1969), in my files.

16. Colyar's remarks in *Nashville Daily American* (Oct. 18, 1876), paraphrased in Constantine G. Belissary, "Behavior Patterns and Aspirations of the Urban Working Classes in Tennessee in the Immediate Post–Civil War Era," *Tennessee Historical Quarterly,* XIV (1955), 38.

17. *Annual Report of the Tennessee Coal, Iron & Railroad Company for the Fiscal Year Ending January 31, 1893* (Nashville, 1893), 4.

18. Facts are mainly from Ethel Armes, *The Story of Coal and Iron in Alabama* (Birmingham, 1910). For additional reference see footnote 12 in the previous chapter.

19. *Annual Report* . . . (1891), 20; (1892), 13.

20. Edward T. Luther letter to me, Nov. 25, 1968. A map of Tracy City mines showing East Fork and Reid Hill (close to Lone Rock) appears in Wilbur A. Nelson, *The Southern Tennessee Coal Field* (Nashville, 1925), 118.

21. Harry S. Avery letter to me, Oct. 4, 1968.

22. TCI records are not presently housed in a designated archive nor does the name Charlie Medlick appear in available documents. Letters to me from H. E. Conrad, Fairfield, Ala., Oct. 30 and Nov. 20, 1970.

23. Interviews, Oct. 10, 1970, supplemented by subsequent correspondence. Mrs. Roberts gives the variant spelling Eli and James's birth and death dates: Dec. 16, 1873–Mar. 10, 1963.

24. Pete Seeger, "The Coal Creek Rebellion," *Sing Out,* V (Summer, 1955), 19.

25. See, for example, William R. McDaniel, *Grand Ole Opry* (New York, 1952). Other sketches are found in Robert Shelton and Burt Goldblatt, *The Country Music Story* (Indianapolis, 1966), and Bill C. Malone, *Country Music, U.S.A.: A Fifty-Year History* (Austin, Tex., 1968). See also Ralph Rinzler and Norman Cohen, *Uncle Dave Macon: A Bio-Discography* (Los Angeles, 1970).

26. Interviews, Aug. 5, 1961.

27. Interview, Aug. 30, 1961.

28. Copies of Lomax holograph manuscript and typescript transcription of Library of Congress field disc 174 are in my files.

29. Holograph manuscript (received Dec. 31, 1968), in my files.

30. Interview, Oct. 10, 1970.

31. Interview with Jake Hargis, Laager, Tenn., Feb., 1937, in Dombrowski, original field notes. . . .

32. Data on Mrs. Brown in Hulan letter to me, Oct. 24, 1970.

33. Data on Brooks in Hulan letter to me, Oct. 24, 1970.

34. Hampton letter to me, Jan. 24, 1971.

35. Peter Tamony, "Bop: The Word," *Jazz,* I (Spring, 1959), 114.

36. Mike Seeger letter to me, Sept. 15, 1968, supplemented by interview with Charles Seeger, Nov. 25, 1968.

37. Henry M. Belden, *Ballads and Songs Collected by the Missouri Folk-Lore Society* (Columbia, 1940), 292. Belden cites nine additional "Irish Girl" texts.

38. Elisabeth B. Greenleaf, *Ballads and Sea Songs of Newfoundland* (Cambridge, Mass., 1933), 198; Helen Creighton, *Songs and Ballads from Nova Scotia* (Toronto, 1933), 175; Ruby Duncan, "Ballads and Folk Songs Collected in Northern Hamilton County" (master's thesis, University of Tennessee, Knoxville, 1939), 310.

39. *The Frank C. Brown Collection of North Carolina Folklore,* III (Durham, 1952), 487.

40. Harry Smith, brochure notes to *American Folk Music* (Folkways FA 2953-55).

41. Interview, Apr. 15, 1958.

42. I cite one item only on the Kingston Trio's show-business role: "Fourth Man Makes the Trio Tick," *Business Week* (Feb. 23, 1963), 57.

CHECKLIST FOUR

"Convict Song." William H. Stevens, Biltmore, N.C., Nov. 16, 1925. Robert W. Gordon, Gordon Collection N.C., record AFS A-107.
Transcribed: Gordon Collection N.C., typescript AFS 159.
Reprinted: *NYTM* (June 19, 1927), 20. Song untitled. Also reprinted in mimeographed book of Gordon's *Times* articles, *F S A* (1938), 50.

"Chain Gang Special." Watts and Wilson, Paramount 3019 (4432). Mar., 1927, Chicago. Parallel issue: Weaver and Wiggins, Broadway 8114.
Transcribed: Blackard, *J E M F Q*, V (1969), 126.

"Buddy Won't You Roll Down the Line." Uncle Dave Macon, Brunswick 292 (C 2127). July 25, 1928, Chicago. Macon, banjo; Sam McGee, banjo-guitar.
Reissued: *American Folk Music,* Folkways FA 2953.
Transcribed: *Sing Out,* V (Summer, 1955), 19, m. Prefaced by Pete Seeger article, "The Coal Creek Rebellion." Also in *Reprints from Sing Out,* 3 (1961), 33, m.
Reprinted: Foner, *H L M U S* (1955), 219. First stanza of text only.
Transcribed: Cohen and Seeger, *N L C R S B* (1964), 220, m. Macon disc, music transcribed by Hally Wood.
———. Pete Seeger, *American Industrial Ballads,* Folkways FH 5251. June, 1956, New York. Brochure includes text and headnote.
———. The Gateway Singers, *The Gateway Singers at the Hungry I,* Decca DL 8671. Apr., 1957, Hollywood. Lou Gottlieb, bass; Jerry Walter, banjo; Travis Edmonson, guitar; Elmerlee Thomas, vocal.
———. Pete Seeger, *Pete Seeger and Sonny Terry,* Folkways FA 2412. Dec. 27, 1957, New York. Brochure includes text and transcribed spoken introduction to song at Carnegie Hall concert.
———. Pete Seeger, Highlander Folk School, Monteagle, Tenn., ca. 1957. A Seeger concert tape, includes song and spoken introduction. This Macon item is identified as "Lone Rock Song" in the "Zilphia Horton Folk Music Collection," Tennessee State Library and Archives, Nashville.
——— ("Buddy Better Get on Down the Line"). Kingston Trio, *String Along,* Capitol T 1407. Apr. 21, 1960, Hollywood. Dave Guard, banjo; Nick Reynolds, guitar; Bob Shane, guitar. Very freely arranged.
Reissued: *A Tribute to the Kingston Trio,* Capitol T 20922 (England).
———. Rooftop Singers, *Rainy River,* Vanguard VRS 9190. 1967, New York. Parallel issue: Fontana TFL 6065 (England).
———. Hedy West, *Serves Em Fine,* Fontana STL 5432. 1968, London, England.

"Roll Down the Line." Allen Brothers, Victor 23551 (62993). Nov. 22, 1930, Memphis.
Reissued: Bluebird 6148; released 1935.
———. Austin Allen, Southern Music Publishing Company, New York (May 23,

1931), E 40344. Coypright renewed: Peer International Corporation, New York (May 23, 1958), R 215545.

"Hey Buddy, Won't You Roll Down the Line." Allen Brothers, Vocalion 02818 (16111). Oct. 5, 1934, New York.

"Rollin' Down the Line." Negro prisoners, Memphis, 1933. John and Alan Lomax, AFS 174.

Transcribed: Lomax holograph manuscript and typescript AFS.

"Lone Rock Song." William Ely James, Palmer, Tenn., Mar. 27, 1937. James Dombrowski, typescript, Tuskegee Institute, Tuskegee, Ala. Original field notes and interviews for "Fire in the Hole."

Copy: "Zilphia Horton Folk Music Collection," Tennessee State Library and Archives, Nashville.

"Roll Down the Line." Thaddeus Goodson and Belton Reece, Brevard Plantation, Adams Mill near Columbia, S.C., 1939. Charles Seeger, AFS 3792. Goodson, bones; Reece, banjo.

"Lone Rock Mine Song." Ned C. Arbuckle, Tracy City, Tenn., Dec. 26, 1968. Holograph manuscript, Green files.

Recorded: Tracy City, Oct. 10, 1970. Green tape files.

"Humpy Hargis." Mrs. Ethel Brown, Tracy City, Tenn., Oct. 23, 1970. Richard Hulan, typescript, Green files.

APPENDIX FOUR

JAMES DOMBROWSKI'S INTERVIEW NOTES

William Ely James ("Uncle Jesse James") 3-27-37, Palmer, Tennessee, 66 years of age, gave me the Lone Rock convict song.

This morning Teffie [Ralph B. Tefferteller] and I drove over to Palmer 20 miles away in the north end of Grundy County. Leaving the main highway about 10 miles north of Tracy City, you go east on a gravel dusty road that stretches straight before you for another 10 miles. Passing through Greutli, known by the sign on a roadside cabin, and Henley's Switch, a store, there is nothing more but fine woods, plenty of pine and an occasional cabin, and church until you come to the mining village of Palmer. Drab, unpainted cabins, in sharp contrast to the beautiful white house of the superintendent. His wife is president of the garden club. But miners' wives do not have the time or the money to go in for landscaping on the scale enjoyed by the superintendent's family. Just before coming to the company store you turn sharp left and continue to the Miners Hall, a large bare room over a store. It is cold. We ascend the dark stairway and knock. The warden says for us to remain downstairs until the local business is over. A late comer passes us, whispers the pass word in the ear of the warden and is admitted. We sit around the stove in the store below until a messenger asks [us] to come above. We are asked to speak. We talk about the HFS [Highlander Folk School], the CIO campaign in the South, the April 1st rally in Palmer. There are questions about the recent broadcast, [BBC, January, 1937], do we endorse John L. Lewis, there has been some criticism recently of Brother Ross, president of Local 5881 and Brother Cheeck, member of the Grievance Committee, for their visit to the school. There is a great deal of interest in the recent broadcast. Following the meeting old Uncle Jesse James gives us some "dots" on the early days in the miners' struggle for a union. He is a small, explosive, little man, small head, flashing black eyes, talks quickly and with lots of gestures. Now 66 years of age. Started to work in the mines of Grundy County on January 20, 1890. Outside of strikes and lockouts has worked in the mines ever since. "I worked five days this week. Yesterday I loaded 5 cars. (? tons) For 47 years I have worked in artificial light. My eyes are not so good close up. But I've a squirrel rifle at home. And Buddy if you put a cross on a stick at 80 yards, and I don't hit it, you'll know I'm a hittin' right around it. I've worked in the saw mills, cut timber, in the mines, and I've never scabbed yet, and (hitting Teffie a blow on the shoulder for emphasis) by God I'll never be a scab if I go to hell for it. Organized labor brought switches instead of tables (turning tables when the men had to use a stick for a lever to turn the cars by hand) it brought them iron tracks, instead of wood, it brought *freedom*. It used to be that I was told, 'If you don't like your job, leave it,' but they can't do it now. No sir! I've seen it [the union] come, and I've seen it go; I've seen it come, and I've seen it go; I've seen it come agin, and I've seen it go agin; and now I've seen it come, and if it goes, I'll help to bring it agin."

BREAKER BOYS

Mother Jones 7

WITHIN THE American language, the term *labor song* is employed at two levels: broadly to include all items which flow from work; narrowly to cover only pieces which comment on unionism as a socioeconomic movement. It has not been difficult for scholars to accept as folksongs such diverse work chants as "Reuben Ranzo" and "Lining Track" or such dramatic occupational ballads as "The Jam on Gerry's Rock" and "Little Joe the Wrangler." However, it has been quite difficult for many folklorists to cope with the specific song lore of unionism. Trade-union pieces are present in good number in accessible popular anthologies (cited in my bibliography) edited by Edith Fowke and Joe Glazer, Waldemar Hille, Alan Lomax, Irwin Silber, and others. Their books, in the main, are more concerned with presenting songs than with theoretical formulations about included items.

Only John Greenway in *American Folksongs of Protest* moved beyond a standard collection in his attempt to stretch formal definitions to cover considerable topical and polemical material. Greenway's book received a mixed reaction from his peers. The eminent folk-tale scholar Stith Thompson wrote: "Here is a book called *American Folksongs* which contains not a single example of what a competent folklorist would call by that name. Folksongs are songs that are traditional, that are handed down from singer to listener, and that are still alive. The songs in this collection are not anonymous and most of them are dead, preserved only in museums. They are not and never were folksongs."[1]

Thompson's succinct definition is useful; his rejection of Greenway's selections may be questioned. In 1953 what was called for by Greenway's provocative book was an intense and careful application of Thompson's criteria to given songs, as well as an attempt to frame new queries about the folkloric role of modern social institutions. For example, was the labor movement in the United States to some degree a folk-like association — a *quasi-folk society* in Robert Redfield's language — capable of nurturing and sustaining traditional material? Did labor songs in fact live in tradition for any length of time? Were union members or their leaders concerned that the public image of their movement be colored by folklore? These rhetorical questions were hardly raised, let alone pondered, within the labor movement, even in the decades when knowledge of folklore as a discipline seeped out of the academy. Only George Korson, of all American collectors, had official union support in his field investigations. Today it is extremely difficult to speculate on the future attention by unionists to their lore. Not all groups are able to cope with folklore, any more than are all individuals who have crossed ethnic or cultural barriers able to handle their former traditions. A part of the price paid by a people for social mobility is a concomitant loss or transformation of symbolic language and expressive forms.

My case study of "The Death of Mother Jones," one of Greenway's inclusions, is in part a response to Thompson's allegation that *American Folksongs of Protest* "contains not a single example" of a folksong. Also, I present and contrast two commercial recordings which hold in their physical grooves the memory of a charismatic woman — one of the few American unionists around whom a body of legend actually clustered.

Mary Harris was born on May 1, 1830, in Cork County, Ireland, long before May Day was proclaimed an international radical holiday. Her family history was that of the fight for Ireland's freedom, but poverty determined that she would play her role in the United States. Richard Harris, her father, left the old country in 1835 to work on American and Canadian railway-construction

MOTHER JONES

gangs. After a childhood in Toronto, Mary worked as a seamstress and convent-school teacher in various communities in the United States. In 1861 she married Frank Jones, an iron molder at Memphis, Tennessee. During the yellow fever epidemic of 1876 she lost her husband and four youngsters; for the rest of her years "Mother Jones" devoted herself to countless "adopted children" in mine and mill, factory and sweatshop.

Her formal connection with the Knights of Labor began shortly after the Chicago Fire of 1871. Thereafter her life illustrated the dramatic scenes in a labor-history chronology. If she were not actually present at a bloody strike, she hastened to the scene to marshal support by challenging injunction-granting judges and by going to jail for her cause. She participated in the turbulent Baltimore & Ohio strike (Pittsburgh, 1877), Chicago's Haymarket

243

Riot (1886), the Pullman strike (Birmingham, 1894), the great Pennsylvania anthracite strike (1902), the Chicago founding convention of the Industrial Workers of the World (1905), the Ludlow, Colorado, massacre (1913), and, finally, the nationwide steel strike (1919). Mother Jones never retired to inactivity; rather, old age itself kept her away from picket line and prison cell.

The *Autobiography of Mother Jones* was edited by her friend Mary Field Parton and issued in 1925 by the socialist publisher Charles H. Kerr. Clarence Darrow introduced the book with an insightful view of Mother Jones's crusading individualism — a conviction not often perceived in supposed collectivists. The highly impressionistic *Autobiography* was strong on color and weak on ideology. It revealed that sentimentality and socialism, passion and philosophy, innocence and invective were equally mixed in one personality. Beyond fighting literally for bread and milk for her "children," Mother Jones also involved herself in the labor movement's ever-present internal political wars, generally favoring rank-and-file activists against established leaders. Even while bed-ridden in her declining years, she spoke out for various factionalists among the strife-torn miners' unions of the late 1920's.

Nearly a decade before her death, a *Nation* correspondent had nominated Mother Jones as one of the twelve greatest women in the United States, and stated that "her life is an epic and it is the shame of America's writers that it has never been told."[2] To this day, aside from the *Autobiography*, we have no scholarly published account of her full activities, although she was not overlooked in her lifetime. Her exploits and rhetoric are scattered in a thousand publications, from legalistic congressional hearings to fragile strike handbills. The best single gathering and overview of such material is found in Judith Mikeal's University of North Carolina thesis, "Mother Mary Jones."[3] Miss Mikeal, fortunately, supplemented historical research by interviews with her father, a Carbon, West Virginia, coal miner and veteran of the Cabin Creek labor struggles.

Following Mother Jones's death in her hundredth year (November 30, 1930) at Hyattsville, Maryland, her casket was carried from Washington, D.C., to Mt. Olive, Illinois, for burial in the Union Miners' Cemetery. This long train trip echoed Lincoln's final return from the nation's capital to Springfield. Mother Jones had

Funeral Notice

Entered Into Rest, at Silver Grove, Maryland, Sunday,
November 30, 1930, at 11.55 p. m.

Mother Jones

Aged 100 Years, 6 Months and 30 Days

The body will arrive in Mt. Olive, Ill., on the Wabash
R. R. at 7:37 p. m. Thursday, Dec. 4, 1930, and will
lie in state until Monday morning at the Odd Fellows Temple, where Rev. Father McGuire, of
Kankakee, President of St. Viator College,
will deliver a Panegyric on Sunday
afternoon at 2:00 o'clock.

Funeral services will be conducted Monday morning,
December 8, 1930, at 10 o'clock at the Church of
the Ascension, by Rev. Father McGuire, assisted by Rev. Father Hogan and
Rev. Father Knaperek.

Interment Mt. Olive Union Miners' Cemetery.

All members and friends of organized labor
invited to attend.

FUNERAL NOTICE

requested that her remains be placed alongside the graves of the
Virden Martyrs — four coal miners who were shot during a strike
in 1898. The site also contained the grave of "General" Alexander
Bradley, an English-born organizer in the Illinois coal fields known
for his picaresque life and naive devotion to his fellows. It is an
ironic commentary on American unionism that a rural cemetery in
Macoupin County, Illinois — a hallowed labor shrine — has been
maintained for three decades by a handful of Progressive Mine
Workers, the last band of dual unionists who had fought bitterly in
the 1930's against the United Mine Workers of America.[4]

In my view there is some connection between the obscurity of
Mother Jones's resting place, the status of her hardly remembered
memorial song, and the labor movement's attitude toward folklore.
I shall use this chapter to explore such connections, and shall pref-

245

ace my remarks with a few brief portraits of Mother Jones by her contemporaries. Marlen Pew, the editor of *Editor & Publisher,* identified himself as a young reporter who had covered coal-field strikes at the turn of the century. For many years after his initial meeting with Mother Jones, she used to drop into his New York office "for a bit of gossip and perhaps a couple of dollars if she chanced to be broke." Pew's sketch of the organizer, written immediately after her death, is representative of many similar portraits:

> She was then [anthracite strike of 1902] nearly 70 years of age, with figure so slight that I doubt if she would weigh 100 pounds, hair white as snow and skin deeply lined with criss-cross wrinkles. But her little blue eyes, deep-set and sparkling, told of mental vigor and dauntless zeal. Sometimes a torrent of harsh language would flow from the mouth of this old woman, in strange contrast to her general appearance which was that of a grandmother, wearing a shabby watered-silk dress to which bits of lace were pinned, with a tiny black bonnet stuck up the back of her head. Mother Jones was intelligent, but in speaking to a crowd would often spoil her argument by raving. When she was among friends and with plenty of time to spare she could regale you with astonishing stories, smacking of Irish wit and invariably carrying a point which illustrated her contempt of rich and comfort-loving people who consciously or unconsciously prey on the weak and poor.[5]

Although Mother Jones's natural setting was a mine camp or a mill town, she could also comport herself in high society. At one time she organized a march of a hundred young pottery workers in Trenton, New Jersey, for a call on President Theodore Roosevelt's summer home at Long Island's Oyster Bay. Upon learning that former President Grover Cleveland lived in Princeton, she had her boys detour in order to camp on his lawn, and induced Mr. Cleveland to feed the lads in the morning. During 1915, Mother Jones visited a well-to-do family of "exploiters" to ask for funds in support of her "brothers of the mine and lumber camp." Addressing her host and hostess as "comrades," she regaled them with tales of industrial life. Her hostess remained anonymous but set down her impressions:

> Are her tales all true? In a sense, yes; undoubtedly she believes every word she speaks. But upon reflection you conclude that life can never have moved so dramatically as in her narration. These stories have

been told by her again and again with propagandist intent. Cumbering details have been suppressed, and telling points have multiplied. To Mother Jones truth is not a photograph; it is something that lives, but above all, something that stirs.

The world Mother Jones sets before you is one of mercilessly oppressed workers quartered in company villages, cheated in company stores, robbed in company gambling halls, arrested and sentenced by company police and company judges whose cruelty and injustice are glossed over by company preachers and explained away by company newspapers. And in distant cities, full-fed beasts of prey, scheming at ease, heap up the spoils of exploitation, or lay them at the feet of perfumed and bejeweled women, arch-parasites upon the blood of the poor. This is the "System." And to Mother Jones the System is characteristic of all modern industrialism. Either it must be destroyed or it will destroy mankind.

Not that Mother Jones attempts to set forth the System in bald analysis. Her method is narrative; she pictures for you the bull pens of Colorado where men and women not charged with crime were herded in stockades without cover and without screen, in shameless disregard of the most elementary decencies of civilized life. She introduces you to fine, manly young fellows, fit material for leadership, goaded into resistance and mercilessly shot down. Whether you believe her or not, your blood begins to boil as you listen.[6]

Mother Jones's patrician "comrade" viewed her sympathetically; this same empathy was felt by countless workers. During 1912-13 Mother Jones participated in the violent industrial disputes at the Paint and Cabin Creek coal fields in West Virginia. This long strike was marked by the murder of miners, as well as their women and children, by gun thugs and private Baldwin-Felts detectives. Mother Jones witnessed the birth and death of babies in improvised tent colonies established to house evicted strikers. At a Charleston mass meeting she harangued the audience: "You have it inscribed on the steps of your capitol, 'Mountaineers are free' [*Montani semper liberi*]. God Almighty, men, go down through this nation and see the damnable, infamous condition that is there. In no nation of the world will you find such a condition." Following the bloody Logan County strike of 1923, Mother Jones poured out her accumulated love and bitterness at West Virginia: "Medieval West Virginia! With its tent colonies on the bleak hills! With its grim men and women! When I get to the other side I shall tell God Almighty about West Virginia."[7] Not only did the mountain state's labor strife impel Mother Jones to talk to the Lord, but the Paint and Cabin Creek atrocities also inspired some of unionism's most tormented poetry, as well as its anthem "Solidarity Forever." Ralph Chaplin's poems, gathered in *When the Leaves Come Out*, complement Mother Jones's invective and turn some of her passion into literature.[8]

A Fairmont, West Virginia, coal miner and carpenter, William M. Rogers, served as president of his state's federation of labor during 1917-20. To close his report at the group's Thirteenth Convention, he recited an untitled poem on Mother Jones.[9] Needless to say, it was applauded by the delegates, many of whom had walked with their feminine organizer over narrow trails to reach isolated camps. Rogers' piece is typical of many poems for Mother Jones in labor journals of the day, which I have listed in Appendix Five. Like them, it stands as an example of folk poetry, unaided by music, without life in tradition:

> The patriotic soldiers came marching down the pike,
> Prepared to shoot and slaughter in the Colorado strike;
> With whiskey in their bellies and vengeance in their souls,
> They prayed that God would help them shoot the miners full of holes.
>
> In front of these brave soldiers loomed a sight you seldom see —
> A white-haired rebel woman whose age was eighty-three.
> "Charge!" cried the valiant captain, in awful thunder tones,
> And the patriotic soldiers "CHARGED" and captured Mother Jones!
>
> 'Tis great to be a soldier with a musket in your hand,
> Ready for any bloody work the lords of earth command.
> 'Tis great to shoot a miner and hear his dying groans,
> But never was such glory as that "charge" on Mother Jones!

Early in the century, the Colorado union historian Emma Langdon penned an effusive testimonial to Mother Jones: "What Holy memories cluster around the woman Re-Christened Mother in the hearts of the workers of the new world. . . . Let no granite shaft rest on her, but let the flowers tell the sweetness of her life and prattling children, wrested from mine and mill and given back to childhood's joys sing her praise."[10] Could anyone have anticipated that Mother Jones would eventually have a granite shaft and a song of praise, too? We do not know who among Mother Jones's "children" expressed grief at her death and composed a simple elegy characteristic of the hillbilly rhetoric of the period. Whether it was, literally, someone wrested from mine or mill or perhaps a professional bard employed in the music industry we may never know. One expects mystery in songs of bygone ages, but "The Death of Mother Jones" can be no older than November 30, 1930. We can pick up its threads on February 21, 1931, the day when Gene Autry recorded the piece in the American Record Corporation's New York studio.

At that time, Autry had not emerged yet as a popular-culture idol for young Americans. His rise began in 1932, when one of his recordings, "That Silver Haired Daddy of Mine," started its climb toward a five million sales figure. This disc led to subsequent cinema and television fame. Before his first hit, Autry was but one of many talented westerners making the transition from folksinger to mass-media entertainer. The 1920's saw the discovery by the commercial entertainment industry of cowboy recording figures, from the now-forgotten pioneer Charles Nabell through remembered traditional performers such as Carl Sprague, Jules Allen, and Harry McClintock. Legend has it that Autry was inspired to a public career after Will Rogers heard this young railroad telegrapher playing his guitar and singing ballads to while away the lonely nights in the Chelsea, Oklahoma, depot. Rogers urged Gene to leave the Morse key behind and go east.[11] Actually, Autry had already picked up a glimmer of show-business life as a teenage busker, when he worked briefly for the Fields Brothers Medicine Show in rural Texas.

When Autry recorded "The Death of Mother Jones," he accompanied himself on the guitar in a simple manner already fixed as appropriate for cowboy balladry. Wilber Ball, a Kentuckian, seconded him on the Hawaiian steel guitar. Similarly, Autry's vocal delivery — straightforward and unornamented — was close to the traditional music he had heard in his Tioga (Grayson County), Texas, childhood. Whether or not Autry had a special association with Mother Jones as a labor unionist is unknown to me. Railroad telegraphers in the 1920's were generally organized and worked closely with other operating and maintenance craftsmen, also in

249

GENE AUTRY

unions. The Frisco (St. Louis–San Francisco Railway Company) ran directly through Oklahoma's coal-producing counties. Autry worked up and down the line and could hardly have avoided contact with organized coal miners. Little has been written of Autry's formative years which might suggest a clue to labor-oriented values or a special feeling for Mother Jones.

I queried Autry about "The Death of Mother Jones" but learned only that he obtained the song from his A & R man, William R. Calaway, a Boone, North Carolina, native.[12] Shortly after the recording session, Calaway mailed the song — unpublished manuscript and simple musical lead sheet — to the Library of Congress Copyright Office. It was registered (E 36010) on March 9, 1931, in Calaway's name, but never published in sheet-music or

250

song-folio form. Legally, Calaway was the song's author and owner, but it is wise to question the compositional claim of any talent scout.

My curiosity about Calaway's role was stimulated upon first hearing Gene Autry's disc in 1957 and finding the A & R man's name listed as composer on the label. However, Calaway, who died in 1949, had not been interviewed by any folklorist and it is now difficult to assess his practices. His wife Florence, a record-firm employee in the 1920's, told me that her husband did not compose "The Death of Mother Jones" but bought it on the road, or had it sent to him for use by one of his performers.[13] This suggestion was confirmed by Cliff Carlisle, a country performer from Kentucky, who also recorded for the American Record Corporation. Carlisle wrote of the song: "I tried to get this from Calaway but failed, as he said he had already promised it to Autry. To my knowledge, W. R. never wrote or composed anything although he bought and picked up a lot of stuff. He could have gotten this almost anywhere; most likely in the south, as this was, more or less, his territory."[14]

Records by obscure cowboy singers were not issued in large quantities during the pit of the Great Depression. In 1931 ARC utilized about ten labels. "The Death of Mother Jones" was pressed on at least seven: Banner, Conqueror, Jewel, Oriole, Perfect, Regal, Romeo. (See Checklist Five for details.) Only a few copies have survived, mainly in the hands of collectors intent on gathering all Autry's discs. My personal copy was presented to me by Eugene Earle, the president of the John Edwards Memorial Foundation. In listening to it over the years, I have always been excited by the juxtaposition of my feeling for Mother Jones and my awareness of Autry as the dean of the singing cowboys.

The text and tune of Conqueror 7702 are transcribed here.

THE DEATH OF MOTHER JONES

The world today's in mourning
O'er the death of Mother Jones;
Gloom and sorrow hover
Around the miners' homes.
This grand old champion of labor
Was known in every land;
She fought for right and justice,
She took a noble stand.

O'er the hills and through the valley —
In ev'ry mining town;
Mother Jones was ready to help them,
She never turned them down.
On front with the striking miners
She always could be found;
And received a hearty welcome
In ev'ry mining town.

She was fearless of every danger,
She hated that which was wrong;
She never gave up fighting
Until her breath was gone.
This noble leader of labor
Has gone to a better land;
While the hard-working miners,
They miss her guiding hand.

May the miners all work together
To carry out her plan;
And bring back better conditions
For every laboring man.

THE DEATH OF MOTHER JONES

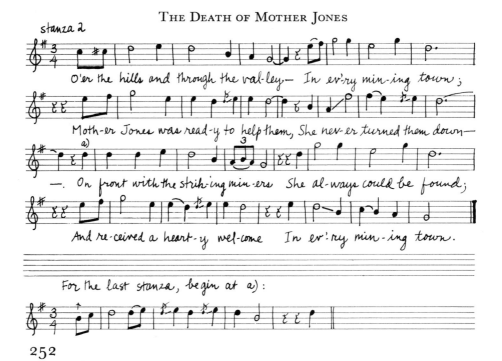

This song is not a poetic gem nor does it narrate any details of Mother Jones's intensely dramatic life. Although some elegies fall into ballad patterns, "The Death of Mother Jones" is rather an elegiac lyric folksong. We are not exposed to a snapshot of a little woman in black satin and lace defying armed gun thugs and troopers. Instead, we hear the clichés "she was fearless of every danger" and "she fought for right and justice." A strong folk ballad has the potential of turning commonplace language into a vivid montage of visual emblems. This was not done by the composer of Mother Jones's song. However, it is the miracle of folksong that a weak poem can be infused with vitality when set to music. Gene Autry's understated cowboy singing style, proper to burial on the lone prairie, was fully appropriate for the death of a woman perceived as labor's Joan of Arc.

Almost miraculously, in the year of its recording, Autry's disc was heard by a miner-writer, Tom Tippett, who had known Mother Jones intimately since childhood and had attended her two funeral services at Washington and Mt. Olive. While still a young man, Tippett had left the pits of Belleville, Illinois, to become a teacher organizer for Brookwood Labor College at Katonah, New York. This Westchester County campus, some forty miles north of New York City, was the major American residence-school committed to workers' education in the 1920's. It did much to create and perpetuate labor tradition, but not from any stated belief that folklore per se was a valued substance. Rather, Brookwood's leader, the Reverend A. J. Muste, inspired his students to act as if trade unionism itself were a primitive religious sect in a folk society. It is not my intent to reduce Muste's philosophy to a conservative or fundamentalist plane; on the contrary, he was a liberal theologian as well as an ecumenicist in action. Nor do I wish to compress Brookwood's broad role as a cultural force into a folkloric capsule simply because its students used union songs and stories with great effect. The special role of Brookwood and sister workers' education centers in adding a dimension of esthetic expression to unionism awaits exploration.[15]

Muste's autobiographical sketches are included in *The Essays of A. J. Muste*. This book forms an excellent base for understanding the intellectual environment of many labor activists — such as Tom

Tippett — during the Depression. Considerable labor history and folklore are included in Tippett's Illinois coal-mining novel, *Horse Shoe Bottoms* (1935), as well as in his previous book, *When Southern Labor Stirs,* a description of the Marion and Gastonia, North Carolina, textile strikes of 1929-30. It was in a Piedmont mill village that Tippett introduced his small son to regional folk music via a portable phonograph. More than two decades later he wrote to me:

> We could obtain some of the native folksongs of the area, now and then, on records, and we always got them from the small notion or 5 & 10 cent store. One day, on such an errand, as we walked up to the record counter, the clerk was playing the Mother Jones record. I was dumbfounded, of course. It happened to be the only copy in the store; the clerk said it had been in demand and he hoped to have more later.
>
> I bought the record and left the area. In every other record store I enquired, but found no more. I took the record to Brookwood and when I left the school some years later, I left it there.
>
> I don't remember who the singer was who recorded it. I am ashamed to confess this. He was a real or pretended hillbilly singer. It was the typical sorrowful hillbilly brand of song, and sounded exactly as the untrained voice of a coal miner in the hills would sing it. And, therefore, it was a good recording.[16]

Tippett's work carried him from the textile industry to coal, and, with fellow Brookwooders, he was very active in West Virginia during 1931. Starvation then stalked the miners in the Kanawha Valley. Not only did children die of malnutrition, but parents were menaced by company guards, as they had been two decades before in this same region. During the Depression, which began much earlier in coal than other industries, the United Mine Workers of America could not enforce its agreements, and wages were slashed north and south. Consequently, the Union disintegrated or was torn by dissension, and many workers turned to dual or radical rival groups. Unable to hold the fabric of industrial government together in the coal fields, miners desperately turned on each other. In 1931 Frank Keeney, the former president of UMWA District 17, organized Kanawha coal diggers into an independent West Virginia Mine Workers Union, itself very loosely related to an anti–John L. Lewis "Reorganized" group centered in Illinois. It is one of the many ironies in union history that Keeney is not fully portrayed

TOM TIPPETT ORGANIZING

in any scholarly monograph, and that his name has also dropped out
of the classic labor song "We Shall Not Be Moved." Originally this
piece centered on the strike and Charleston hunger march he led,
and contained the line "Frank Keeney is our captain, we shall not
be moved."[17]

In this West Virginia setting of meager living and intense labor
rivalry, Tippett met Walter Seacrist, a Baptist lay preacher and
miner from Holly Grove, near the junction of Paint Creek and the
Kanawha River.[18] Like other hill folk, young Seacrist had an ear
for traditional Appalachian lore. As he grew, he poured his impressions into new ballads and poems. He remembered from childhood the brutal killing of miner Cesco Estep by gunmen from the
"Bull Moose Special," an armored train used to attack the Holly
Grove tent colony in 1913. When the independent miners struck in
1931, Seacrist composed a song for his companion, Clifford Estep.
He titled it "The Strikers' Orphaned Child" and used as his model
the sentimental piece, "The Drunkard's Child." The new ballad
helped bridge the similar events of 1913 and 1931.

255

Tippett taught Seacrist the words and music of the Mother Jones song, which were not in print. The music sounded to Seacrist like "Three Leaves of Shamrock," and in his mind he reworked Tippett's contribution to the more familiar Irish tune. In 1932 Seacrist went from his home at Holly Grove to nearby Charleston, and in a private studio recorded "The Death of Mother Jones." It was paired with "The West Virginia Hills," a militant labor piece of his own composition based on the unofficial state anthem of the same name. This disc was played at West Virginia union meetings and later in Illinois by members of the Progressive Mine Workers. Southern Illinois historian John W. Allen recalled hearing the elegy in the Harrisburg coal fields of Saline County during the early 1930's.[19] Whether this "Little Egypt" singing had sprung from Seacrist's disc or Autry's then-available record is but one of the many mysteries encountered in my Mother Jones song-history reconstruction. I know of no one today who has a copy of the private recording; its recovery would be important to indicate the extent of Seacrist's textual and melodic change in the song so recently learned from Tippett. Also, the Charleston studio pressing may have been the first record specifically made for and used in a union organizational campaign.

In his constant travel between southern textile and mining areas and Brookwood Labor College, Tippett carried hillbilly discs north and union songbooks south. Not only did he bring Gene Autry's record to Katonah, he also brought an unusual item which coupled "The North Carolina Textile Strike" and "The Marion Massacre" (Paramount 3194). These 1929 topical numbers were composed and sung by Frank Welling and John McGhee but released under a pseudonym, the Martin Brothers. However, records and books were not the only means of song transmission in labor circles. In the fall of 1931 Seacrist and three fellow strikers traveled to Brookwood. The interchange in labor song between country singer and city organizer was an active process in the 1930's.

It is not often that we can document the actual interaction so well as we can in this case study. Brookwooders were teaching "Solidarity Forever" to coal miners in West Virginia in 1931; Seacrist, in return, moved "The Death of Mother Jones" into urban circles, where the young miner's style struck a responsive chord for

256

many listeners. Helen Norton, also on the Brookwood staff, presented at Vassar and other colleges Tippett's play, "Mill Shadows," which dealt with the 1929 Marion textile strike. Both she and Seacrist performed. She recalled: "Walter had a very good voice, quite untrained, but sweet and true. I remember once when we put on 'Mill Shadows' at Vassar College we had dinner with the students, and, during a song session afterwards, Walter was asked to sing 'Mother Jones' and 'The West Virginia Hills.' Among all these upper-class maidens he might have been forgiven some nervousness, but he sang quite without self-consciousness."[20]

Many spirited college students in depression years identified themselves with the labor movement and were moved by union song. I have touched on this theme previously, in noting that Don West was drawn to the Kentucky coal fields and that James Dombrowski was drawn to the Piedmont textile region. Throughout this period, some students went into West Virginia's Kanawha Valley with the League for Industrial Democracy and the Pioneer Youth — groups close to the Socialist party — to conduct educational and recreational programs for the coal-camp children.[21] One of the band of youthful teachers, Agnes Martocci, a Hunter College graduate, went to live in a Ward, West Virginia, tent colony during 1932, where she heard Walter Seacrist sing "Mother Jones" and other songs.[22] Agnes was deeply impressed. Years later, after World War II, she met Joe Glazer, a Textile Workers Union of America staff member. Apart from his regular educational duties, Glazer sang, swapped, taught, and composed labor songs. He had traveled both picket line and convention circuit with his giant Martin guitar and his rich store of topical songs. One of Glazer's favorites became "The Death of Mother Jones," learned from Agnes' singing.[23]

About 1955 Glazer and Edith Fowke, a Canadian folklorist, began compiling an anthology, *Songs of Work and Freedom,* for which they selected 100 pieces — occupational ballads, union songs, work chants. The compilers went beyond the range of previous labor collections by adding to the lyrics and music extensive headnotes based on interviews and correspondence. For "The Death of Mother Jones" Fowke and Glazer used Mary Jones's *Autobiography* to recall her history; for the song itself they indicated that

257

Agnes (Martocci) Douty and Mark Starr had helped in its circulation. Until this juncture I have followed Autry's disc in a straight line to Tom Tippett, Walter Seacrist, Helen Norton, Agnes Douty, and Joe Glazer. A single rendition of a song can be likened to a pebble dropped into a pool with a consequent circle of ripples. However, separate pebbles create patterns of distorted and converged rings. Ideally a scholar ought to be able to "read" each singer's ripples until the pool's surface is finally placid.

The knowledge that Mark Starr, the educational director of the International Ladies' Garment Workers' Union, was also involved in the dissemination of "The Death of Mother Jones" added, metaphorically, a new set of ripples for me to observe.[24] Previously I had known of Starr's long interest in labor lore by virtue of the ILGWU's extensive cultural program, and upon seeing the Fowke-Glazer manuscript was eager to learn Starr's interest in Mother Jones's elegy. Starr had been a coal miner in his native England before becoming involved in American unionism. From 1928 to 1935 he taught at Brookwood, leaving to assume his ILGWU position.

Starr had also heard the Mother Jones song at Katonah, initially from the Autry disc and soon after directly from Seacrist. Some fifteen years later he requested a colleague, Mrs. Slawson, to set down the words and music as he recalled them. This transcription by an ILGWU staff person was mimeographed as a single-page broadside with Starr's headnote, "Made from memory of W. Va. miners, Brookwood Labor College, 1929." The error in placing the date of collecting ahead of Mother Jones's death is symbolic perhaps of the speed with which labor buries and forgets its dead. However, the reading of symbolism into Starr's dating error is my own. From Mrs. Starr, the former Brookwood faculty secretary Helen Norton, I received a more prosaic explanation. Walter Seacrist, Columbus Ball, and other West Virginia miners at Brookwood had played roles in "Mill Shadows," Tippett's drama concerning 1929 events. When Mark Starr prepared the Mother Jones broadside in 1946, he unconsciously substituted the date of the strike in the play for the time of Mother Jones's passing.

Starr, like Seacrist, was unaware of the elegy's original source. When the song sheet was issued, it carried the line "copyright by the ILGWU," but the union never pressed its claim in Washington. Had it done so, Starr might well have reached Calaway while he was still alive and learned whether or not he was the original composer of "The Death of Mother Jones."

There are fashions in labor song as well as folksong. In 1946 Mark Starr took a few copies of the Mother Jones broadside to an ILGWU summer institute at the University of Wisconsin. At this time the worker-students rejected the number as "too mournful for modern taste."[25] However, if the song distressed trade unionists it did not distress John Greenway, a University of Pennsylvania graduate student gathering material for a thesis, "American Folksongs of Social and Economic Protest." Greenway, who obtained the broadside from Starr, eventually used its text in his book *American Folksongs of Protest* without indicating its source.

In October, 1955, while a faculty member at Denver University, Greenway journeyed to New York to record some sixty songs for the Riverside label. "Mother Jones" was released on his first LP, *American Industrial Folksongs*. This was edited by Kenneth S. Goldstein, as part of a series which proved to be highly influential in the "folksong revival" of the 1950's. Riverside's proprietors, Bill Grauer and Orrin Keepnews, jazz enthusiasts of wide taste, used their firm to reissue many race records by artists of the 1920's such as Blind Lemon Jefferson and Ma Rainey. Parallel to such reissues, Riverside also produced new LPs aimed at urban buyers of folk-music recordings.

In noting Riverside's role in making available to a 1956 audience a text and tune of "Mother Jones," it is worth remembering that Autry's phonograph disc was not only forgotten but virtually nonexistent in that year. Autry himself had not retained a copy. The American Record Corporation had not issued the original in great quantity, and it had effectively vanished by the New Deal period. However, the song itself had not disappeared before it reached at least one traditional folksinger, Walter Seacrist.

No quantitative method has been devised to tell ballad scholars exactly how many persons a song reaches in any folk community. We document the process of transmission and variations only after we learn that certain items which interest us are in tradition. The song on Autry's disc was conveyed by Tippett to Seacrist orally, and the latter's text-tune was not fixed in print until Starr used it for a 1946 ILGWU broadside. Greenway and Glazer followed with formal book printings of this version in 1953 and 1960, respectively. However, these were not the first appearances of "The Death of Mother Jones" in book form. In 1943 George Korson had presented the song in *Coal Dust on the Fiddle* from the singing of James Farrance, a Monongah, West Virginia, miner. Farrance's tune on his 1940 acetate field disc was not transcribed. Consequently, Greenway, in his book, was able to comment on Korson's text by correcting an incoherent line, but was unable to compare Starr's broadside melody to Farrance's.

When I undertook to explore the story of "The Death of Mother Jones," Korson generously made available to me a copy of his Farrance field recording. The style once more was hillbilly, the guitar in the background subdued, and the melody close to that of Greenway's Riverside LP. But Korson, like Greenway, could add little to my knowledge of the song's background. Neither had known of Autry's 1931 disc. Korson's self-imposed task of rescuing coal minstrelsy before its demise has been touched in my introductory chapter. He was aware that song histories might be lost, but gave priority to collecting the material itself. Upon my expressing particular interest in the story for Mother Jones's song, Korson suggested that I write to James Farrance. In the summer of 1958 I reached him and was rewarded with a warm document telling not only how "The Death of Mother Jones" came to the coal digger while he worked at Cecil, West Virginia, but also why it lived in his memory:

> I did not compose it. I found it in a Woolworth 5 & 10 cent store in Grafton, West Virginia, in 1919 or 1920. It was on an Orles record and was sung by some one like the Tennessee Plowboy, a very good singer. I learned it from the record. My brother was a fine guitar player, and I was a pretty good singer at that time.
>
> The song was new and nobody had ever heard it before. Everywhere I went people wanted me to sing it for them. It is real pretty if it is sung right. I sang it at union mass meetings of the United Mine Workers when we was on strike. The miners went wild over it.
>
> I saw her (Mother Jones) many times, and heard her speak here in Monongah on Labor Day. She sure was a grand old lady with her

hair turning white in the later years. I've been told the reason she became a fighter for union organization was that her husband and her son was killed by coal company yellow dogs, and she became angry at all non union outfits.

I saw her one time here in Monongah. We was trying to organize our mines. She came down Pike Street in a buggy and horse. Two company thugs grabbed the horse by the bridle and told her to turn around and get back down the road. She wore a gingham apron, and she reached under it and pulled out a 38 special pistol and told them to turn her horse loose, and they sure did. She continued on to the park, and spoke to a large bunch of miners. She wasn't afraid of the devil.[26]

There are several curious parallels in the experiences of Tippett and Farrance. Both found the record when it was current in similar stores, and both responded to the song because they had known and identified with the heroine. Farrance, in memory, placed the date of discovery a full decade too early, but remembered the "Orles" (Oriole) label. Like Tippett he forgot the unknown or then-obscure singer, but hazarded a good analogy in Eddie Arnold, the Tennessee Plowboy, who did not achieve fame until long after Gene Autry's disc had vanished.

Farrance's personal story is much like that of Seacrist. Their West Virginia heritage was held in common. Neither drew a sharp line between labor song and folksong. Coal mining was a way of life and it was as natural for them to sing about a strike as an explosion. Both had musical talent — Seacrist as a balladeer, and Farrance as a slide trombonist in his UMWA Local 1643 band. It is interesting to note that Mother Jones appealed across union lines to all her "children." In 1931 Seacrist temporarily cast his lot with the dissident West Virginia Mine Workers Union. Farrance was a life-long United Mine Workers member and one-time president of his Monongah local. He noted in a letter to me that he sang "The Death of Mother Jones" for 2,000 assembled miners in Constitution Hall at the 1938 UMWA convention in the nation's capital. The date of his field recording for collector Korson is stamped in his memory as the day when John L. Lewis spoke in Monongah. For both James Farrance and Walter Seacrist, their impressions of Mother Jones and their perception of union experience are fused in a set of remembered images clustered around a song.

We are seldom able to roll back time and reveal a folksong in the making. Seacrist and Farrance, as singers, recalled for me the impact of "The Death of Mother Jones" upon themselves. Fortunately there is also preserved a written impression by an outsider of the elegy's early meaning in a folk community. Lucile Kohn, a sensitive observer and listener, was teaching circuit school to the West Virginia tent-colony miners in 1932. She wrote of the scene:

> The great moment for the class comes when, a hundred strong, students and teachers, grizzled miners with their tired wives, nursing babies at their breasts, and children of all sizes stand under the trees with dusk coming on singing "The Death of Mother Jones" or "Solidarity Forever." Columbus Ball, himself a miner, with a guitar leads the song and it is lustily taken up by the children who have spent part of their hour of class-room learning these songs. It is a ragged crowd, inarticulate and downtrodden, but for the moment there is an exaltation that fills the spirit of all who participate in the gathering.[27]

In my four previous case studies, I have transcribed several versions of each basic text to illustrate variation. There is no need to reprint either Seacrist's or Farrance's "The Death of Mother Jones" from Greenway, Korson, or Fowke and Glazer's books. The three texts are close to Gene Autry's original. Hence, this chapter centers on but one "original" rendition.

However, some comments on the music of the available versions may bring together a few stray threads which illustrate melodic variation. Mark Starr's ILGWU worker-students rejected the song's mournful quality. Lucile Kohn heard exaltation in the voices of the Kanawha Valley singers. Obviously, any given folksong is capable of quite divergent interpretations. The Autry music transcribed in this chapter is melodically simple enough to fit itself to the moods of many traditional southern and western singers. When I listen to Autry's disc, I find it close to a group of familiar hillbilly standards: "Bad Companions," "Girl in the Blue Velvet Band," "I've Got No Use for the Women." Of course there is considerable musical difference in the many recorded and printed versions of these ballads, but there is enough of a common core to suggest that a member of the "Bad Companions" tune family inspired the composer of "The Death of Mother Jones."

I have already indicated that we know nothing of William

JOE GLAZER AT UMWA CONVENTION

Calaway's source for "The Death of Mother Jones." Nor do we know whether he purchased — if indeed he did — only a text or a combined text and tune. Possibly Calaway obtained a text and fitted it to a traditional mountain melody. It is highly unlikely that he or the author made up an original tune for the song. Regardless of such speculation, we do have some comments by others on the music. Seacrist identified it in terms of "Three Leaves of Shamrock." Glazer, who learned Seacrist's melody from Agnes Douty's singing, informed me that his young son, upon hearing him sing the elegy, likened it to Glazer's own composition, "The Mill Was Made of Marble." Glazer had composed this piece after a 1947 Rockingham, North Carolina, textile strike. He had no conscious memory of using this tune for his mill song, but there is a discernible aural relationship. Glazer's music for the two pieces can be compared in *Songs of Work and Freedom.*

Early in this study I quoted Stith Thompson's assertion that none of the items in John Greenway's *American Folksongs of Protest* were actually folksongs. Interestingly, this position was also advanced by San Francisco music critic Alfred Frankenstein when Greenway's LP was released. The critic wrote of the disc: "Greenway's 'American Industrial Folksongs' are primarily documents of sociology. These are songs about strikes, hard times among miners, farmers and factory workers, and ghastly happenings on the labor

263

front like the Ludlow Massacre. . . . The songs are important for what they record about certain aspects of American life, but there is no evidence to show that they are really folksongs."[28]

During 1960 I presented in *Labor History* an article in which I attempted a response to the Thompson-Frankenstein position by demonstrating that "The Death of Mother Jones" had moved from singer to singer and had functioned vitally in a folk-like community. In turn, the distinguished collector Mrs. Sidney Robertson Cowell questioned my notion of the elegy as a folksong, partly because I had not shown variation for its tune, and partly because the melodies of the "Bad Companions"–"Girl in the Blue Velvet Band"–"I've Got No Use for the Women" type did not meet her criteria of folk music. She defined hillbilly tunes as a "layer of music [which] is printed, commercially promoted and circulated, 19th and early 20th century music — what I call Broadway, for short."[29] Mrs. Cowell's reservations about the "Broadway" nature of hillbilly music would seemingly preclude any of the material considered in this book from folksong status, whether or not any textual or melodic variation was demonstrated.

I have offered Mrs. Cowell's view to enable readers not only to judge specifically "The Death of Mother Jones" but to make evaluations of the kinds of old-time and country tunes transcribed for the various case studies in this work. It is my personal belief that hillbilly music is fully capable of entering tradition and that melodic variation, however slight, can be found when the movement of a given song is demonstrated in a folk community. In short, musical and textual variation are concomitant with a song's life in folk society.

I have employed Thompson's twin standards of movement from singer to singer and vitality in tradition — echoed by Frankenstein — to demonstrate my notion that "The Death of Mother Jones" is indeed a folksong, despite my lack of examples of transcribed musical variation as suggested by Mrs. Cowell. Nor have I felt it necessary to "prove" that hillbilly tunes by definition are folk music. I hold these positions knowing fully that the variation is slight from Walter Seacrist's text to James Farrance's. But the measure of folksong does not rest on melodic or textual variation alone. The context of change is at least as significant as change

264

itself. By any criterion, the two West Virginians are traditional folksingers. We know more about the movement of Seacrist's piece than Farrance's, but from the latter we have a better statement of the song's meaning. Both imparted an emotional tone to Mother Jones's elegy greater than that possible for Gene Autry. Also, each learned the piece when he was part of a coal-camp community — a place where individuals respected the struggle for unionism as part of their heritage.

I am not, however, wedded to the notion that any given folksong lives forever. Certainly, folksongs go out of tradition when folksingers die, no longer retain them in memory, or more important, when audiences disappear. During 1958 Farrance sent to me in a letter his remembered text of "The Death of Mother Jones" with an added comment: "This song is sung with feeling and in the key of G." During 1966 Seacrist sent me his own fine tape recording of the piece. Farrance is now dead; when Seacrist follows the song will no longer reach new listeners in a traditional context.[30] Here, of course, I raise the problem of the labor movement's use of folklore. Perhaps it should be said that in the 1970's American trade unions, as socioeconomic institutions, are too far removed from their roots, as well as from Mother Jones's spirit, to give singers like Seacrist and Farrance significant living audiences.

It is relatively easy to identify a given item as a folksong by an agreed standard, however static or dynamic is the utilized definition. It is far more difficult to define a specific song's role in a large and pluralistic social movement. Accordingly, it did not particularly matter to John Greenway in the 1950's and 1960's whether or not Mother Jones's elegy was a folksong when he related her deeds to "revival" audiences, nor to Joe Glazer when he similarly regaled groups of labor-convention banqueteers. The professor and the labor educator reached sophisticated listeners who accepted "The Death of Mother Jones" as a valued reminder of past ideals.

It was quite another experience for Seacrist or Farrance to communicate via mail with a scholar, after each had been deprived of an audience of peers who knew Mother Jones and who accepted her as a heroic figure. Farrance's statement that "miners went wild" over his singing is highly significant, but it must be placed in the context of New Deal years, when the United Mine Workers re-

JOHN L. LEWIS

emerged in America by utilizing all the techniques associated with a revitalization or a religious movement. There are no studies by anthropologists on John L. Lewis' rebuilding of the miners' union in the 1930's comparable to Anthony Wallace's analysis of Handsome Lake's work among Iroquois Indians.[31] If such attention is ever paid to American trade unionism, the singing of Seacrist and Farrance will be seen as a highly functional role, not unlike that of tribal medicine men or hymnleaders at frontier camp meetings.

In the very decade of unionism's massive growth under the aegis of John L. Lewis and the Congress of Industrial Organizations, Mother Jones was "lost" to a new membership. In time, the many partisans who had known her firsthand retired or died. Beyond attrition in the ranks of early activists, it became extremely difficult for labor leaders in post–World War II years to cope with a radical past. Also, commitment to Cold War politics in the 1950's precluded sympathetic retention of socialist or syndicalist ancestor figures. This study is not the place to probe Mother Jones's highly individualistic response to class-struggle ideology, or to pin her in a specimen case of exotic militants. It is important to note here that in her declining years she had aligned herself with some of Lewis' factional enemies within the UMWA, and that she died before the Union's period of regeneracy began. Could she have stretched her long life beyond the century mark, she might well have assumed a mantle of CIO sainthood.

Parenthetically, it can be noted that in the 1930's and 1940's many communists — themselves shapers of labor lore — had no

266

trouble "appropriating" previous heroic figures, such as Albert Parsons of the Haymarket anarchists or Joe Hill of the Industrial Workers of the World. However, Communist party members found it difficult to accept Mother Jones. Following her death, Vern Smith, using the hysterical language of his party, tempered his respect for her heroism by stating that "the catholic church [claimed] her as a partisan," that her "money [had gone] to the choicest gang of labor traitors that ever sold out the miners," and that she was "used as an agent of reaction."[32] It must be remembered that Smith's invective was penned in a leftist sectarian period when communists were engaged in revolutionary dual unionism and bitter attacks on "misleaders of labor." By the time the party adopted its Popular Front line embracing Americanism, Mother Jones was lost to unionists and radicals alike.

My view of Mother Jones's brief life in tradition is keyed to a double formulation: her rank-and-file "children" were taken from her after World War II as the labor movement established itself in large society; and the circumstance of her death date denied her any official status either within the structure of unionism or that of the national community. One can compare the circulation of Mother Jones's song with the transformation of the birthday of John Mitchell, an early UMWA president, into a contractual holiday, or the marking of Eugene Victor Debs's home as a National Historical Landmark.

Ideally, we need a comparative study of labor heroes of all sorts — Mother Jones, Eugene Victor Debs, Wesley Everest, Andrew Furuseth, Joe Hill, Frank Little, John Mitchell, Albert Parsons, Harry Simms, William Sylvis — before we can place any of them in a frame somewhere between work and patriotic figures. No union heroes were able to appeal beyond their movement to all Americans, as did tunnel-stiff John Henry or silversmith Paul Revere. Further, I do not believe that any laborites who achieved the status even of local heroes in the last century could survive the fantastic growth and ideological shifts within twentieth-century American unionism.

To preface Mother Jones's elegy I offered a few brief prose portraits and a poem to illustrate how she appeared to her associates. No mourning song for her would have lasted even a day if

JOHN MITCHELL MONUMENT

Mother Jones had not previously acted in a manner which insured that her deeds would inspire expressive forms capable of life in tradition. Here I separate the life span of her song from the era of active memory focused on Mother Jones by unionists. Obviously Mother Jones acted out a flamboyant life, not necessarily to prepare herself for eternity but rather out of a sense of urgency in assisting her "children." A few examples of her flair follow.

Long before she inspired an elegy, she had utilized song in a 1911 dispute in the coal fields of Pennsylvania's Westmoreland County.[33] Mother Jones commanded a group of miner's wives to sing themselves out of jail: "Sleep all day and sing all night and don't stop for anyone. Say you're singing to the babies, I will bring the little ones milk and fruit. Just you all sing and sing." A report by Fred Mooney, a West Virginia coal miner, brings another aspect of Mother Jones's style to the surface. Mooney was standing on the Cabin Creek Junction bridge when Mother Jones entered that troubled community guarded by coal-baron gunmen. He stated:

> She surveyed the scene with a critical eye and walked straight up to
> the muzzle of one of the machine guns and patting the muzzle of the
> gun, said to the gunman behind it, "Listen here, you, you fire one shot
> here today and there are 800 men in those hills (pointing to the almost
> inaccessible hills to the east) who will not leave one of your gang alive."
>
> The bluff worked; the gunmen ground their teeth in rage. Mother
> Jones informed me afterwards that if there was one man in those hills
> she knew nothing of it. Her comment in regard to this day was, in part,
> as follows:
>
> "I realized that we were up against it, and something had to be
> done to save the lives of these poor wretches, so I pulled the dramatic
> stuff on them thugs. Oh! how they shook in their boots, and while they
> were shaking in their boots I held my meeting and organized the miners
> who had congregated to hear me."[34]

Bluffing in another tactical context was reported by John
Herling. When local newspapers in mining towns would refuse to
run ads for Mother Jones's meeting, "two miners would walk down
main street, one feigning deafness, the other yelling into his ear the
news that 'Mother Jones was going to speak tonight at the local
hall.' By the time he got through yelling, and the deaf man asking
what he was shouting about, the whole place knew that Mother
Jones was going to be there to talk about miners liberation."[35]

Not only did Mother Jones ably handle the stock devices such
as songs which convey folklore, and not only did she persuade
miners on the street to perform traditional theatrical bits, but folkloric detail accreted to her. When Laurence Todd, a Federation
Press correspondent, described the agitator's hundredth birthday,
he credited her with coining the labor slur *yellow dog,* which re-
placed the term *iron-clad agreement.* However, his main concern
was not so much etymology as image-making: "Staunch Old War-
rior Cries to Workers to 'Raise Hell' with Yellow Dog."

> Whether or not the stout-hearted little Irishwoman with the compelling
> blue eyes and the fiery speech was the first to use that term of scorn for
> the anti-union shackles placed upon the helpless coal miners by their
> bosses, she at least has used it with a jolting, re-dignifying force that no
> senator can ever achieve in mere debate. Coal miners heard her use
> it with every intonation of rebellious scorn, with appeal to their man-

hood, with a defiance of the company officials and their political servants that seemed to run straight back to curse their ancestors for three generations. "Yellow dog contract" was a declaration of war which she accepted, met halfway, and with which she gave the West Virginia slaveholders a grim realization that they have invited the doom of all slaveholding classes the world around.[36]

There is no need to recapitulate once more Mother Jones's dramatic deeds, except to suggest that her use of song and trickster's bluff as organizational tools seems to have been a highly conscious mastery of rhetorical forms in trade-union society. I raise this point only to underscore the meaning of her elegy to singers such as Farrance and Seacrist. They were drawn to her life-style partly because she was brave and good, but also because she integrated and enacted their abstract notions of labor's goals and values.

A few recent comments and actions, within and without the labor movement, are appropriate to draw this chapter to an end. John Brophy, born in a Lancashire, England, mining family, began his own work in Pennsylvania's central coal field at the age of ten in 1893. Some six years later he first saw Mother Jones. "She came into the mine one day and talked to us in our workplace in the vernacular of the mines. How she got in I don't know; probably just walked in and defied anyone to stop her." Brophy was aware of the superstitious belief that it is bad luck for women to enter mines, but his zeal as a unionist made this knowledge pale in comparison to his acceptance of her sympathetic role. In his autobiography (1964) he closed his keen sketch of Mother Jones with a simple requiem: "She had spent her life in God's work for the poor and oppressed."[37]

Another parting thought was expressed in 1958 by literary critic and novelist Edmund Wilson, when he reissued a series of his early travel essays, *The American Jitters,* including "Frank Keeney's Coal Diggers."[38] Mother Jones, in this firsthand report from the Kanawha Valley during 1931, had appeared as a sharp and vital personage standing in the wings behind the strikers. When Wilson rewrote his Depression essay for new readers, he felt compelled to identify Mother Jones in a laconic footnote: "A then well-known labor leader." Seldom has so much militancy and devotion been interred with so brief a phrase.

Brophy's requiem and Wilson's footnote sum up Mother Jones's contribution as well as large society's current view of her position. It has been the burden of this chapter to show that the modern labor movement in the United States could not retain Mother Jones as a legendary figure. Yet she stubbornly refuses to die in imagination, and, curiously, our memory of her is now invoked by a variety of persons far wider in ideological position than that held by the devoted band at her funeral. During 1969 the Arno Press, a service unit of the *New York Times,* reissued her out-of-print *Autobiography.* This was complemented in the same year by Irving Werstein's *Labor's Defiant Lady,* an attractively printed biography designed for high school students. On Mother's Day, 1970, the International Ladies' Garment Workers' Union placed a full-page, union-label advertisement in the *New York Times Magazine,* in which Mother Jones marched down an American street flanked by a flag-carrying lad. Her words, "I reside wherever there is a good fight against wrong," matched the determination revealed in this turn-of-the-century photograph.

In the summer of 1970 another strong portrait of the "patron saint of the picket lines" appeared on the cover of *People's Appalachia,* a research report issued by intellectuals/activists working to "decolonize" their region. For this journal Keith Dix, in an excellent sketch, introduced Mother Jones to New Left leaders and suggested the need for a documentary film on the "folk heroine's" life. Newspaper accounts from Madison following the bombing of a University of Wisconsin building on August 24, 1970, reported that among the splinter groups which had broken from the radical SDS (Students for a Democratic Society) were the Weathermen, the White Panthers, and the Mother Jones Revolutionary League. To close this kaleidoscopic impression of recent usages of Mother Jones's name, I note the paper on her achievement read by Philip Taft, a distinguished economist-historian, to the Illinois Labor History Society on November 21, 1970. The paper itself was a prelude to a Sunday morning visit by trade unionists and historians to the Mt. Olive Union Miners' Cemetery, toward the end of securing recognition of the shrine as a National Historical Landmark. It can be noted that the social distance from an ILGWU-prepared Mother's Day ad in the *New York Times* to a revolutionary league

271

"I reside wherever there is a good fight against wrong."

Mother Jones was a labor organizer. For more than half a century she was, as some called her, the Joan of Arc of the coal fields.

One newspaper described her as "the most dangerous woman in the country." Another stated: "There is no more patriotic citizen in America."

"Her personal non-resistance," wrote Clarence Darrow, "was far more powerful than any appeal to force."

Asked where she lived, she replied: "I reside wherever there is a good fight against wrong."

Today, as the nation observes Mother's Day, the members of the International Ladies' Garment Workers' Union (80% women) salute the memory of Mother Jones who died just forty years ago.

Their signature is the ILGWU label.

sewn in women's and children's apparel. It represents progress made; and more to come.

Look for it when you shop.

1900-1970
SEVENTY
YEARS OF
PROGRESS
AND MORE
TO COME.

For 64-page publication containing historic photographs, send 50¢ to ILGWU, Union Label Dept., 275 7th Ave., N.Y.C. 10001, Dept. T-5.

ILGWU AD

gathered in a Madison "collective" is considerable, yet both the established union and the student extremists feel it appropriate to invoke Mother Jones's spirit.[39]

This contrastive overview of treatment of Mother Jones in 1969 and 1970 by some of her "children" makes a convenient closing point for my study of her song. Specifically, I have placed the elegy in a field between two recordings by such disparate singers as cowboy-telegrapher Gene Autry and anthropologist-folklorist John Greenway. In spite of research, the song's author is still unknown, but this fact is not particularly significant in view of our knowledge that "The Death of Mother Jones" has moved in tradition, has involved its hearers in a network of institutional values, has been collected and archived, and has provided an interpretive vehicle for a glimpse of the labor movement's ambivalence about its most charismatic heroine.

1. Review by Stith Thompson, *American Historical Review,* LIX (1954), 454. See also Howard Mumford Jones, *Midwest Folklore,* IV (1954), 48; Ben Gray Lumpkin, *Western Folklore,* XIII (1954), 142; W. Edson Richmond, *Journal of American Folklore,* LXVII (1954), 96; Claude M. Simpson, Jr., *Southern Folklore Quarterly,* XVIII (1954), 197.

2. George P. West, "Correspondence: Mother Jones among the Twelve," *Nation,* CXV (July 19, 1922), 70.

3. Judith Mikeal, "Mother Mary Jones: The Labor Movement's Impious Joan of Arc" (master's thesis, University of North Carolina, Chapel Hill, 1965). Priscilla Long Irons of Cambridge, Mass., is gathering data for a Jones biography. Mrs. Irons has suggested that Mother Jones was actually born some time after May 1, 1830.

4. John H. Keiser, "The Union Miners Cemetery at Mt. Olive, Illinois," *Journal of the Illinois State Historical Society,* LXII (1969), 229. For reporting on Mother Jones's funeral see all issues of the Chicago Federation of Labor's weekly *Federation News* for Dec., 1930.

5. Marlen Pew, "Shop Talk at Thirty," *Editor & Publisher,* LXIII (Dec. 6, 1930), 56.

6. "Mother Jones: An Impression," *New Republic,* II (Feb. 20, 1915), 73.

7. Charleston speech, Aug. 1, 1912, included in Mikeal, "Mother Mary Jones," 159; Logan response in Mary Harris Jones, *Autobiography of Mother Jones,* ed. Mary Field Parton (Chicago, 1925), 235.

8. Ralph Chaplin, *When the Leaves Come Out* (Cleveland, 1917). See also his autobiography, *Wobbly* (Chicago, 1948).

9. West Virginia State Federation of Labor, *Proceedings of the Thirteenth Annual Convention* (Charleston, 1920), 34.

10. Emma Langdon, *The Cripple Creek Strike* (Denver, 1908), 488.

11. For variation in anecdote see Ken Michaels, "Wait Up, Gene," *Chicago Tribune Magazine* (May 28, 1967), 18; Alva Johnson, "Tenor on Horseback," *Saturday Evening Post,* CCXII (Sept. 2, 1939), 18; Ben Botkin, *A Treasury of Western Folklore* (New York, 1951), 519.

12. Letter to me, Dec. 27, 1957.

13. Interview, June 7, 1959.

14. Letter to Eugene Earle, Aug. 31, 1959.

15. Brookwood's folkloric role is unexplored. For Muste's values see *The Essays of A. J. Muste,* ed. Nat Hentoff (Indianapolis, 1967). For a brief view of the school see James O. Morris, *Conflict within the AFL* (Ithaca, N.Y., 1958), 86.

16. Letter to me, Feb. 6, 1958, supplemented by interview, June 16, 1958.

17. There is no single history of the WVMWU. Useful theses are Charles P. Anson, "A History of the Labor Movement in West Virginia" (University of North Carolina, Chapel Hill, 1940), and Thomas E. Posey, "The Labor Movement in West Virginia" (University of Wisconsin, Madison, 1948). See also Evelyn Harris and Frank Krebs, *From Humble Beginnings* (Charleston, W.Va., 1960). For an interview with Keeney see Homer L. Morris, *The Plight of the Bituminous Coal Miner* (Philadelphia, 1934), 123. For a report on a WVMWU strike see Winifred L. Chappell, "Embattled Miners," *Christian Century,* XLVIII (Aug. 19, 1931), 1043.

18. Seacrist correspondence dates from Dec. 7, 1957, and is supplemented by a tape recorded by him, Aug. 22, 1965.

19. Interview, Feb. 16, 1960. See also John W. Allen, *It Happened in Southern Illinois* (Carbondale, 1968), 18.

20. Letter to me, Dec. 18, 1958.

21. Lucile Kohn, "Solidarity in Kanawaha Valley," *Labor Age,* XX (Sept., 1931), 11, and "Pioneer Youth and the Labor Movement," *ibid.,* XXI (Nov., 1932), 20. These reports were illuminated for me by an interview with Miss Kohn, Mar. 7, 1960.

22. Interview, May 16, 1959.

23. Interview, Nov. 20, 1957. See also Edith Fowke and Joe Glazer, *Songs of Work and Freedom* (Chicago, 1960), 58.

24. Starr correspondence dates from Dec. 10, 1953, and is supplemented by an interview with Mr. and Mrs. Starr, June 12, 1959. For an example of Mrs. Starr's labor reportage see Helen G. Norton, "Feudalism in West Virginia," *Nation,* CXXXIII (Aug. 12, 1931), 154.

25. Letter to me, May 9, 1958.

26. Letter to me, June 16, 1958.

27. Lucile Kohn, "There Are Classes in the West Virginia Hills," *Labor Age,* XXI (Sept., 1932), 11. An unsigned report, "Students Teach West Virginia Class," *Brookwood Review,* XI (Dec., 1932), 4, confirms Columbus Ball's singing of the Mother Jones elegy, but I have been unable to locate Ball. His views on the song's early transmission would be valuable.

28. Review by Alfred Frankenstein, *San Francisco Chronicle, This World* (Feb. 10, 1957), 20. See also W. Edson Richmond, *Journal of American Folklore,* LXXI (1958), 179; D. K. Wilgus, *Kentucky Folklore Record,* III (1957), 41.

29. Letter to me, Oct. 12, 1960.

30. James Farrance died Mar. 28, 1965.

31. Anthony F. C. Wallace, *The Death and Rebirth of the Seneca* (New York, 1969). See also his "Revitalization Movements," *American Anthropologist,* LVIII (1956), 264.

32. Vern Smith, "From an Era That Has Passed: Mother Jones," *Labor Defender,* VI (Jan., 1931), 16. For a revisionist view see Joseph Leeds, "The Miners Called Her Mother," *Masses and Mainstream,* III (Mar., 1950), 38.

33. Mary Jones, *Autobiography,* 145.

34. Fred Mooney, *Struggle in the Coal Fields* (Morgantown, W.Va., 1968), 28.

35. John Herling, "Women's Lib — Bah," *John Herling's Labor Letter* (Sept. 26, 1970).

36. Laurence Todd, "Mother Jones, 100 May 1, Honored by Labor," *Labor's News* (May 10, 1930), 6.

37. John Brophy, *A Miner's Life* (Madison, Wis., 1964), 74, supplemented by interview, Mar. 21, 1960.

38. Edmund Wilson, *The American Earthquake* (Garden City, N.Y., 1958), 318, and *The American Jitters* (New York, 1932), 150.

39. Material cited on Werstein, the ILGWU ad, Dix, the University of Wisconsin account ("Officials Fear Renewal of Campus Violence"), and the Taft paper is found in the bibliography.

CHECKLIST FIVE

"The Death of Mother Jones." Gene Autry, Banner 32133, Conqueror 7702, Jewel 20053, Oriole 8053, Perfect 12696, Regal 10311, Romeo 5053 (10477). Feb. 25, 1931, New York.

————. William R. Calaway, New York (Mar. 9, 1931), E 36010.

Transcribed: Green, *L H,* I (1960), 78. Article also includes Farrance-Korson text and Seacrist-Starr-Greenway text.

————. Walter Seacrist, private studio recording. 1932, Charleston, W.Va. No located copies known to me.

————. Walter Seacrist, Mims, Fla., Aug. 22, 1965. Self-recorded. Green tape files.

————. James Farrance, Monongah, W.Va., Apr. 2, 1940. George Korson, Green tape files.

Transcribed: Korson, *C D F* (1943), 348.

"Mother Jones." Mark Starr, ILGWU, New York (1946). Mimeographed broadside of text and tune states, "Made from memory of W. Va. miners, Brookwood Labor College, 1929." Green files.

Text reprinted: Greenway, *A F P* (1953), 154.

Previously used: Greenway's University of Pennsylvania dissertation, "American Folksongs of Social and Economic Protest" (1951).

Recorded: John Greenway, *American Industrial Folksongs,* Riverside RLP 607. Oct., 1955, New York.

Transcribed: *Sing Out,* X (Apr., 1960), 20, m.

"The Death of Mother Jones." Fowke and Glazer, *S W F* (1960), 58, m.

APPENDIX FIVE

POEMS ABOUT MOTHER JONES

1. "Welcome, Mother Jones" by Jenkin D. Reese. *United Mine Workers Journal,* Oct. 16, 1902. Reprinted in George Korson, *Coal Dust on the Fiddle,* 347.
2. "Who visited, one certain day." *Appeal to Reason,* Oct. 16, 1909. Reprinted in Judith Mikeal, "Mother Mary Jones," 98.
3. "Fie, mammon, base and cruel, fie!" by John Ward Stimson. ca. 1911. Mother Jones Papers, Catholic University of America. Reprinted in Mikeal, "Mother Mary Jones," 142.
4. "Mother Jones" by Gerald J. Lively. *Solidarity,* May 10, 1913, 3.
5. "They've put an injunction on old Mother Jones" by Oscar Langford. *Miners Magazine,* ca. May, 1913. Reprinted in Mikeal, "Mother Mary Jones," 141.
6. "Mother Jones" by a Paint Creek miner. *International Socialist Review,* Apr., 1914, 604.
7. "The patriotic soldiers came marching down the pike" by William M. Rogers. West Virginia State Federation of Labor, *Proceedings of the Thirteenth Annual Convention,* 1920, 34. Reprinted in Mikeal, "Mother Mary Jones," 86.
8. "I reckon her greater than lord or prince" by Terence V. Powderly. Aug., 1922. Mother Jones Papers. Reprinted in Mikeal, "Mother Mary Jones," 141.
9. "To Mother Mary Jones" by Martha Shepard Lippincott. *Federation News,* Jan. 17, 1931, 10.

COMPANY TOWN

Two by Travis 8

"FROM HERE TO ETERNITY," a motion picture depicting GIs in World War II, starred Frank Sinatra, Montgomery Clift, and Burt Lancaster; it also featured Merle Travis as a soldier performing a memorable "Re-enlistment Blues." The film, released in 1953, reached a wide audience not previously acquainted with Travis, a successful singer and composer of such country-western hits as "No Vacancy," "Divorce Me C.O.D.," "So Round, So Firm, So Fully Packed," and "Smoke, Smoke, Smoke That Cigarette." The film also reached a few viewers who identified the guitar-picking private in terms of his 1947 Capitol album *Folk Songs of the Hills*. This 78 rpm set held eight songs: "Nine Pound Hammer," "John Henry," "Sixteen Tons," "Dark as a Dungeon," "That's All," "Over by Number Nine," "Muskrat," "I Am a Pilgrim." All the numbers included spoken introductions which placed six of the pieces in a Kentucky coal-mining locale. These anecdotal openings, intrinsically entertaining, suggested the same homespun feeling Carl Sandburg had conveyed in his prefaces while presenting folksongs to concert groups throughout the land.

At the war's end Capitol Records was a fledgling Hollywood firm, experimental and eager to explore novel trends not readily perceived in the East. The company had established itself during 1942-43 when major competitors were suffering effects of the

279

"Petrillo ban" — a strike by the American Federation of Musicians against the inroads of mechanical performance via jukebox and radio. Not only had Capitol's young executives quickly come to terms with the union, but, as their little firm grew, they searched for artists with fresh appeal. In a sense, Capitol deliberately aimed Travis' *Folk Songs of the Hills* not at his previous country-western fans, but rather at an enlarged "Sandburg audience" — a group of consumers already committed to folksong on the stage or from recordings by then-popular performers: Richard Dyer-Bennett, Burl Ives, Frank Luther, John Jacob Niles, Susan Reed, Josh White.

In Chapter 2 I alluded to *Smoky Mountain Ballads,* a Victor set released a few months before Pearl Harbor and reviewed in the *New York Times.* This reissue contained a brochure by John Lomax introducing the selections by artists such as J. E. Mainer's Mountaineers, Gid Tanner and His Skillet Lickers, and the Monroe Brothers to northern, intellectual auditors. In the years immediately prior to World War II, the sound-recording industry learned that it could reach new folksong enthusiasts with race and hillbilly records by packaging three, four, or five-disc sets in stiff paper-board albums which included inside and outside cover pictures and annotative data. Such albums, of course, gave way in the 1950's to ten- and twelve-inch LP discs in illustrated jackets, sometimes with extensive back-liner notes or elaborate insert brochures. This development of graphic and scholarly accouterments for folksong records invites its own study. Here I touch the theme only to underscore the fact that *Folk Songs of the Hills,* the first album in Capitol's Americana series, was consciously aimed at an anticipated audience which might welcome an aural portrait of coal-mining life comparable to previous issues of sailor or cowboy lore by other firms.

According to normal commercial standards, Travis' first album was not a great success, although a Capitol release prepared late in 1949 confirmed that the firm's strategy to reach urbanites had worked: *Folk Songs of the Hills* "registered its greatest sales in New York."[1] Before the industry converted from 78 rpm discs to LPs, however, it was deleted from Capitol catalogs. Yet two of Travis' new coal-mining songs, especially composed for *Folk Songs of the Hills,* endured and their story is the subject of this chapter. "Dark as a Dungeon" and "Sixteen Tons" made their way into a wide variety of repertoires: "folksong revival," popular, bluegrass, traditional. Today these two songs are widely recognized in and out of the United States as representative of American mining lore by a public which never heard "The Death of Mother Jones," "Coal Creek Troubles," or "Only a Miner." Travis himself is known to many folk-music enthusiasts not for his fine industrial compositions or even his country-western hits, but rather for his complex guitar style. "Travis picking" has itself been studied in terms of both technique and source, but I shall not dwell on it here.[2]

After "Sixteen Tons" was catapulted into the million-seller category by a Tennessee Ernie Ford television show in 1955, Travis received considerable attention which lifted him from the ranks of other talented country musicians. While Ford's disc was at the top of the sales charts, the *United Mine Workers Journal* printed a short autobiographical sketch by Travis as the "saga of every coal miner's family." In 1966 Travis wrote a second and longer account detailing his growth as a public entertainer. It was entitled "I Have a Sick Sister in Texas," a stock line used by the young guitarist to solicit change while riding the rods, and riverboats too, during lean years. The autobiographies of many Nashville stars are marred by the clichés of public-relations ghost writers. By contrast, Travis' writing is fresh and reflects a keen ear for southern rural locutions as well as backwoods humor. The earliest Capitol press release on Travis, before any of his discs were hits, stated perceptively that as a youngster he had absorbed Negro and backwoods lore and adopted "philosophies" found in such material into his music.[3] Below I shall quote from his writings to illustrate facets of the song histories under consideration, as well as to demonstrate the folk roots of a participant who himself helped broaden and nationalize country music.[4]

Merle Robert Travis was born on November 29, 1917, at Rosewood, Muhlenburg County, Kentucky. While Merle was still a little boy, his father switched from tobacco farming to coal mining, a transition similar to that made by countless Americans in the century of our nation's rapid industrialization. Merle's parents, known as "Uncle Rob" and "Aunt Etter," as well as his older brothers and sister — Taylor, John, and Vada — were all musical as singers or instrumentalists. Young Travis learned to pick the five-

281

string banjo in his eighth year, but even before this he had heard his first guitar played by a miner near the family home at Browder. About 1926 Rob Travis transferred from the Browder Mining Company to the Beech Creek Coal Company near Ebenezer. Here Merle completed the eighth grade in a one-room schoolhouse, receiving the same education allotted to coal-camp children during hard times.

It was literally outside his schoolroom, at the nearby home of family friend Mrs. Bunnie Baugh, that Merle first met two coal miners from Drakesboro, Mose Rager and Ike Everly, who were his best extracurricular teachers. Rager and Everly taught the eager youngster their bouncy Negro-influenced style, and thereby helped establish his professional life away from the mines. An enlistment at the age of sixteen in the New Deal's Civilian Conservation Corps helped round out Merle's education, and soon afterward he left home for good to begin the life of a public entertainer. His radio debut in Evansville, Indiana, during 1935 featured a Mose Rager-styled "Tiger Rag"; his long apprenticeship included a stint with country-music pioneer Clayton McMichen and the Georgia Wildcats. In this formative period, Merle's earliest published song, "The Dust on Mother's Old Bible," appeared in the *Drifting Pioneers Song Folio Number One* (1939). During the early war years, Travis was involved in considerable radio broadcasting from Cincinnati's WLW with "Grandpa" Jones and the Delmore Brothers (Alton and Rabon), as the Brown's Ferry Four. After a World War II hitch in the Marine Corps, Travis made Hollywood his base. Before coming to California he had recorded under pseudonyms; his debut under his own name was for Atlas and Ara, two minor labels in Los Angeles. During March, 1946, at the suggestion of his friend Cliffie Stone, a Pasadena radio performer (KXLA), Travis signed an exclusive contract with Capitol Records.

When Lee Gillette, Capitol's country-western A & R man, asked Travis to record an album of Kentucky folksongs, Merle's deprecatory, and far from true, response was that he didn't know any. To which Gillette retorted, "Write some!" A recording session which leads to a historic record, a new stylistic trend, a fresh artist, or a national hit eventually is very likely to produce its own body of reportage. The Hollywood session at which Travis recorded "Nine

MERLE TRAVIS

Pound Hammer" and other numbers required no special attention for some nine years. However, when Tennessee Ernie Ford's rendition of "Sixteen Tons" excited the nation late in 1955, journalists began to interview Ford and Travis in order to interpret the song's phenomenal attraction. At this time the then-distant *Folk Songs of the Hills* session became the cluster point for its own lore. Merle shared a number of recollections about his songs with me during a long visit in 1967. The lapse of two decades permitted him to view this session and its compositions as if he himself were the detached historian. To my query on his negative response to the proposed album, Travis suggested that many Kentucky folksongs had already been recorded by Bradley Kincaid, Cousin Emmy, Doc Hopkins, Bob Atcher, and others, and that there was no need to cover their songs.

Travis had put off the composing assignment until the last minute, but he could not put it completely out of mind since he did have a strong desire to write original songs. Actually, the released album was a compromise, with four folksongs which showed varying degrees of arrangement or recomposition ("Nine Pound Hammer," "John Henry," "Muskrat," "I Am a Pilgrim"), a jazzy gospel song also in tradition ("That's All"), and three fresh compositions ("Sixteen Tons," "Over By Number Nine," "Dark as a Dungeon"). The music, text, and spoken introduction of the last are transcribed from Capitol 48001 at this point.

Dark as a Dungeon

(Sung) It's as dark as a dungeon way down in the mine.

(Spoken) I never will forget one time when I was on a little visit down home in Ebenezer, Kentucky. I was a-talkin' to an old man that had known me ever since the day I was born, and an old friend of the family. He says, "Son, you don't know how lucky you are to have a nice job like you've got and don't have to dig out a livin' from under these old hills and hollers like me and your pappy used to." When I asked him why he never had left and tried some other kind of work, he says, "Nawsir, you just won't do that. If ever you get this old coal dust in your blood, you're just gonna be a plain old coal miner as long as you live." He went on to say, "It's a habit (chuckle) sorta like chewin' tobaccer."

> Come and listen you fellows, so young and so fine,
> And seek not your fortune in the dark dreary mines.
> It will form as a habit and seep in your soul,
> 'Till the stream of your blood is as black as the coal.
>
>> It's dark as a dungeon and damp as the dew,
>> Where danger is double and pleasures are few,
>> Where the rain never falls and the sun never shines,
>> It's dark as a dungeon way down in the mine.
>
> It's a-many a man I have seen in my day,
> Who lived just to labor his whole life away.
> Like a fiend with his dope and a drunkard his wine,
> A man will have lust for the lure of the mines.
>
> I hope when I'm gone and the ages shall roll,
> My body will blacken and turn into coal.
> Then I'll look from the door of my heavenly home,
> And pity the miner a-diggin' my bones.
>
>> Chorus:

284

DARK AS A DUNGEON

stanza 1

a)

Come and lis-ten you fel-lows, so young and so fine, And

seek· not your for-tune in the dark drear-y mines. It will

form as a hab-it and seep in your soul, 'Til the chorus

stream of your blood is as black as the coal. It's

dark as a dun-geon and damp as the dew, Where

dan-ger is dou-ble and pleas-ures are few, Where the

rain nev-er falls and the sun nev-er shines, It's

dark as a dun-geon way down in the mine.

a) stanzas 2-3   b) stanza 3   rit. _____

"Dark as a Dungeon's" poignant imagery speaks eloquently and links this piece to the body of lyric folksongs known to Travis from his youth. The introduction reveals a natural use of dialect and characterization which is neither pejorative nor cloying. Travis himself perceptively wrote of his father's speech: "Dialect is sometimes hard to read, and impossible to set down on paper, but I'll do my best to write it as I've heard him say it."[5] Travis' introductions were more than local-color bits, for in the context of the record

285

DARK ENTRANCE

album they served to place coal miners on the same level as other folksong heroes. Travis understood the need to surround his songs with the anecdotes which would delineate a folk community, much in the way George Korson placed the songs he collected in a frame of history and ethnography.

I was fortunate to learn the author's explanation for the composition of "Dark as a Dungeon." Shortly before his Hollywood recording session, Travis was returning from a Redondo Beach date. While reminiscing with his girlfriend about his childhood, the song's images as well as a tune had come to his mind. On the way home, he pulled his car up under a street lamp and scribbled the stanzas on the back of an old envelope. Later, in the studio, he transferred the text to a cardboard propped against the microphone stand and worked out the melody on his guitar. When he related this anecdote to me he seemed a bit distressed to reveal that the song

286

was not penned in a Kentucky mine chamber by the light of a carbide lamp. Of course Merle was sophisticated enough to enjoy his
own telling of a tale which violated urban stereotypes about the folk.
On my part, I was intrigued to hear him set the actual composition
of a nostalgic mining song into a congenial California evening.
Something had to trigger Travis' writing assignment and uncap the
bittersweet memories of boyhood.

Some of these memories are in print, and a few Travis para-
graphs (1955) reveal a child's perception of the fluctuations in mine
employment as well as the drama in strikes. These lines also illustrate the fact that Travis' writing style is part of a long tradition
which shaped so much frontier experience into local-color literature. Commenting on his father's job as an "outside" sulphur picker,
Travis wrote:

> The roar of the shakers finally affected his hearing and many is the
> time he'd call my brother John and myself out on the porch of the
> company farm we lived on, three miles from Beech Creek, and say as
> he pulled from his overall pocket a huge Elgin watch, "Now boys,
> you've got better ears than I have, so listen for the whistle. I heard a
> coal-drag switchin' around over there today, and they jus' might run
> tomorrow."

> When the whistle from ol' Number Five came drifting over the hills
> at five o'clock in the afternoon Dad would brighten up like a child
> anticipating a fishing trip only one night away. This didn't happen too
> often in the summer when the demand for coal was at its lowest ebb.
> At these times a gloom would shroud the big man like a gray sky before
> an all night drizzle. He'd return his watch to his pocket and remark,
> "Well boys, I reckon we'll hill them beans in the garden tomorrow."

> When the opposite occurred, and the thin sound of the whistle
> drifted to our alert ears, it was a different scene. Uncle Rob Travis was a
> happy man. He'd kiss his watch, return it to his bib-pocket and say,
> "Well boys, looks like ol' man Kirkpatrick [operator of Number Five
> and Number Nine mines] has peddled some more rocks." The Travis
> household was a brighter abode. Maybe dad would take the old five-
> string banjo from the nail on the wall and pick and sing:

> > "Jenny Weaver clumb a tree
> > Hopin' for her Lord to see.
> > Th' limb it broke and she did fall,
> > Never got to see her Lord a'tall."

287

Then there were the strikes! To us and all the people we knew it meant "Root, hog, or die!" I became well acquainted with the "aid-hall." There we'd go to get whatever was to be given in the way of food to the miners on strike. Just enough beans and salt-pork to keep body and soul together. It seemed a festive time to me as a boy in my early teens, for there were the mass-meetings. Hundreds would gather and sit on slabs of wood laid across carbide cans and listen to the speeches. The promise of miners becoming united was music to the ears of the miners and their wives, but the entertainment they'd have between speeches was more musical to my young ears.

I'll never forget four Negro boys by the name of the Dean Quartet (although one was named Doolin). With a sound that reminded me of the I.C. train whistle on a winter's night, they'd lean four black heads together and sing in perfect harmony.

> "When we get our union
> When we get our union
> There'll be no more scabbin in District 23
> And won't we be glad, Oh Good Lawd."[6]

It can be assumed that most American folksong enthusiasts, as well as some from other parts of the world, have heard "Dark as a Dungeon" during the last two decades. Checklist Six reveals the song's spread to some three dozen singers of widely different backgrounds, for example Harry Belafonte, Glen Campbell, Rose Maddox, the Stoneman Family. An effective use of Joe Glazer's recording of this song was made in a TV documentary on the life of John L. Lewis, filmed by CBS News for "The Twentieth Century" and televised on March 22, 1964.

However, I shall not detail the full spread or use of "Dark as a Dungeon"; only its initial movement need concern us here. The composition was recorded in Capitol's Hollywood studio on August 8, 1946, but not released in *Folk Songs of the Hills* (AD 50) until June 9, 1947. This period of nearly a year in readying the set seems to be an unusual lapse of time, and I have learned of no reason for it. However, Cliffie Stone has suggested to Ken Griffis that albums were somewhat of a novelty to the industry at that time. While Capitol was still geared to "singles," the Travis production "just had to wait its time."[7]

It is doubtful whether the official release date meant that the album was actually on sale in many music stores. In November the

FOLK SONGS OF THE HILLS

Louisville Courier Journal Magazine included a Bill Ladd feature on Travis' return to Drakesboro High School to perform at a benefit for a new playground. Ladd identified Travis by "Smoke, Smoke, Smoke That Cigarette" and other country-western hits, rather than by his recent mining songs, some of which were localized to tipples within school-bus distance of Drakesboro. It can be presumed that *Folk Songs of the Hills* was not actually available in Kentucky until after the *Courier Journal* story was printed.[8]

Travis, in 1947, apparently expressed no concern at the time span in producing the set. He was busy in that year as a country-music performer, and rather casual in his relationship with friends at Capitol. More than two decades after the album's release, he recalled for me the humor of the sitting when he was called to pose for a cover portrait. Riding his motorcycle to the studio during a rainstorm, he was photographed "wringing wet" in a black Stetson and a loud checkered shirt. The resulting album design seemed to Merle to be more appropriate to cowboys or lumberjacks than to miners, but it may well have reflected the then-current music industry's image of folksingers. Travis was considerably pleased when *Folk Songs of the Hills* (augmented by four items) was reissued on an LP record in December, 1957, as *Back Home* (Capitol T 891). This time the LP jacket cover featured a huge rustic waterwheel — still far removed from coal-mining symbolism, but close in tone to Travis' poetry.

The delay in marketing Travis' first album after it was recorded was compounded by a much longer lapse in coprighting any of its numbers. It was not until after Tennessee Ernie Ford's "Sixteen Tons" became a hit that Sylvester Cross, the owner of American Music, Incorporated, in Hollywood, undertook to register the *Folk Songs of the Hills* material at the Copyright Office. "Dark as a Dungeon" was received in Washington on February 27, 1956, but retroactively identified as a June 9, 1947, publication (EP 97185). The arrangement was legally proper; it meant only that Travis' song had been "unprotected" for nearly a decade.[9] I do not know whether the American Music lead sheet used for copyright purposes was actually based on an early rendition or whether it represented a 1956 performance, inasmuch as the Copyright Office version included a stanza not heard on the original recording:

> The midnight, the morning, or the middle of day,
> Is the same to the miner who labors away.
> Where the demons of death often come by surprise,
> One fall of the slate and you're buried alive.

To my knowledge, none of the singers who recorded "Dark as a Dungeon" after 1947 used this stanza. However, at a University of Chicago concert during 1966, Travis himself dropped the "lure of the mine" couplet in favor of "the demons of death–fall of the slate" couplet. Whether or not Travis, in a live concert for a congenial audience, discarded his "dope-drunkard" comparison out of dissatisfaction with it, or whether he made the change unconsciously by drawing on an unused layer of language, is difficult to say with any degree of certainty. Although I was present at Travis' Chicago evening, I did not "hear" his changed lines until I subsequently

290

transcribed the concert tape.[10] This reinforced for me the knowledge of how difficult it is to assert that one has heard fully any given text in a familiar song.

Perhaps the very first of Merle Travis' "new fans" in 1947 was Alan Lomax, one of the earliest students to treat race and hillbilly material as folksongs. While Alan aided his father John in editing their last joint anthology, *Folk Song U.S.A.,* Travis' album appeared. It was noted immediately in the book's discography: "Work songs of the East Kentucky coal camps, perfectly performed. A new album, one of the ten best." Lomax demonstrated this enthusiasm by playing the set's numbers in the spring of 1948 on his Mutual Network radio series, "Your Ballad Man." This Sunday noon program, produced by Elsie Dick, reached a huge small-town audience with the latest recordings of native as well as foreign-language folksongs, and it helped many urban dwellers over the threshold of folk-style acceptance.[11]

Folklorist Ben Botkin also found considerable pleasure in Travis' songs and purchased the album for his son's birthday in 1949.[12] Further, Botkin secured permission from American Music to print "Dark as a Dungeon" in *A Treasury of Southern Folklore* (1949).[13] Botkin transcribed the words as well as the spoken introduction; Herbert Haufrecht transcribed the music. In the *Treasury,* the item was properly identified by song and album title, record number, album copyright date, and publisher — a practice not always followed by other users of Travis material. Botkin was the first editor to place any Travis song in a folklore anthology. This acceptance itself indicates how broadly defined the term *folksong* had become in the New Deal and postwar period.

My personal criterion is more liberal than that of many colleagues, but it is not so free as to have permitted me to share Botkin's judgment. By comparison to "The Death of Mother Jones" in 1932, for example, there was no evidence in 1949 to demonstrate that traditional singers had accepted "Dark as a Dungeon." Until we intensify our attention to the traditions spawned by mass media and employ *poplore,* or a better term, to chart a new discipline centered in popular-culture studies, we shall be unable to separate intelligently the folk from the folk-like material netted by recent collectors and editors.

When I questioned Botkin about his use of "Dark as a Dungeon," he indicated that he liked all the numbers in the Travis album, and that he was drawn to them particularly by the spoken introductions, which he compared to material he had previously categorized as *folksay*. He knew, of course, that "Nine Pound Hammer," "Muskrat," and other songs from the set were traditional, but he wanted to transcribe a new Travis item which might become a folksong. Botkin's stance was unusual in that he looked to the future, while most folklorists are preoccupied with the past. Interestingly, Botkin consciously bypassed "Sixteen Tons," which he believed had less potential for life in tradition than "Dark as a Dungeon."

In the previous chapter I introduced Walter Seacrist and James Farrance as folksingers and commented on how quickly "The Death of Mother Jones" had moved from Gene Autry's disc to their repertoires. It is entirely possible that Travis' *Folk Songs of the Hills* was purchased in various coal-mining communities and that some of its songs were learned by traditional singers. In 1963 the *Kentucky Folklore Record* included "Nine Pound Hammer" and "Way Down in the Mines" ("Dark as a Dungeon") as "folksongs." Earlier, Ed Kahn and I had enjoyed hearing coal miner Bob Garland sing "Sixteen Tons" on his porch near Arjay in Clay County, Kentucky, but he associated the piece with Tennessee Ernie Ford rather than Merle Travis.[14] Apparently the earliest persons to learn any songs directly from the Travis album were fellow country-western artists, semi-professional bluegrass performers, and "folksong revival" singers. At least this must be inferred from records listed in Checklist Six.

The first artist to cover "Dark as a Dungeon" was Travis' close friend Louis Marshall "Grandpa" Jones, who recorded it in the summer of 1950 for King, a Cincinnati firm. King 896 was released in the fall of the year, and, curiously, the disc's printed label credited the song to composer Jones — Lois Music, BMI. This ascription on the part of King and the Lois Publishing Company, which had copyrighted the song in Jones's name on August 31, was a form of careless borrowing all too common in country-music publication. It was particularly uncalled for in that Jones clearly knew that he was using a friend's piece and could have informed

"GRANDPA" JONES

the Lois or King staff had they asked.[15] Ironically, the Lois registration in Washington (EU 213915) was the very first for "Dark as a Dungeon" in that American Music had not actually copyrighted Travis' piece at its time of composition, recording, or release.

Like Travis, Jones grew up in a Kentucky rural community; however, the latter's experiences were that of a farm boy near Smith Mills in Henderson County. As a young man Jones also turned to the professional country-music field, in which he featured old-time banjo songs and related barnyard humor. Both men worked together on the radio in the Brown's Ferry Four during 1941, and continued to swap songs and stories, as well as to hunt and fish together, in subsequent decades. This study is not the place to delineate "Grandpa" Jones's important forty-year role in linking folksong and country-music genres, nor to comment on his droll use of traditional anecdotal material on the popular TV production "Hee-Haw." Here I intend only to stress that his early disc of "Dark

293

as a Dungeon" was the first recorded cover of any Travis coal-mining song.

The second person to take this song into a studio was Cisco Houston, long associated with Woody Guthrie and other People's Artists–People's Songs figures. Houston, an actor and merchant seaman, helped build the bridge between the radical movement of the 1930's and the "folksong revival" of the 1950's. During 1951 Folkways Records issued a ten-inch LP of work songs, *This Land Is My Land,* which contained selections by seven singers, including a "Down in the Mines" sung by Houston. This was, in reality, Travis' number uncredited to him. It is difficult to believe that neither Houston nor the Folkways staff knew the source and identity of the renamed piece. Some years after Houston's death (April 27, 1961), I queried Moe Asch, the Folkways proprietor, about "Down in the Mines." He hazarded only that Cisco had learned Merle's song while doing Denver radio broadcasting, and that Travis and Jack Guthrie were, in Asch's judgment, the two country-western singers fully accepted as "folk" by radicals and "folksong revivalists" in the post–World War II years.[16]

Sing Out, which frequently transcribed Folkways material, in 1953 presented the text and tune of "Dark as a Dungeon," also without credit to Travis. This process of appropriation, not of anonymous or time-worn songs but of recent identifiable compositions, continued with the issuance of still another uncredited "Dark as a Dungeon" sung by Bob De Cormier and Pete Seeger on a *Hootenanny Tonight* LP recorded at two New York "hoots" in 1954. Obviously, the movement of a song to Houston, De Cormier, and Seeger was not part of the folk process as the concept is normally understood by scholars.

"Grandpa" Jones and Cisco Houston were good representatives of the many country and "revival" singers to whom "Dark as a Dungeon" appealed. A third type was John Greenway, a singing professor, who included it in his book *American Folksongs of Protest* as well as his subsequent Riverside LP *American Industrial Folksongs.* This early spread suggests that the number was well on its way to becoming a "revival" standard, if not a folksong, when Tennessee Ernie Ford threw a giant spotlight on another Travis coal-mining piece. The transcription of Merle Travis' original recording of "Sixteen Tons" (Capitol 48001), including his descriptive introduction, is presented at this point.

SIXTEEN TONS

You load sixteen tons and what do you get?
Another day older and deeper in debt.
Saint Peter, don't you call me 'cause I can't go,
I owe my soul to the company store.

(Spoken) Yessir, there's a-many a Kentucky coal miner that pretty near owes his soul to the company store. He gets so far in debt to the coal company he's a-workin' fer that he goes on fer years without being paid one red cent in real honest-to-goodness money. But he can always go to the company store and draw flickers or scrip — you know, that's little brass coins that you can't spend nowhere only at the company store. So they add that against his account and every day he gets a little farther in debt. (chuckle) That sounds pretty bad, but even that's got a brighter side to it.

Now, some people say a man's made out of mud,
But a poor man's made out of muscle and blood,
Muscle and blood, skin and bones,
A mind that's weak and a back that's strong.

Chorus:

Well, I was born one mornin' when the sun didn't shine.
I picked up my shovel and I walked to the mines.
I loaded sixteen tons of Number Nine coal,
And the straw-boss hollered, "Well, bless my soul."

Chorus:

Well, I was born one mornin', it was drizzlin' rain.
Fightin' and trouble is my middle name.
I was raised in the bottoms by a mama hound.
I'm mean as a dog, but I'm as gentle as a lamb.

Chorus:

Well, if you see me a comin' you better step aside.
A lotta men didn't and a lotta men died.
I got a fist of iron, and a fist of steel.
If the right one don't get you, then the left one will.

Chorus:

295

SIXTEEN TONS

This text represents the song as it was first heard by purchasers of *Folk Songs of the Hills* and by listeners to radio stations whose disc jockeys played the set. However, some stations played a slightly different "Sixteen Tons." In the period before taped programs were

296

widespread on the airwaves, some record companies and many advertising agencies produced sixteen-inch electrical transcription discs at various speeds for broadcast purposes. Such discs were commonly called ETs, and were frequently leased for stated time periods rather than offered for direct sale. ETs included fully packaged dramatic or musical programs with or without commercials, as well as straight groups of songs virtually identical to present-day LPs. The role of ETs is hardly known to folklorists, in that these products were not sold to the public and almost never were deposited in archives. Fortunately, some were assiduously gathered by private collectors and discographers. Bob Pinson holds nearly 100 Capitol ETs which contain more than 1,000 songs or instrumentals, many of which were never released on records. Obviously such a private collection is of priceless value to students of folksong. Hence, I have appended to this chapter a list of Travis ETs in Pinson's possession.

In order to illustrate the ET's function in song transmission via radio, collector Pinson generously made available to me a number of Capitol ETs in which Travis appeared as a solo self-accompanied performer, in duets with Texann, and as part of the Coonhunters, a string band.[17] When Merle Travis recorded "Sixteen Tons" on an ET, he altered his "mama hound" couplet to state, "I was raised in a cane-brake by a big mama lion / Cain't no high tone woman break this heart of mine." This improved the rhyme scheme. Also, he altered the song's introduction to bring it closer to home:

> Down in southwest Kentucky where I was born and raised up, they have a little sayin' around the coal mines that they get so far in debt that they owe their soul to the company store. That's almost a fact because a lot of the boys works for years and never really sees any United States money — it's all coal miner's money they call flickers or scrip. Here's a little song about sixteen tons and you'll notice that the line in there says he owes his soul to the company store.[18]

Like "Dark as a Dungeon," "Sixteen Tons" was recorded in Capitol's Hollywood studio on August 8, 1946, and released a year later. Similarly, the latter song was not registered in the Copyright Office until October 31, 1955, when it was retroactively identified as a June 9, 1947, publication (EP 93930). The actual "Sixteen Tons" sent by American Music to Washington for copyright pur-

16 TONS

poses was the published sheet music of the then-new hit bearing Tennessee Ernie's picture on the cover.

When *Folk Songs of the Hills* was released late in 1947, Alan Lomax began to play "Sixteen Tons" on his "Your Ballad Man" radio broadcasts, comparing Travis to Woody Guthrie in each one's ability to compose fresh songs true to his respective folk heritage. This accolade to Travis was not followed by *Sing Out,* which printed the text and tune of "Sixteen Tons" without credit to anyone or indication of source.[19] Nor was the transcriber identified. *Sing Out*'s headnote read, "This traditional miner's song speaks a sharp language — with a real worker's imagery in its poetry." The note on language was excellent, but the completely unsupported

298

ascription of traditional status to "Sixteen Tons" was disturbing in a magazine that had long fought against Tin Pan Alley's exploitation of "the folk." During 1954 *Sing Out* offered its readers "some revisions in the lyrics of 'Sixteen Tons' " by Bill Oliver, again without reference to Travis. It was not until a year after Tennessee Ernie Ford's "Sixteen Tons" became a hit-parade favorite that *Sing Out* announced that Merle Travis had composed this "hard hitting miner's song." Interestingly, reviewer Pete Seeger suggested that Travis, in Hollywood, had known Earl Robinson — composer of "Ballad for Americans," "Sandhog," "The Lonesome Train," and other folk operas and folk cantatas. Travis had been "impressed with Earl's manner of explaining an old folk song to make it come alive to the audience." Seeger was but one of many commentators who helped surround "Sixteen Tons" with its own body of reminiscences and exegesis.

Unlike "Dark as a Dungeon," no recording artist covered "Sixteen Tons" before Ford's Capitol disc was released in mid-October, 1955. Ford, who appealed to country-western and popular-song audiences alike, has written a homiletic autobiography, *This Is My Story — This Is My Song* (1963), which ironically fails to mention his most successful song. Its rise to popularity is sketched here.

Although Ford sang "Sixteen Tons" on radio in the Los Angeles area well before he recorded it, the song was literally launched on television, a medium not previously treated in these studies. "Sixteen Tons" soared to public attention after it was seen "at home." I stress the verb *to see* because in the mid-1950's Negro blues performance styles were beginning to seep out of black communities to reach mass audiences of white teenagers. On the surface there is little to connect Tennessee Ernie Ford to Bill Haley and Elvis Presley or "Sixteen Tons" to "Rock Around the Clock" and "Hound Dog." Yet the twin spectacles of Haley on the film screen in "Rock Around the Clock," after his record of this near-bawdy song had become a hit, and of Presley with his then-outlandish (for TV) long hair and sideburns as well as his near-erotic gyration while singing on Ed Sullivan's hour, are excellent visual symbols to mark the transformation of rhythm-and-blues (formerly race) music into rock-and-roll forms palatable to white America. Television viewers in the fall of 1955 were ready for the semi-rock or rock-abilly treatment in which Ford offered Travis' coal-mining brag to a huge audience. Travis himself, on receiving a BMI "Citation of Achievement (December 5, 1955) for "Sixteen Tons," shrewdly noted that it took "a-hold" partly because it was "a cousin to those ragin' rhythm and blues songs that are rockin' rockin' 'round the clock."[20]

Ernest Jennings Ford, born in Bristol, Tennessee, on February 13, 1919, began his work as a home-town radio announcer in 1939. His musical heritage was primarily that of Methodist hymn singing, reinforced by the folk music known to his farming grandparents. As a young man he aspired to a career as a basso in opera and received some vocal training in Cincinnati. His enrollment in the Army Air Corps during World War II led to work as a radio disc jockey in San Bernardino, California. A move to a similar job in Pasadena (KXLA) brought him closer to Hollywood's Capitol Records studio, where he began to record in 1948, achieving moderate success with such numbers as "Mule Train" and "Shotgun Boogie." It was at KXLA on Cliffie Stone's "Hometown Jamboree" that Ford met Merle Travis, Molly Bee, Harold Hensley, Speedy West, and other country radio performers also involved in records, films, and television. Ford was particularly successful in the latter, in part because his musical training helped ease the transition from east Tennessee's rural church values to pop standards, and in part because it was relatively easier for a Hollywood-based than a Nashville star to break out of the Grand Ole Opry mold and appeal to a national audience. Ford aptly placed himself musically: "You know I couldn't top Roy Acuff's stuff, and I couldn't beat [Perry] Como. So I mix 'em, and the people like it fine."[21] In addition to his skill in mixing forms, Ford also had an entertaining way with the colorful metaphoric speech of his kinfolk. He worked on stage in an easygoing manner, reminiscent of the cowboy-philosopher Will Rogers, and this style earned Ford the tab "pea-pickin' Plato." Like Rogers, Ford appealed to overseas audiences, and he was the first country-western artist to appear in London's Palladium Theatre.

On January 3, 1955, the National Broadcasting Company inaugurated the "Tennessee Ernie Ford Show," a weekday, half-hour television program originating in Hollywood. Actually this morning program had partially evolved out of the "Kay Kyser Kollege of Musical Knowledge," in which Ford had already appeared as a professor but had been unable to display his country bent. Throughout 1955 Ford constantly sought fresh songs for his own show, and late in August he first offered "Sixteen Tons" to a television audience.[22] Ten days later he repeated it as a tribute to workingmen in a special Labor Day telecast, and at this time calls began to reach him for a record. The Capitol disc (3262) was made on September 20 and assigned master number 14296.

It is axiomatic that television pushes both old and new material into quick obsolescence. Fortunately, while the royalties from "Sixteen Tons" were still pouring in, the singer gave Pete Martin, a *Saturday Evening Post* reporter, an account of how he found and presented the Travis piece. Ford's story is not only important in a mining study, but it is highly valuable as one artist's perception of the hit-song process. For Martin, Ford recalled:

> When you do a show five days a week and one night a week, the way I was doing, you use up so much music every day that pretty soon you find yourself hustling for material. You do repeats and you do songs in the top twenty — that way you keep current — but if you do six songs a day five days a week, pretty soon you're scratching for stuff you can use as hard as a starving hen in a concrete barnyard.
>
> Still, it takes more than just desperate looking through old material to make a smash of an eight-year-old song. You can keep rummaging around until you find a song you like, but you can't predict whether it'll hit or not. Sometimes it's a new twist that boosts one of those songs up into the million sales class. Sixteen Tons was written eight years before I recorded it, too. I'd sung Sixteen Tons years before [on radio], but it hadn't been any blockbuster, and Merle Travis, who'd written it, had put it in an album of his songs called *Folk Songs of the Hills*. Nothing happened then either. Then we decided to do some of Merle's things with modern instrumentation [on television]. When Merle did them, he'd used a straight guitar music background. When we did them we used a flute, a bass clarinet, a trumpet, a clarinet, drums, a guitar, vibes and a piano. They gave it a real wonderful sound.
>
> "But what gave Sixteen Tons its hammerlike rhythm?" [Martin] asked, "It sounded like a chain gang pounding on a hard-top road."
>
> It had a good solid beat to begin with. In addition, I snapped my

fingers all through it. Sometimes I set my own tempo during rehearsal by doing that. The orchestra leader asks me, "What tempo do you want, Ernie?" I say, "About like this," and I begin to snap my third finger and thumb together. After I was through rehearsing that song, Lee Gillette, who was in charge of the recording session for Capitol Records, screamed through the telephone from the control room, "Tell Ernie to leave that finger snapping in when you do the final waxing."

They liked Sixteen Tons, all right, at Capitol, when I brought it over and suggested that they record it, but nobody threw a fit over it. Nobody said, "We're glad you brought this along because it's sure to sell a million copies in twenty-one days." They didn't say that because anybody in his right mind knew that wouldn't happen. Yet that's exactly what did happen.[23]

Ford was completely right to stress the difficulty of anyone at Capitol anticipating a smash success with his finger-snapping treatment of a 1947 mining song. I have already suggested that wide audiences in 1955 were ready for semi-rock music, however refined. Conductor-arranger Jack Fascinato, who led Ford's television-studio orchestra and who backed him in recording sessions, must be credited with the right music at the proper time. I am unaware whether or not Fascinato was especially drawn to race-music models or whether he has ever claimed any share in the rise to fame of "Sixteen Tons."

At this point it is worth noting that Ford and Fascinato not only provided an up-tempo rhythmic treatment for the song, underplaying its melodic tone, but that Ford further altered Travis' modified "mama hound" couplet. Ford sang, "I was raised in a canebrake by an ole mama lion / Cain't no high toned woman make me walk the line." It is characteristic of popular-music publishing practices that a hit's text drives earlier forms off the marketplace. During 1956 American Music issued Merle Travis' first song folio containing nineteen of his country-western numbers and "Sixteen Tons."[24] Although this song — the first in the folio — carried a 1947 copyright date, its text was the one changed by Ford in 1955.

It did not take long in the fall of 1955 for Ford's Capitol disc, boosted by television programming, to pass the million-seller mark. At this point Travis allegedly mused, "Well, it's taken eight years."[25] He was accurate in measuring the time span between his and Ford's recordings. However, less than eight weeks elapsed during which Ford's television song became a national hit. In previous chapters I have not stressed disc sales figures for the 1920's and 1930's largely because they are unavailable except in the most generalized terms. By the time Ford recorded "Sixteen Tons," *Billboard* had developed a complex system of ratings to mark the rise and fall of popular, country-western, and rhythm-and-blues material. Songs in each of the categories were marked on separate charts based on store sales, jukebox performance, and radio playing time. In turn, the interaction of movement in the three categories led to an over-all Honor Roll of Hits. From *Billboard* (1955) I have summarized the rise of "Sixteen Tons" with date and page numbers cited for the steps:

October 15: 40 — Review of new pop records (Tennessee Ernie Ford's "Sixteen Tons," Capitol 3262), "This is a wonderful arrangement of a tune with a great folksong flavor. It is a lament that moves all the way, and Ford gives it his best."

November 12: 78 — Honor Roll of Hits, first appearance of "Sixteen Tons" in position # 13.

November 19: 26 — # 6.

November 26: 26 — # 1.

This phenomenal rise in three weeks was, of course, noticed in *Billboard*'s news columns:

November 5: 34 — "This week's territorial charts show Ford bustin' out all over; Minneapolis–St. Paul, Milwaukee, Pittsburgh, and Dallas–Fort Worth are the cities that number this disc in their top [popular] 10. In addition to these, however, there was hardly a major market that did not report the record a strong seller. The singer's many country fans are not overlooking this record; sales to them are also reported to be unusually good."

December 3: 21 — "The disc — possibly the fastest rising platter ever to hit the charts. . . . The song, which has already passed the 1,000,000 disc sales mark. . . ."

Precise sales figures are not published by recording firms; rather, outstanding discs are marked by various intra-industry rewards. I cite but one example from a Capitol publicity brochure,

Record, issued as a service to disc jockeys and reviewers. The January 9, 1956, issue carried a cut of Ford receiving from Capitol's Lee Gillette a gold record of "Sixteen Tons" in honor of the million seller.[26] The photo was not dated; however, early in January a *New York Times'* Hollywood correspondent reported a sales figure of two and a half million, and very appropriately labeled the disc a "backhanded testimonial to TV." In August *TV Guide* raised the sum to three, and on May 27, 1957, *Time* reported four million copies sold.[27]

Not only was "Sixteen Tons" a monetary blockbuster, but Tennessee Ernie Ford continued to feature it on television after it became a record hit, giving it a continuous dramatic impact. Eventually this song led to Ford's promotion from his daytime show to a highly rated Thursday evening "Ford Show" for the Ford Motor Company, beginning on October 4, 1956. But even before the new exposure, other singers had moved in to cover the hit. The first in the recording field was Johnny Desmond, whose Coral 78 rpm and 45 rpm pressings of "Sixteen Tons" were featured in a full-page *Billboard* advertisement (November 12) in which the pop singer thanked disc jockeys for "all those spins."

In time, more than two dozen performers offered their own interpretations. Details are listed in Checklist Six, but it is worth noting that the artists represented a fantastic cross section of talent, for example Eddie Arnold, Jimmy Dean, Bo Diddley, Tom Jones, Mickey Katz, B. B. King, Ewan MacColl. The song was subject to parody and was also translated for recording in Japanese, and Spanish, and other languages. While the industry was apparently offering "Sixteen Tons" to every American home with a record player, and to many overseas, a number of commentators attempted to explain why this industrial song had become a hit.

Denver University folklorist John Greenway, previously acquainted with Merle Travis' *Folk Songs of the Hills,* was amazed at the rise of "Sixteen Tons." He stated, "It just doesn't make sense. It would have made sense back in the depression days, but not now."[28] In addition to his comment on topicality, Greenway suggested that "the song reflected conditions up to about 1932 in Kentucky," that it "probably was written during the past fifty years," and that "stanzas of other Kentucky folksongs apparently

COMPANY STORE: OUTSIDE

were freely incorporated into 'Sixteen Tons.' " To my knowledge, Greenway was the first scholar to cast doubt on Travis' originality, but no evidence was advanced to back the assertion.

This theme of surprise that "Sixteen Tons" should appeal in a prosperous era was voiced by others. Walter Reuther, presiding at the CIO's final convention before its merger with the AFL, reported to the assembly: "When you hear Tennessee Ernie sing 'Sixteen Tons' you begin to understand what has happened in the twenty years of the CIO. There are millions of Americans who hear that song sung and who don't appreciate its social significance — who have no understanding of a coal-mining town in which the employer, the coal-mining company, not only owns the mines and the roads and the schools and the courthouse and the company store, but also the lives of the coal miners themselves."[29] Amusingly, when delegates called on Reuther to sing "Sixteen Tons," he demurred. Reuther liked the song because it pungently recalled a past when millions of workers occupied an economic position like that of Merle Travis' father in Ebenezer, Kentucky, and when such workers were impelled to organize dynamic industrial unions.

Other listeners felt that the song was peculiarly appropriate in 1955 and not just a retrospective portrait. *Time*'s feature on "Sixteen Tons" ended with an anonymous capsule: "We all live on credit and owe our souls to some sort of company store."[30] This emblematic view of America — the land of glittering promise and perpetual debt — represented my personal response to the song's appeal, when it was fresh on the air and in the jukeboxes. Ralph J. Gleason, the *San Francisco Chronicle*'s feature writer on the lively arts, reflected on "Sixteen Tons" in terms of its strong contrast to inane Tin Pan Alley ditties such as "Three Iddy Fishes" and "Doggie in the Window." He identified Travis incorrectly as a "Western singer born in Harlan County" and characterized his hit as "strong as a belt of Kentucky moonshine." Gleason shrewdly noted that "Senator [Joseph] McCarthy might not appreciate the general tenor of the song," and added that "a year or two ago, a song with the overtones of 'Sixteen Tons' wouldn't have gotten enough air play to get it started as a hit."[31]

These comments by Greenway, Reuther, and Gleason — folklorist, labor leader, and journalist — touch a good deal of the response to "Sixteen Tons" but hardly all of it. Rather than exhaust every strand in the number's appeal, I shall note Merle Travis' statement on its meaning. Editor Justin McCarthy of the *United Mine Workers Journal* had heard Tennessee Ernie sing "Sixteen Tons" on his Labor Day (1955) television show.[32] McCarthy was happy to learn that the song's composer came from a UMWA family, and featured the first Travis article to shed light on the background of his mining songs. Travis sagely noted for *Journal* readers the important role of the UMWA organ during his childhood: "In our home in Kentucky the miner's *Journal* ranked alongside the family Bible and the 'wish book' (Sears-Roebuck catalogue)." For readers of this influential labor paper, Travis reported that his songs were set in Muhlenberg County's mines. However, the scenes dramatized in the songs were those of his father's and brother's lives and not his own except by association. Travis also made a good statement on the breakup of the mine community exemplified in his family experience. His brother Taylor was driven out of the industry by the fate of the mines: "An electric motor pulling coal on the 'lie-away' rolled him against the 'rib,' the bulkhead of the interior of the mine, and practically broke every rib in his body. . . . My older brother, John, just drifted away from the coal fields. . . . I left home with a guitar under my arm. . . ."

COMPANY STORE: INSIDE

In noting the meaning of "Sixteen Tons," Travis identified Cliffie Stone, his radio friend who also served as Tennessee Ernie's manager, as the person who had suggested to a *Time* reporter that "most everybody owed most of their money to some sort of company store." Travis was not completely certain that Cliffie's view was "logical." Perhaps Travis was leery of anyone reading too much symbolism into his personal song. In the relatively prosperous decade of the 1950's, he noted for *Journal* readers that "the sinking sun no more reminds the weary miner that he's 'Another day older and deeper in debt.'" The problem of poverty in coal-mining Appalachia, explored in such influential books as Harry Caudill's *Night Comes to the Cumberlands*, lies beyond my study; however, I do not feel that the question of the timeliness of "Sixteen Tons" will ever be resolved as long as some miners are unemployed. Travis' hard-hitting song is no longer on the hit parade but it is still useful as a keen statement on the condition of work.

One recent citation of the meaning of "Sixteen Tons" underscores its continuing function as a symbol of status. During the 1970 political campaign, *Steel Labor* ran a feature on ethnic power aimed at blue-collar workers of immigrant stock. Monsignor Geno Baroni, who had involved Catholics in the civil-rights movement of the 1960's, asserted a "new" position of unity based on his own roots:

307

I think those of us in the ethnic bag can learn from the blacks about the importance of cultural identity. In our eagerness to "make it" we cut ourselves off from our roots too fast. My family came to this country [from Italy] with a strong family setup, a strong work ethic, a fantastic culture, and hope for life in America. . . . I come from a working class family in a company town between Johnstown and Altoona, Pennsylvania. The town is Acosta, and the mine is Mine 120. It was one of the last areas in coal country to be organized. We moved from a shack to a company house. The company owned the electricity, the water, the outhouses. We bought everything at the company store. Remember that song, "Sixteen Tons." My father loves that song; he sang it practically every day.[33]

In my interviews with Merle Travis, I was curious to learn whether "Sixteen Tons" stemmed from an earlier song or was newly composed for his Capitol 1946 session. Parenthetically, I might state that in fifteen years of talking to country musicians I have met few persons as perceptive as Travis on the thorny problem of composition / recomposition and as clear as he in the recall of precise sources.

Travis knew that his father had sung a rare Kentucky local ballad on a Browder mine explosion (February 1, 1910) which involved a black miner walking out of an entry playing a banjo. This represented a layer of tradition beyond Merle's recall, for he could not piece together the text. He could recall Vernon Dalhart's "Dream of the Miner's Child" because his sister Vada played it on her wind-up Edison phonograph, but he didn't want to sing it because it seemed to him to be stylistically inappropriate. He had learned "I Am a Pilgrim" from Mose Rager, whose elder brother Lyman had heard a black prisoner sing it in an Elkton, Kentucky, jail. Travis and his friend "Grandpa" Jones had heard "That's All" at a Negro revival meeting in Cincinnati during their days as youthful buskers. Not only did the song's jazz beat appeal to Merle but he relished its actual learning: he and his pal were the only two white boys at the affair. "Muskrat," a traditional animal song, belonged to fellow performer and fiddler Harold Hensley, who had sung it in 1946 on the beach at Santa Monica, California. It came to Harold from his mother at White Top, Virginia, and Travis, exercising poetic license, placed it in his Capitol album with the comment that an old fellow had carried it to Kentucky from Virginia.

I cite these several points made by Merle Travis to illustrate that he is a folksong purist in his careful attention to origin and transmission. When Ed Kahn and I visited him at home in 1960, he demonstrated a "non-folksong" in process by showing us the scribbled notes for "Loading Coal," which he had just written "on assignment" for his friend Johnny Cash.[34] His technique was to fashion a good punch line and build the text around it. To my query on the melody, he laughed, "It just suits itself to the words."

This description of "Loading Coal's" genesis also fitted Travis' situation in 1946. Lee Gillette and Cliffie Stone had been prodding Merle to write coal songs. During the war his brother John had written him a letter containing the cliché "another day older and deeper in debt." Travis also noted that John was an avid reader of war correspondent Ernie Pyle and perhaps reflected the latter's commonsense values. The Saint Peter fragment came from Merle's memory of his father's ironic reply to a friendly query about his health: "I can't afford to die. I owe my soul to the company store." The "strong back and weak mind" quip belonged to the proverbial speech of all miners as well as other craftsmen. (During my apprenticeship I was told constantly that a "woodbutcher" needed only a strong back and his brains knocked out.) With these keys Travis put "Sixteen Tons" together a few days before the June recording session.[35] Had the song not become a fabulous hit late in 1955, I doubt that anyone would have raised any question about its origin.

There are many instances of song hits which give rise to rival ownership claims. This seems particularly true in the case of folklike numbers where linguistic formulas, performing style, and ideas are held in common by members of a given community. Since "Sixteen Tons" had limited circulation in 1947, it must have seemed an ancient song during 1955 to some listeners upon hearing it for a second time. My preparation of a coal-mining discography was undertaken before "Sixteen Tons" became a hit, and I can recall reading or hearing comments that it was traditional. For example, Russell Ames in *The Story of American Folk Song* (1955) printed two stanzas and the chorus of "Sixteen Tons," which he labeled a "traditional miner's song."[36] Subsequently a labor journal stated, "This old tune which for years has been sung throughout the mining areas, has suddenly mushroomed into a national hit."[37] During 1956 I raised this problem with D. K. Wilgus, then on the staff at Western Kentucky State College in Bowling Green, some fifty miles from Muhlenberg County. He too was "investigating the reports that it was sung at miners' meetings in Kentucky before Travis recorded it. Latest reports say that he composed it as a boy many years before he recorded it."[38] In several field trips Wilgus could not confirm any of these accounts, which of course were contradictory to the fact of composition in California during 1946.

It was not until 1968 that a rival but retroactive claim was seriously advanced on the origin of "Sixteen Tons." At this time, an LP edited by John Cohen, *When Kentucky Had No Union Men* (Folkways FTS 31016) by George Davis, was released. This is an excellent production and by any standards one of the most important American industrial-song documents prepared in recent years. Davis, born August 19, 1906, in La Follette, Tennessee (close to Coal Creek), moved to Kentucky for trapper-boy employment at the age of thirteen. In this period he began to write poems but did not set one to music until about 1937, when he composed his first song, "Harlan County Blues," which was closely related in style and melody to the "Harlan Town Tragedy." This latter item, about a local crime or possibly feud ballad involving two coal miners, was commercially recorded in 1938 by Asa Martin (Vocalion 04894).

During 1940 George Korson collected a number of Davis' pieces, and "Harlan County Blues" was subsequently included in the Library of Congress *Songs and Ballads of the Bituminous Miners*. In 1949 Davis recorded two coal items for Rich-R-Tone, an obscure Johnson City, Tennessee, label. For the liner notes of Davis' Folkways LP, which included a personalized "Sixteen Tons," Cohen wrote: "Davis claims to have composed 'Sixteen Tons' during the 1930's and feels that Merle Travis and Tennessee Ernie capitalized on his song, though changing the chords somewhat."

I do not in any way wish to diminish Davis' creativity or the significance of having an LP of industrial songs performed by a miner. However, Cohen offered no evidence to support Davis' claim. Perhaps the matter is unimportant and only of pedantic interest to scholars who burrow into the song-origin underground. I commend *When Kentucky Had No Union Men* to all listeners who enjoy aural documentaries, but I retain my belief in Merle Travis' claim to "Sixteen Tons."

To close my discussion of "Sixteen Tons," I summarize an interview with a former Drakesboro miner who lived in Muhlenberg County when Travis was a youngster "crazy about a guitar as soon as he was old enough to hold one." Jay Watkins had worked at the Beech Creek mines from 1926 to 1928 while "Uncle Rob" Travis was still alive, but, like many other miners, Watkins left Kentucky in "tough times" for the auto industry.[39] When I met Jay he was a staff official in the United Automobile Workers. I value his comments on Travis' album because Watkins had no special folkloric or country-music axe to grind. He had purchased *Folk Songs of the Hills* out of a sense of identity with a home-town boy and also with fellow worker Mose Rager, who "taught Merle to play the guitar." Watkins accepted implicitly the notion that the Capitol album's numbers reflected Beech Creek life.

In Travis' autobiographical sketch previously quoted as background for "Dark as a Dungeon," we heard through the composer's ears the good sound of Number Nine's whistle calling the elder Travis to work. Watkins himself associated this same tipple whistle with the wonderful smell of fried potatoes. When Watkins first played the record of "Over By Number Nine," which was based on the sounds of Travis' childhood, Watkins could "taste the savory potatoes in the pan." It is one of the mysteries of sound-recording circumstance that no performer has ever covered "Over By Number Nine," my personal favorite on Travis' album, and one of the most evocative aural reports to come out of a coal camp. Watkins also reported that he enjoyed Travis' reworking of "Muskrat" to include the sound of miners slapping their mules while driving them to above-ground stables at the end of the workday. In the mid-1920's the Beech Creek mines were hardly mechanized and mules worked both above and below ground.

Watkins was delighted to inform me that the line in "Sixteen Tons" which said "I was raised in the bottoms by a mama hound" was a local reference to Pond Creek, flowing between Ebenezer and Greenville, the county seat. All the mine children played in the bottoms, where they came to swim and fish. Watkins further pointed out to me a Beech Creek local custom which I had never heard Merle Travis relate or encountered in any article on "Sixteen Tons." The specific usage *sixteen tons* referred to the on-the-job practice of initiating a new miner. In the mid-1920's a man usually loaded eight to ten tons. According to "turn-of-the-mine" informal rules, work was evenly divided in order that each man might reach but not exceed his quota. Naturally union men despised "hogs," "ratebusters," and other "scissorbills" who broke the rules. However, when a youngster came to work, the old-timers slacked off on their loads so that the newcomer could "make sixteen" on his very first day. It was a sign of manhood to be initiated by reaching this excessive figure. Jay Watkins was proud that he had loaded his sixteen tons in Beech Creek long before he could possibly dream that "Uncle Rob's" boy would turn the local custom into a song known to a worldwide audience.

Something of the affinity which ex-miner Watkins felt for Merle Travis' compositions as soon as his album became available was later expressed by thousands of miners on June 29, 1956, in Ebenezer, Kentucky. While "Sixteen Tons" was at the height of its phenomenal popularity, one of Travis' boyhood chums suggested a local marker and celebration for the man and song.[40] Mrs. Bunnie Baugh, who had befriended young Merle and who had clerked in the company store where his parents had exchanged scrip for food, donated a strip of land adjacent to the Missionary Baptist Church, the Travis family place of worship. A local committee of Muhlenberg County citizens, including Central City newspaper and radio men, UMWA officials, and Raymond Kirkpatrick, the operator of Number Nine, where "Uncle Rob" had worked, undertook arrangements. The group secured a one-ton native limestone monument holding a bronze plaque on which Travis' likeness, in relief, was flanked by a crossed pick and shovel and guitar. Underneath the facsimile was lettered the chorus of "Sixteen Tons."

On the day of tribute — the second day in the UMWA contractual bituminous vacation period — visitors by the thousands poured into Ebenezer for rounds of speeches, music, and barbecue. Travis, who returned home in a Cadillac, was joined for the festivities by Gene Autry, Chet Atkins, and the Everly Brothers. Autry

HAND LOADING

and Atkins personified Travis' professional standing as a country-western star. Phil and Don Everly, exponents of rockabilly and folk-rock music, were the sons of Travis' Drakesboro friend Ike Everly, who along with Mose Rager had given "Uncle Rob's" boy his initial guitar lessons.

This celebration, which brought country musicians and coal miners as well as sound-recording personnel and Kentucky political figures literally into Mrs. Baugh's front yard, exemplified the multiple strands of "Sixteen Tons." During 1956 the song had come to speak both for old folk values and current entertainment-industry profits. While UMWA official Harvey Bell could dramatically tell the celebrants that "Sixteen Tons" was a reminder of "the good old days" of company-store exploitation, Capitol Records executive Ken Nelson could quietly contemplate the song's fantastic profit to the music industry. There is no contradiction between Bell's and Nelson's perceptions. Both men ably related to Travis' song in terms of their roles. Precisely because America is a plural society of hundreds of groups at every associational level is it possible to see "Sixteen Tons" in a kaleidoscopic light. To the extent that Travis' other pieces from *Folk Songs of the Hills* never became smash hits, they are far easier to view in narrow perspective.

313

Of the handful of items which I have selected for close examination in this book, "Dark as a Dungeon" and "Sixteen Tons" are the most recent in time of composition, but they are comparable to the older "Only a Miner" in fixing a few certainties of mining life into American consciousness. In the sense of stereotype, theme, and style, Merle Travis' two numbers resemble folksongs without evidencing movement in tradition as the process normally is understood by scholars. I do not see much value in seeking scraps of data to demonstrate that the folk embraced either song. It may well be that in the next decade some collectors will net these pieces from folksingers. For the present I have felt it sufficient to note the role of the sound-recording and television industry in popularizing Travis' folk-like material. Capitol Records aimed *Folk Songs of the Hills* at folksong enthusiasts in a period when the firm had reason to believe the album would be well received. I have never seen sales figures for the 78 rpm set but at least one reporter termed it a "flop."[41]

This harsh judgment implies that sales alone give a record its worth. Holding to monetary consideration, nothing happened to Travis' songs until Tennessee Ernie Ford presented "Sixteen Tons" to television viewers. Yet "Dark as a Dungeon" had already reached many "folksong revival" and country singers before Labor Day, 1955. Additionally, Merle Travis' recomposition of "Nine Pound Hammer" (the subject of the following chapter) also reached new audiences before "Sixteen Tons" became a hit. From 1956 to the present day, it has been difficult to separate the stories of these three Travis items. Each song is accepted by a wide range of listeners as an authentic portrait of mining life. In this sense *Folk Songs of the Hills* must be judged an aural document of import.

Beyond the matter of song history, this chapter has touched on Merle Travis' deep roots in tradition. By whatever standards we frame the term *folk society,* we can use such norms to encompass his childhood in a Kentucky mining community. Yet Travis, as an adult composer of country-western hits as well as a professional trouper, has placed himself squarely in the realm of popular culture and urban society. Many Americans have made such a transition; few are as qualified as Travis to describe the shift. Those of us who are intrigued by his skill as a guitarist, his superb ear for folk speech,

HAROLD LEVENTHAL presents

Country Music
at Carnegie Hall

Lester Flatt &
Earl Scruggs

and The Foggy Mountain Boys

and First New York Appearance of the
popular country songwriter and singer

Merle Travis

Saturday Eve. December 8th, at 8:40 P.M.
at Carnegie Hall 57th STREET & SEVENTH AVE., N.Y.C.

TICKETS: $4.50, 4.00, 3.50, 3.00, 2.50

on sale at Carnegie Box office

also on sale at:

Melody Lane Record Ranch, 73 Franklin Ave., Franklin Square, L. I., PR-5-5151

Folklore Center, 110 Macdougal St., New York, GR 7-5987

CARNEGIE HALL CONCERT FLYER

315

his compositional technique, and his warm performing style will be deeply rewarded if he writes a full autobiographical sequel to his *Folk Songs of the Hills.*

1. "Merle Travis Biography," Capitol Records Information Bureau (1949), a two-page mimeographed release.

2. For sources see D. K. Wilgus, "On the Record," *Kentucky Folklore Record,* VII (1961), 126. For technique see Happy Traum, *Finger-Picking Styles for Guitar* (New York, 1966), 41.

3. "Merle Travis Biography," Capitol Records Information Bureau (ca. 1946), a two-page mimeographed release.

4. Merle Travis, "The Saga of 'Sixteen Tons,' " *United Mine Workers Journal* (Dec. 1, 1955), 5, and "I Have a Sick Sister in Texas," in *Country and Western Keepsake,* ed. Larry Moeller (Nashville, 1967), 18. These two sketches are supplemented by my interviews with Travis: Apr. 20, 1960, Oct. 28, 1966, June 15, 1967, July 6, 1969, as well as with Bunnie Baugh, Mose Rager, and Ike Everly, respectively: Aug. 2, 1961, Aug. 2, 1961, Aug. 3, 1963. I have also benefited from an unpublished paper by Ed Kahn, "Merle Travis: Folk Informant" (1965).

5. Travis, "I Have a Sick Sister," 19.

6. Travis, "The Saga of 'Sixteen Tons,' " 5.

7. Ken Griffis letter to me, July 24, 1969.

8. Bill Ladd, "The Home Town Smokes Travis Out," *Louisville Courier Journal Magazine* (Nov. 16, 1947), 6. The *National Hillbilly News* (Nov.-Dec., 1947), 21, included a photo of Capitol's top A & R men displaying Travis' *Folk Songs of the Hills.* Presumably this publicity at year's end marked the actual appearance of the album.

9. Until Cross submitted Travis' songs to the Copyright Office in 1956 they had been protected by common law rather than statutory law.

10. Dan Auerbach kindly made available to me the tape of the Travis Chicago concert.

11. Lomax noted the late Elsie Dick's radio production skills in a letter to me, Jan. 14, 1969.

12. Interview, Jan. 3, 1965.

13. In 1949 American Music had not yet copyrighted "Dark" and its granting of reprint rights was ambiguous. Correspondence on this permission grant for *A Treasury of Southern Folklore* is not now available. Botkin letter to me, May 3, 1971.

14. Don Carlos Amburgey, "Folk Songs," *Kentucky Folklore Record,* IX (1963), 11; Bob Garland interview, Aug. 27, 1961.

15. Jones letter to me, Jan. 23, 1969.

16. Moe Asch interview, Aug. 6, 1969. See also Bill Wolff, "For Cisco Houston — the End of the Road," *Sing Out,* XI (Oct., 1961), 8.

17. Texann's full name was Sydna Jacqueline Nation; friends called her Lois. For a time she was married to country entertainer Buck Kelly. Two of the Coonhunters were guitarist Wesley Tuttle and fiddler Charlie Linville.

18. Transcribed from Capitol ET G 109, in possession of Bob Pinson.

19. *Sing Out,* II (Nov., 1952), 3. See also *ibid.,* IV (Fall, 1954), 6, and Pete Seeger, "Record Review: 'Sixteen Tons,'" *ibid.,* VI (Winter, 1956), 40.

20. "Whatever Happened to Love? Coal Mining Song No. 1 on Hit Parade . . . ," *News from BMI* (ca. Dec., 1955), a five-page mimeographed press release.

21. "High-Priced Pea Picker," *Time,* LXIX (May 27, 1957), 72. For Ford's metaphoric style see also Richard G. Hubler, "That Pea-Pickin', Philoso-phizin' Tennessee Ernie," *Coronet,* XL (Aug., 1956), 115.

22. I am unable to document the first television performance of "Sixteen Tons" by a studio log. The late August date is drawn from "A Hit on the Double," *Newsweek,* XLVI (Nov. 28, 1955), 110.

23. Pete Martin, "I Call on Tennessee Ernie Ford," *Saturday Evening Post,* CCXXX (Sept. 28, 1957), 124.

24. *Merle Travis Hit Parade Folio No. 1* (Hollywood, 1956).

25. "Merle Travis' 'Sixteen Tons' Took Eight Years to Become Smash Hit," *Music Views* (Jan., 1956), 4, a Capitol Records Magazine.

26. "Beaming Tennessee Ernie Ford Is Presented . . . ," *Record* (Jan. 9, 1956), a Capitol Records brochure.

27. Oscar Godbout, "On TV from Hollywood," *New York Times* (Jan. 8, 1956), sec. 2, 11; "Housewives' Hillbilly," *TV Guide,* IV (Aug. 25, 1956), 17; *Time,* LXIX (May 27, 1957), 72.

28. "'Sixteen Tons,' Hit Parade Topper, Amazes DU Song Authority," [Denver] *Rocky Mountain News* (Dec. 4, 1955), 17.

29. Ed Townsend, "People at Work: 'Sixteen Tons' Impact," *Christian Science Monitor* (Jan. 7, 1956), 9.

30. "The Wild Birds Do Whistle," *Time,* LXVI (Dec. 19, 1955), 78.

31. Ralph J. Gleason, "The Lively Arts," *San Francisco Chronicle* (Jan. 3, 1956), 19.

32. Travis, "The Saga of 'Sixteen Tons,'" 5.

33. Monsignor Geno Baroni, "I'm a Pig, Too," *Steel Labor* (Sept., 1970), 9.

34. Johnny Cash, *Ride This Train* (Columbia CL 1464). "Loading Coal" was also performed by Cash on his TV program, Saturday, July 12, 1969.

35. Every article on "Sixteen Tons" late in 1955 and through 1956 gave some account of its origin. I have not attempted to cite them all. In addition to articles and interviews already mentioned see "What Made 'Sixteen Tons' a Hit," *Cowboy Songs,* no. 46 (May, 1956), 4, and Bill Ladd, "Beech Creek Coal Miner Gave Son Idea for 'Sixteen Tons' Song Hit," *Louisville Courier Journal* (Nov. 30, 1955).

36. Russell Ames, *The Story of American Folk Song* (New York, 1955), 201. When I queried Ames about "Sixteen Tons," he wrote that Travis' *UMWJ*

article (Dec. 1, 1955) "leaves no room for assuming anything except that the words are wholly his." Letter to me, Nov. 3, 1957.

37. "Sixteen Tons and Deeper in Debt," *March of Labor,* VII (Dec., 1955), 21.

38. Wilgus letter to me, Nov. 22, 1956.

39. Interview, Sept. 26, 1957.

40. Two Central City, Ky., newspapers, the *Messenger* and the *Times-Argus,* carried extensive reports and photographs on the Travis festivities before and after June 29, 1956. See also Rex Lauck, "Merle Travis Day," *United Mine Workers Journal* (July 15, 1956), 10; Joe Creason, "One-Ton Honor Given Composer of 'Sixteen Tons,' " *Louisville Courier Journal* (June 30, 1956); Joe Creason, "Sixteen Tons — What Do You Get?" *Louisville Courier Journal Magazine* (July 15, 1956), 13.

41. Townsend, " 'Sixteen Tons' Impact," 9.

CHECKLIST SIX

PART I: "DARK AS A DUNGEON"

————. Merle Travis, Capitol 48001 (1334). Aug. 8, 1946, Hollywood; released late in 1947 in album *Folk Songs of the Hills* (AD 50).

Reissued: *Back Home,* Capitol T 891; released Dec., 1957. Parallel issue: EAP 1-891.

> *The Best of Merle Travis,* Capitol T 2662.

> *21 Years a Country Singer,* Capitol T 21010 (England).

————. Merle Travis, American Music, Hollywood (June 9, 1947), EP 97185. Lead sheet received at Copyright Office Feb. 27, 1956, but backdated to 1947.

Transcribed: Botkin, *T S F* (1949), 729, m.

> *Sing Out,* III (Apr., 1953), 8, m. Uncredited. Also reprinted in *Sing* (England), III (Aug., 1956), 43, m, under title "Lure of the Mines."

> Greenway, *A F P* (1953), 172, m.

> Fowke and Glazer, *S W F* (1960), 49, m.

> Lomax, *F S N A* (1960), 295, m.

————. Grandpa Jones, King 896 (3013). July, 1950, Cincinnati.

Reissued: *Sixteen Sacred Gospel Songs,* King 822; released 1963.

————. Marshall Louis Jones, Louis Publishing Company, Cincinnati (Aug. 31, 1950), EU 213915.

"Down in the Mines." Cisco Houston, *This Land Is My Land,* Folkways FC 1027; released 1951. Brochure includes text.

————. Bob De Cormier and Pete Seeger, *Hootenanny Tonight,* HLP 201. Apr., 1954, New York. Parallel issues: Topic TRC 98 (England, 78 rpm); Topic TOP 37 (45 rpm).

Reissued: Folkways FN 2511; released ca. June, 1959.

————. John Greenway, *American Industrial Folksongs,* Riverside RLP 607. Oct., 1955, New York.

————. Tennessee Ernie Ford, *This Lusty Land,* Capitol T 700. Hollywood. Parallel issue: EAP 2-700. Ford's version also released on a single, Capitol 4531, and an LP, *The Great Ones,* Capitol T 1718.

————. Lee Moore, Cross Country 522. ca. May, 1956.

————. Maddox Brothers and Rose, Four Star 1540 (3890). ca. June, 1956.

————. Bobby Hill, Sparton 306 (Canada). ca. Mar., 1957.

————. Charlie Gore, King 4879. ca. July, 1957, Cincinnati.

————. Glen Yarborough, *Come and Sit by My Side,* Tradition TLP 1019. ca. Nov., 1957, New York. Parallel issue: *Folk Sampler,* TSP 1.

319

————. Grandpa Jones, Decca 30264. ca. Feb., 1957. Parallel issue: Brunswick 05676 (England).

Reissued: *An Evening with Grandpa Jones,* Decca DL 4364; released 1963.

————. Kitty White, *Folk Songs,* Mercury MG 20183; released ca. Jan., 1958.

————. Children of Adam, *One More Round,* Ikon 571. ca. May, 1959, Boston.

————. Cisco Houston, *The Cisco Special,* Vanguard VRS 9057. ca. July, 1959, New York. Parallel issues: Top Rank 30-028 (England); Fontana TFL 6007 (England).

————. Odetta, *Odetta Sings the Ballad for Americans,* Vanguard VRS 9066. ca. Aug., 1959, New York.

————. Steve Benbow and others, *Rocket Along,* HMV DLP 1204. ca. Jan., 1960, England.

"Down in the Mines." Reivers, *The Reivers,* Top Rank JAR 283. ca. Feb., 1960, England. Parallel issue: JKP 2062 (45 rpm).

————. Danny Dill, *Folk Songs of the Wild West,* MGM E 3819. ca. Mar., 1960.

————. Reno and Smiley, *Country Songs,* King 701. ca. July, 1960, Cincinnati. Parallel issue: King 5369 (45 rpm).

————. Mac Wiseman, Dot 16194 (9028). ca. Feb., 1961.

————. Joe Glazer, *Songs of Work and Freedom,* Washington WR 460. ca. Mar., 1961, Washington, D.C.

"Down in the Mines." Gateway Singers, *Down in the Valley,* MGM E 3905. ca. Apr., 1961, Hollywood.

————. Tarriers, *Tell the World about This,* Atlantic 8042. ca. Apr., 1961, New York.

————. Journeymen, *Coming Attraction — Live,* Capitol T 1770. ca. Mar., 1962.

————. Robin Christenson, *You Can Sing It Yourself,* Folkways FC 7625. ca. July, 1962. Brochure includes text and tune transcribed by Alan Beuchner.

————. Harry Belafonte, *The Many Moods of Harry Belafonte,* Victor LPM 2574. New York.

————. Newcastle Trio, *Newcastle Trio,* Grand Prix K 179. ca. Oct., 1962. A "budget" LP probably also issued under other labels and artists' names.

"Way Down in the Mines." Amburgey, *K F R,* IX (1963), 19.

————. Green River Boys, Capitol 4990. ca. July, 1963.

————. Glen Campbell, *Twelve String Guitar,* World Pacific WP 1812. ca. Sept., 1963. Parallel issue: Fontana 688008 ZL (England).

————. Big Three, *The Big Three,* FM 307. ca. Oct., 1963.

"Down in the Mine." Wray Family, Lawn 220. ca. Feb., 1964.

————. Joan Baez. *Joan Baez in San Francisco,* Fantasy 5015. ca. July, 1964.

————. Stonemans, *Big Ball in Monterey,* World Pacific WP 1828.

————. Joe Glazer, *Songs of Coal,* Sound Studios 12-1137. Sept., 1964, Bal Harbour, Fla.

————. Jim Glaser, *Just Looking for a Home,* Starday SLP 158. ca. Oct., 1964, Nashville.

————. Lee Moore, Arc 606. ca. Feb., 1965, Canada.

————. Don Gibson, *Too Much Hurt,* Victor LSP 3460.

————. Chad Mitchell, *Chad Mitchell — Himself,* Warner Brothers WS 1667. July, 1966, New York.

————. Johnny Cash, *Johnny Cash at Folsom Prison,* Columbia CS 9639.

PART II: "SIXTEEN TONS"

————. Merle Travis, Capitol 48001 (1333). Aug. 8, 1946, Hollywood; Released late in 1947 in album *Folk Songs of the Hills* (AD 50).
Reissued: *Back Home,* Capitol T 891; released Dec., 1956. Parallel issue: EAP 1-891.
    The Best of Merle Travis, Capitol T 2662.
    21 Years a Country Singer, Capitol T 21010 (England).
————. Merle Travis, American Music, Hollywood (June 9, 1947), EP 93930. Printed sheet music received at Copyright Office Oct. 31, 1955, but backdated to 1947. Sheet music issued by American Music has cover photo of Tennessee Ernie Ford.
Transcribed: *Sing Out,* III (Nov., 1952), 3, m. Uncredited.
    Fowke and Glazer, *S W F* (1960), 52, m.
    Lomax, *F S N A* (1960), 294, m.
————. *Merle Travis Hit Parade Folio No. 1,* Merle Travis, American Music, Hollywood (1956), 6, m. Folio includes biographical data.

————. Merle Travis, Capitol G-109. An electrical transcription made in Hollywood. Date unknown.

————. Tennessee Ernie Ford, Capitol 3262 (14296). Sept. 21, 1955, Hollywood. This hit record was released Oct. 15 on 78 and 45 rpm discs. Subsequently it was reissued many times from its original master. It was also re-recorded, both in studios and at live performances. In the absence of a Ford discography citing master numbers I have included all post-1955 discs below.
CL 14500 (78 rpm, England).
EAP 1-693 (45 rpm).
EAP 1014 (45 rpm, England).
6007 (45 rpm).
Gold Record, T 830.

Ford Favorites, T 841.

Sixteen Tons and Other Favorites, T 1380.

Tennessee Ernie Ford Invites You to Come to the Fair, T 1473. Live recording made at Indiana State Fair, 1960.

Today's Top Hits, T 9130.

This Land Is Your Land, United Automobile Workers UAW 2. Master leased for anthology.

"Special Commemorative Pressing of Sixteen Tons," S-1-EFS. Feb., 1969. Capitol promotional 45 rpm, not for sale.

————. Johnny Desmond, Coral 61529. Oct., 1955. The first released cover of Ford's hit. Note: Eight items below issued on 78s and 45s as further covers of hit.

————. Bob Caroll, Camden 306.
Reissued: *The Biggest Hits of 56,* Camden CAL 318.

————. Eugene Church, King 5715.

————. Buddy Durham, Emperor 204.

————. B. B. King, RPM 451.

————. Bill Long, Sparton 193 (Canada).

————. Ewan MacColl, Topic TRC 97 (England).

————. Marvin and the Chirps, Tip Top 202.

————. Red Sovine, Decca 29739. Parallel issue: Brunswick 05513 (England).
Reissued: *Country Music Time,* Decca 4736.

————. Fred Hellerman, *The Weavers at Carnegie Hall,* Vanguard VRS 9010. Recorded at Christmas Eve concert, 1955.

————. Eddie Arnold, *Tennessee Waltz,* Victor LPM 1293. Parallel issue: EPA-915.

————. Snooky Lanson, *Ten Years of Great Hits,* Dot DLP 3279.

————. Mac Wiseman, *Twelve Great Hits,* Dot DLP 3313.

————. Frankie Laine, *Balladeer,* Columbia CL 1393. Parallel issue: Philips BBL 7357 (England).

————. Four Lads, *The Four Lads,* Kapp KL 1224.

————. Hi-Lo's, *The Hi-Lo's Happen to Folk Songs,* Reprise R 6034.

————. Three Young Men from Montana, *Folk Song Favorites,* Cameo C 1025.

————. Troubador Singers, *Sing Out on the Beach,* Horizon WP 1619.

————. Jimmy Dean, *Big Bad John and Other Fabulous Songs and Tales,* Columbia CL 1735. Parallel issue: Philips BBL 7537 (England).

————. Oscar Brown, Jr., *In a New Mood,* Columbia CL 1873.

————. Dave Dudley, *Songs about the Working Man,* Mercury MG 20899.

————. Billy Vaughn, *Another Hit Album,* Dot DLP 3593.

————. Lorne Greene, *The Man,* Victor LPM 3302.

————. Bo Diddley, *Bo Diddley Is a Gunslinger,* Checker LP 29777; released ca. June, 1965.

————. Frank Chacksfield, *Great Country & Western Hits,* London 3436.

————. Hank Thompson, *Hank Thompson,* Warner Brothers WS 1686.

————. Billy Ward, *Eighteen King Size R & B Hits,* Columbia 2667; released ca. June, 1967.

————. Big Bill Broonzy, *Big Bill Broonzy,* Archive of Folk Music FS 213.

————. Stevie Wonder, *Down to Earth,* Tamla S 272; released ca. 1967.

————. Tom Jones, *Funny Familiar Forgotten Feelings,* Press 61011; released ca. July, 1968.

Parodies

"Sixteen Pounds." Gloria Becker, Real 1304. Parallel issue: Sparton 203 (Canada).

"Ballad of the Salt Spreader." Richard Peters Hagan, Happy Hearts 115.

————. Homer and Jethro, *Homer and Jethro at the Country Club,* Victor LPM 2181. Parallel issue: Victor EPA 716.
Reissued: *The Humorous Side of Country Music,* Camden CAL 768.
    The Best of Homer and Jethro, Victor LPM 3474.

"Sixteen Tacos." Spike Jones, Verve 2003.

————. Mickey Katz, *All Mish Mash,* Capitol T 779. Parallel issue: Capitol 3342.

————. Lou Monte, *The Great Italian American Hits,* Reprise 6005.

"Sixteen Tons Rock and Roll." Jimmy Murphy, Columbia 4-21534.

"The Teacher's Lament." Pete Seeger, *Gazette,* Folkways FN 2501.

Translations

"Sixteen Tons." Kazuya Kosaka, Nippon Columbia JL 170 (78 rpm); SB 1 (45 rpm).

"Dieciseis Toneladas." Candelas Quartet, Colonial Latin CNL 164. A Los Angeles release.

"Dieciseis Toneladas." Loco Gomez, Victor 23-6886.

"Dieciseis Toneladas." Reyes Hermanos, *Reyes Hermanos con Teresita,* Victor MKL 1050.

Note: A slightly rearranged, copyrighted sheet-music version of "Sixteen Tons" was issued by Larabee Publications, New York (1963). Credited to Albert Gamse and Stephen Sechak.

APPENDIX SIX

MERLE TRAVIS CAPITOL ELECTRICAL TRANSCRIPTIONS

The area of ETs is largely unexplored by discographers. Bob Pinson has collected nearly a complete set of Capitol ETs through G-184. The list below represents only his Travis Capitol ET holdings. It is unknown whether more Travis Capitol ETs were made than are represented here. However, Travis did record ETs for other uses such as Armed Forces radio recruiting. Unknown to me are the precise dates of the Travis Capitol ETs which were produced at Radio Records in Hollywood.

The Coonhunters included Wesley Tuttle on rhythm guitar, Charlie Linville on fiddle, and Texann on vocals. Some of the selections indicate that the string band also included a bass and a banjo player; their names are unknown to me. Texann's full name was Mrs. Sydna Jacqueline Nation Kelly.

CAPITOL G-1 (The Coonhunters)
    Midnight Special — M. T. & duet
    Old Joe Clark — M. T. & duet
    Jim Crow — M. T. & duet
    Glendy Burke — M. T. & duet
    Jim Crack Corn — M. T. & duet
CAPITOL G-2 (The Coonhunters)
    Sourwood Mountain — M. T. & duet
    Bile That Possum — M. T. & duet
    Fiddlin' Dan — M. T.
    She'll Be Comin' Round the Mountain — M. T. & duet
    I'm Goin' Back to Dixie — M. T. & duet
CAPITOL G-3 (The Coonhunters)
    Higgin's Farewell — inst.
    Ham Bone Am Sweet — M. T. & duet
    Sally Goodwin — inst.
    Oh Dem Golden Slippers — M. T.
    Off She Goes — inst.
    Fisher's Hornpipe — inst.
CAPITOL G-4 (The Coonhunters)
    Detour — M. T. & duet
    You Are My Sunshine — M. T. & duet
    I'm Sick and Tired of You, Little Darlin' — M. T. & duet
    Footprints in the Snow — M. T. & duet
    Grey Eagle — inst.
CAPITOL G-5 (The Coonhunters)
    Nellie Bly — M. T. & duet
    I'll Remember You Love, in My Prayers — M. T.

Liza Jane — M. T. & duet
Comin' Home from the Wake — M. T.
You're the Apple of My Eye — M. T. & duet
CAPITOL G-6 (The Coonhunters)
False Hearted Girl — M. T. & duet
John Henry — M. T.
Nancy Till — M. T. & duet
Polly Waddle Do — M. T.
Methodist Pie — M. T. & duet
CAPITOL G-7 (The Coonhunters)
Stonewall Jackson — inst.
Possum up a Gumstump — inst.
Man Eater — inst.
The Gal I Left Behind Me — inst.
Devil's Dream — inst.
Old Bill Campbell — inst.
CAPITOL G-8 (The Coonhunters)
I Don't Love Nobody — inst.
Ragtime Annie — inst.
Old Joe Clark — inst.
Turkey in the Straw — inst.
Soldier's Joy — inst.
Cripple Creek — inst.
CAPITOL G-9 (The Coonhunters)
Cactus Jig — inst.
Sailor's Hornpipe — inst.
Rakes of Mallow — inst.
Miller's Folly — inst.
Waggoner — inst.
CAPITOL G-10 (The Coonhunters)
Coonhunters Jig — inst.
Smash de Window — inst.
Curly's Cakewalk — inst.
Stoney Point — inst.
Rattlesnake Jig — inst.
CAPITOL G-11 (Merle Travis)
Walkin' the Strings — inst.
Saturday Night Shuffle — inst.
Cannonball Stomp — inst.
Blue Smoke — inst.
Goodbye My Bluebell — inst.
Rose Time — inst.
CAPITOL G-12 (Merle Travis)
I Am a Pilgrim

325

Little David Play on Your Harp
Everly Rag — inst.
That's All
Lost John
CAPITOL G-77 (Merle Travis)
Pigmeat Stomp — inst.
Louisville Clog — inst.
Old Aunt Dinah — inst.
Fuller Blues — inst.
Green Bay Polka — inst.
On a Bicycle Built for Two — inst.
CAPITOL G-78 (Merle Travis and Texann)
Grandad's Cuspidor — duet
Heaven Bound Train — duet
Travis Trot — inst.
Why'd I Fall for Abner? — duet
Dream Train Engineer — duet
Old Kentucky Home — inst.
CAPITOL G-79 (Merle Travis and Texann)
Baby Don't Cry No More — duet
Honeybunch — duet
The Dutchman's Wife — duet
Someone to Call Me Honey — duet
Go Where I Send Thee — duet
CAPITOL G-80 (Merle Travis and Texann)
The Life of the Party — duet
Wild Goose — duet
Dear Little Wifey at Home — duet
Hi Ho Hi Ho — duet
The Dust on Mother's Old Bible — duet
The Courtin' Song — duet
CAPITOL G-81 (Merle Travis and Texann)
Turkey in the Straw — duet
My Worst Worry — duet
Peg Leg Jack — duet
God Put a Rainbow in the Clouds — duet
Jenny Weaver — duet
CAPITOL G-82 (Merle Travis and Texann)
The World Is Such a Dreary Place — duet
Hubbin' It — duet
Paper of Pins — duet
Cane Brake Blues — duet
Did You Ever Go Sailing? — duet
Thumbing the Bass — duet

326

CAPITOL G-83 (Merle Travis and Texann)
  I'm Goin' Down the Mountain — duet
  Lolly To Dum Dey — duet
  Sourwood Mountain — duet
  The Wise Old Owl — duet
  Shady Brook Lane — duet
CAPITOL G-84 (Merle Travis and Texann)
  Muskrat — duet
  I'd Like to Go Back — duet
  Nickelty Nackelty Now — duet
  They Made It Twice as Nice as Paradise and They Called It Dixieland — duet
  Tomorrow (I'll Be in My Dixieland Home Again) — duet
CAPITOL G-109 (Merle Travis)
  Sixteen Tons
  John Bolin
  Jordan Am a Hard Road to Travel
  Barbara Allen
CAPITOL G-110 (Merle Travis)
  Nine Pound Hammer
  Darby's Ram
  Possum up a 'Simmon Tree
  Dry Bread
  Take My Hand, Precious Lord
CAPITOL G-127 (The Coonhunters)
  Heard a Whistle Call My Name — M. T. & duet
  When I Walked with My Love in the Dew — M. T. & duet
  Rocky Road to Glory — M. T. & duet
  Ballad of the Knotted Pine — M. T.
  Old Cow Found a Muley Calf — M. T. & duet
  Long Journey Home — M. T.
CAPITOL G-128 (The Coonhunters)
  One More Rainy Morning — M. T. & duet
  Darlin' Cora — M. T.
  The Dark Dreary Woodland — M. T. & duet
  Adrie Hill — M. T. & duet
  The Shoe Cobbler — M. T. & duet

MINE-CAR WHEELS

Nine Pound Hammer 9

"NINE POUND HAMMER," the lead piece in Merle Travis' *Folk Songs of the Hills,* contained a curious request that the singer's tombstone be made out of Number Nine coal. This thought recalled Travis' wish in "Dark as a Dungeon" that future miners might dig his coal-fossil bones, and his boast in "Sixteen Tons" of loading Number Nine coal. We know, of course, that as a youngster he lived within hearing distance of Number Nine's tipple at Beech Creek, Kentucky. We do not know exactly when he first associated this particular mine with the already-traditional "Nine Pound Hammer," but his adaptation of the old song in 1946 was entirely appropriate as an opener in a set which a Capitol publicist termed "authentic folk music . . . handed down for generations."

Well before Travis' album was released, the phrase "nine pound hammer" had served in at least three capacities: (1) the proper name of a fairly specific lyric folksong arising out of the hammer's many functions in railroad building, mining, and other industries; (2) a designation for a motif, significant or peripheral, in the John Henry ballad; (3) one element in an amorphous work-song complex including widely diverse titles such as "Roll On Buddy," "Driving Steel," "Swannanoa Tunnel," or "Take This Hammer." Items in the complex, though generally linked by the hammer element as well as by structural and melodic ties, at times sloughed off the basic hammer reference. Paradoxically, there were some hammer songs in which the tool itself was unmentioned. To illustrate the source of Travis' "Nine Pound Hammer" as well as its movement after composition, I shall comment on material of all three types.

Attention to Negro work song in the United States began when early travelers in the South reported on the rhythmic boatsmen chants and field calls of slaves. Formal collection and study of cabin and plantation material, however, was reserved initially for religious music. It was not until 1903 that the *Journal of American Folklore* printed its first eyewitness account of black laborers at work.[1] Charles Peabody and a fellow Harvard archeologist had spent two summers excavating an Indian mound near Clarksdale, Coahoma County, Mississippi. Peabody was pleased to hear the hired men sing while digging or wheeling on the mound and to listen to them sing with guitar accompaniment at their quarters. He reported that "our ears were beset with an abundance of ethnological material in song."

Negro music has been gathered assiduously in all the decades of this century, and the names of collectors such as Harold Courlander, Guy B. Johnson, John and Alan Lomax, Howard W. Odum, E. C. Perrow, Dorothy Scarborough, and Newman Ivey White are familiar to every folklore student. It is likely that the decade ahead will witness a reexamination of this corpus by scholars employing new perspectives gained in the area of black-culture study. Here I wish only to touch on the base behind Travis' "Nine Pound Hammer," as well as to mark his particular contribution to the cluster which bears this name.

Presently, Norman Cohen of the John Edwards Memorial Foundation is engaged in a discographic investigation of railroad songs, giving some attention to hammer numbers.[2] Checklist Seven reveals how influential was Travis' contribution, inasmuch as more than two dozen artists either covered it on records directly or incorporated some of his special language into their versions. Cohen's study and the checklist together suggest how rich is the subject for future exploration.

Out of the total literature on work songs, I shall cite but a few position points to help locate "Nine Pound Hammer" in time and

WHEELING

place. Gates Thomas of Southwest Texas State Teachers College had noted in 1891 six couplets of "Roll On, Johnnie" from the singing of a Fayette County levee-camp man who began, "Oh, roll on, Johnnie; you rolls too slow / For you roll like a man never rolled befo'."[3] Although this piece lacked a specific hammer reference, it was the earliest collected version in the general complex presently related to hammer songs by virtue of the "roll on (John, boys) buddy" phrase. Thomas' pioneer text, however, was not published until 1926, after several other roll items were in print.

The first sojourner in the South to observe actual hammermen singing at work and to attempt to transcribe their music was, to my knowledge, William Eleazar Barton (1861-1930), a teacher-minister and Lincoln biographer, who offered during 1898-99 three articles on plantation hymns in the *New England Magazine*.[4] He notated some seventy pieces as examples of "heart religion" which might "disappear before the swift coming 'book religion,'" but he also went on to describe "railroad songs" which were sung by large bodies of men in railroad construction and other public works. Barton correctly noted that much of this material dated to the Civil War building of army fortfications and had little to do with the iron horse's progress.

Between 1880 and 1887 Barton, a Berea College faculty member, apparently visited a tunnel site or heard steel-driving chants elsewhere. He wrote: "I wonder if the reader can imagine the effect of it all, the powder smoke filling the place, the darkness made barely visible by the little lights in the hats of the men, the echoing sounds of men and mules toward the outlet loading and carting away the rock thrown out by the last blast, and the men at the heading droning their low chant to the *chink! chink!* of the steel."

For *New England Magazine* readers, Barton transcribed three measures of an untitled syncopated line, "O-o! Lu-lah! Lu-lah!," which accompanied the metallic chinking in the tunnel. Also, he presented six couplets and the music for an "interminable" work song, "Walk Jerusalem Jes' Like John." Additionally, he transcribed an evening service hymn, "The Christians' Hymn of the Crucifixion." Of this graphic item, which portrayed Christ hammered to the cross, Barton stated: "I do not know that it is used as a song to work with, but suspect that the 'ham-mer-ring!' which is the constant response, may be used sometimes to time the descent of the pick or sledge." One senses Barton's enthusiasm for work songs and one speculates whether or not in his lifetime he heard any songs about John Henry at the Big Bend Tunnel, constructed only a few years before Barton undertook his mission.

The first actual printing of any hammer fragment in a folklore journal occurred in 1909, when Louise Rand Bascom submitted to the *Journal of American Folklore* a couplet heard in Watauga County, North Carolina: "Johnie Henry was a hard-workin' man, / He died with a hammer in his hand."[5] It can be assumed that some of the John Henry ballad texts — subsequently published by Guy B. Johnson of the University of North Carolina and by Louis Chappell of West Virginia — dated to the period immediately after the Chesapeake & Ohio Railroad's Big Bend Tunnel was completed in 1872. It can also be assumed that some of the generalized work songs found by Johnson and Chappell preceded this tunnel's construction. In short, hammer songs were composed and recomposed throughout the South, and apparently moved from black to white workers long before a John Henry fragment surfaced in any folklore publication.

332

During 1911 Miss Bascom's item was followed in the *Journal of American Folklore* by a hammer stanza not associated with the heroic tunnel driller. Howard W. Odum, in a conglomerate "Pick-and-Shovel Song" unidentified by a specific singer, time, or community, included a stanza:

> This ole hammer, this ole hammer,
> Lord, it's 'bout to kill me dead, O Lord!
> Lord, it's 'bout to kill me dead.[6]

Two years later, in the same publication, E. C. Perrow offered the first two musical transcriptions of actual hammer songs, "Drivin' Steel" and "John Henry." Both notations were from the University of Louisville professor's memory of hearing east Tennessee mountain whites sing these pieces in 1905. He also offered a long "John Henry" text from a Kentucky correspondent's manuscript received in 1912. One stanza, which Perrow judged to be "out of shape" or "brought in from some other song," read:

> If I die a railroad man,
> Go bury me under the rail ties,
> With my pick and my shovel at my head and feet,
> And my nine-pound hammer in my hand.[7]

I do not know when or where the first tunnel driller, road laborer, or section hand commented in song on his hammer's weight, sound, or power and found solace in singing to it. To my knowledge, Perrow's Kentucky correspondent was the first to write down in a song the phrase "nine pound hammer," although this particular verbal combination could well have appeared orally decades before 1912. Perrow's various contributors and their home locales demonstrate that Afro-American work chants were incorporated into the Anglo-American ballad and frolic (banjo) idiom before the close of the nineteenth century.

In 1918 Natalie Curtis Burlin issued four folksong booklets drawn entirely from Hampton Institute (Virginia) student sources. Mrs. Burlin used an Edison phonograph and made wax cylinders on campus. Her book selections were from the singing of male quartets and were transcribed in four parts with added notes for the piano. Considerable controversy exists on the subject of arranged folksongs offered by choral and concert groups in Negro colleges, and judgment of this practice is found elsewhere. Particularly useful in this study, however, is the "Hammerin' Song" brought to Hampton by George Alston, who had sung it in the mines of Virginia.[8] Very likely his lengthy piece of twenty-seven stanzas was extended by various students. Nevertheless, it was the first full text-tune of the hammer type presented with an explanation of how the song functioned on the job, its improvisatory nature, and its symbolism. Mrs. Burlin perceptively labeled such folk poems of black laborers "gems in the literature of the United States."

During 1924 Robert Winslow Gordon published in *Adventure* a series of six work fragments heard in southern railroad and other construction camps by Charles Miller of Waycross, Georgia. Gordon neither attempted to collate nor to title Miller's contribution, but printed it as submitted. One of the six portions read:

> I looked at the sun, and the sun looked high,
> I looked at the boss, and the boss looked shy.
>
> > And it's roll on, buddy,
> > What makes you roll so slow?
> > Your buddy is almost broke
> > Down on the K.N.O.
>
> In a few more days, and that won't be long,
> Till the roll will be called, and I'll be gone.[9]

Miller's "sun-high" figure had already been printed in 1912 as part of a Texas "Skinner's Song," but the special combination "roll on buddy" had escaped print until 1924.[10] Although my chapter on "Roll Down the Line" indicates that the sentence "buddy won't you roll down the line" appeared about 1890 in a Tennessee convict song's chorus, and although the words "roll on, Johnnie" were sung in Texas during 1891, I find no printed use of the phrase "roll on buddy" in a song until Gordon. Actually, the roll work song was widespread in the South before "Roll On Buddy" emerged as a discrete title.

In addition to the Texas "Roll On, Johnnie" already cited, it is important to mention a North Carolina "Some of These Days and It Won't Be Long," first printed in the Frank C. Brown anthology in 1952 but obtained by the collector many years earlier. This number was given a title from its first line, but the chorus

RAILROAD CONSTRUCTION GANG

read: "On, boys, don't roll so slow. / When the sun goes down you'll roll no more." Newman Ivey White had previously received a Georgia fragment of this same item in 1915: "Some o' these mornings, and 't won't be long / Capt'n gwine ter call me and I be gone."[11] I shall comment on these "non-hammer" work lyrics below.

Songs parallel to Gordon's and Brown's numbers, as well as to White's fragment, unstructured in terms of Anglo-American poetic forms, must have been sung for decades before they were placed in neatly titled bins, conventionally named. It is difficult to imagine how pioneer collectors — sometimes trained as ballad scholars — isolated amorphous black work material. One becomes aware, while checking early articles and anthologies, that some folklorists were content to include fragments, however discontinuous, and that others could not rest until functional chants were either compressed or extended into tight poems. There has always been a conflict between those who favored publishing song texts exactly as found and those who favored restoration or literary emendation. This conflict is nowhere more apparent than in the publication of hammer songs.

335

It is one of the strengths of Dorothy Scarborough's *On the Trail of Negro Folk-Songs* that she was willing to include odds and ends of song fragments, and reminiscences about them from her Texas childhood. Also, she published such bits contributed by friends throughout the South. A Virginian, hearing a Bedford County road worker's piece which contained exactly forty-two words, sent it to Miss Scarborough. To my knowledge it was the first song in print to be titled "Nine Pound Hammer." Interestingly, she also presented the text and tune for a "spiritual adapted to use as a work song." Reverend Barton had suspected that some of the hymns he had heard in the 1880's served as work songs. Miss Scarborough noted that Noah's ark-building hammer had preceded John Henry's exploits, and she suggested the spiritual "Noah's" function: "The antiphonal questions and responses mark the rhythmic strokes of the hammer — which tool here is given power of thought and speech."[12]

In the mid-1920's Professor Scarborough's book was but one of many excellent, academically published folklore collections. In December, 1927, Carl Sandburg's *The American Songbag* appeared, and it reached a wider audience than university press studies could capture. The poet-singer's sweep was broad and he placed in his book "Drivin' Steel" and "My Old Hammah." He also included such chants in public concerts, thereby presenting to an extremely wide range of folksong enthusiasts hammer songs from east Tennessee mountain whites and Georgia-Alabama blacks.

Coincidentally, a half-year before *The American Songbag* appeared, Brunswick Records released in its "Songs from Dixie" (hillbilly) series two discs, "Roll On John" by Buell Kazee and "Nine Pound Hammer" by Al Hopkins and His Buckle Busters. These songs, recorded in April and May, 1927, respectively, were the first commercial records to present to an audience beyond Scarborough and Sandburg a full textual-musical form of the "non-hammer" work-song complex, as well as the specifically named hammer song itself. Prior to 1927 the hammer motif had appeared only in recorded versions of the John Henry ballad by Fiddlin' John Carson, Earl Johnson, Riley Puckett, Welby Toomey, and other old-time performers, as well as by one or two race-record artists. Also, Franck C. Brown had recorded some field cylinders of "John

Henry" and related work chants at Durham, North Carolina, as early as 1919.

I feel that the Brown cylinders and the early commercial discs by Carson and his peers properly belong in a discographical appraisal of the John Henry ballad rather than in a study of general hammer songs. My position assumes that the John Henry ballad and lyric song types can be isolated for analytic purposes. Folklorists are divided in their opinions about the interdependence of the John Henry branches. Briefly, Guy B. Johnson suggested that the ballad had evolved slowly out of fluid work songs. By contrast, Louis Chappell felt that the narrative form was separately and quickly composed around the particular dramatic conflict of a man and a steam drill, and hence was not dependent on the lyric complex for its vitality. I subscribe to the latter position; accordingly, my major concern is with hammer songs per se.

The earliest commercial recording to bear the name "Nine Pound Hammer" was Brunswick 177. Its melody, very close to Travis' tune, and text follow.

NINE POUND HAMMER

Somebody stole my nine pound hammer,
Baby took it and gone, baby took it and gone.

>   Nine pound hammer, just a little too heavy,
>   Baby, for my size, baby, for my size.
>   Roll on buddy, don't you roll so slow.
>   Baby, how can I roll when my wheel won't go?

Nine pound hammer killed John Henry,
Ain't a-gonna kill me, ain't a-gonna kill me.

>   Nine pound hammer, just a little too heavy,
>   For my size, baby, for my size.
>   So long buddy, don't you roll so slow,
>   And how can I roll when my wheel won't go?

Goin' on the mountain, for to see my darlin'
And I ain't-a comin' back, and I ain't-a comin' back.

>   Nine pound hammer, just a little too heavy,
>   Baby, for my size, baby, for my size.
>   Roll on buddy, don't you roll so slow,
>   And how can I roll when my wheel won't go?

337

NINE POUND HAMMER

The Buckle Busters' language in "Nine Pound Hammer" presents no special interpretive problem. The theft of the hammer, its weight, and its role in John Henry's death are explicit. Also stated without ambiguity is the hammerman's wish to leave his job in favor of seeing his woman — a fantasy previously encountered in the "Chain Gang Special." An aspect of the "Nine Pound Hammer" which is not immediately clear is structural: the unusual splicing of separate *hammer* and *roll* figures of speech in the chorus. Normally, in early railroad construction, hammers were used for two basic functions: spike driving, and rock drilling by hand preparatory to exploding charges of powder. Drill hammers were similarly used at other work sites: canals, open road-cuts, tunnels, quarries, mine shafts and chambers, foundation excavations, dam footings. Whether in preparing the railroad right-of-way or in other building and construction, a hammerman necessarily would be involved if rock had to be penetrated and removed.

The act of drilling, already touched on in the Reverend Barton's report, was performed by two buddies, a driller or striker and a turner or shaker. The shaker held and turned the steel drill, which was frequently given a phallic name such as *bull prick*. The driller struck the drill with his hammer repeatedly as the shaker turned the long steel tool. This rhythmic act demanded intense coordination between two buddies. Such work was generally labeled *single jacking;* when two drillers worked with a solitary turner the appropriate term was *double jacking*. After drilling was finished to the requisite depth of the hole, powder was inserted, tamped, and detonated. At this time it was necessary to haul away the rubble, and hand-propelled wheelbarrows were rolled into action.[13]

The earliest work songs which invoked the word *roll* stemmed from pushing such implements filled with rock, sand, gravel, clay, or mud. In 1909 E. C. Perrow received a Mississippi song manuscript: "Captain, captain! my feet are cold / Doggone your feet! let them wheelers roll." For an educated audience, the folklorist glossed *wheelers* as "the wheelbarrows with which the Negroes are moving dirt." In 1960 a Hillsville, Virginia, folksinger explained the title "Roll On, Boys" to a young collector: "Now these words were uttered over a hundred years ago by an old man who'd worn himself out in a wheelbarrow gang workin' in the ore mines."[14] Although

339

such imagery implied a hand barrow initially, it was not difficult to extend the *roll* phrase to chants by muleskinners and teamsters as soon as mechanical graders, scrapers, and draglines became prevalent.

In river-bank levee building, when fill was obtainable from open pits of loose strata, the act of rolling or moving material either by hand or by mule power might be completely divorced from the acts of hammering, drilling, and dynamiting. It can be recalled that the earliest "work song" to reach a wide audience was the popular "I've Been Working on the Railroad" ("Dinah"). At least one version was arranged and published in sheet music in 1900 under the title "Levee Song," a juxtaposition which bothered some listeners who visualized a precise relationship between locomotive and levee.[15]

Fascinating but untouched, the subject of levee folksong and folklore invites exploration. The French word *levée* as a river embankment was used in New Orleans before 1719. Eventually this noun also acquired a secondary meaning as a lively place swarming with saloons and brothels. Curiously, Mitford Mathews in *A Dictionary of Americanisms* does not note the usage *levee camp* either as a river-bank or general construction site. Although early Mississippi Valley travelers must have observed levee-camp life, I do not find the term in print until 1912. When the Texas Folklore Society's first publication appeared, Will Thomas included in "The Railroad Blues" the lines: "Oh! where were you when the rolling mill burned down? / On the levee camp about fifteen miles from town." During August, 1925, Ma Rainey recorded "Levee Camp Moan" (Paramount 12295), the earliest song title to use the combination *levee camp*. To my knowledge, Gates Thomas (Will's brother) was the first scholar to gloss *levee camp* as any construction camp, and not just an actual levee site.[16] Appendix Seven, which follows this chapter, offers a brief recollection by a levee-camp man. Here I wish to note only that the levee camp itself, whether actually along the river or inland at a construction site, was a place where many roll songs originated. Gates Thomas' "Roll On, Johnnie," sung in 1891 by a Texas teamster, was such a levee-camp piece.

During 1927 Texas Alexander from Normangee, Leon County,

340

MULESKINNERS

recorded two chants titled "Section Gang Blues" / "Levee Camp Moan Blues" (Okeh 8498). The pairing of these construction items by Alexander is significant. In the former, the singer related that he was working on the railroad for a dollar and a quarter a day and asked his captain for a plug of Battle-Axe tobacco; in the latter, he reported his search for a mule with his "shoulder well" — unchafed by harness.[17] These verbal work referents were freely associated with other scenes and moods: loneliness, women, murder, reflection on race. From listening to this more than forty-year-old disc today, one senses that Texas Alexander worked in a levee camp or on a section gang. Perhaps he used *levee camp* to designate railroad construction. Hypothetically, he could have learned his material from others; however, I know of few recordings, field or commercial, which ring as true as Alexander's. He died in the 1950's before any folksong enthusiasts queried him about his life or repertoire. His thoughts on the nature of songs arising at earthmoving jobs would have been most welcome.

My focus on the extension of the levee camp *roll* phrase into the hammer-song complex returns me to the contrast between Brunswick's first roll and hammer recordings. Well before 1927 an early singer confronted by a new type of wheelbarrow had sung: "Well, dey makin' dem wheelers on de Western plan, / Dey mos' too heavy for a light-weight man."[18] Buell Kazee, in a mournful

341

"Roll On John," accented by his old-time banjo style, extended this complaint against weight to the point of a worker's very defeat by his wheelbarrow or team. Kazee's number is transcribed from Brunswick 144 at this juncture, not only because it complements previous roll citations but also because it is an excellent example of the general work song which eventually was fused into the hammer complex.

ROLL ON JOHN

Oh, roll on John, and make your time,
For I'm broke and can't make mine.

Oh, I dreamed last night, oh, Lu was dead,
With her apron string tied around her head.

Oh, whose been here since I've been gone?
It's ole Aunt Jenny with her night cap on.

Oh, up to my chin, and under my nose,
Where a-many of a quart and a gallon goes.

Oh, roll on John; don't roll so slow,
When the sun goes down, we'll roll no more.

These five stanzas are either interchangeable with or repeat images in other roll songs — a certain way to establish their traditional status.[19] Buell Kazee, born in Magoffin County, Kentucky, on August 29, 1900, was a Brunswick recording artist of the 1920's with deep traditional roots. Unlike most early old-time performers, Kazee was college-educated. He had received excellent musical training, which he used in directing church choirs or teaching voice when free from his calling as a Baptist minister. Reverend Kazee's comments on "Roll On John" help establish its lineage:

It is among my first memories [Burton Fork, Kentucky, 1900-1910] and I have no idea how long before that it was sung. Like most of the songs which we knew it had come down with the heritage. It is connected with no historical event that I know. The tune follows the pattern of "Roll On Buddy" although the time and mood are radically changed. This I attribute to the old style of banjo playing which I and others did. All stanzas that I know of "Roll On John" were definitely sung with this song from my first memory, but I had never heard of "Roll On Buddy" in those early years. That probably was being sung over on some other creek. I heard it first in Corbin, Kentucky, about the time I was recording [after 1927].[20]

BUELL KAZEE

To underscore the lack of association between the roll and hammer songs before 1927, I indicate that in 1929 Buell Kazee recorded "Steel a Goin' Down" (Brunswick 330), a piece of his own composition. It was based on his work during 1917 in the railroad yard at Williamson, West Virginia, where he saw and heard Negro rail carriers chanting as they lifted and moved steel, as well as hammermen spiking rails to the ties. He recalled: "I saw this type of work giving way to the machine, and I wrote this song in memory of some great steel drivers I knew." Kazee identified his steel chant as a work song, but did not place "Roll On John" in this same category. Because the latter was an old number when he learned it as a boy, he accepted it without curiosity as to origin. About 1949 he composed "The Wagoner's Lad," an operetta on Kentucky mountain themes, in which he used "Roll On John" as a choral background number without implying a work task.[21]

Kazee's "Roll On John," which seems peripheral to any specific job, does, however, present a neat philosophic package. Men pushing or hauling loads of earth from sunrise to sunset were not held to the precise rhythmic tension of single-jack drilling or spiking ties. Accordingly, roll songs freely brought many non-occupational

343

images to consciousness. This point had been put aptly by Lamar Stringfield in transcribing Kazee's Brunswick disc in 1931: "The whole song is expressive of the mental changes of a laborer during a day's work."[22] On listening, we perceive at once that Kazee's first and final stanzas are work-centered, but that his three middle stanzas deal with Lu, Aunt Jenny, and gallons. Need one comment on the Viennese formula of wine, women, and song?

Because many work numbers touch on the pleasures of life, there is a tendency in some folksong analysis to treat work terms so casually that they lose their value as referents to labor itself. Having spent part of an apprenticeship on road construction in the Siskiyou Mountains of California, where I experienced single-jack drilling, endless wheelbarrow rolling, and even breaking rocks into gravel by sledgehammer (our CCC foreman would chuckle, "Boys, let's make little ones out of big ones"), I tend to interpret the "roll on buddy" phrase quite literally. I am aware that a treatise could be developed on roll songs, possibly beginning with wheelbarrows but extending to railroad numbers in which the injunction "see the drivers roll" refers to locomotive engine wheels, and to the huge body of sea chanties in which *roll* vies with *blow* as a nautical, all-purpose word. Of course no such study could avoid the sexual imagery in rock-and-roll lyrics, or the question of when these words were first linked. A widespread chanty, more than a century old, holds the line "O do, me Johnny Bowker, come rock'n'roll me over."[23]

During a 1961 visit with Charles Bowman, a member of the Buckle Busters string band, Ed Kahn and I learned how Bowman and Al Hopkins had put "Nine Pound Hammer" together in Brunswick's New York studio. This reference to place of composition is not intended to imply that their song was not traditional. "Nine Pound Hammer" stemmed directly from locutions and a melody used by black railroad-construction laborers early in the century.

Bowman was born July 30, 1889, on a farm some ten miles from Johnson City, Tennessee. In his words, he was a backwoods mountain boy. When he was fourteen years old, the C C & O (Clinchfield, Carolina & Ohio Railroad, being built from Spartanburg, South Carolina, to Elkhorn, Kentucky) reached his community, which was then named Gray Station. For two years (1903-

344

05) the construction crews were in the area — surveying, brushing, drilling, blasting, grading, laying and lining track, spiking and tamping ties. Whenever he could escape home chores, young Charlie got away to listen to the laborers sing. Like other mountain boys he grew up in a ballad and fiddling tradition, and was instantly drawn to the strange new music. He never forgot the everyday chants of the muleskinners, steel drivers, and track spikers. On Sunday he sauntered to their quarters to listen to "nigger love songs" about "gals leaving camp to go down the line." Here Bowman first heard guitarists picking the blues, although he was careful to indicate that he never learned the word *blues* until the 1920's, when he first heard W. C. Handy's pieces on the radio.

Bowman's interest in Negro music was not unique. Many of the mountain whites would sit for hours watching and listening to the steel drivers and other gang workers. From this experience Charlie retained a certain tune and such lines as "One of these mornin's / I'm a-gonna leave here, / And I ain't a-comin' back, / I ain't a-comin' back."[24] After the railroad-building crews departed from Gray Station, Bowman saw few blacks; occasionally, on a visit to Johnson City, he would hear street singers and itinerant guitarists. Possibly because the C C & O entered his life at an impressionable age, and possibly because of his limited contact with black music after 1905, Bowman never forgot "his" work song. In 1925 he joined Al Hopkins, "Tony" Alderman, and other musicians in an influential string band called both the Buckle Busters and the Hillbillies. Elsewhere I have told something of this group's history; here I wish to note only that the band handled a heavy schedule of appearances at fiddlers' conventions, county fairs, school commencements, and political rallies.[25] Road tours, north and south, were correlated with New York recording sessions for Brunswick and Vocalion, parallel firms at the time. The Buckle Busters' records included an unusually wide range of lyric folksongs, ballads, breakdowns, and novelty or humorous items contributed by all the members out of their respective backgrounds.

While in New York during May, 1927, Bowman taught his remembered words and tune for "Nine Pound Hammer" to the group. He was careful to tell me, in 1961, that he had no full-blown piece in mind before the session and that others present

345

helped round out his phrases. I take this to mean that some of his fellow Buckle Busters had heard hammer songs traditionally, and had retained fragments which fit Bowman's. If he was aware that he had fused language which stemmed from steel drilling, spike driving, and wheelbarrow moving, he did not reveal it to me. I be-lieve that he saw the multiple operations of the laborers as a flowing process, and his song seemingly reflected a single visual-aural con-figuration. It is possible that a worker at Gray Station had already juxtaposed the *hammer* and *roll* expressions, but we lack knowledge of such an act.

Bowman credited band leader Al Hopkins, a gifted country piano player and creative musician, with arranging the piece for the six performers involved: Al Hopkins, lead voice; John Hopkins, singing with ukulele; Charles Bowman, singing with guitar; Elvis Alderman, singing with fiddle; Jack Reedy, banjo; Elbert Bowman, hammer effects. In addition to these musicians, another band mem-ber, Walter "Spark Plug" Hughes from Cranberry, North Caro-lina, was present and performed without his name being entered in the New York session's ledger sheets.[26] Hughes, when only ten or eleven years old, had begun to entertain professionally with an older fiddler and balladeer, Clarence Greene. While the Hillbillies (Buckle Busters) were appearing at a Spruce Pine (Mitchell County, North Carolina) fair, the band "adopted" the young mu-sician — too little to spark the girls — and took him on the road. In 1963 he played and sang for Ed Kahn and me the original "Nine Pound Hammer," contrasting his performance with a second one of Merle Travis' more intricate version. Hughes's memory of the song's birth was that the boys had "fixed that number up right in the hotel room — the Knickerbocker Hotel."

Two details supplement my story of this disc. On June 29, 1927, the Brunswick-Balke-Collender Company copyrighted "Nine Pound Hammer" in the names of Al Hopkins and Charles Bowman (E 665883). Two years later, Guy B. Johnson included the text and tune of a stanza and chorus from the record in his book *John Henry*. This represented one of the earliest properly credited tran-scriptions from any hillbilly record in an academic publication. Johnson also made an interesting stylistic comment: "Although it is sung by a quartet in regular tempo, one can easily make a hammer song out of it by inserting appropriate pauses, hammer strokes, and grunts."[27]

By meeting Charles Bowman, I traced the first recorded "Nine Pound Hammer" to an east Tennessee Negro crew of the years 1903-05. It is relatively easy for a folklorist to assert that a given item is traditional; it is difficult to find a performer at one time poised on the line between Anglo and Afro traditions and also conscious of his role in a dynamic acculturation process. In regard to "Nine Pound Hammer" I was unusually lucky to complement Bowman's account with that of his younger brother Elbert, who had made the hammer-driving effects heard on the song by striking his banjo hoop with a small steel rod.[28] One detail, puzzling to me, stood out in Elbert's memory of the recording session. He recalled that it had occurred during Charles Lindbergh's transoceanic flight to Paris, May 21, 1927. However, the session's ledger sheets indicate May 13. I do not know what particular association caused this time shift in Elbert's mind.

Elbert also remembered the genesis of his brother's song, for he had been one of the avid listeners to the steel drillers near Gray Station. For example, one tune he recalled from this experience was "K C Blues," long associated with railroading in country repertoires. The full story of Charles and Elbert Bowman and their respective careers in hillbilly music will have to be told elsewhere. Both were typical of traditional mountain musicians, fully folk in background and life-style, who made a partial accommodation to the commercial-music medium in the 1920's and 1930's but who were not completely engulfed by it. Elbert alternated for many decades between neighborhood entertainment and his regular work as a furniture finisher. His last major employment, for twenty years, was with Eastman Kodak at Kingsport, Tennessee. Charles was also a music maker as long as it was remunerative. Among his other jobs in the late 1930's he was an oil-field roustabout, working as far from home as Bakersfield, California. I note this occupational duality for the brothers because too many feature articles about folk musicians present idyllic portraits of artists suspended in a realm of composition or performance, never threatened by the economic facts of life except in terms of possible recording or festival fees.

THE BUCKLE BUSTERS

Happily for the Buckle Busters, "Nine Pound Hammer" sold well, and along with the band's other records was a source of royalties until the Brunswick firm went under in the Depression. Within the total body of American work songs known to folksingers of both races, Brunswick 177 played a small but influential role, illustrative of how a single recording could help stabilize a number of fluid elements into a fairly structured form. I have been fortunate in having interviewed four persons present when "Nine Pound Hammer" was first recorded for Brunswick, but not fortunate enough to obtain a coherent explanation about the welding in this song of the *roll* and *hammer* figures of speech. "Tony" Alderman knew that Bowman or Hopkins had drawn the latter image from the John Henry tradition, but was at a loss to explain the former. In a 1969 visit with Alderman, after his performance at a "fiddlers' convention" on the Washington Mall, he confessed that from 1927 until the time of my questioning, the chorus of "Nine Pound Hammer" made no sense to him: "I don't know what the wheels have to do with that damn hammer."[29]

Between 1927 and 1947 some thirty lyric hammer songs, commercial or field, were recorded, exclusive of John Henry ballads. More narratives were recorded about the heroic steel driver's adventures than all other recorded hammer pieces combined. Here I

348

shall isolate but a few stanzas (and comments) to trace the path from Charles Bowman to Merle Travis. The first group to cover the Buckle Busters' disc was Frank Blevins and His Tar Heel Rattlers, a Marion, Virginia, string band, in spite of its name. This band was fully rooted in the broad Blue Ridge Mountain range which sweeps through Virginia and the Carolinas. I am at a loss to know why Blevins copied the Brunswick item so closely, melodically and textually. Frequently, when traditional performers learned new songs from records, they reached back into memory for formulas or situations to alter their offerings. The Tar Heel Rattlers' "Nine Pound Hammer" (Columbia 15280-D), recorded on April 17, 1928, was the first indication that the Buckle Busters' disc had become a model for others.

In previous chapters I noted that folklorists had not talked to many old-time musicians when they were alive. I do not believe that any collector ever interviewed Blevins, but I am intrigued by the fact that in 1928 Abbe Niles reviewed his "Nine Pound Hammer" and compared it to the then-popular "Water Boy," widely sung by Paul Robeson and fellow concert artists.[30] There is a small measure of poetic justice in this apt linkage by Niles, for very few consumers of hillbilly records were Robeson fans in the 1920's.

In strong contrast to Blevins' obvious cover of the Brunswick "Nine Pound Hammer" was "Roll On Buddy" by Charles Bowman and His Brothers (Columbia 15357-D), also recorded in 1928. Few early country musicians were held by exclusive contracts, and when Columbia A & R man Frank Walker met Bowman in Johnson City, Tennessee, it was easy to arrange a quick recording session in a loft over the Brading Lumber Company. In this improvised studio Charles, Elbert, and Walter Bowman "rigged up" a new song for Mr. Walker. Whether out of a sense of loyalty to the Buckle Busters, or whether in response to the A & R man's desire for a fresh piece rather than an exact cover, the resulting "Roll On Buddy" departed completely in language and melody from "Nine Pound Hammer." Only the single phrase "roll on buddy" was held in common by the two pieces. Whereas "Nine Pound Hammer's" tune had originated in the singing of Gray Station Negro laborers, the Bowmans seem to have modeled the new number on a mountain frolic melody usually called "Rock About My Saro Jane."

349

ROLL ON

It can be noted here that the tune used by the Buckle Busters as well as by Travis for "Nine Pound Hammer" is close to the one obtained in 1916 by Cecil Sharp for "Swannanoa Town."[31] This tunnel song's music is an integral part of the hammer complex treated here. By contrast, Charles Bowman's tune for "Roll On Buddy" may have been ultimately derived from black stevedores, or even the minstrel stage, but it is very likely that the Bowmans learned it as a breakdown or barn-dance piece in their community.

Whereas all the expressions in "Nine Pound Hammer" were found in tradition before it was recorded, most of the phrases in the new "Roll on Buddy" were apparently put together during 1928 in a Johnson City loft. I would not stress these differences, except for the fact that the Bowmans' "Roll On Buddy" appealed to traditional musicians and it intertwined in the 1930's, to some extent, with older hammer songs. Between 1937 and 1939 six field recordings titled "Roll On Buddy" were deposited in the Library of Congress. These items included such diverse fare as William C. Handy singing a cotton-stowing song and Aunt Molly Jackson singing a poignant work chant, the setting of which was the L & N Railroad. Aunt Molly's version, which can be heard on the Library of

350

Congress *Railroad Songs and Ballads* (L 61), offers eight couplets associated with traditional work songs but without a hammer reference. It would be a formidable task today to sort out all the influences of the two songs which Charles Bowman helped put together.

In my 1963 visit with Mr. and Mrs. Elbert Bowman, they told me, with some amusement, that in recording "Roll On Buddy" the brothers had included the name of Elbert's wife in the final stanza. The full text of Columbia 15357-D follows.

ROLL ON BUDDY

I'm going to the East, Karo,
I'm going to the East, Karo,
I'm going to the East, I'm going to the West,
I'm going to the land I love best.

> Roll on buddy, roll on, roll on my buddy, roll on.
> You wouldn't roll so slow,
> If you knew what I know.
> Yes, roll on my buddy, roll on.

You'd better quit your rowdy ways,
You'd better quit your rowdy ways,
You'll get killed some day — you'll be laid in your grave.
You'd better quit your rowdy ways.

> Chorus:

My home's down in Tennessee,
My home's down in Tennessee,
In Tennessee is where I always want to be.
Way down in sunny Tennessee.

> Chorus:

I've got a good woman just the same,
I've got a good woman just the same,
Woman just the same, Fannie Bowman is her name.
I've got a good woman just the same.

> Chorus:

During 1937 Bill and Charlie Monroe covered the Columbia record either directly or from someone else's singing of it, and in time their disc (Bluebird 6960) became a model for subsequent

351

bluegrass versions. The Monroe Brothers' "Roll On Buddy" retained the original Bowman text except for Fannie's line, which was altered: "A woman just the same, says sh' gonna change her name." The alteration is slight but represents the kind of precise change which can be demonstrated by the comparison of related recordings.

To transcribe all recorded hammer songs and to prepare a classificatory paper on thematic content would be rewarding in many fields. Even in casual listening, one perceives that each transient line which originally functioned to time a hammer blow or to pace another thrust at the wheelbarrow's handles also may have expressed a psychological state or social position. I do not mean to imply that work songs were conscious expressions of emotion or ideology, but how is one to interpret a couplet from the Carolina Tar Heels' "Roll On Boys" (Victor 40024)?[32] "Oh, some of these days and it won't be long, / You'll call for me and I'll be gone" in a work song might be a defiant statement by a laborer against his boss or it might represent merely a half-muttered threat to quit, arising from a sense of defeat. Perhaps it is neither work-defiance nor resignation, but rather a challenge to an unresponsive woman. How many workmen eased anxiety by moaning about the joys and sorrows of love to their tools, draft animals, and machines? The Tar Heels' couplet, it must be noted, had appeared earlier in work songs collected by Frank C. Brown and Newman Ivey White as well as in blues and spirituals.

Ernest V. "Pop" Stoneman in his "Nine Pound Hammer" (Okeh and Vocalion 02655) sang: "Some of these days 'bout courtin' time / Gonna pack my grip, go down the line."[33] This surely is an open statement by a construction man that he will not be deprived of sex for the job's length but must affirmatively set his own departure time. A railroad worker's "Roll On Buddy" collected at Cox's Mill, West Virginia, explicitly locates "Pop" Stoneman's "down the line" in terms of progression from the job to "the taverns and brothels at night." One couplet rings with warning but hides a boast: "Look out boys, and mind your eye / When you go home with Anna Marie."[34] Despite my stated propensity to view work songs as direct commentaries on labor, I heard substantial on-the-job bawdy humor during employment in the maritime and building trades. The subject of such humor is peripheral to this

"POP" STONEMAN

study, but a single Stoneman couplet, also from "Nine Pound Hammer," merits attention. "Well I want somebody for to grease my buggy / So the wheel will go, so the wheel will go" is a quip of double meaning. Wheelbarrows, humorously called *buggies* on the job, literally had to be greased for effective operation. Figuratively, the "grease my buggy" metaphor is a sexual call.

To return to a central problem in "Nine Pound Hammer," I shall comment briefly on the 1928 recording by G. B. Grayson and Henry Whitter, who came from Laurel Bloomery, Tennessee, and Fries, Virginia, respectively. Following the Buckle Busters' and the similar Tar Heel Rattlers' version, Grayson and Whitter, in their "Nine Pound Hammer" (Victor 40105), retained the melody and some of the motifs of the previous discs, but not all of them. Hence the duo can be credited with adding several important traditional elements to the development of the hammer complex, insofar as it is documented on commercial records. In capsule form, we can

353

reduce the original (Brunswick) "Nine Pound Hammer" to the formulaic phrase "roll on buddy" and four motifs: the hammerman's escape wish; the hammer's weight; the hammer's theft; the hammer's use as a killing device. Grayson and Whitter retained the *roll* term as well as the motifs of escape, weight, and killing, but they dropped the theft couplet.

Additionally, Grayson and Whitter brought to their song two familiar motifs: the worker's pride in his hammer and his challenge to the boss. Either Grayson or Whitter — perhaps both — had previously heard the hammer song's "shines like silver, rings like gold," and this proud simile was incorporated into their Victor recording. Also, the duo used the now-familiar couplet "Take this hammer, take it to the captain, / Give it to the captain, tell him I'm gone." I have not traced this provocative passage in texts of race records prior to December, 1928, when Mississippi John Hurt used it in "Spike Driver Blues" (Okeh 8692). The expression, which so neatly fuses an aggressive thrust and an escape wish, could date to any early hammerman's chant, but like much imagery in this genre, it was late in getting fixed in manuscript or print. While Newman Ivey White was teaching at Alabama Polytechnic Institute, Auburn, in 1915, he received a Pickins County manuscript, probably from a student, containing these lines: "Take this hammer, take it to the Captain, / Tell him I'm gone, babe, tell him I'm gone." It should be unnecessary to digress in order to cite the tremendous circulation given to "Take This Hammer" in urban circles after Huddie Ledbetter's version became known in 1942.

During 1936 the Monroe Brothers recorded "Nine Pound Hammer Is Too Heavy" (reissued on *The Railroad in Folksong,* Victor LPV 532). This rendition thoroughly mixed elements both from the Buckle Busters and the Grayson and Whitter versions, indicating that the two early discs, out of print in the 1930's, had not vanished without a trace but had pulled together into a "new" and relatively stable hillbilly piece. I do not think it is useful to construct an archetypal "Nine Pound Hammer" sung by an idealized, but nonexistent, singer. Nor do I think we can chart separate courses after 1927 for field-recorded and commercial versions of this song.

One illustration of the interdependence of the commercial

recording and its traditional roots will suffice. Dependent as they were on the Bowman-Hopkins-Grayson-Whitter text and tune which located "Nine Pound Hammer" on "the mountain," Bill and Charlie Monroe placed their song in a special work site: "Ain't one hammer in this tunnel / That rings like mine, that rings like mine." We know the long history of tunnel references in John Henry ballads, lyric folksongs, and scholarly analysis. We know also that as early as 1922 Bascom Lamar Lunsford made a field cylinder of "Swannanoa Tunnel" for Professor Frank C. Brown of Trinity University, Durham, North Carolina. This was the first of many field recordings Lunsford made of the hammer song, but, strangely, he did not record it in his sessions for Brunswick in the late 1920's. Apparently no performer placed a specific tunnel reference in a "Nine Pound Hammer" or "Roll On Buddy" recording prior to the Monroes in 1936. It can well be advanced that such an association was integral to the John Henry corpus, and hence casual or normal on the part of the Monroe Brothers.[35] Nevertheless, there is a given time when any traditional fragment must be captured in sound or print if it is to be known beyond the ears of folksingers, and if it is to serve in extending large society's awareness of folk culture.

In any complex as loosely integrated as the handful of lyric work songs brought together in this chapter, the investigator's role must be perceived as an arbitrary one. Hammer songs cannot be placed in a ballad-like continuum of either sequential growth or slow decay. Neither can a scholar assert that a single mode of analysis is better suited than another for the hammer group. I have selected only a few early printed texts as well as some hillbilly discs to illustrate the range of material in this category; however, there remain numerous hidden questions in this corpus which await future study. For example, a perplexing problem which I can pose but not probe is: Why were there more hillbilly than race recordings of hammer songs? This query is linked to a parallel question: Why did white performers initially record more John Henry ballads than did black artists? Implied in these discographical questions is the concern with the crossover in American folksong of Anglo and Afro forms and styles.

A fairly specific query which can be answered here is that of

355

how a generalized hammer-wheelbarrow song became identified as a coal-mining piece after 1947. Manifestly, these two tools were common in and around coal mines, but no version of "Nine Pound Hammer" or "Roll On Buddy" was localized to mining until Merle Travis effected the transplant. It can well be stated that some John Henry ballads were physically set in coal regions by virtue of the many references to the driller's wife Polly Ann, who accepted money (or garments) from a man (or driver) in the mine. However, Professor Chappell has carefully noted that nineteenth-century tunnel workers, north and south, were referred to as miners without implying the coal industry. A technical report on the Hoosac Tunnel (Massachusetts), constructed between 1855 and 1873, noted that its underground workers were "regularly bred miners . . . the very best Cornish miners." One of the few contemporaneous accounts by a Big Bend Tunnel (West Virginia) worker contained the line: "And the miners hoarsely singing."[36] There is no precise connection between these references to tunnel laborers as miners and the singing of hammer songs by coal miners. Very likely such numbers were carried directly into bituminous mine camps by the crews who built railroad spurs into the coal-bearing Appalachian Mountains, as well as by spike drivers who actually laid underground tracks for the coal cars within mines.

I have been unable to establish an exact date for a miner singing a hammer song, but can suggest the decade 1890-1900 on the basis of a "Yew Pine Mountains" printed by Josiah Combs (1925) and by John Harrington Cox (1927). This song was given to the two collectors by Carey Woofter of Glenville, West Virginia, during 1924.[37] Woofter asserted that it had been sung in the coal camps near Fairmont "years ago." The song itself contained such familiar elements as the hammer's killing function, the hammer's tone, and the hammerman's desire to return home. West Virginians called the red spruce tree the yew pine and named a Nicholas County range after these evergreens. There is no question that the "Yew Pine Mountains" was sung by coal miners well before 1924; I stress only that it was not internalized within the coal industry. Such an action awaited a Kentucky performer who knew a traditional hammer song but who was impelled to give it a fresh twist prior to a Hollywood recording session.

356

Merle Travis' "Nine Pound Hammer," recorded on August 8, 1946, like "Dark as a Dungeon" and "Sixteen Tons," was not sent in to the Copyright Office until the latter piece became a hit. The lead sheet for the hammer number was received in Washington on March 23, 1956, but the song was copyrighted (EP 98030) effective June 9, 1947 — the official release date for *Folk Songs of the Hills*. Interestingly, "Nine Pound Hammer," the album's opener, contained a spoken introduction localizing the piece to east Kentucky rather than to the singer's home in Muhlenberg County. The text has much in common with that of the Buckle Busters offered earlier in this chapter, but of course the Travis version is unique in its coal references. The words and music from Capitol 48000 follow.

NINE POUND HAMMER

Roll on buddy, don't you roll so slow.
How can I roll when the wheels won't go?

(Spoken) Up in East Kentucky around Harlan and Perry County, the coal miner sings a little song called the "Nine Pound Hammer." Now just picture yourself a-driving four-inch spikes in hard black-oak track-ties about five miles back under the mountain — where the top's so low in the mines that you cain't straighten up to rest your back jest for a minute. And lotsa time the air gets so foul back there that you jest cain't get a good deep breath. (sigh)

This nine pound hammer is a little too heavy,
For my size, honey, for my size.
I'm a-goin' on the mountain, gonna see my baby,
But I ain't comin' back, Oh, well, I ain't comin' back.

Roll on buddy, don't you roll so slow,
How can I roll when the wheels won't go?
Roll on buddy, pull a load of coal,
How can I pull when the wheels won't go?

It's a long way to Harlan, it's a long way to Hazard,
Just to get a little brew, just to get a little brew.
When I'm long gone, you can make my tombstone,
Out of Number Nine coal, out of Number Nine coal.

Chorus:

357

NINE POUND HAMMER

In the preceding chapter on Travis' newly composed mining songs, I touched upon radio's role in using electrical transcriptions to supplement records from the *Folk Songs of the Hills* album. Also, I noted the artist's textual variation in songs found on these ET

358

HAND DRILLING

mechanical forms. The new verbal introduction which Travis used for his ET "Nine Pound Hammer" shifted the stress of the original disc opening from workers singing in the mines to miners entertaining themselves to fill in leisure time:

> You know 'round the coal mines, when the boys ain't a-workin' in the mines they don't have a whole lot to do. They ain't a whole lot of farms and they ain't a lot of moving picture shows they can go to so lots of 'em just gits 'em a guitar, and they learn to pick and sing. Here's an old song that lots of boys around in East Kentucky sings. It's a song about a nine pound hammer.[38]

Travis' "Nine Pound Hammer" can be likened to "Dark as a Dungeon" rather than to "Sixteen Tons," inasmuch as no particular singer turned Travis' hammer song into a hit but many singers assimilated it into their repertoires. The first person to cover "Nine Pound Hammer" for recording purposes was Buffalo Johnson, whose version was released in 1952 on Rich-R-Tone 1023. This minor label belonged to James Hobart Stanton of the Rich-R-Tone Music Center in Johnson City, Tennessee. Stanton was one of the last entrepreneurs to record country music on 78 rpm discs in a mountain locale and he can be credited with helping such artists as the

359

Stanley Brothers and Wilma Lee and Stoney Cooper at the start of their careers. The exact circumstances of Buffalo Johnson's recording of "Nine Pound Hammer" are unknown to me. However, discographer Pete Kuykendall has suggested that Johnson probably knew it traditionally but refreshed his memory from Travis' disc, which was available in Kentucky-Tennessee during 1947-51.[39] The significant clue in identifying Johnson's version is his acceptance of Travis' new "Harlan-Hazard" phrase. A secondary clue is conveyed by the musicians who backed Johnson, for his lead guitarist imitated Travis' distinctive picking style.

I do not wish to single out Buffalo Johnson's cover of "Nine Pound Hammer" for special attention. Checklist Seven reveals that many artists were drawn to Travis' song to such a degree that it supplanted earlier variants. In the repertoires of bluegrass and old-time musicians today, it is difficult to find any performers who sing "Nine Pound Hammer" without either the Harlan-Hazard or Number Nine coal references. In fact, just two or three traditional versions of "Nine Pound Hammer" unrelated to coal were recorded after 1947. A good example of such a number not influenced by Travis is "Nine Pound Hammer" by Bill and Earl Bolick on *The Blue Sky Boys* (Starday SLP 205), an LP edited from electrical transcriptions originally made by the Bolicks to advertise Willys Overland Jeeps via an Atlanta radio show.

To a folklorist, Travis' role in fixing "Nine Pound Hammer" as a coal song is worthy of attention since there are few documented instances of given songs crossing industrial lines. To Travis himself, the piece seems primarily of interest in that it removed him by association from his home county. Although Travis had named his childhood home, Ebenezer, in "Dark as a Dungeon," and his father's work site, Beech Creek, in "Over By Number Nine," these two hamlets were completely overshadowed by the Harlan-Hazard references in "Nine Pound Hammer." Actually, "bloody Harlan" had become a forboding symbol throughout the United States during the violent labor disturbances in that area in the 1930's.[40] Harlan is still a significant name-on-the-land in trade-union lore, comparable to Haymarket Square in Chicago, Ludlow, Colorado, or Homestead, Pennsylvania. Merle Travis was a teenage boy when he first heard his father and other union miners talk in muted tones about defeats

HARLAN COUNTY PAMPHLETS

in Harlan. His adult recollection to me of his earliest feeling about the place was that it was rough and tough — a dark and bloody ground. I was curious to learn how this somber association became linked in Merle Travis' mind with a cheerful, rhythmic hammer song, but apparently there was no special connection until the eve of his 1946 recording session.

Travis' first conscious memory of hearing any persons sing "Nine Pound Hammer" was that of Texas Ruby, with whom he had worked briefly on the road before World War II. She had chanted it one night on "The Galloping Goose," an old bus used by the Boone County Jamboree touring troupe for trips to and from radio station WLW in Cincinnati. Ruby Owens, born on a Decatur,

361

Texas, ranch, had had considerable experience as a radio cowgirl before her marriage in 1939 to Tennessee fiddler Curly Fox. Ruby and Curly together formed a Grand Ole Opry team until Ruby's tragic death in a Nashville fire in 1963. During my visit with Travis a few years later he was pleased to be able to name Texas Ruby as his source for the hammer song.[41] He could still recall, and imitate in 1967, her rhythmic, knee-patting rendition. I took it as a mark of Travis' sophistication that he carefully credited Texas Ruby with "Nine Pound Hammer" and did not ascribe the piece to a mythical strike veteran from Harlan. When Travis accepted the assignment from Capitol Records in 1946 to put together an album of coal-mining folksongs, he pulled Texas Ruby's traditional song out of memory and extended it with a Harlan-Hazard stanza from his own sure knowledge that Harlan conjured up visions of coal and mountaineers to many Americans.

The mark of his success in giving an old hammer number a specific locale was demonstrated as early as 1948, when Alan Lomax cited *Folk Songs of the Hills* as "work songs of the East Kentucky coal camps." Few performers resisted this association. In a personal sense, I recall my first pleasant meeting with La Jolla's marine biologist Sam Hinton at the University of California, Berkeley, when I complimented him on singing several of Merle Travis' "Harlan" songs but informed him that actually Travis came from south central Kentucky. Travis himself, after many years of publicly singing "Nine Pound Hammer" and telling people he was not from Harlan, made his position explicit in an autobiographical sketch:

> In 1947 I made a record of a song by the title of NINE POUND HAMMER. One of the verses in part has these words.
>
> > "It's a long way to Harlan
> > It's a long way to Hazard."
>
> It's flattering that so many folks must have heard the old recording, for constantly I meet people who got the wrong impression from the song.
>
> "I'm from your neck of the woods, Merle," they'll say, "up around Harlan and Hazard."
>
> When I explain that I'm from the other end of the State, and was never in East Kentucky until I was grown, they look a little confused.

"But you sung about it," they'll say, "in that song about the Nine Pound Hammer!"

Let me explain to folks from other states that in Kentucky, like in Ireland, a person first mentions the county he's from, and gets around to the town later.

It's strange that folks would get mixed up about the old hammer song. I've sung about Heaven all my life, and nobody ever thought I was from there.[42]

As the crow flies it is 200 miles from Ebenezer to Harlan — a distance never traveled by Merle Travis until he left home to begin the life of a professional country musician. This chapter has suggested only some of the sites from Texas to Virginia where "Nine Pound Hammer" was shaped. Travis heard the song originally about 1939 from Texas Ruby on a bus returning to Cincinnati. It is unlikely that we shall ever know where she learned her version except to state that, regardless of locale, it resembled the one recorded by Al Hopkins and His Buckle Busters in 1927. This Brunswick number, in turn, had stemmed via Charles Bowman's memory from the singing of black railroad workers at Gray Station, Tennessee, about 1903-05. It is, indeed, in Travis' hammer folksong a long way to Harlan. However, "Nine Pound Hammer's" journey in becoming a coal-mining song was significantly longer than the physical distance overland from Ebenezer to Harlan, for it was a journey which brought together separate work experiences and widely diverse people.

1. Charles Peabody, "Notes on Negro Music," *Journal of American Folklore,* XVI (1903), 148.

2. Norman Cohen, "Railroad Folksongs on Record — a Survey," *New York Folklore Quarterly,* XXVI (1970), 91.

3. Gates Thomas, "South Texas Negro Work-Songs," in *Rainbow in the Morning,* Publications of the Texas Folklore Society, no. V, ed. J. Frank Dobie (Hatboro, Pa., 1965), 154.

4. My comments on and quotations from Barton are drawn from his reprinted article, "Recent Negro Melodies," in *The Negro and His Folklore in Nineteenth-Century Periodicals,* ed. Bruce Jackson (Austin, Tex., 1967), 302.

5. Louise Rand Bascom, "Ballads and Songs of Western North Carolina," *Journal of American Folklore,* XXII (1909), 249.

6. Howard W. Odum, "Folk-Song and Folk-Poetry as Found in the Secular

Songs of the Southern Negroes," *Journal of American Folklore,* XXIV (1911), 386.

7. E. C. Perrow, "Songs and Rhymes from the South," *Journal of American Folklore,* XXVI (1913), 165.

8. Natalie Curtis Burlin, *Negro Folk-Songs,* Hampton Series, III (New York, 1919), 22.

9. Robert Winslow Gordon, "Old Songs That Men Have Sung," *Adventure,* XLIV (Jan. 10, 1924), 191.

10. Will Thomas' "Skinner's Song" was included in an early Texas Folklore Society pamphlet, "Some Current Folk-Songs of the Negro and Their Economic Interpretation" (1912), and reprinted as an addition to *Rainbow in the Morning* (1965).

11. *The Frank C. Brown Collection of North Carolina Folklore,* III (Durham, 1952), 267; Newman Ivey White, *American Negro Folk-Songs* (Cambridge, Mass., 1928), 139.

12. Dorothy Scarborough, *On the Trail of Negro Folk-Songs* (Cambridge, Mass., 1925), 220, 222.

13. For drilling and related hand labor see Otis E. Young, Jr., *Western Mining* (Norman, Okla., 1970).

14. "Wheelers" from Perrow, "Songs and Rhymes from the South," 172; "Roll On, Boys" from Herbert Shellans, *Folk Songs of the Blue Ridge Mountains* (New York, 1968), 47.

15. Scarborough, *On the Trail of Negro Folk-Songs,* 248.

16. This extension of the term *levee camp* to general construction is noted by Thomas, "South Texas Negro Work-Songs," 168. However, the usage is not found in Mitford M. Mathews, *A Dictionary of Americanisms* (Chicago, 1951). For an excellent account of levee history rich in folkloric leads see Robert W. Harrison, *Levee Districts and Levee Building in Mississippi* (State College, Miss., 1951).

17. "Levee Camp Moan Blues" was reissued in 1964 on *The Country Blues* (RBF 9). For Texas Alexander see Samuel Charters, *The Bluesman* (New York, 1967), 197.

18. Odum, "Folk-Song and Folk-Poetry," 382.

19. A "Roll On John" text from Knott County, Ky., similar to Kazee's is found in the Josiah H. Combs Collection of the Western Kentucky Folklore Archive, University of California, Los Angeles.

20. Letter to me, Jan. 31, 1969, supplemented by interview, Mar. 21, 1969. See also John Edwards, "Buell Kazee," *Caravan,* no. 17 (June, 1959), 42, and Charles G. Bowen, "Buell Kazee: The Genuine Article," *Sing Out,* XX (Sept., 1970), 13.

21. A copy of this operetta is in my files.

22. Lamar Stringfield, "America and Her Music," *University of North Carolina Extension Bulletin,* X (Mar., 1931), 21.

23. Stan Hugill, *Shanties from the Seven Seas* (London, 1961), 289; William Main Doerflinger, *Shantymen and Shantyboys* (New York, 1951), 8.

364

24. Interview, Aug. 10, 1961, supplemented by correspondence with Charles Bowman beginning Feb. 13, 1961. See also Dorothy Hamill, "Bowman Band Recalls 'The Good Old Days,' " *Johnson City* [Tenn.] *Press-Chronicle* (Feb. 5, 1960), 2A.

25. Archie Green, "Hillbilly Music: Source and Symbol," *Journal of American Folklore*, LXXVIII (1965), 204.

26. Interview, Aug. 14, 1963.

27. Guy B. Johnson, *John Henry: Tracking Down a Negro Legend* (Chapel Hill, N.C., 1929), 79.

28. Interview, Aug. 8, 1963.

29. Interview, July 5, 1969.

30. Abbe Niles, "Ballads, Songs and Snatches," *Bookman*, LXVIII (Oct., 1928), 214.

31. Cecil Sharp, *English Folk-Songs from the Southern Appalachians*, II (London, 1932), 42. See also Mellinger E. Henry, *Folk-Songs from the Southern Highlands* (New York, 1938), 448.

32. For the Carolina Tar Heels' background see Ralph Rinzler's two brochures to *Old Time Music at Clarence Ashley's* (Folkways FA 2355) and *Old Time Music . . . Part Two* (Folkways FA 2359). See also my brochure to *The Carolina Tar Heels* (Folk-Legacy FSA 24).

33. For Stoneman see Norman Cohen and others, *The Early Recording Career of Ernest V. "Pop" Stoneman: A Bio-Discography* (Los Angeles, 1968).

34. Michael E. Bush, *Folk Songs of Central West Virginia* (Glenville, 1969), 48.

35. For Bill Monroe see Jim Rooney, *Bassmen: Bill Monroe and Muddy Waters* (New York, 1971).

36. Quotations in Louis W. Chappell, *John Henry: A Folk-Lore Study* (Jena, Germany, 1933), 63, 64.

37. Josiah H. Combs, *Folk-Songs of the Southern United States*, ed. D. K. Wilgus (Austin, Tex., 1967), 166; John Harrington Cox, " 'The Yew Pine Mountains,' a 'John Hardy' Ballad," *American Speech*, II (1927), 226. For Woofter see also D. K. Wilgus, "The Oldest (?) Text of 'Edward,' " *Western Folklore*, XXV (1966), 77.

38. Transcribed from Capitol ET G 110, in possession of Bob Pinson.

39. Letter to me, Jan. 14, 1969.

40. See, for example, Theodore Dreiser, *Harlan Miners Speak* (New York, 1932). For a fresh review on the book's reprinting see Harry Caudill, "The Appalachian Tragedy," *New York Review of Books*, XV (Nov. 19, 1970), 17. For an early view of Harlan events see John F. Day, *Bloody Ground* (Garden City, N.Y., 1941), 287; for two recent overviews see Irving Bernstein, *The Lean Years* (Boston, 1960), 377, and Tony Bubka, "The Harlan County Coal Strike of 1931," *Labor History*, XI (1970), 41.

41. Interview, June 15, 1967.

42. Merle Travis, "I Have a Sick Sister in Texas," in *Country and Western Keepsake*, ed. Larry Moeller (Nashville, 1967), 18.

CHECKLIST SEVEN

This list is restricted to "Nine Pound Hammer" versions directly from Merle Travis or utilizing some of his language.

————. Merle Travis, Capitol 48000 (1332). Aug. 8, 1946, Hollywood; released late in 1947 in album *Folk Songs of the Hills* (AD 50).
Reissued: *Back Home,* Capitol T 891; released Dec., 1957. Parallel issue: EAP 1-891.
> *The Best of Merle Travis,* Capitol T 2662.
> *21 Years a Country Singer,* Capitol T 21010 (England).

————. Merle Travis, American Music, Hollywood (June 9, 1947), EP 98030. Lead sheet received at Copyright Office Mar. 23, 1956, but backdated to 1947.

————. Merle Travis, Capitol G-110. An electrical transcription made in Hollywood. Date unknown.

————. Buffalo Johnson, Rich-R-Tone 1023 (1414). Early 1952, Johnson City, Tenn.

————. Tex Williams, Decca 29764 (88921). Nov., 1955.
Reissued: *Country Music Time,* Decca DL 4295.

————. Tennessee Ernie Ford, *This Lusty Land,* Capitol T 700. Hollywood. Parallel issue: Capitol EAP 2-700.

————. *150 Old Time Folk and Gospel Songs,* Bill Clifton, Adams Printing Company, North Wilkesboro, N.C. (1956), 34.

————. Bob Green, Milburn, Carlisle County, Ky., July, 1956. Jerry and Marcie Williams, typescript, Western Kentucky Folklore Archive, UCLA, Tape 7-10.

————. Sanford Clark, Dot 15534. ca. 1956. Parallel issue: Reo 8143 (Canada).

————. Billy Faier, *Travelin' Man,* Riverside RLP 657. Aug., 1958, New York.
Reissued: Washington VM 740.

————. Smiley Hobbs, *Mountain Music Bluegrass Style,* Folkways FA 2318; released 1959.

————. Dick Curless, Event 4274. ca. 1960.

————. Merle Travis, Capitol 2176. A single 45 rpm, released in 1960, which may represent his second recording of this song.

————. Brothers Four, *Rally Round,* Columbia CL 1479. ca. 1960, New York.
Reissued: *Greatest Hits,* Columbia CL 1803.

"Roll on Buddy." Lomax, *F S N A* (1960), 284, m. Lomax includes "Harlan-Hazard" stanza.

366

————. Hank Thompson, *At the Golden Nugget,* Capitol T 1632. ca. 1961, Las Vegas.

————. Lou Rawls, Capitol 4669 (36658). ca. 1962.

————. Greenbriar Boys, *The Greenbriar Boys,* Vanguard VRS 9104. New York. Parallel issue: Fontana TFL 6019 (England).

————. Flatt and Scruggs, *Folk Songs of Our Land,* Columbia CL 1830.

————. Johnny Cash, *Blood, Sweat and Tears,* Columbia CL 1930. Aug. 22, 1962.

————. Bluegrass Hillbillies, *Pickin' n' Grinnin',* ABC Paramount ABC 446. ca. 1963, Hollywood.

————. Don Carlos Amburgey, east Ky. Amburgey, *K F R,* IX (1963), 16.

————. Country Gentlemen, *Hootenanny,* Design DLP 613; released 1963.

————. Country Gentlemen, *The Country Gentlemen,* Zap MLP 101.

————. Homesteaders, *Railroad Bill,* Riverside RM 7537. ca. 1963, New York.

————. Tex Williams, *Tex Williams in Las Vegas,* Liberty 3304.

————. Tom Rush, *Got a Mind to Ramble,* Prestige FL 14003. ca. Aug., 1963.

————. Reno and Smiley, *The World's Best Five-String Banjo,* King 861. ca. 1963, Cincinnati.

————. Hank Ferguson, *Behind These Walls,* Folk-Legacy FSA 13. Indiana State Penitentiary, 1964.

————. Kentucky Colonels, *Appalachian Swing,* World Pacific WP 1821.

————. Lorne Greene, *The Man,* Victor LPM 3302.

————. Traum, *F P S G* (1966), 42, m.

————. Dick Curless, *Tombstone Every Mile,* Tower T 50005.

————. Tex Williams, *Tex Williams,* Sunset 1144.

————. Don Reno, *Don Reno & Bill Harrell with the Tennessee Cut-Ups,* Rural Rhythm RRDR 171. ca. 1967.

————. Beau Brummels, *Triangle,* Warner Brothers WS 1692.

APPENDIX SEVEN

LEVEE-CAMP RECOLLECTION

This is a portion of a transcript by Mody Boatright of Walter Cline's recollection. Cline, born in Louisiana, went from rice-canal work to the oil fields, where he became a driller, drilling contractor, and producer. The interview was taped at Cline's home in Wichita Falls, Texas, on August 13, 1952. The original tape and transcript are deposited in the University of Texas Archives, Austin, and the selection used here is by permission. For an extensive book drawn from memories of oil-field pioneers see Mody C. Boatright and William Owen, *Tales from the Derrick Floor* (New York, 1970).

I left school in my senior year in order to help in the education of my two younger brothers. My first employment was on a rice canal south of Crowley, Louisiana, the Ferris Canal, where I was a mule skinner, and then worked in a shovelling wheelbarrow gang and later was put in charge of a carpenter gang building flood gates and flumes and short bridges across the canals and laterals. And from this job I was promoted, through my experience, to a somewhat better job with the Grand Canal Company who was building a new canal out north of Jennings, Louisiana. On this canal I was placed in charge of the levee building crew, consisting of some 200 to 225 Negroes and about 200 to 225 mules, and about half that many mule skinners and lumpers and dumpers that are necessary in every building crew. This was the crew that we worked from camp to camp and we began work as soon as we can see and worked until we can't see, and then came into camp and treated the sore shoulders of the mules and fed them, and I had to take personal care of my riding pony and give him just the amount of oats that he could eat, cause some folks don't know it, but you can just cut sacks of oats in an open trough in front of these jugheads, and they're smart, and they won't eat enough to hurt them. But a horse, if you leave a half a sack of oats in front of him, he'll flounder himself. I enjoyed this work very much because you can plow in the first furrow and you can look back over the canals when the water began to run down it and see homes and churches and schools and civilization coming along, and you felt like you'd pioneered in it and contributed in a small way to help develop this section of your home state. While I was on the Grand Canal the well diggers discovered oil at Evangeline, Louisiana [September 21, 1901]. Not very far distance from where I was. It was north of Jennings, too. And hearing that the pay was better in the oil fields, I quit the canal business and went over and got a job in the oil field.

Well, in running my levee camp, I'd learned a bit of that. I was the only man, only foreman the levee company had that didn't carry a Winchester rifle in a scabbard strapped onto the sweatleather on his horse, a six shooter strapped around him and a big hickory stick. I didn't carry anything. And yet I'd move more cubic yards of dirt per unit of man and mule and had fewer mules hurt, and tore up less equipment than anybody that worked for the company because, rather than have all this firearms and things, I set up an emergency medical tent and if they'd fall out in a cooncan game — you know, a little crap shooting or something and razor each other up a little bit — I got to be pretty good at this first aid and things; I just doctored them up. If I loaned them a dollar, I didn't expect two dollars Saturday. I just got my dollar back, and it wasn't but a little while until I had a hundred-odd Negroes. If they got in jail, I'd go down and pay their fines, never charge them anything. Just take a wagon and usually have the wagon loaded in jail every weekend, too.

WORK TOMORROW?

Blues and More Blues 10

NO CATEGORY of native-American folksong has gathered to itself more varied commentary than the blues. Anthropologists, musicologists, historians, cultural nationalists, and poets all have offered definitions and analysis. Blues are frequently identified in terms of form (twelve-bar structure, three-chord progression, three-line stanza), content (joys and sorrows of love), ethnic origin (unique contribution of the Negro in the United States), and mode of dissemination (race, rhythm-and-blues, or soul records). Fortunately, numerous blues recordings of the past five decades have been reissued on current LPs, and these aural documents are well complemented by recent books of enthusiasts such as Samuel Charters, LeRoi Jones, Charles Keil, Paul Oliver, Harry Oster, and Eric Sackheim. To add to my listening pleasure I have used their books (cited in the bibliography), and here I wish to note only two which are striking visual productions: Oliver's *The Story of the Blues* is a gathering of rare photographs; Sackheim's *The Blues Line* is an anthology of texts freely arranged typographically, themselves enhanced by Jonathan Shahn's fine drawings of bluesmen.

In this closing case study I shall present and contrast three songs which stemmed from bituminous-mining life in the South: "Mining Camp Blues," "Coal Mountain Blues," "Coal Miner's

371

Blues." The first two were pressed on race records and might be identified respectively as "urban" and "country." The third is a "mountain" piece originally released on a hillbilly disc. I am aware that terms such as *urban, city, uptown, country, rural, native,* and *folk* all have been extended to try to convey nuances of structural and stylistic distinction within the blues. In the main, students have attempted to separate folk (or country) from city blues by stressing the primitive, unpolished, or spontaneous style of the former against the standardized, theatrical, or formal quality of the latter. Pete Whelan and Bill Givens, co-producers of the Origin Jazz Library reissue series, have suggested that the word *country* "causes more confusion and hard-feeling among collectors and commentators on the blues than any other term. . . ." Their own gloss: "[Country] does not primarily mean rural, but native, as in the normal English fellow countryman. But over and above this, it means close-to-home, earthy, vital, familiar, powerful, lacking airs, and most important, in full measure. Used this way, the expression is quite familiar to American baseball fans as a country mile, and through the use of country as an epithet reserved for such over-powering and all-out ball players as "Country" Slaughter."[1]

It is not my prime interest to place "Mining Camp Blues," "Coal Mountain Blues," or "Coal Miner's Blues" along a continuum: folk to non-folk. Rather, I find each of these three songs — representative of urban, country, and hillbilly categories — to be a compelling human document which reveals aspects of American coal miners' working conditions and value systems. In addition to viewing a blues as a mining commentary, it is my hope that this three-branched chapter will contribute to the unexplored area of the blues as industrial folksong.

Some Negroes, among them George W. Johnson, Bert Williams, the Fisk Jubilee Singers, and James Europe, had appeared on cylinders and discs in the two decades before World War I. Their offerings included comic novelties, coon songs, polished spirituals, and "modern" dance music. However, the genre which was denominated *race records* in the immediate postwar years was based largely on previously unrecorded jazz and blues material. In the halcyon days of the early 1920's, *jazz* and *blues* were almost synonymous tags. With the perspective of time, it becomes easy to distinguish, for example, an intricate jazz performance by John Coltrane from an anguished blues by Robert Johnson. Such distinctions were not yet called for in 1920, when Mamie Smith recorded "Crazy Blues" and other numbers which marked the birth of race records. This genre, tremendously important to the entire music industry, and to black people both as consumers and citizens striving for racial progress, is touched upon in a variety of works noted in my bibliography.

A perusal of blues reissued on LPs in the 1960's reveals that among the predominant songs of love are varied occupational items: "Working Man," "WPA Blues," "Levee Camp Blues," "Hard Time Killin' Floor Blues," "Labor Blues," "Electrician Blues." The titles point to work; the lyrics, however, range from descriptions of given job sites or experiences to songs of sexual innuendo in which virile handymen play double roles. Only after close listening to many race records representing different artists and areas can one begin to feel the texture of toil in farming, domestic employment, and factory life that occupied most of the Negro work force in the 1920's and 1930's.

George Korson was the first folklorist to gather consciously field recordings of black miners in Alabama and West Virginia, although Newman Ivey White had collected a number of fragments when he taught school in Alabama in 1915. These latter attested to the richness of this previously hidden tradition. One couplet alone is selected here to represent the early corpus: "Captain, Captain, give me my time / Tired of workin' in damned old mine."[2] Korson and White were buoyed up in their quest by the knowledge that black workers had a long and distinct singing tradition. Slaves had worked commercial mines along the James River in Virginia during colonial times, and had supplied coal to ammunition makers for the Continental Army. Booker T. Washington, while a boy slave recently freed, worked in a coal mine at Malden, West Virginia. During 1969 black miners in West Virginia were active in the campaign against the "black-lung" disease (pneumoconiosis). Despite Negro involvement in the coal industry for more than two centuries, we have few recorded coal songs from black miners at hand except those gathered by Korson.

The only other source for such material is race records. As

373

near as I can determine, about a dozen mining songs, listed in Appendix Eight, were issued on discs, although in some the industrial content is peripheral. A few items, such as "Coal Woman Blues" by Black Boy Shine (Vocalion 03757) and "Coal Man Blues" by James Hall (Vocalion 04231), are excluded from my list because they comment on the selling of coal and other less prosaic goods rather than mining itself. Two race records which spring directly from coal as an extractive industry are selected for specific investigation here.

Early in February, 1925, Trixie Smith, one of the many queens of the blues, accompanied by her Down Home Syncopators, recorded in a New York studio "Mining Camp Blues (Paramount 12256). The 1920's were both productive and exhilarating for Lucille Hegamin, Sara Martin, Ma Rainey, Bessie Smith, Victoria Spivey, Sippie Wallace, Ethel Waters, and other female stars of the recording studio, the cabaret, and the stage.[3] Some of these women owed their success entirely to the then-new race-records enterprise, but others were tested show-business figures. For example, Daisy Martin had been billed as the "bronze Eva Tanguay" in 1910 and Ma Rainey in this same year was already an experienced tent-show and vaudeville star.

Trixie Smith merits attention as a successful early urban blues performer, yet she has been neglected by jazz historians. No account is known to me of her apprenticeship in the South on the TOBA (Theater Owners Booking Agency) circuit. However, on the night of January 20, 1922, she won a silver loving cup at the Manhattan Casino in a well-publicized and well-attended "National Blues Singing Contest."[4] The gala event was sponsored by a group of Harlem American Expeditionary Force veterans, and drew such notables as Irene Castle, Madame Enrico Caruso, Mrs. H. Payne Whitney, and Major Fiorello La Guardia. Noble Sissle, then appearing in his Broadway hit "Shuffle Along," was master of ceremonies. Miss Smith won with her personal "Trixie's Blues" and soon made her recording debut with this song on Black Swan, a short-lived Negro-owned and -managed firm organized by Harry Pace. When Black Swan failed, its masters and other assets were acquired by Paramount, and Trixie continued her association with the Wisconsin Chair Company's recording subsidiary through 1926.

374

IRENE CASTLE AND TRIXIE SMITH.

Photograph By Robt. McDougald, The Age Photographer.
Mrs. Castle presenting Silver Loving Cup to Miss Trixie Smith,
winner of 15th Regiment "Blues" Singing Contest at
Manhattan Casino, January 20th.

TRIXIE SMITH AND IRENE CASTLE

Trixie Smith's repertoire was typical of that demanded of
nightclub and recording performers in the mid-1920's: "Everybody's Doing That Charleston," "Voodoo Blues," "Messin'

375

Around," "Don't Shake It No More," "Railroad Blues," to name a few. Curiously, one title anticipated the recent generic term *rock-and-roll:* "My Man Rocks Me with One Steady Roll." It is highly unlikely that Trixie's "Mining Camp Blues" would have lived beyond its period of initial sales had it not been for her accompanists, the Down Home Syncopators. Nearly all popular female songsters in the first years of race records were backed by small jazz bands, either casually gathered for recording sessions or held together by dance-hall and speakeasy employment.

In the fall of 1924 Louis Armstrong, reaching New York from New Orleans by way of Chicago, joined the Roseland Ballroom band of Fletcher Henderson, a precursor of swing. Armstrong's career is as well documented as that of any jazz figure. Here I need state only that he, Henderson, Buster Bailey, Charlie Green, and Charlie Dixon backed Trixie on "Mining Camp Blues." Consequently this disc and other Down Home Syncopator numbers became important to Armstrong enthusiasts as examples of his early work with Henderson. I can still recall my surprise when, on a 1962 visit to Arlington, Virginia, record collector Richard Spottswood casually asked if I had ever heard a jazzy mining song. Upon eliciting a negative reply, he played for me Trixie's "Mining Camp Blues," complementing the music with a brief history of the Paramount race series.

During 1968 Riverside Records issued in the United States a "Classic Jazz Masters" set originally released in Europe, including the LP *Louis Armstrong in New York 1924-1925* (Riverside RM 8811) edited by Professor H. R. Rookmaaker of the Netherlands. This was followed by the American LP *Louis Armstrong, an Early Portrait* (Milestone MLP 2010). Both albums were used in transcribing the tune and text of Miss Smith's song:

MINING CAMP BLUES

Once I had a daddy and he worked down in a hole,
Once I had a daddy and he worked down in a hole;
Diggin' and a-haulin', haulin' that Birmingham coal.

Many times I wondered when they took my daddy down,
Many times I wondered when they took my daddy down;
Will he come back to me, will they leave him in the ground?

376

Something like the pitcher that they sent down in the well,
Something like the pitcher that they sent down in the well;
Wond'rin' will they break it, Lawdy, Lawdy, who can tell?

It was late one evenin' I was standin' at that mine,
It was late one evenin' I was standin' at that mine;
Foreman said my daddy had gone down for the last, last time.

He was a coal miner, from his hat down to his shoes;
He was a coal miner, from his hat down to his shoes;
And I'm nearly dyin' with these minin' camp blues.

MINING CAMP BLUES

The text requires little explication. In the manner of many tightly structured and polished early jazz blues, it does not depart from a three-line stanza and an a a a or a a b rhyme scheme. Within this form it builds strongly to the level of grief expressed by every miner's woman — wife, girlfriend, mother, daughter, sister — at the loss of her man. The contrast between this blues and most mining-disaster ballads found in Korson's books is a good reflection of differences in compositional options open to black miners in the South and Anglo-Celtic miners in the North. To illustrate, "The Avondale Mine Disaster" commented on an 1869 happening

377

in Pennsylvania and is as concrete in all vital details as a cinema newsreel. Upon hearing or reading "Mining Camp Blues," however, we have no way of knowing whether or not it sprang from an actual event. This blues whispers of death in the dark via a foreman's matter-of-fact message: "My daddy had gone down for the last, last time." In part, Miss Smith universalized the tension generated in mining life from the imminence of danger by resorting to a proverbial analog of her man and the pitcher broken on its journey to or in the well.

I do not know enough about Trixie Smith's early life to document the Birmingham passage in her "Mining Camp Blues."[5] It can be recalled that the "Coal Creek Troubles" chapter held references on the employment of black convicts in Alabama's Pratt mines during the 1890's. Unlike Tennessee, Alabama retained this system through the 1920's. A half-year before "Mining Camp Blues" was recorded, James Knox, a convict at the Flat Top Prison camp near Birmingham, was brutally tortured to death. His murder aroused citizens in Alabama finally to end their convict-lease system.[6] It is entirely possible that Trixie Smith was aware of the public scandal which stemmed from Knox's death, although her song is not a commentary on the use of convicts in mining. Unless some clue comes to the surface concerning this specific item's composition, it is difficult to know how much Alabama mining history stands behind the song. Even the question of whether this blues had sprung from Miss Smith's direct experience or came to her already formed by another person is a mystery.

One detail remains. On January 30, 1925, the musical lead sheet and a professionally typed text of "Mining Camp Blues" reached the Library of Congress and was copyrighted in Trixie Smith's name (E 605721). (Interestingly, it held two stanzas not sung on the record; the deletion presumably was caused by the three-minute limitation normal to 78 rpm discs.) The *Catalogue of Copyright Entries* added the information that Porter Grainger had arranged the song. Grainger is remembered as a New York pianist who accompanied many of the blues queens of the 1920's, and as a highly successful composer and arranger in the idiom disseminated by race records. With a colleague, Robert W. "Bob" Ricketts, he published a booklet, *How to Play and Sing the Blues Like the*

378

MINING CAMP BLUES

By Trixie Smith

Once I had a daddy and he worked down in a hole,
Once I had a daddy and he worked down in a hole;
Diggin' and a-haulin'--haulin' that Birmingham coal.

Ev'ry time he left me and went down into that mine,
Ev'ry time he left me and went down into that mine;
Hung my head in sorrow and I couldn't help from cryin'

Many times I wondered when they took my daddy down
Many times I wondered when they took my daddy down;
Will he come back to me--will they leave him in the ground.

Something like the pitcher that they sent down in the well,
Something like the pitcher that they sent down in the well;
Wond'rin' will they break it, lawdy, lawdy, who can tell;

It was late one evenin' I was standin' at that mine,
It was late one evenin' I was standin' at that mine;
Foreman said my daddy had gone down his last, last time;

Ev'ry day I've waited, sad and worried as can be,
Ev'ry day I've waited, sad and worried as can be;
Waitin' for my daddy, thinkin' he'd come back to me;

He was a coal miner, from his hat down to his shoes
He was a coal miner, from his hat down to his shoes;
And I'm nearly dyin' with these mean camp-minin' blues.

Copyrighted 1925 by Trixie Smith

"MINING CAMP BLUES"

Phonograph and Stage Artists. The team wrote perceptively of the newly demanded style: "If one can temporarily play the role of the oppressed or the depressed, injecting into his or her rendition a spirit of hopeful prayer, the effect will be . . . natural and successful."[7] As I listen in 1970 to "Mining Camp Blues," I hear a vocalist's deliberate singing set off by a blue trombone and expressive cornet, and I am transported to the Harlem jazz realm of 1925. But when I focus on this number's clearly enunciated words, I become aware that Trixie Smith, in Grainger's terms, caught the timeless spirit of oppressed laborers and their loved ones depressed by work of great danger.

Trixie Smith grieved for just one miner without indicating whether his death resulted from an individual accident or a mass holocaust. In this sense she sang for all diggers, black and white, who had given their lives on the industrial battlefield. It is well to note that America's earliest documented major coal disaster (March 18, 1839) at the Black Heath pit near Richmond, Virginia, occurred close to the original James River open-faced mine where slaves had inaugurated commercial coal production in the New World. An observer of this grim Richmond event wrote: "Of the fifty-four men in the mine, only two who happened to be in some crevices near the mouth of the shaft escaped with life."[8] Did a Black Heath victim's woman in any way articulate her loss in song? I ask this rhetorical question to underscore the timelessness of Trixie Smith's blues, which could also have been penned or sung as recently as year's end 1970 on Hurricane Creek, Leslie County, Kentucky, when thirty-eight workers were killed in a volcanic explosion in the Finley mine.

Accidental loss of life was not, and is not, the only destiny of the coal miner. A constant fear in this industry of boom and depression, spiraling good and bad times, and technological change has been, and is, unemployment. The havoc caused by lack of work and by shifts in productive technology are detailed in statistical reports and novels alike, and are all too available in public and private libraries. In this study I shall offer but a single text which bitterly illuminates an individual miner's response to joblessness — a response made doubly tragic by the narrator's expressed willingness to work in spite of illness.

380

Sonny Scott's harsh, mournful melody for "Coal Mountain Blues" (Vocalion 25012) and text follow.

COAL MOUNTAIN BLUES

(Spoken) I'll play it just like I feel.

Oh, I went on Coal Mountain; saw the men pulling coals from the
    mine;
Lord, I went on Coal Mountain; saw the men pulling coals from the
    mine;
I saw the men wearing their mine lamps where all the lights did shine.

Lord, I went to the mine foreman; told him I need a job mighty bad;
Lord, I went to the mine foreman; told him I need a job mighty bad;
But he said, "You have to go up to de doctor, and, boy, you sure won't
    pass."

Lord, I left that mining section; went towar' a seashore town;
Lord, I left that mining section; went towar' a seashore town;
I believe I've got the TB, I'm gonna jump overboard and drown.

(Spoken) Oh shucks, what is this, you reckon? I couldn't care what it's
    all about.

Lord, I've seen a seagull flying, baby, over my wat'ry grave;
Lord, I've seen a seagull flying, baby, over my wat'ry grave;
And it seemed to say that you goin' away to stay.

COAL MOUNTAIN BLUES

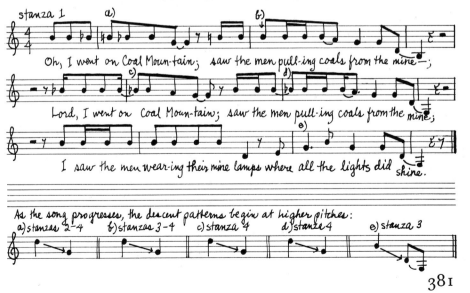

Without having any facts at hand about Sonny Scott's life history, one can still comment on his text and compare it to "Mining Camp Blues." Scott's piece is somewhat freer than Trixie Smith's in that his lines are both longer and shorter than hers. Also, his spoken interjections break the stanzaic regularity demonstrated by her tightly structured poem. I have suggested that her broken-pitcher figure was traditional; similarly Scott employed at least one image common to many blues: the seagull flying over the watery grave. Early in 1928 Okeh advertised "Dead Sea Blues" by Blue Belle (Bessie Mae Smith) with a sketch of a gull, or perhaps a pterodactyl, hovering over a floating corpse.[9]

Apart from Scott's closing stanza, his song is a unique industrial document. At least I know of no parallel in race or hillbilly records, and George Korson encountered nothing like it during his field investigations. This number is singular in that suicide was not usually suggested as a resolution for the dilemma posed in most blues. Despite the rhetorical call for self-immolation in some blues, and despite the very heavy stress in the genre on amatory failure, bluesmen generally held to a belief that by clinging to life they might regain love. Yet, contrary to this pattern, Scott contemplated self-destruction as an answer to the problem of his rejection for mine employment. Does this not seem a heavy price for joblessness?

Aside from the general problem of suicide, "Coal Mountain Blues" is most unusual in its portrait of a worker being declared unfit by a doctor. I presume that Scott meant a company doctor, for until very recent times most miners received all medical attention in company infirmaries. Here one can again note obvious differences between ballad and blues as literary forms. Scott's episodic line stated by the foreman, "You have to go up to de doctor, and, boy, you sure won't pass," has the potential of being expanded into a full narrative. One longs to ask for the doctor's name and the time and place of examination. The hidden question to anyone who has experienced any type of job discrimination is whether or not Scott was in fact diseased. Did he really have TB? Was it "miners' con" — a legacy of virulent consumption from previous employment? Was it projected by the doctor as a technique to withhold work?

The role of paid company doctors in refusing employment to "troublemakers" (union men) is briefly touched upon in standard

BIG JOE WILLIAMS

labor histories, but it is not something confined to the misty past. Part of the 1969 "Black Lung Rebellion" in West Virginia stems from radical differences among physicians over the very diagnosis of the disease. Doctor Lorin E. Kerr of the United Mine Workers of America has stated that the "medical denial of the existence of danger of coal dust has continued to be the position throughout the years of company-oriented physicians motivated by enlightened self-interest and a desire to save money for the industry."[10]

I have presented "Coal Mountain Blues" in terms of its text's meaning to me, without any background on its composer-singer's life. I acquired this record in 1958 and in nearly a dozen years have met only one person who claimed to know Sonny Scott. Big Joe Williams, a Mississippi bluesman who wandered from ministrel-show stages to recording studios as well as college "folksong revival" concert halls, told me that Scott had stayed at New York's Avenue Hotel — two blocks from Madison Square Garden — for a few days in October, 1961. More important, Williams identified Scott as coming from Birmingham, Alabama.[11] This fact would place "Coal Mountain" in proximity to the mining camp where Trixie Smith's man was lost.

383

The discographical information available on Scott seems to confirm his Alabama origin. His first recording session for the American Record Corporation took place in New York on July 18-20, 1933. He was in the studio with Walter Roland, whose nickname was "Alabama Sam," and with Lucille Bogan, a race-records pioneer originally from Birmingham. It is possible that Miss Bogan, who used the pseudonym Bessie Jackson, arranged for the recording debut of Scott and Roland. Scott made a number of vocal discs, accompanying himself on the guitar. On a few numbers he was backed by Roland on either guitar or piano. On others both performers backed Miss Bogan. Scott and Roland, as the Jolly Two, can now be heard on *Bessie Jackson & Walter Roland 1927-1935* (Yazoo L 1017). Scott is also heard on two other LPs holding reissues: *Alabama Country Blues* (Roots RL 325) and *New Deal Blues* (Mamlish 3801).

"Coal Mountain Blues" was Scott's first recorded vocal selection. Whether this is pure coincidence, or whether it signifies that he or an A & R man felt it to be an unusual song, I do not know. During 1933 Scott complemented his mining song with a "Working Man's Moan" (Vocalion 25013), which contained a stanza holding a significant statement on his probable occupation:

> I dug coals in the mine until my hands got cherry red;
> I dug coals in the mine 'til my hands got cherry red;
> I gave you all o' my money, woman, and you ought to be dead.

Among the handful of pieces recorded by Scott, a few stand out which were particularly appropriate in the period before the then-recent New Deal had reached black workers in great numbers. From some of Scott's record titles alone — "Fire Wood Man," "Hard Luck Man," "Naked Man Blues" — one senses that Scott had not only been disqualified from mine employment in a medical examination but that his hard luck had been severe and lengthy.

The major problem in the analysis of socioeconomic content in race records lies beyond the scope of my investigation. In a nutshell, partisans divide on the question of latent protest in the blues. Obviously, most blues seemed on the surface only to be love laments ending in self-ridicule, resignation, or veiled hope that joy might return. Yet some blues mixed ironic social commentary into their

CHERRY RED HANDS

standard humor or fantasy. A few made explicit near-political criticism directed at the grotesque and degrading life-patterns imposed by discriminatory employment and meager compensation. It was difficult to lose a woman; it was more difficult to go hungry.

Russell Ames has made the effective point that many bluesmen who could not raise protest to an objective, ideological pitch could and did offer political (but ambiguous and even surrealistic) images in an intense, strident vocal style backed by talking guitars. He stated "that the primary emotion [in blues] is not expressed verbally but is left to the music, to the use of the voice, and to implied scenes that the listeners can imaginatively develop out of their own experience or knowledge."[12]

Ames's formulation is useful in closing my comments on "Coal Mountain Blues." Scott's text, standing alone, is not a statement of conscious protest. He did not respond to job disqualification and unemployment by seeking out a union organizer or political leader. Seemingly, his suicide wish was the ultimate negation of class consciousness. Yet Scott's voice and guitar did express a poignant musical cry against company doctors, joblessness, and poverty. Hence, I am suggesting that "Coal Mountain Blues" is at one and the same

385

time a formal verbal statement of a worker's personal failure fused with a highly charged and volatile social message. Further, I feel that such a view of the blues may prove helpful in relating a large number of race records to particular socioeconomic groups and events, if only listeners will seek out the very tradition that led bluesmen, consciously or unconsciously, to cloak and muffle their ideological positions.

Perhaps in the context of a future study of race records as social documents, many such discs will be transcribed and evaluated. Pete Welding, a blues scholar and collector, has observed that topical-journalistic material stands outside the main blues lyric folksong tradition, and that items similar to those by Trixie Smith and Sonny Scott may have been suggested to race artists by A & R men of the 1920's who had observed the success of hillbilly news-broadside recordings.[13] Hopefully, a student in the 1970's will seek out many industrial blues, however peripheral they seem, and will go beyond my case study's perspective.

Of the coal-mining race records listed in Appendix Eight, I shall identify only a few at this juncture in order to show their distance from "Mining Camp Blues" and "Coal Mountain Blues." Merline Johnson, a Chicago honkytonk singer known as the "Yas Yas Girl," recorded "Got a Man in the 'Bama Mine" during 1937. In a song which boasted of her man's prowess as well as his prosperity, she neatly added to a conventional blues of sexual innuendo an indirect comment on the New Deal climb by Alabama miners to unionization and economic security. That her song achieved some popularity is attested by the fact that it was covered by Addie "Sweet Peas" Spivey and answered by "Jazz" Gillum in a lusty "I'm That Man Down in the Mine."

Far removed from these near-bawdy items were two earlier records which drew on the reservoir of traditional work songs: "Ninety-nine Year Blues" by Julius Daniels and "Rolling Mill Blues" by Peg Leg Howell. Each number contained a brief mention of Joe Brown's mine, but in widely separate contexts. Daniels referred to this Georgia convict-lease mine in a piece related to "The Coon Can Game," a criminal-pattern blues ballad which is the subject of a study by Marina Bokelman. Daniels' blues is close to several hillbilly discs, such as Morgan Dennon's "I've Still Got

Ninety-nine" (Okeh 45105), in which a prisoner is sentenced to a mine rather than a jail. In contrast, Howell's reference to Joe Brown's mine is found in a song which is itself part of the complex commonly titled "In the Pines" or "The Longest Train." Recently, Judith McCulloh traced the history and musical structure of this pines-train lyric folksong.[14] It can be seen from the Merline Johnson disc alone that an apparent industrial title may offer but an oblique view of mining life. Likewise, "Ninety-nine Year Blues" and "Rolling Mill Blues," which on the surface are far removed from coal, actually hold important references to a coal operator in part remembered for exploiting black convict labor.

I have already noted George Korson's attention to Negro miners' folklore. One of the intriguing aspects of his Library of Congress disc, *Songs and Ballads of the Bituminous Miners,* is the fact that it includes six blues — "Mule Skinnin' Blues," "Harlan County Blues," "Coal Diggin' Blues," "Coal Loadin' Blues," "Drill Man Blues," "Hignite Blues" — all recorded by white miners from Kentucky and West Virginia. At first thought, one associates blues not with mountain and hillbilly music but only with Negro life. This linkage has been, and continues to be, made by white reviewers and scholars as well as black performers and nationalists. Two typical formulations, made forty-two years apart, demonstrate the point:

> The blues sprang up, probably within the last quarter-century, among illiterate and more or less despised classes of southern Negroes: barroom pianists, careless nomadic laborers, watchers of incoming trains and steamboats, street corner guitar players, strumpets and outcasts.

> Nobody can sing blues but black people. Nobody can sing a gospel song but black people. Nobody in the whole world.[15]

How did this musical genre, only given its formal published title *the blues* about 1912 and first issued on commercial race records after 1920, penetrate the southern highlands and sink into the consciousness of mountain folk grown up with centuries-old musical patterns of their own? From the beginning of hillbilly recording, some white singers included a few blues in their repertoires. Were these blues carried into the hills by black railroad laborers and riverboat roustabouts and given to mountain singers directly, before blues were published in sheet music or on disc? Or did hillbilly blues blossom largely in the 1920's, when race records disseminated this idiom widely and inexpensively? When and where did black and white folk musicians first begin to play together across the color line in local entertainments, medicine shows, carnivals, rural taverns?

Such interaction must be seen as a phenomenon structured by more than formal entertainment. Persons of both races throughout the South gathered at country stores on Saturday night to rest after toil in the fields or mills. Here they would gossip and observe, as well as absorb the sounds of harmonica and guitar, the poetry of the blues, the story of a ballad. This puzzling and challenging history of the musical borrowing between two sets of singers has yet to be fully documented; a start is made in Tony Russell's *Blacks, Whites and Blues* (1970).

My chapter on "Nine Pound Hammer" indicated that Charles and Elbert Bowman were influenced by Negro song well before they heard blues on records. The discussion of "Roll Down the Line" told something of the life in both Anglo- and Afro-American tradition of a particular convict song. I am aware that I have but hinted at the complexity of this musical amalgamation so important to folk and popular culture. At least two reissued sets, *Mountain Blues* (County 511) and *Mister Charlie's Blues 1926-1936* (Yazoo L 1024), edited by David Freeman and Nick Perls respectively, offer listeners twenty-six early recordings by hillbilly performers drawn to this cross-cultural form.

To my knowledge, the most widely circulated mining blues to be recorded by white artists was "Coal Miner's Blues," first performed on record by the celebrated Carter Family — Alvin Pleasant Delaney Carter, his wife Sara Carter, and his sister-in-law Maybelle Carter. Hence an account of the song's background provides a useful addition to the yet-unwritten story of mountain blues. "Coal Miner's Blues" is on the surface only a cheerful and catchy rhythmic piece, but it is as well an accurate social reminder of primitive bituminous-mining days in the South. The recorded performance itself — a vocal duet with two accompanying guitars (lead voice by Sara and lead guitar by Maybelle) — was made June 8, 1938, in New York and released on a 78 rpm disc, Decca 5596. It was also issued for mail-order sale on Montgomery Ward 8072 and sepa-

CARTER FAMILY HANDBILL, 1929

rately in Canada on Melotone 45280. After World War II, Decca kept the record in print in America as well as in Great Britain; discographical details are found in Checklist Eight.

The song was not covered by others until 1960, when Ed Romaniuk and his sister Elsie Pysar, two Carter Family fans in Canada, recorded it for release on a 45 rpm disc, Acme 104. Actually, Roma-

389

niuk was drawn to the song not only because of his affection for the Carters but also because of his "Coal Branch" childhood in Foothills, Alberta, on the eastern flank of the Canadian Rockies.[16] Ed's immigrant father and four brothers were all miners and his sister Elsie was married to a miner. Following this semi-private "fan" rendition, "Coal Miner's Blues" was also covered by blue-grass groups: Lester Flatt and Earl Scruggs, Harry and Jeanie West, Hazel Dickens and Alice Foster.

In spite of the song's initial popularity and the fact that it was kept on the market by Decca, the Carters never included it in any of their published folios. But in 1956 a gifted young singer and gui-tarist from Maryland, Bill Clifton, published *150 Old Time Folk and Gospel Songs,* based on early songsters and on his own field collection from the singing and playing of rural entertainers.[17] He printed the words to "Coal Miner's Blues" without credit to A. P. Carter, although over the years Clifton has been generous in acknowledgement of debt to the family. The transcribed music for "Coal Miner's Blues" was found not with its words but in connection with a Clifton composition, "Parris Island Blues," a com-mentary on the state of U.S. Marine Corps life in 1951. The words and music of the Carter song transcribed from Decca 5596 follow.

COAL MINER'S BLUES

Some blues are just blues, mine are the miner's blues.
Some blues are just blues, mine are the miner's blues.
My troubles are coming by threes and by twos.

Blues and more blues, it's that coal black blues.
Blues and more blues, it's that coal black blues.
Got coal in my hair, got coal in my shoes.

These blues are so blue, they are the coal black blues.
These blues are so blue, they are the coal black blues.
For my place will cave in, and my life I will lose.

You say they are blues, these old miner's blues.
You say they are blues, these old miner's blues.
Now I must have sharpened these picks that I use.

I'm out with these blues, dirty coal black blues.
I'm out with these blues, dirty coal black blues.
We'll lay off tomorrow with the coal miner's blues.

COAL MINER'S BLUES

This Carter Family blues holds even less narrative content than Trixie Smith's lament over the loss of her man or Sonny Scott's account of his failure to qualify for employment. Although the Carters conveyed but a few fragmentary feelings instead of a story, their song's text did establish a time setting in the premechanized days of pick-and-shovel mining. "Coal Miner's Blues" also hinted at anticipation of layoff and expressed clearly the fear of a cave-in. But mainly, behind these few articulated details there is, in the poetry of the lyrics, a poignant expression that miners' blues are by definition more basic, more severe, than other blues. One singer has projected his personal lament into a generalized song meaningful to all diggers who have toiled underground and to others who share their condition.

Who made up "Coal Miner's Blues?" From whom was it collected by the Carter Family? Bill Clifton, at my suggestion, queried A. P. Carter and reported: "He learned it from several miners in Wise County, Virginia, some years back. Naturally he does not recall the names of the men who taught it to him, but it existed as a true mining song, and I imagine that it served a useful purpose around the local Wise County coal mines."[18]

A. P.'s collecting techniques were quite unscholarly, for he failed to note names, places, or other pertinent data. However, the body of American folksong is richer for his effort; he helped his listeners share some of the experiences of his unnamed miner friends in southwestern Virginia. Their songs mirror their time and place. Can we look into the glass and re-create something of the life of the unknown pick-and-shovel miners who gave their blues to Carter years ago?

We lack a precise clue as to whether the song itself was of black or white origin, although Maybelle Carter recalls that it was obtained from a white man.[19] But we do know that Negro miners came early to this area — the richest coal county in Virginia. Thomas Jefferson wrote about Wise County coal, and coal was mined for local use from Revolutionary through Civil War days. After 1880 it became an imporant center for coke production and attracted European immigrants, some directly from overseas and some from northern coal fields, as well as black workers from southern agriculture. "The population of Wise County in 1920 was 46,500 consisting mainly of whites, but including several settlements of Negroes in the mining districts."[20]

Unlike some of the Carter Family's classic recordings, "Coal Miner's Blues" evidences neither life in oral tradition nor variation. It seems completely local to a corner of Virginia, and the extent of A. P.'s alteration for recording purposes is unknown. By definition it is neither folksong, broadside, nor popular song. It can only be labeled a commercial hillbilly or mountain blues of folk origin. Like many blues, it is much more than a personal document of feeling, for it is a graphic and moving statement of five or six decades of Wise County work lore compressed into a single rhythmic song.

To establish the origin of any Carter Family song is a complicated matter. Because traditional tunes and texts were altered to suit the Family's characteristic style, A. P. would respond to queries on sources that he or they "worked up" the songs. He did not distinguish between direct borrowing, recomposition, and original creation. To collector Ed Kahn he indicated that he worked up "Coal Miner's Blues."[21] Sara recalled in 1958 that they came across it in a "piece of poetry."[22] Maybelle's memory of this song is sharpest, for she remembers a drive in the spring of 1938 from A. P.'s home at Maces Springs through Pennington Gap to nearby St. Charles,

Lee County, Virginia, where A. P. got the words from an old man.[23] Lee County is adjacent to Wise County and lies directly south of the rich coal fields of Harlan County, Kentucky. Before the Decca recording session in New York, Maybelle and Sara set the words of "Coal Miner's Blues" to their own tune, one also used for their "Bear Creek Blues."

The memories of A. P., Sara, and Maybelle, when joined, round out the story of how their blues was collected. A. P. erred in moving the Pennington Gap–St. Charles area a few miles across the line into Wise County. Sara's reference to "poetry" meant that the song was found without music, and that it was either specifically written down for them as a "ballet" or previously printed. Very likely it was handwritten, for there is no clear evidence that it was in print on a slip, in a newspaper, folio, or booklet prior to their Lee County visit.

Up to this point I have discussed the text and locale of "Coal Miner's Blues" without attention to the biographies of Carter Family members. Shortly after A. P. Carter's death on November 7, 1960, in Kingsport, Tennessee, and his burial at Maces Springs, Virginia, I wrote a brief report on his life coupled with a partial description of his mining blues.[24] Subsequently, both Robert Shelton and Bill Malone presented useful accounts of the Carter Family. In 1970 Ed Kahn's thesis, "The Carter Family: A Reflection of Changes in Society," focused on the trio members as symbols of agrarian America's transformation during their lifetimes. My remarks here are intended to bring to the attention of a general audience some key features in the account of a group whose phonograph records have sold, since 1927, in the millions and continue to sell on current reissue LPs. These discs perpetuated a particular Negro-influenced beat in country music, preserved striking instrumental patterns developed to complement sounds of vocal music previously sung unaccompanied, and introduced many American folksongs throughout the world.

The Carter Family, in its recording years, was well known and fully accepted by its folk and folk-derived audience. For example, when MacEdward Leach was song hunting in the Blue Ridge Mountains, he found that the Family's records were artifacts which helped direct traditional music into new channels.[25] For many

393

MAYBELLE CARTER AND FRIENDS

enthusiasts over a four-decade span, the Family epitomized excellence in mountain and rural music.[26] Although known to the academic community prior to A. P.'s death, there is still to be assayed the Carters' performing style, their role as folksong collectors and transmitters, their influence on the development of bluegrass as well as on commercial country-western music, and their part in the mid-century urban "folksong revival."

A. P. Carter was born December 15, 1891, close to Maces Springs, Scott County, Virginia, in an area where his family name seemed as old as the land itself. In 1784 his pioneer ancestors had built Carter's Fort, a station on the Wilderness Road from North Carolina to Kentucky, near present-day Rye Cove. A. P.'s life-long affection for his early community was ingrained; as a child he lived in Poor Valley between Pine Ridge and Clinch Mountain, and he could follow the clear water of Blue Springs Branch down to the North Fork of the Holston River. It was here, in a mountain farming pocket, that young Carter absorbed the familiar songs and ballads rooted in his culture.

While visiting relatives on Copper Creek in Scott County, A. P.

met an accomplished young singer and instrumentalist, Sara Dougherty. She was born July 21, 1898, at Flat Woods, near Coeburn, Wise County, where her father worked in a forest sawmill. Upon her mother's death, little Sara went to live with relatives, Aunt Melinda and Uncle Milburn Nickles, on Copper Creek. There she took up the banjo, autoharp, and guitar, and began singing with Uncle Milburn, a fiddler, and her cousins Madge and Maybelle Addington. Family tradition has it that when A. P. met Sara she was singing the railroad-disaster ballad, "Engine One-Forty-Three" ("Wreck on the C & O"). They were married on June 18, 1915, and settled at A. P.'s home.

A decade later the group that emerged as the Carter Family was formed, when Sara's cousin Maybelle Addington married A. P.'s brother, Ezra J. Carter, on March 13, 1926, and came to live in Poor Valley. Maybelle, the trio's youngest, was born May 10, 1909, on Copper Creek at Nickelsville. While still a child, she had begun to play and sing with the many talented family performers in the close-knit community. Upon her marriage, she brought her own instruments — guitar, banjo, autoharp — to Maces Springs, and in a short time the new trio of A. P., Sara, and Maybelle was pleasing friends at church socials and neighborhood entertainments with spirited singing and playing. Three children — Gladys, Janette, Joe — were born to A. P. and Sara, and three — Helen, June, Anita — to E. J. and Maybelle. In time the children were to join their parents as performers.

Late in July, 1927, A. P., Sara, and Maybelle journeyed to Bristol, on the Tennessee-Virginia line, where Ralph Peer, Victor's country-music scout, had set up portable recording equipment in an improvised office-building studio to audition local singers. By one of the fascinating coincidences in recording history, Peer discovered Jimmie Rodgers and the Carters in Bristol on the same midsummer expedition. Much has been written about the Carters' first recording session on Monday, August 1, 1927. Here are Sara's words: "So there was an ad come out in the Bristol, Va.-Tenn., paper for all talent to come to Bristol to try out on records. So we three decided to go. We made three records. 'Single Girl, Married Girl' tipped it off. The Carter Family and Jimmie Rodgers made a hit out of the talent that went."[27]

Like other successful performers, the Carters followed their records out of the hills and into the world — southern radio stations, northern recording studios, rural entertainments in between. Perhaps their most influential broadcasting began in 1938 when the Carters relocated, temporarily, at Del Rio, Texas, for a stint on XERA, the powerful Mexican border station.[28] At that time the radio station belonged to millionaire John R. Brinkley, the "goat-gland doctor." During the Depression Brinkley had perfected a lurid advertising formula that wedded Carter Family and other hillbilly music to radio evangelism as well as to the sale of patent medicine, junk jewelry, and inexpensive Bibles.

Late in 1932 A. P. Carter and Sara had drifted apart and some years later they were divorced, but they continued to work together with Maybelle, partly guided by their mentor Ralph Peer. Sara married Coy Bayes on February 20, 1939, in Brackettsville, Texas, and shortly thereafter moved to his California home in the Sierra Nevada Mountains. However, she returned for recording sessions and radio work until 1943, when the trio disbanded while at station WBT in Charlotte, North Carolina. Without formal work as an entertainer, A. P. retired to his old home at Maces Springs and Sara remained in California. Meanwhile, Maybelle moved to Richmond, Virginia, where she formed a new unit with her three daughters. On station WRVA's Old Dominion Barn Dance, Mother Maybelle and the Carter Sisters achieved considerable popularity. In 1948 they moved on to radio work at Knoxville, Tennessee, and Springfield, Missouri. Finally they reached the Grand Ole Opry, entertaining in the new idiom of country-western and rockabilly music. The first released record to feature Helen, June, Anita, and their mother, "Kneeling Drunkard's Plea" / "My Darling's Home at Last" (Victor 21-0029), was recorded February 2, 1949, in Atlanta.

During 1952 and 1956 Sara joined A. P. for a series of "come back" recordings on the small Acme label. For these sessions Joe and Janette joined their parents to form a quartet, issuing material made popular by the early trio. Since A. P.'s death, many original Carter Family discs have been reissued in the United States, Japan, and elsewhere. In 1963 Maybelle recorded an excellent LP with bluegrass artists Lester Flatt and Earl Scruggs, and in 1967 she and

Sara recorded a memorable reunion disc for Columbia. Throughout the 1960's Maybelle presented the best of the Carter Family tradition to "revival" audiences as far apart as the University of California's student body and the Smithsonian Institution's Festival of American Folklife. At the decade's end she and her daughters reached a huge new audience via the dramatic Johnny Cash television hour, a production geared in part to the rural nostalgia evoked by the original Carter Family.

Before the era of records and radio, what types of songs had the Carters learned from their neighbors in that cluster of the Appalachians where five states —Virginia, North Carolina, Tennessee, Kentucky, West Virginia — converge in a complex of mountain ridges and twisting valleys? Maces Springs, Virginia, is less than sixty miles from the four bordering states. The terrain limited communication, but songs moved about as to defy geography.

When the Carters began to record, they sang old hymns, new gospel songs, timeless secular ballads, sagas of bad men, current journalistic pieces, stories of unrequited love, recomposed sentimentalities of the popular stage, and occupational songs of cowboys, railroaders, and hoboes. The initial numbers obtained from the Family's treasury were popular among local mountain entertainers and audiences. The Carters' first disc was "Wandering Boy" / "Poor Orphan Child" (Victor 20877). For Victor between 1927 and 1934 they recorded "East Virginia Blues," "Engine One-Forty-Three," "John Hardy Was a Desperate Little Man," "Little Moses," "Wabash Cannon Ball," "Wildwood Flower," and other widely known folksongs. Victor material was also released and reissued on Bluebird, Montgomery Ward, and a few minor labels. From 1935 to 1940 they recorded for various firms songs that were put out on a kaleidoscope of labels: Banner, Columbia, Conqueror, Coral, Decca, Melotone, Okeh, Oriole, Perfect, Romeo, Vocalion. In those years their repertoire on discs was extended to include a considerable number of new songs, as well as variants of the British traditional ballads "Black Jack David" and "Sinking in the Lonesome Sea." Before the start of World War II they returned to Victor, and on October 14, 1941, the final Carter Family songs, "Rambling Boy" / "Waves on the Sea" (Bluebird 33-0512), were recorded in New York City.

CARTER FAMILY FIRST FOLIO

Beginning in 1929, many of the Carter Family's pieces were published in song folios and copyrighted by A. P. Carter, usually under the watchful eye of Ralph Peer. Copyright laws often mask the normal process of growth and change in folk music by making that which is inherently fluid seem static. In a sense, every time A. P. Carter recorded a song or published it in folio, he "collected" a variant, as does any folklorist in the field with his notebook, acetate disc, or tape machine. Carter, of course, made no pretense to scholarship and hence claimed most songs as his own. The "Coal Miner's Blues," obtained from an old man not far from home, was registered in A. P.'s name by the United Publishing Company of New York on October 26, 1938 (E 179384). This previously unreported blues was assimilated by Carter and copyrighted just as he had claimed as his own compositions "Sinking in the Lonesome Sea" and other venerable ballads.

In remarks on "Mining Camp Blues" and "Coal Mountain Blues" I have indicated that I do not know whether these numbers were composed by Trixie Smith and Sonny Scott or, possibly, came to them from other persons. Regardless of the facts of composition, all three blues considered in this chapter are personal laments by commercial recording artists reaching to paying audiences. Additionally, each song is a general statement on the nature of bituminous miners' expectations.

The literature of coal mining is rich in prose portraits of poverty and danger. Throughout these chapters I have refrained from extensive quotations drawn directly from miners' writings in favor of secondary sketches in song texts. However, there is at hand a graphic eyewitness account from Wise County which not only provides the specific background out of which "Coal Miner's Blues" was shaped, but also serves indirectly to substantiate my evaluation of "Mining Camp Blues" and "Coal Mountain Blues."

James Taylor Adams (1892-1954), a miner-printer-writer from Big Laurel, Virginia, worked in Wise County from 1905 to 1930, when he left the mines to collect sketches, short stories, poems, and songs descriptive of the southern highlands.[29] He edited his own quarterly magazine, *The Cumberland Empire,* to perpetuate this lore. In 1941 he published a little book, *Death in the Dark: A Collection of Factual Ballads of American Mine Disasters with Historical Notes.* In addition to printing songs collected from his fellow miners, he poured something of the meaning of his life's work into the book's introduction. His stark, honest story was intimately known to and felt by all his companions. Coal miners, no less than other workers, were given to petty complaint, but work conditions beyond endurance and beyond dignity generated emotions which in turn were expressed in oratory and organization, poetry and song. Adams wrote:

> I was born in Letcher County, Kentucky, when the first entries were being driven into the coal seams here in Wise County, Virginia just twenty-five miles to the south. When I was thirteen I crossed Pine Mountain, with my fifteen year old cousin, John Sherman Adams, to find a job. . . . We joined the industry as coke loaders for the Stonegap Colliery Company at Glamorgan. This was in the fall of 1905. . . .
>
> In those days conditions in the Virginia coal fields were awful.

399

Cooperation among the mine owners had never been thought of. A miner's union was something beyond heaven. It was not even hoped for. Coal was gotten from under the sagging mountains by haphazard methods, at mighty risk to life and limb, crushed into dust by makeshift machinery, and dumped into ovens from which it emerged forty-eight hours later as coke. There was but a limited demand for this product and the result was that the producers resorted to cheap methods to find a market. Prices were cut to such a level that either the corporations must go broke or the workers must go hungry. The workers went hungry.

There was no attempt at standardization. Wages were, apparently, whatever the companies wanted to pay. Coal loaders made about two dollars a day. . . . There was a sort of loose understanding for a ten hour shift, but it was so loose that men sometimes worked thirty-six hours without a stop save for food. I have worked twenty-four hours without stopping, and on one occasion I did not have my shoes off my feet from Monday morning till Saturday night. . . .

"Get the coal!" was the cry from the man with the big cigar in the head office right down to the man with the pick and shovel at the face of the coal. "Get the coal!" the manager told the superintendent; "get the coal!" the "super" told the mine foreman; and "get the coal!" the foreman told the coal loader, "or get the hell out of here!" And this order was carried out regardless of the cost in toil, danger and death.

Foremen were hardboiled. They did not necessarily have to know much about coal mining, but they had to know how to handle men. And when I say "handle men" I mean just that. They were men with an iron nerve, capable of instilling fear into "white folks," "hunks" or "niggers" with a look or a pick handle. In 1924, I heard an old mine superintendent boasting of how he used to knock a pick off the handle and beat his men over the head with it. . . .

If there was any system at all in the coal industry it was the efforts of the men in charge to work up hard feelings between the Negroes, foreigners and native white Americans. Particularly did they play upon the feelings of the mountaineer who had sold his land with half a million dollars worth of coal under it for seventy-five or a hundred dollars, and then, when the money was spent, was forced to go to work in the mines digging the coal he once owned, to keep himself and family from starving.[30]

Did a mountaineer who sold his land before becoming a coal

digger compose "Coal Miner's Blues" out of the fullness of his heart? Or did a black miner beaten with a pick handle first put these troubled lines together? Who taught it to whom? When? Where? How many miners knew it in memory and found solace in the song? My questions are framed in regard to a specific Carter Family blues. It has been more than three decades since "Coal Miner's Blues" was originally recorded, and the present chance to learn more about it than has been stated in this case study is remote. Likewise, I am not sanguine about unearthing significant additional data on "Mining Camp Blues" or "Coal Mountain Blues" (although surely we should obtain some biographical facts about their performers). Why are rhetorical queries posed in case studies? I feel that those raised here are the kinds that we must continue to ask about other blues — past and present — where there is still hope of obtaining answers.

Black and white miners, like fellow Americans, have shared the blues throughout this century. Names of artists and their modes of presenting songs change rapidly in our urban, technological society. Yet, as I complete this book's final case study late in 1970, I cannot dim out the sound of Trixie Smith and Sonny Scott when I listen to memorial broadcasts for Janis Joplin and Jimi Hendrix. Queries which extend or deepen understanding about given blues or blues performers — whether from the 1920's or 1970's — are worth posing in themselves; answers which bring singers and listeners together across culture lines hold intrinsic value.

1. Liner notes for *Really the Country Blues* (Origin Jazz Library OJL 2).
2. Newman Ivey White, *American Negro Folk-Songs* (Cambridge, Mass., 1928), 258.
3. For an introduction to these artists see Derrick Stewart-Baxter, *Ma Rainey and the Classic Blues Singers* (London, 1970).
4. Lucien H. White, "Fifteenth Infantry's First Band Concert and Dance," *New York Age* (Jan. 28, 1922), 1. See also Samuel Charters and Leonard Kunstadt, *Jazz: A History of the New York Scene* (Garden City, N.Y., 1962), 98.
5. In Albert McCarthy and others, *Jazz on Record* (London, 1968), 269. Paul Oliver notes Miss Smith's dates (ca. 1900-1943) without identifying her early home.

6. For Alabama events see George Korson, *Coal Dust on the Fiddle,* 2nd printing (Hatboro, Pa., 1965), 164.

7. Porter Grainger and Bob Ricketts, *How to Play and Sing the Blues Like the Phonograph and Stage Artists* (New York, 1926). See also Victoria Spivey, "My Porter Grainger," *Record Research,* no. 79 (Oct., 1966), 8.

8. Ben A. Franklin, "The Scandal of Death and Injury in the Mines," *New York Times Magazine* (Mar. 30, 1969), 25. See also H. B. Humphrey, *Historical Summary of Coal-Mine Explosions in the United States, 1810-1958* (Washington, 1960), 7.

9. Ronald C. Foreman, Jr., "Jazz and Race Records, 1920-32" (thesis, University of Illinois, Urbana, 1968), 250.

10. Robert G. Sherrill, "West Virginia Miracle: The Black Lung Rebellion," *Nation,* CCVIII (Apr. 28, 1969), 531.

11. Interview, Mar. 23, 1962. I am indebted to Goddard Graves and Jeff Titon for attempts to trace Sonny Scott.

12. Russell Ames, "Implications of Negro Folk Song," *Science and Society,* XV (1951), 171.

13. Pete Welding, "Mail," *Living Blues,* I (Autumn, 1970), 38, and letter to me, Jan. 29, 1971.

14. Judith McCulloh, " 'In the Pines': The Melodic Textual Identity of an American Lyric Folksong Cluster" (thesis, Indiana University, Bloomington, 1970).

15. Abbe Niles, Introduction, in *Blues: An Anthology,* ed. William C. Handy (New York, 1926), 9. "Nobody" statement made by a vocalist at a Southern Christian Leadership Conference meeting in Atlanta, 1967, and reported in Dan Wakefield, *Supernation at Peace and War* (Boston, 1968), 98.

16. Letter to me, May 11, 1961.

17. Bill Clifton, *150 Old Time Folk and Gospel Songs* (North Wilkesboro, N.C., 1956). For a series of recent interviews between Clifton and Richard Spottswood see *Bluegrass Unlimited,* II (Mar.-May, 1968).

18. Letter to me, Apr. 24, 1957.

19. A forthcoming LP of Lesley Riddle edited by Mike Seeger will document some of the Negro influence on the Carters. My first direct evidence of such borrowing came from Brownie McGhee, who described A. P. Carter's visits to him at Kingsport, Tenn., between 1932 and 1939 in search of songs. Interview, Apr. 26, 1961.

20. James Brian Eby, *The Geology and Coal Resources of the Coal-Bearing Portions of Wise and Scott Counties, Virginia* (Baltimore, 1922), 3.

21. Kahn letter to me, Feb. 27, 1961.

22. Griffith Borgeson tape interview with Sara Carter Bayes at Angels Camp, Calif., Apr. 1, 1958.

23. Mrs. Louise Scruggs queried Maybelle Carter and reported her recollection in a letter to me, May 17, 1961. Subsequently I interviewed Mrs. Carter, Aug. 31, 1961, and Sept. 9, 1962.

24. Archie Green, "The Carter Family's 'Coal Miner's Blues,'" *Southern Folk-lore Quarterly,* XXV (1961), 226. See also my "A Carter Family Bibliography," *Sunny Side Sentinel,* no. 2 (Jan., 1963), a mimeographed "fanzine" edited by Freeman Kitchens at Drake, Ky.

25. MacEdward Leach and Horace Beck, "Songs from Rappahannock County, Virginia," *Journal of American Folklore,* LXIII (1950), 258.

26. Three persons who shared with me, via correspondence and interviews, their impressions of the Carters were Harvey Fink of Watertown, Wis., Luis Kemnitzer of El Sobrante, Calif., and Freeman Kitchens of Drake, Ky. Also helpful was my interview with Janette Carter Jett, Aug. 25, 1961.

27. Letter to John Edwards, Dec. 27, 1955.

28. For the role of Mexican border stations see Ed Kahn, "The Carter Family: A Reflection of Changes in Society" (thesis, University of California, Los Angeles, 1970), 120-173.

29. I am indebted to Luther F. Addington, principal of Kelly High School, Wise, Va., and Mrs. Naomi Mullins, Adams' daughter, for data on Adams. Interviews, Aug. 26, 1961. See also Frederick D. Vanover, *James Taylor Adams* (Louisville, Ky., 1937).

30. James Taylor Adams, *Death in the Dark* (Big Laurel, Va., 1941), 4.

CHECKLIST EIGHT

"The Coal Miner's Blues." Carter Family, Decca 5596 (64104). June 8, 1938, New York. Parallel issues: Montgomery Ward 8072; Melotone 54280 (Canada).

Reissued: Decca 46086; released 1946 (78 rpm).

        Brunswick OE 9168; 1956 (England, 45 rpm).

        A Collection of Favorites by the Carter Family, Decca DL 4404; released June, 1963.

Transcribed: Green, *S F Q,* XXV (1961), 226.

————. A. P. Carter, United Publishing Company, New York (Oct. 26, 1938), E 179384. Copyright renewed: Peer International Corporation, New York (Nov. 8, 1965), R 372805.

————. *150 Old Time Folk and Gospel Songs,* Bill Clifton, Adams Printing Company, North Wilkesboro, N.C. (1956), 34, m on 59.

————. Ed Romaniuk and Elsie Pysar, Acme 104. Taped in Canada in 1960 and released on a Greenville, Tenn., 45 rpm.

————. Lester Flatt, Earl Scruggs, and the Foggy Mountain Boys, *Hard Travelin',* Columbia CL 1951. 1963, Nashville.

————. Harry and Jeanie West, *Songs of the Southland,* Folkways FA 2352. 1963, New York. Brochure includes text and headnote.

————. Hazel Dickens and Alice Foster, *Who's That Knocking?* Verve-Folkways FV 9005. 1965, New York.

APPENDIX EIGHT

COAL-MINING SONGS ISSUED ON RACE RECORDS

1. "Mining Camp Blues," Trixie Smith, Feb., 1925, New York. Paramount 12256 (2016-1-2). Smith vocal acc. by Down Home Syncopators: Louis Armstrong, trumpet; Charlie Green, trombone; Buster Bailey, clarinet; Fletcher Henderson, piano; Charlie Dixon, banjo.
   Reissued: *Louis Armstrong in New York 1924-1925* (Riverside RM 8811).
   Louis Armstrong, an Early Portrait (Milestone MLP 2010).

2. "Ninety-nine Year Blues," Julius Daniels, Feb. 19, 1927, Atlanta. Victor 20658 (37932-2). Daniels vocal self-acc. on guitar.
   Reissued: *American Folk Music* (Folkways FA 2953 C).

3. "Rolling Mill Blues," Peg Leg Howell, Apr. 10, 1929, Atlanta. Columbia 14438 (148237-1). Howell vocal self-acc. on guitar; unknown violin.
   Reissued: *The Georgia Blues: 1927-1933* (Yazoo L 1012).

4. "Cave Man Blues," Memphis Jug Band, May 21, 1930, Memphis. Victor 38605 (59962). Charlie Nickerson vocal acc. by Will Shade, guitar; Milton Robie, violin; Charlie Burse, guitar.
   Reissued: *The Party Blues* (Melodeon MLP 7324).

5. "Coal Camp Blues," Taylor's Weatherbirds, June 11, 1931, Louisville. Victor 23309 (69425-1). Walter Taylor vocal and guitar; banjo and mandolin acc. unknown.

6. "Coal Mountain Blues," Sonny Scott, July 18, 1933, New York. Vocalion 25012 (13555-1). Scott vocal self-acc. on guitar.

7. "Poor Coal Loader," Springback James, July 15, 1935, Chicago. Champion 50076 (90153-A). James vocal self-acc. on piano; guitarist unknown.

8. "Poor Coal Passer," Springback James, Dec. 21, 1936, Chicago. Bluebird 7116 (01893-1). James vocal self-acc. on piano; Willie Bee (James) on guitar.
   Reissued: *Favorite Country Blues, Piano-Guitar Duets* (Yazoo L 1015).

9. "Got a Man in the 'Bama Mine," Merline Johnson, July 30, 1937, Chicago. Conqueror 8924; Vocalion 03722 (C 1976). Johnson vocal acc. by Horace Malcolm, piano; Big Bill Broonzy, guitar; Fred Williams, drums.

10. "I Got a Man in the 'Bama Mines," Sweet Peas (Addie Spivey), Oct. 11, 1937, Aurora, Ill. Bluebird 7224 (014348-1). Spivey vocal; piano and drum acc. unknown.
    Reissued: *Women of the Blues* (Victor LPV 534).

11. "I'm That Man Down in the Mine," Bill "Jazz" Gillum and His Jazz Boys, June 16, 1938, Aurora, Ill. Bluebird 7718 (020819). Gillum vocal and harmonica; Big Bill Broonzy, guitar; string bass unknown; probably Washboard Sam, washboard.

TODAY'S MINER

Singles, LPs, and the "Revival" *11*

THERE ARE FEW precedents in the United States for academic book-length investigations based exclusively on sound recordings. Sound frozen into artifact — cylinder, disc, perforated roll, wire or plastic tape, film track, cartridge, cassette — is a very recent phenomenon, a second in time when compared to the age of the cave drawings at Lascaux. Because sound technology was perfected well after folklore became an established discipline in Europe, the notion that a recording might be a useful tool was slow in reaching folklorists.

While it is true that some collectors such as Bela Bartok, Frances Densmore, J. Walter Fewkes, Percy Grainger, and E. M. von Hornbostel embraced the new technique and were early in the field with primitive accoustical equipment, and while it is true that the *Journal of American Folklore* has carried record reviews since 1948, it is a lamentable fact that a folkloric literature based primarily on recordings is just emerging as we move toward the twenty-first century. The appearance of scholarly works in language and literature studies, anthropology, and other social sciences using recordings to reveal text, tune, style, and linguistic pattern as well as life history, symbolism, and commentary on culture is an exciting prospect for the decades ahead. In narrow terms of the sound recording merely as a physical object, my book has focused chiefly on ten-inch discs recorded at 78 rpm speed. This chapter deals with smaller and larger parallel forms: the seven-inch 45 rpm disc and the twelve-inch 33 rpm disc in the context of the "folksong revival" of recent decades.

To many folklorists the most fascinating problem in dealing with sound recordings is their role as objects suspended between the separate traditions of print and verbal art. In the centuries from Gutenberg and Caxton to the present day, it has been possible to note that songs on broadsides entered tradition and to contrast broadside style with its "pure" predecessor forms. At one level a phonograph record is a direct extension of the printer's slip or sheet — in short, the plastic disc itself is the broadside. At another level the disc is an aural experience more vivid and lifelike than print. Hence, when a scholar extends the term *broadside* to a product of the recording industry, he refers either to the disc's physical grooves, which hold a text, or to the total process whereby a song is taped, pressed, and distributed inexpensively and quickly.

Leslie Shepard's *The Broadside Ballad* is an excellent background primer for persons concerned with post-Edison broadsides in wax and vinyl. Shepard's illustrations of items from his personal collection give the novice a quick view of the printed broadside in its multiple shapes and sizes. We know that the slips which poured from the presses of "Jemmy" Catnach and his fellows in London's Seven Dials district during the nineteenth century were so cheap as to be tagged *catchpennies*. Apparently this name was given to a Catnach broadside by irate buyers who had been tricked into believing that a murderer, Weare, was alive when the printer issued a song on the crime with the title in bold type, "WE ARE ALIVE AGAIN," conveniently eliminating the space between the words *we* and *are*. It is said that Catnach's fortune, based on selling tens of millions of broadsides, was accumulated in coppers and conveyed from his shop in huge bags via hackney coach to the Bank of England.[1] Of course not all issues sold in the millions or made their merchants wealthy. Many ephemeral slips came from tiny one-man shops in small runs meant only for distribution in the close vicinity of the printery.

Most of the songs included in this book were initially released on 78 rpm discs intended for wide regional or national sale, although

AIR–SHAFT FIRE

some were subsequently reissued on 33 rpm LPs. A few songs were first gathered on archival field recordings, which in turn were commercially released or served as sources for fresh LPs. None of my case studies was based on 45 rpm discs of the 1950's and 1960's, the form most comparable to the locally printed, limited-circulation broadside. Such 45s, generally named *singles,* can be rushed to radio stations or tavern jukeboxes within weeks of song composition and initial recording on a "demo" (demonstration tape). A consideration of the technology and marketing of 45s can be found elsewhere. Here I shall cite a few coal-song singles only to note the continuity in the music industry's use of mining events and themes.

A few months after the March, 1960, mine holocaust in Logan County, West Virginia, two disaster songs were taped, pressed, and offered for sale: "Island Creek Mine Fire" by the Wright Brothers (Golden Leaf 106), and "Holden 22 Mine" by Benny Reed (Cool 155). The former text was traditional enough in style to have perhaps been accepted by George Korson or James Taylor Adams as a ballad indigenous to Logan County had it been penned three decades previously. To my knowledge, however, these two songs were only "printed" in the plastic compounds of their respective discs. One substantial difference between most local broadsides and these records was that the records were apparently not sold in Logan County itself.[2]

Lenny Wright, the composer of "Island Creek Mine Fire," was a bluegrass musician from the Grandfather Mountain area in North Carolina (Avery County). While working as a country-music performer and disc jockey in Ohio, he learned via Akron radio and television newscasts of the dramatic rescue of some of the entombed Island Creek miners. He composed his song in thirty minutes and set it to a mournful tune "which just came to him."[3] The Golden Leaf Record Company, a small Cleveland firm, pressed enough copies of Wright's disc for radio-station distribution, and the song received some word-of-mouth publicity from bluegrass enthusiasts. Essentially, most singles are not geared for initial over-the-counter sales but are fed into radio channels in the hope that they will emerge as hits. "Island Creek Mine Fire" did not so emerge.

"Holden 22 Mine," after its release on the Cool label, was copyrighted on July 7, 1960 (EU 631144) by the Queen Music Company of Harrison, New Jersey. Its rock-and-roll tempo seemed to direct it to urban teenagers rather than West Virginia miners and raised the question, in my mind, of the intent of the song's composer. Curiously, this offering was complemented by five other pieces all copyrighted during 1960: "Holden 22," "Holden W. Va. Mine," "Holden Mine Disaster," "Holden Twenty-two," "The Holden Mine Disaster." I have no evidence that these five items were recorded, printed, or disseminated in any manner beyond the submission of their musical lead sheets to the Library of Congress. It is possible that these compositions stemmed from a song-writing contest in a periodical advertisement which furnished the facts of the disaster. Such contests, generally announced in pulp magazines and promoted by "song sharks" and "fast-buck operators," have functioned for nearly a century without close examination by folklorists. Should the circumstance of inspiration for the various Holden songs come to hand, we might be rewarded by a fascinating glimpse at a topical or broadside expression completely divorced from locality and group association.

Joseph C. Hickerson of the Library of Congress Archive of Folk Song has called to my attention an important song complex,

"The Titanic," whose origin seemingly parallels that of the Holden numbers:

> The sinking of the Titanic on April 14, 1912, a tragedy of immense and universally publicized proportions, produced a host of songs, 106 of which I have thus far discovered through the files of the Copyright Office for the years 1912-1915. Of the 106, 44 were published by H. Kirkus Dugdale Co., Inc., 14th and U Streets, Washington, D.C. Of these 44, the music for 22 was composed by M. C. Hanford, and the music for 9 was composed by Charles J. W. Jerreld. The Dugdale Co. apparently had a particularly active and effective method for soliciting songs, usually lyrics only, through some such "come-on" as "Have your song published" or "Earn thousands," perhaps with a contest for the best Titanic song. Of course, the author of the song had to submit a "fee" which "covered" (actually exceeded) the cost of copyright registration (always in the author's name) and a minimal printing. A summary description of the well-known Titanic event need not have accompanied Dugdale's solicitations, although it does seem surprising that the reported facts through a multiplicity of sources should have given rise to the universal use of "Nearer My God to Thee" in all of the 106 Titanic pieces which contain words.[4]

To summarize, neither the bluegrass "Island Creek Mine Fire" nor the rock-and-roll "Holden 22 Mine" was composed, produced, or distributed by coal miners in or near Logan County. Yet each disc had broadside attributes. A contrasting single, "The Mine Explosion" by the Baker Brothers (Ark 284), did come from a coal miner's experience and was distributed to some extent in mining territory, but it was not based on an actual accident. Bob (Robert L.) and Jesse L. Baker grew up near Mount Vernon, Rockcastle County, Kentucky, their present home.[5] To collector Neil Rosenberg the Bakers reported that they, their brothers, and father were all coal miners, and, like many youngsters, Bob and Jesse saw country music as one way out of the mines. The brothers worked on the Renfro Valley Barn Dance after their overseas service in World War II. Bob composed "The Mine Explosion" about 1962 from experience of "bad air" in his early work underground. At year's end, 1964, the Bakers broke into records with a single of "The Mine Explosion" backed with the traditional "Make Me a Pallet on the Floor." The disc was pressed by a Cincinnati

PRICE $1.00   ARK No. 284

The Baker Brothers

Side No. 1: MAKE ME PALLET ON THE FLOOR
Side No. 2: THE MINE EXPLOSION

45 RPM SLEEVE

firm, but the Bakers purchased enough copies to sell at various live appearances at Kentucky country-music parks and similar local entertainments. In correspondence with me concerning his knowledge of other mining songs, Bob Baker identified "Sixteen Tons" recorded by Tennessee Ernie Ford as "a good one." This suggested that in the 1960's American musicians who might still be labeled *folk* were highly dependent for referential ideas and values on the mass media.

A full study of current locally composed and distributed 45s, particularly those continuing the race and hillbilly subjects and styles first waxed in the 1920's, would be of great value in throwing light on the contemporary interaction of folk and popular-culture processes. "Island Creek Mine Fire" sounds like a folksong not because composer Wright was a miner, but because his childhood in a North Carolina mountain community gave him an opportunity to absorb a specific folksong tradition. That his song reached a few bluegrass fans rather than any Logan County families is a function of the present structure of the entertainment industry. Benny Reed's "Holden 22 Mine" was textually related to the long narrative tradition of mine balladry; nevertheless, his melody did not sound like West Virginia folk music, probably because Reed was unfamiliar with or rejected hillbilly style.

Although Bob Baker's "The Mine Explosion" was distributed in some Kentucky mining counties, it apparently never caught on with either miners or country-music fans. It is much more difficult to hazard a guess about a song's failure to enter tradition than to reconstruct the path of its entrance. I believe that "The Mine Explosion" represents the same imaginative projection in composition as that employed by Andrew Jenkins in "The Dream of the Miner's Child." Also, the pieces are similar in rhetoric. Quite apart from the matter of the almost hand-to-hand distribution of Baker's record, it is possible that "The Mine Explosion" was stylistically and musically too frozen into a Dalhart ambience to catch on in the 1960's as did the comparable heart songs of the 1920's.

My commentary upon the relationship of 45 rpm records to printed broadsides is limited to the three examples above. However, I do not wish to imply that the production of coal-mining broadsides ended in 1964 with "The Mine Explosion." On the contrary, the process continues, and such recent titles as "Little Mining Town in Walker County" (Zone 1091), "The Coal Mines of West Virginia" (Music Town 023), "Black Lung Blues" (Rem 449), "Black Lung Cadillac" (Big Whiz 25721), "Hyden Miners' Tragedy" (Sunrise 109), and "A Coal Miner's Life" (Silver Star 1042) attest to its vitality. Only one current 45 need be selected to conclude my report on the production and distribution of these "new" broadsides.

During 1969 Howard Bramlett composed, copyrighted, and recorded "Harlan County," a nostalgic piece in which he expressed the desire of many displaced miners to return home to their native mountains for final rest. The song, recorded at Red Bank, Hamilton County, Tennessee, was custom pressed in Nashville, and released at Old Fort, Polk County, Tennessee, on Rymer 90003. Had "Harlan

413

County" been printed as a poem in a Harlan job shop it would have had some resemblance to a nineteenth-century broadside and it could have been hawked personally to persons within the county either by its composer or printer. Because it was issued on a 45 rpm disc, its initial taping was in a sound studio near Chattanooga and its physical manufacture was in Nashville. Hence it can be seen that even "home-made" discs are dependent on a technological system more complex than that of a neighborhood print shop. Interestingly, in correspondence with Bramlett I learned that at the time of distribution of "Harlan County" he was working far from home.[6] Bramlett and a number of his friends performed regularly in the "Cherokee Folk Gatherin' " — a mountain-music, gospel, square-dance, Saturday happening — sponsored by the Polk County 4H Clubs at their Camp McCroy in the Cherokee National Forest.

Unlike many single discs which are offered for sale in a plain sleeve or one decorated only with the name of the issuing label, "Harlan County" came in a printed paper jacket showing two photographs: Howard's childhood mountain-cabin home in Harlan County, and Howard's brother Elmer in front of a tipple, with the explanation that he had "dug the black gold for thirty-five years." This song, dedicated to Elmer Bramlett's memory and to "former miners everywhere," was perceived as a folksong by its producer/publicist, who used the jacket to express "hope that [listeners] will enjoy these down-to-earth simple folk songs." Just as most printed broadsides neither entered tradition nor remained in this state of movement and change long enough to become folksongs, I do not believe that "Harlan County" will move beyond the grooves of its limited pressings. Yet unless a collector in the 1970's retraces Korson's path into Appalachian mine homes to ask, firsthand, for new and old coal songs, it is likely that Howard Bramlett's Rymer single — and others on the commercial market like it — will have to represent current modes in mining-song lore.

In viewing this selection of a few 45 rpm discs as sample broadsides springing from activities in or reflecting the values of folk society, it must be understood that the overwhelming number of single pressings in the 1950's and 1960's was strictly "pops." Because American folksong is still separated from popular music (despite denominative difficulties), most folksong enthusiasts, inside and outside the academy, have depended on the 33 rpm long-playing disc rather than the 45 single. To the extent that we perceive a 45 as a printed broadside, we also can accept an LP as a literary anthology or published folksong collection. Folksong LPs, either by traditional singers or by interpreters who cleave to folk style, are directed alike by the large music industry and by small specialist producers mainly to urbanites who treasure folk music. In short, consumers of "folk" LPs — whether by mail from specialty distributors or by normal commercial channels — also purchase books by Child, Lomax, Sandburg, Bronson, or Fife.

These generalizations about print and sound recordings can be qualified by noting that the use of relatively inexpensive tape recorders and access to cash-and-carry pressing services have enabled some singers in folk society to produce fully "authentic" LPs for friends and neighbors. Also, contemporary technology has permitted dedicated amateurs at times to produce limited-edition LPs superior to the efforts of the music industry as well as to those of scholarly archives. Hence, the range of folksong material available to purchasers is found on discs issued under at least four sets of labels: major companies, country firms, folk "revivalists," and archival institutions. Consequently, one unexplored area concerning the shape and direction of American society is the present-day mix of its folksong "family" — producer, seller, buyer — across a complex network of affiliation.

In turning to a discussion of more than a dozen LPs holding coal songs — the kind offered to an audience ranging from working miners to young folksong enthusiasts — I must restate that preceding chapters focused on songs issued on individual discs, some of which were incidentally reissued on LP. When readers of these case studies wish to hear a particular ballad or blues they will very likely turn not to the rare-record market for old 78s, but rather to present-day record stores and mail-order services which specialize in folk, blues, or country LPs.

Without question, the two best recorded coal-song documents in the United States are George Korson's Library of Congress LPs: *Songs and Ballads of the Anthracite Miners* (L 16) and *Songs and Ballads of the Bituminous Miners* (L 60). I have already mentioned them in my introductory chapter; here I shall elaborate on their

415

OLD MINER

background, content, and style. Korson and Melvin LeMon first used field-recording equipment in Pennsylvania's anthracite counties in 1935; between 1938 and 1940, supported by a United Mine Workers' grant, Korson extended his search to southern bituminous regions, using portable equipment. Early in 1946 he returned to Pennsylvania's hard-coal area, accompanied by Arthur Semmig, a Library of Congress engineer. Two years later the Archive of American Folk Song issued a 78 rpm set (five twelve-inch discs) based on this trip. In 1958 the set was remastered at 33 rpm speed as L 16. Late in 1965 the archive issued L 60, which was drawn from Korson's previous bituminous field work.

These two discs are the only American LPs devoted solely to

416

field-recorded mining material. L 16 includes twelve songs and two fiddle tunes; L 60 includes seventeen songs and one fiddle-guitar duet. Both discs contain identifiable folksongs as well as pieces with no demonstrated life in tradition. While all the material on the two albums is industrial, nine pieces are marked by special labor-union content (three on L 16, six on L 60). The time span for L 16 is 1869 ("Avondale Mine Disaster") to 1944 ("Union Man"); for L 60 it is 1876 ("Two Cent Coal") to 1937 ("Harlan County Blues"). No singer on L 16 used instrumental accompaniment; several on L 60 used the guitar to second the voice. The predominant musical style on the anthracite disc is Celtic; that of the bituminous disc is mainly hillbilly and blues. Such a bare recital, however, establishes only the mechanical differences and similarities between the discs; to hear Irish brogue, Negro rhythms, mock-Slavic dialect, and southern highland locutions all expressed in mining idiom one must listen to Korson's friends.

It is possible that many new listeners to Korson's LPs in the years ahead will be at a loss to appreciate the trade-union songs in contrast to the more universal disaster ballads. During the 1960's much so-called "protest" material was legitimized by the entertainment industry. Singers of folksong and singers in rock bands learned to accommodate the poetry of political nihilism and personal alienation to the music of various idioms: pop, blues, soul, rock-and-roll, country-western. To one raised on Mick Jagger's convulsive aggression, the labor songs found on L 16 and L 60 may seem quaint or even camp, in that Korson's friends expressed their intense loyalty to unionism in such simple rhetoric:

> Union man! Union man!
> He must have full dinner can!
>
> The strike is nearly o'er,
> And with joy I'm near insane.
>
> We will have a good local in heaven,
> Up there where the password is "Rest."[7]

Obviously, the coal diggers who recorded for the Library of Congress experienced directly much of the tension which can be heard today in the music of the Rolling Stones or Country Joe and the Fish, to name but two of many groups. Although folk music is at times internally complex, the parameters of poetic and melodic style available to American anthracite and bituminous miners seem very ordinary by contemporary folk-rock standards. Regardless of this stylistic contrast and regardless of the fate of Korson's LPs in the hands of new listeners, the message songs on the two albums are highly relevant in grasping the notion of folk society knitted together partly by political and social ideals.

I shall close my remarks on the Library of Congress LPs by calling attention to an unusual feature of *Songs and Ballads of the Bituminous Miners*. This LP contains several union pieces by Negro folksingers. Many blues anthologies — print and sound — hold work songs from agriculture and railroading as well as laments about hard times and the trauma of relocation in the urban North, but songs by black artists touching on unionism are extremely rare. Students of labor history know that the United Mine Workers of America was far ahead of sister groups in breaking discriminatory bars. Historian Herbert Gutman in an excellent article has traced the UMW's non-exclusionary role to the belief by its pioneer British organizers in industrial unionism, evangelical egalitarianism, and reform ideology.[8] Fortunately, these concepts come alive when we hear, via L 60, the Evening Breezes Sextet of Vivian, West Virginia, harmonize in gospel style on "The Coal Loading Machine," or Sam Johnson of Pursglove, West Virginia, offer "We Done Quit" to the spiritual tune "I Can Tell the World." Particularly useful in the on-going struggle for civil rights and black power is a ballad, "This What the Union Done," composed by Uncle George Jones of Trafford, Alabama, and recorded at his cabin home on March 19, 1940. Although blind Uncle George memorializes both Mr. Roosevelt and President John L. Lewis, his composition can best be understood as a black worker's ode to freedom.

George Korson had the opportunity to reach working miners in their homes and union halls. In my second chapter I noted that miners such as Dock Boggs reached commercial studios in the 1920's but recorded no coal songs, while miners such as Frank Hutchison did. During the 1950's and 1960's coal songs issued on LPs were recorded by former miners, as well as by relatives or friends of miners, rather than by workers still active in the industry. Perhaps the best LP by a former coal digger is George Davis' *When Ken-*

tucky Had No Union Men (Folkways FTS 31016), a disc already discussed in connection with Davis' claim to "Sixteen Tons." This LP contains some non-mining material; here I wish only to stress this album's value as a supplement to and continuation of the Library of Congress bituminous LP. In fact, Davis' "Harlan County Blues" recorded by Korson in 1940 appears on L 60; the same item recorded by John Cohen in 1966 appears on the Folkways disc.

In classifying folksingers it is convenient, at times, to contrast domestic singers with semi-professional bards or minstrels, who to some degree perform for gain. Polar terms which separate these sets are *insiders* and *outsiders, folk* and *non-folk.* Interestingly, when Korson met Davis the latter was a worker, who wrote "Harlan County Blues" as a mine pumper. "My desk was an old powder box and the light came from my own carbide lamp."[9] This industrial setting, deep underground, can still be perceived as part of a domestic tradition. However, in 1947 Davis began to entertain on Hazard station WKIC. His new work was supplemented by live concert appearances in the mountains, by service as a local MC for visiting country-music shows, and by employment as a disc jockey. For more than two decades George Davis has been part of the music-business world. I commend his LP to listeners who are puzzled by the question of what elements of folk style are retained when mass culture reaches its microphones and transmitters into the hills.

When ballad scholars wish to identify the "pure" Appalachian ballad tradition they frequently cite persons such as Aunt Molly Jackson, Texas Gladden, Almeda Riddle, or Sarah Ogan Gunning. Very early in this book I alluded briefly to Mrs. Gunning's *Girl of Constant Sorrow* (Folk Legacy FSA 26) as a helpful tool in distinguishing topical from traditional items. I had the pleasure of collecting songs from Sarah and editing her LP; hence I shall not comment in detail on FSA 26. However, one can note that it contains six coal-mining songs reflecting the brief life of the communist-led National Miners Union in eastern Kentucky during the early 1930's. Sarah's new labor songs were based fully on folk models; for example, "Down on the Picket Line" stems from the spiritual "As I Went Down in the Valley to Pray," and "Dreadful Memories" stems from the gospel hymn "Precious Memories."

419

Notwithstanding stylistic authenticity in composition and performance, there is no evidence that these items were accepted by Sarah's peers in folk society or entered tradition, however broadly the term is defined. Unionists and radicals alike have composed songs for more than a century which were doomed to instant death because of the press of events, the difficulty in maintaining viable organizations, the failure of causes, the narrowness of sectarian positions, and blindness to the drift in American life. Surely one significance of *Girl of Constant Sorrow* is precisely that it preserves a handful of labor songs, all of which failed to enter tradition but which deeply reveal a wholeness in life, by a singer who could cap oppression with poignant artistry. Sarah Ogan Gunning's album testifies that the lot of a miner's daughter, sister, and wife is not constant sorrow.

I shall end this chapter with one of Mrs. Gunning's incisive pieces which did succeed in reaching a new audience in the late 1960's. At this juncture I shall turn to an anthology holding a few but significant mining items. *Newport Broadside* (Vanguard VRS 9144) was recorded at the Newport Folk Festival in 1963 and included among a group of recent topical songs Jim Garland's provocative "Ballad of Harry Simms," also known as "The Death . . ." or "The Murder of Harry Simms."[10]

Jim Garland, Sarah Gunning's brother, was born at Four Mile, a Bell County, Kentucky, coal camp, on April 8, 1905, into a family which treated Baptism, unionism, and traditional song at the same level of respect. He worked in the mines from boyhood until 1932, when he was blacklisted for National Miners Union activity. In the summer of 1963 Garland traveled from his home on the Columbia River at Washougal, Washington, to Rhode Island to participate in the Newport Folk Festival. The "Ballad of Harry Simms" had sprung from the killing of a nineteen-year-old National Miners Union organizer on Brush Creek, near Pineville, Kentucky, early in 1932. Previous to Newport, this song had been recorded on field and commercial discs by Aunt Molly Jackson (Jim's sister), Pete Seeger, and John Greenway, and touched on in the latter's book, *American Folksongs of Protest.*

Still to be written is a full essay on Simms's memorial song. Born in Springfield, Massachusetts, Harry Hersh took the name

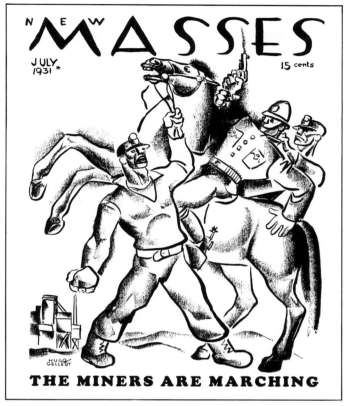

A RADICAL STANCE

Simms when he became an active member of the Young Communist League. In a period when American communists were committed to dual or red unionism, he was assigned to the South, working for a while with black organizer Angelo Herndon. In Kentucky on February 10, 1932, Simms was shot by mine guard Arlin Miller. Subsequently Miller was himself brutally slain on a lonely road. In every sense of the word Harry Simms was a martyr to a cause, but he did not emerge as a legendary figure in either coal-mining, trade-union, or radical movements. To the coal operators and their hired gunmen he was a subversive outsider who deserved to be killed. To NMU partisans he was an idealistic and radiant youth. To one veteran radical, recalling Depression experience, Harry was a symbol of the Communist party's callousness in sending a naive young man, untrained and unprepared, to his death.

421

On February 17 Simms was given an elaborate funeral in the prize-fight arena of the Bronx Coliseum. His coffin, banked by red carnations, was flanked by seven Kentucky miners, whose flickering cap lamps lit the platform from which William Z. Foster and other party functionaries orated. Shortly after the ritual Jim Garland, then living in New York, composed the elegy, setting it to his mother's tune for her Civil War piece, the "Battle of Mill Springs." In time Aunt Molly Jackson appropriated Jim's ballad and recorded it for Library of Congress collectors Mary Elizabeth Barnicle and Alan Lomax. The Seeger and Greenway discs stem from Aunt Molly; the 1963 Vanguard LP represents the first recording of the song by its original composer, Garland.

One problem involved in an analysis of the "Ballad of Harry Simms" is the relationship of radical unionists to the main body of American labor. A philosophic question which also surfaces is the value position of scholars who approach folk and folk-like material associated with communism. Because Communist party members have been under attack for a half-century in the United States, and because of the feeling among apologists for Stalinism that it is always too early to criticize communist subculture, we have no detailed investigation of songs like Garland's elegiac ballad. It is my personal belief that in an America where some young people pay homage to Che Guevara, Frantz Fanon, and Regis Debray we can ill afford to overlook the esthetic and ethical statements in the "Ballad of Harry Simms."

Because of the intense loyalty engendered by coal unionism and the special tone of solidarity displayed by mine laborites, it may come as a surprise to some readers of this book to learn that at least one anti-miners' union song is available on an LP. Fleming Brown, born in 1926 at Marshall, Missouri, presently works as a commercial artist in Chicago. His special contribution to the "folksong revival" of the last two decades is his mastery of five-string banjo picking, a technique learned in part from National Barn Dance star Doc Hopkins (born in Harlan County). During 1962 Folk-Legacy issued *Fleming Brown* as the first record in its Interpreters series (FSI 4). One of the numbers, "Flag of Blue, White and Red," declaims: "Idle men and a roving band / Strike the tools from a miner's hand," and "I tell you boys, it is a crime / That has transpired in many a mine." (For balance, Brown also sings Aunt Molly Jackson's "Ely Branch.") The LP's brochure indicates that Brown learned "Flag" from a Missouri woman who insisted that her name remain secret. The only clue to locale is a reference to strike violence at Donegan Coal and Coke.[11] No other recorded anti-union coal song is known to me. However, it is a commentary on coal-song students that we tend to favor unionism and therefore overlook the anti-labor sentiment always parallel to union loyalty.

A number of LPs by singer-scholars previously referred to in my separate case studies merit listing here. John Greenway's "Mother Jones" appeared on *American Industrial Folksongs* (Riverside RLP 607) recorded in 1955. Pete Seeger's "Roll Down the Line" appeared on *American Industrial Ballads* (Folkways FH 5251) recorded in 1956. Each album offers an industrial panorama; specifically the two contain fifteen coal songs, some never before recorded, and some otherwise available only on archival field discs. Parallel to these LPs is Mike Seeger's *Tipple, Loom & Rail* (Folkways FH 5273), which holds seven coal, five textile, and four railroad songs. "The Hard Working Miner" and "Coal Creek Troubles" as performed by Seeger have already been considered; at this chapter's end I shall touch on his treatment of "Come All You Coal Miners."[12]

Similar to Mike Seeger in sensitivity to Appalachian folksong, and in respect for the scholarship which enhances this music's appeal, is Hedy West. In my chapter on "Only a Miner" I have discussed her rendition of Aunt Molly Jackson's "Poor Miner's Farewell," found on *Hedy West* (Vanguard VRS 9124). Here I shall mention Hedy's *Old Times and Hard Times* (Folk-Legacy FSA 32), originally recorded on the Topic label in England and reissued in America by Sandy Paton. FSA 32 includes among a mixed group of British classic and broadside ballads "The Coal Miner's Child," "The Davison-Wilder Blues," "Lament for Barney Graham," and "Shut Up in the Mines at Coal Creek." Three of these — texts, tunes, and source date — along with a group of textile-mill pieces (and older ballads, too) are offered by Hedy in a German-English songbook, which reveals how far from home many of America's local mining songs have journeyed.[13]

In my treatment of Merle Travis' "Nine Pound Hammer,"

423

"Sixteen Tons," and "Dark as a Dungeon" I noted that his 78 rpm set *Folk Songs of the Hills* was reissued on *Back Home* (Capitol T 891). About 1964 Travis composed a dozen new mining songs, also based on childhood experiences in Muhlenberg County, Kentucky, and each prefaced by a spoken anecdotal introduction. This set was titled *Songs of the Coal Mines* (Capitol T 1956), and it featured back liner notes by Merle's brother John, a former miner, who lauded the experiential reality of the songs. None of the compositions on T 1956 are traditional; the choice was deliberate on Merle's part. To my knowledge, only one of them, "Miner's Strawberries," has moved on to another singer, Joe Glazer. Time will tell whether or not any of the LP's other pieces get away from Travis as did some of his earlier coal-song compositions.

As part of this roundup of coal-song LPs, I have not featured any albums which hold only one mining song. A pleasure in field collecting is finding a rare item previously unknown; related is the sense of discovery on finding unusual material on new records. Two such coal pieces can be cited here.

The Carolina Tar Heels (Folk-Legacy FSA 24) includes Dock Walsh singing "If I Was a Mining Man," a delightful love song which Walsh learned as a lad from his mother in Wilkes County, North Carolina. This lyric was new to me and to Eugene Earle when we taped it in 1962, and to my knowledge it has not been reported elsewhere since. During 1963 Billy Edd Wheeler, a Berea College graduate especially interested in folksong use in dramatic productions and historical pageants, issued a group of his fresh compositions on *Memories of America* (Kapp KL 1425). One of its topical numbers, "Coal Tattoo," was based on unemployment accounts from Wheeler's native West Virginia. It was aided considerably in circulation after it was accepted by several popular singers of folksongs such as Judy Collins. During 1969 "Coal Tattoo" began to reach some of the men whose experience it originally had reported when another West Virginian, David Morris, began to sing it at "black-lung" and miners' political rallies.[14] These citations of "If I Was a Mining Man" and "Coal Tattoo" hopefully may indicate that good coal songs, worthy of search, can be found on a wide variety of general LPs not limited to industrial lore.

I have left for the end three widely different LPs especially important in coal-song study. *Songs of Coal* by Joe Glazer is drawn from the Forty-fourth (1964) Constitutional Convention of the United Mine Workers of America at Bal Harbour, Florida. Although the numbers on the album were taped by technicians hired to record the entire proceedings, the UMWA did not see fit to release the LP on its own label. Rather, Glazer issued it privately through Sound Studios, a Washington, D.C., firm. The disc includes fifteen songs drawn from coal and other industries. Liner notes by Glazer detail the sources of all the pieces; for instance, a hitherto unrecorded and wry "Company Store" learned by Joe from Helga Sandburg is identified as one of her father Carl's favorites.[15] Even better than the notes are Joe's spoken introductions to the songs, in which he draws the delegates into a dialogue in spite of the opulent setting of the hall. It is admittedly difficult to bring the intimacies of a picket-line turn or a back-of-the-saloon meeting to the Americana Hotel's grand ballroom, but Joe mixes vocal stamina, stand-up humor, and audience participation to re-create the spirit of a miners' picnic. The disc is useful as an example of some union classics sung by a partisan. It is also important as an introduction to an institutional source for labor tradition — the convention. In this sense, a union-taped convention disc may be seen as parallel to an LP anthology drawn from festival tapes. Each happening brings together as participants labor activists in the one case and star performers in the other, whose experiences and traditions are presented in highly compressed forms.

In reading the *United Mine Workers Journal* one is struck by the fact that music was an integral part of the union's official life from the beginning. While I was gathering data on "The Death of Mother Jones," James Farrance felt it important to note that he had sung the piece at the 1938 convention. Here I shall refer readers only to formal reports of one convention, held appropriately at Cincinnati's Music Hall (October, 1948). On October 15 the *Journal* stated that four coal-field bands had been present, one of which premiered the "John L. Lewis Chieftain March." On November 1 the editor pictured four Negro miners in the Logan County (West Virginia) quintet which had entertained delegates. On January 15 the *Journal* used photographs of Jerry Byrne, Daniel Walsh, and James Muldowney, three anthracite miners who had

425

LOGAN COUNTY QUINTET

sung and fiddled at Cincinnati. Also, it announced George Korson's Library of Congress 78 rpm set on which the three old-timers, among others, had appeared.[16] I do not know the last time that any traditional singers participated formally in a UMWA convention, but it is important to mention the difference in role, for example, between coal miner Jerry Byrne of Buck Run, Pennsylvania, and Joe Glazer, America's best-known union troubadour.[17]

Glazer grew up in a New York needle-trades family and from his parents learned the traditions of the Jewish socialist movement in Poland. He has been an education director for two groups (Textile Workers Union of America and United Rubber Workers of America); he is currently a U.S. Information Agency official in Washington, D.C. To the extent that there is a given style proper for labor songs, Glazer might be tagged a "pure" union singer. Yet this so-called "purity" is a most eclectic blend of the many musical influences in Joe's life: radio cowboys, Workmen's Circle choruses, collegiate variety-show singers, and southern textile string-band vocalists.

A similar eclecticism is displayed on an unusual LP by the Irish Balladeers, *The Molly Maguires* (Avoca 33-ST 162), released in 1968 by a Westbury, New York, firm specializing in Irish material. The disc's jacket cover is a photo of a quartet (with banjo, guitar, and tambourine) posing in front of a Hudson Coal Company breaker, near Scranton, Pennsylvania. The jacket's back liner

426

JERRY BYRNE AND DAN WALSH

is graced by excellent notes by Anna Cashin, divided equally between Molly Maguire history and background data on the fourteen
mine-song inclusions. The Irish Balladeers are identified as brothers
Chuck, Bob, and John Rogers, and brother-in-law Ted Andrews.
Accompanists to the quartet are Charles Rogers, Sr., on accordion,
and Eddie Lennihan on banjo and guitar. (The tragic account of
the Pennsylvania anthracite miners who resorted to violence in the
nineteenth century is well told elsewhere by Wayne Broehl and other
historians.)

My only criticism of the liner notes is that, despite the 2,000
words in small print, the imposition of a 12″ x 12″ space limit does
not offer enough room for all the data one desires. Because the
Rogers group seems to derive stylistically from the popular Clancy
Brothers rather than from any of the rough-hewn Celtic-based singers encountered by George Korson, I wish to know something about
the Irish Balladeers' song sources and their audience. A few of
their songs seem to come from British "revival" singers influenced
by A. L. Lloyd's and Ewan MacColl's interest in industrial folksong. One ballad, "The Knox Mine Disaster," is original to the
Irish Balladeers; it recounts a Susquehanna River mine flooding at
Port Griffith during 1959.

Several rhetorical questions come to mind: Do the Irish Balladeers perceive their role as domestic entertainers or show-business
figures? How do they relate to George Davis, Joe Glazer, Mike See-

427

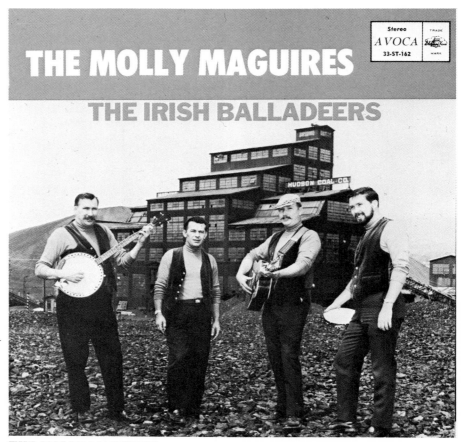

THE MOLLY MAGUIRES

ger, or Merle Travis? Finally, in what spirit is the memory of the Molly Maguires received? Does it kindle Irish-American nationalism; illuminate a page in history; or remind youngsters of trade-union violence? Mrs. Cashin, in correspondence with me, indicated that the LP was produced in response to an announcement of a cinematic "Molly Maguires." She objected in advance of seeing the film to Hollywood's "penchant for depicting Irish people in the past in low, demeaning, rowdy characterizations"; for Avoca's LP she wanted "a sympathetic, truthful account of this incident in American history."[18]

It is ironic that Mrs. Cashin relates the Mollies to genteel cultural nationalism. Of course it is impossible to separate coal-song lore from struggle — constant struggle against underground accident, death in the dark, exploitive conditions, fear of unemployment, and the lash of poverty. Perhaps it is this heritage that has made the life of coal unionism one of continual conflict. At times the rivalry between groups of organized miners has spurred the United Mine Workers to magnificent achievement in collective bargaining and industrial democracy. At times the rivalry has sapped it of vitality and destroyed internal democracy. In this book I have not paid special attention to the songs of dual unionists except to note that the "Coal Creek Troubles" dated back to a time of undercover dualism involving the Knights of Labor and the UMWA, and that "The Death of Mother Jones" was helped into tradition by UMWA as well as independent West Virginia Mine Workers Union members. Also, the compositions of Aunt Molly Jackson, Jim Garland, and Sarah Gunning speak for the short-lived National Miners Union.

It has been nearly forty years since "Which Side Are You On" emerged from a dissident NMU setting to become a general labor song, shorn of its sectarian coloration. As I ready this book for publication, I am conscious that internal conflict once more divides mine unionism. After the killing of Joseph A. (Jock) Yablonski during a race against UMWA president William Anthony (Tony) Boyle, an LP appeared with a song about the former's murder. My remarks on 45 rpm singles had stressed their broadside role. It is precisely this same journalistic role which is served by Michael Kline and John Martin in *The Poverty War Is Dead* (Dillons Run DLP 103). Privately distributed from Kline's home at Capon Bridge, West Virginia, the LP holds eleven topical commentaries on strip mining as well as on the experiences of anti-poverty volunteers in Kentucky and West Virginia during the 1960's. The tone of the songs is summed up aptly by the liner notes' opening words: "All . . . the Vista workers and outsiders . . . ever talk about is white paint for our schools and cultural enrichment for our children in the community. But if we don't do something about the bulldozers stripping the head of this creek, we ain't going to have no community or kids, either one. . . ."[19]

Kline's songs are set appropriately to traditional tunes and performed in a manner acceptable to their intended listeners: poor

429

people of the creeks and coal camps. John Martin is identified as having learned Appalachian music from his family at Troutman, North Carolina. Apparently Kline was drawn to folksong before he journeyed to the mountains to engage in political work. Currently he is associated with the Highlander Research and Education Center at Knoxville, which continues the folk-school program of the 1930's. Some of Kline's broadsides were first "printed" in the Highlander mimeographed songster *Sowing on the Mountain* (1967).

While listening to *The Poverty War Is Dead,* I found three expressive strands among its several pieces: the values of southern social reform, the rhetoric of "peoples' artists" such as Woody Guthrie, and the attention to folk style by recent "protest" composers. One artist to whom Michael Kline is indebted is Jean Ritchie (Mrs. George Pickow), widely known in America and Europe, through her books and records, for her presentation of and affection for Appalachian traditional culture.

It is Miss Ritchie's "Blue Diamond Mines" that is used by Kline to note the Yablonski killing. Actually Jean wrote the "Blue Diamond Mines" in 1964 as a reflective commentary on coal unemployment, and Kline added a topical final stanza in 1970. Originally, the Ritchie item had been issued, along with a few other new numbers, on *A Time for Singing* (Warner Brothers W 1592); at that time it was attributed pseudonymously to "Than Hall." Recently Miss Ritchie re-recorded "Blue Diamond Mines" for *Clear Waters Remembered* (Sire SES 97014), a strong LP offering old ballads and fresh compositions. The latter reflect Jean's response to strip-mining destruction in Kentucky by augers and 'dozers. Jean Ritchie, consciously "old-fashioned," wants this album to help her children recall the beauty in the mountains before smoke and dust came to "hang like a pall of sorrow over the ridges and hollers" of her native Perry County.[20] Michael Kline wants to extend this twin concern (for clear waters and against strip mining) to the internecine struggle within the UMWA. It is in the movement of "Blue Diamond Mines" from singer to singer and from an initial statement on unemployment to a polemic on the politics of murder that we see something of the long-playing record's contemporary function.

COMMITTEE FOR MINERS

presents.

FOLK MUSIC

BENEFIT FOR UNEMPLOYED MINERS OF APPALACHIA

at

THE GATE

featuring

MISSISSIPI JOHN HURT.	HAMILTON CAMP
PHIL OCHS	PETER LA FARGE
PATRICK SKY	LISA KINDRED
ERIC ANDERSON	DAVE COHEN

and other top folk artists
and
POEMS BY — SAM CORNISH

AT
THE VILLAGE GATE : SUNDAY
THOMPSON AND BLEEKER ST.   APR 25 : 2.30 PM.

TICKETS : $2.50 and $3.50
from
COMMITTEE FOR MINERS, 1165 BROADWAY, NY 1, NY : Tel OR97077
IZZY YOUNG'S FOLKLORE CENTER, 381 6TH AVE.

GREENWICH VILLAGE RALLY

Records similar to *The Poverty War Is Dead* and *Clear Waters Remembered* will continue to appear in the future in order to give voice to outside intellectuals and radicals drawn to the southern highlands, as well as to native activists attracted to the life-style epitomized by the term *counter-culture*. The coal industry has always served as a magnet to attract conservationist and planner, reformist and revolutionist. Their schemes and jeremiads are available in yellowed journals of charitable work and child-labor reform, as well as in the ephemera of current leftist groups.[21] Anyone who has the slightest familiarity with the hortatory literature surrounding coal will recognize its rhetoric in the songs collected by Korson,

431

in the LPs mentioned here, and in the lyrics of peripatetic folk-song interpreters (traveling the collegiate-coffeehouse circuit) who equate their very songs with liberation.

There is no reason to believe that coal's black magnet will lose its power to draw rebels for the decades remaining in this century. And it is certain that for years to come some mining songs will be preserved and some new ones composed by traditional singers as well as folksong enthusiasts, who live in a period of inexpensive and instantaneous sound recording. Hopefully, some of my commentary on singles and LPs will prove useful to students and workers, to performers and listeners, in evaluating future coal-song records.

A basic assumption in this chapter has been that consumers could and would purchase discs for home playing. All my judgments of text-tune worth or performance style are based on personal selection of records for my own turntable. Yet today all of us hear through jukeboxes, cinema amplifiers, transistor radios, and television sets many singles and LPs which are arbitrarily selected for us by others. Hence, I end this chapter with a discussion of a television producer's use of one coal-mining disc to establish a needed mood for special visual scenes. From the perspective of staid folklorists who view the entertainment media as destructive of traditional folkways, television is a monstrous instrument. From the perspective of other folklorists, this medium may prove to be an effective source for future lore. Without entering this speculative and on-going debate, I can suggest that attention to TV's usage of recordings may help us perceive clearly the wide mix in the contemporary popular-culture audience, though not the specific nature of folksong origin and transmission.

In this last decade, film and print have helped make Appalachian poverty highly visible throughout the United States, frequently to the acute discomfort of some highland residents who have questioned the right of outsiders to invade their communities. The justification of radical or critical documentary films in democratic society is based on the medium's broad educational role; such a consideration must be set against TV's capacity to hurt a portion of the citizenry. This conflict between rival value positions was tragically acted out in Jeremiah, Kentucky, in September, 1967, when a Letcher County mountaineer, Hobart Ison, murdered a

Canadian filmmaker, Hugh O'Connor.[22] To my knowledge, no folk composer memorialized O'Connor on broadside or disc.

Some thirty-six years before this shooting, the poverty-stricken coal miners of Harlan and neighboring counties witnessed the arrival of a band of radical intellectuals and union organizers from the North. Some came to help miners form locals of the communist-led National Miners Union; some came to work with hungry children; some came to observe and report conditions in "bloody Harlan" to the rest of the nation.[23] This revolutionary intrusion into Kentucky was brief, but it left behind a handful of topical songs using old melodies set to new militant texts which echoed the rhetoric of Karl Marx and Mikhail Bakunin. One such number was Sarah Ogan Gunning's "Come All You Coal Miners." It summed up her feelings about coal operators and company stores as well as the promise of unionism. One stanza declaimed:

> They take our very life blood, they take our children's lives,
> Take fathers away from children and husbands away from wives.
> Coal miners, won't you organize, wherever you may be,
> And make this a land of freedom for workers like you and me.[24]

The tension contained within this song stemmed from the mixture of a mournful traditional tune, usually associated with "The Texas Rangers," and a revolutionary text concluding in the flaming call: "Let's sink this capitalist system in the darkest pits of Hell." Sarah explained to me that at the time of its composition she did not perceive this as a political or protest song. It was written when her first husband, Andrew Ogan, lay dying of miner's consumption. In composing it, she identified her sorrow in sectarian terminology which was at that time new to her and but dimly understood.

This song was first recorded for the Library of Congress in 1937 but it failed to receive the attention, even in radical circles, given to the comparable "Which Side Are You On" or "The Death of Harry Simms." During 1965 Mike Seeger recorded Sarah's piece for *Tipple, Loom & Rail,* a Folkways LP depicting the industrialization of the South. I do not believe that it has yet sold a thousand copies. I detail this commercial fact only to underscore the small present-day audience for traditional material, whether by folksingers themselves or interpreters. However, in November, 1968,

433

TIPPLE, LOOM & RAIL

Seeger's rendition of "Come All You Coal Miners" was heard in hundreds of thousands of American homes by virtue of its inclusion as background music in the National Educational Television documentary, "Appalachia: Rich Land, Poor People."[25]

While editing the NET film, producer-director Jack Willis sought an incisive musical selection "to show the historical continuity between the region and industrial America."[26] He weeded out some twenty recorded items drawn from Folkways and Library of Congress LPs before he decided that "Come All You Coal Miners" was best suited for his already-filmed sequences. Actually, Willis could have gone beyond the disc and reached Sarah herself for a "live" tape if he had desired to do so. What seems much more im-

434

portant to me than the basis of choice, however, is the use itself of a single coal-mining piece to establish a needed tone in a TV film. Sound recordings in the libraries of television and cinema makers' studios are ideal holders of a wide range of human feeling.

Sarah Gunning's Library of Congress field disc of "Come All You Coal Miners" is a poignant statement of her condition, and Mike Seeger's secondary Folkways rendition is a faithful re-presentation of this cry, but in a form available to anyone with a record player. NET producer Jack Willis' use of Seeger's LP widely extends the song's audience, but with much loss of intensity. On a film soundtrack the song functions fleetingly to set mood, and it is part of an impressionistic portrait of American poverty.[27] Perhaps in tracing the movement of Sarah's coal-mining song from a virtually inaccessible, low-fidelity field disc, through a technically fine and inexpensive LP, to a sensitive TV documentary film track, we have wrought a parable on an excellent use of folk material by the mass media, as well as on our own problems in coping with recorded sound at its many levels.

1. G. Malcolm Laws, Jr., in *American Balladry from British Broadsides* (Philadelphia, 1957) and Leslie Shepard in *The Broadside Ballad* (London, 1962) draw on Charles Hindley, *The Life and Times of James Catnach* (London, 1878).

2. Mrs. W. A. Brown, Logan, W.Va., librarian, was unable to find any sound recordings about the March disaster in her community. Letter to me, July 18, 1960.

3. Gilbert Donahue letter to me, Nov. 30, 1962, as well as my telephone interview with Lenny Wright, Dec. 4, 1962.

4. Hickerson letter to me, June 16, 1969.

5. Robert L. Baker letter to me, Mar. 26, 1965. Neil Rosenberg interviewed the Baker Brothers at the Brown County, Ind., Jamboree and reported his findings in a letter to me, Aug. 9, 1965.

6. Letter to me, Aug. 20, 1970.

7. Couplets are from "Union Man," "On Johnny Mitchell's Train," and "A Coal Miner's Goodbye" in Korson's liner notes to L 16 and L 60.

8. Herbert G. Gutman, "The Negro and the United Mine Workers of America," in *The Negro and the American Labor Movement*, ed. Julius Jacobson (Garden City, N.Y., 1968), 49.

9. Liner notes by George Korson to *Songs and Ballads of the Bituminous Miners* (Library of Congress AFS L 60).

435

10. Preval Glusman, "Harry Simms — a Young Revolutionist," *Daily Worker* (May 8, 1934), 5; Mary Elizabeth Barnicle, "The Story Behind This American Ballad," *People's Songs*, II (July, 1947), 12. My comments are supplemented by interviews with Jim Garland, Sarah Gunning, Aunt Molly Jackson, and Pete Seeger. For background see Jack Stachel, "Lessons of Two Recent Strikes," *Communist*, XI (June, 1932), 527.

11. For a comment on "Flag" see Oscar Brand, *The Ballad Mongers* (New York, 1962), 9, 19.

12. For Seeger's approach to material see Jon Pankake, "Mike Seeger: The Style of Tradition," *Sing Out*, XIV (July, 1964), 6.

13. Hedy West, *Hedy West Songbook* (Erlanger, West Germany, 1969).

14. Interview with Morris, Aug. 1, 1970.

15. Joe Glazer liner notes to *Songs of Coal* (Sound Studios 12-1137). For the "Company (Store) Song" see Helga Sandburg, *Sweet Music* (New York, 1963), 60.

16. "Recordings Preserve Colorful Anthracite Folk Ballads," *United Mine Workers Journal* (Jan. 15, 1949), 6.

17. For examples of Glazer profiles in the labor press see Alvin Toffler, "Joe Glazer, Union Songster . . . ," *Labor's Daily* (Apr. 27, 1955), 3, and Harry Conn, "Labor Songs . . . ," *RWDSU Record* (Mar. 18, 1956), 13.

18. Cashin letter to me, Jan. 12, 1971. For two film reviews of "The Molly Maguires" see Pauline Kael, "The Current Cinema: Duds," *New Yorker*, XLV (Feb. 7, 1970), 91, and "Stanley Kauffmann on Films," *New Republic*, CLXII (Feb. 21, 1970), 20.

19. Liner notes, unsigned, to *The Poverty War Is Dead* (Dillons Run DLP 103).

20. For full background on her heritage see Jean Ritchie, *Singing Family of the Cumberlands* (New York, 1955).

21. For an article citing many leftist sources see Paul Nyden, "Coal Miners, 'Their' Union, and Capital," *Science and Society*, XXXIV (1970), 194. For a current criticism of coal unionism see Thomas O'Hanlon, "Anarchy Threatens the Kingdom of Coal," *Fortune*, LXXXIII (Jan., 1971), 78.

22. Calvin Trillin, "U.S. Journal: Jeremiah, Kentucky. A Stranger with a Camera," *New Yorker*, XLV (Apr. 12, 1969), 178.

23. Lawrence Grauman, Jr., " 'That Little Ugly Running Sore,' " *Filson Club Historical Quarterly*, XXXVI (Oct., 1962), 340.

24. My views on Sarah Gunning, based on interviews, are developed in the brochure to *Girl of Constant Sorrow* (Folk Legacy FSA 26). See also my brochure to Mike Seeger's *Tipple, Loom & Rail* (Folkways FH 5273) for "Come All You Coal Miners."

25. No statistics are available on the size of the specific audience for this feature. However, Neilson reports for Oct., 1966, indicate that nearly seven million homes did tune to one or more educational TV stations in an average week. Data in Carnegie Commission on Educational Television, *Public Television* (New York, 1967), 251.

26. Letter to me, Aug. 16, 1969.
27. For representative reviews of this feature see Dean Gysel, "An American Tragedy on TV," *Chicago Daily News, Panorama* (Nov. 9, 1968), 31; Jack Gould, "TV: Appalachia Poverty Documented," *New York Times* (Nov. 13, 1968), 22; Stephanie Harrington, "Living With It," [New York] *Village Voice* (Nov. 21, 1968); James Doussard, "Appalachian Poverty Is Impressive," *Louisville Courier Journal* (Nov. 27, 1968); Robert Lewis Shayon, "A 'No' to Question-Begging," *Saturday Review*, LI (Dec. 14, 1968), 53.

TALKING IT OVER

Slack from the Gob Pile *12*

THE *UNITED MINE WORKERS JOURNAL,* an eight-page labor newspaper, first appeared on April 16, 1891, in Columbus, Ohio, when the United Mine Workers of America was still a fledgling organization. The paper was edited temporarily by a working compositor — a member of the International Typographical Union — until miner-editor John Kane was selected from the ranks. In the *Journal*'s second issue, UMWA secretary-treasurer Patrick McBryde started a little column, " 'Slack' from the Secretary's 'Gob Pile,' " including odds and ends of information and personal comment couched in traditional language and predicated upon an awareness that his readers shared his values.[1] Despite the fact that the feature was not continued for long under this name, the *Journal* in its eight decades has always carried some slack: songs, stories, cartoons, humor, proverbial speech.

In seeking to conclude my views on a handful of recorded coal-mining songs as cultural documents and communicative devices, I have felt it proper to appropriate McBryde's column title. *Slack* is the finest grade of screened coal not commercially useful until it is washed free of slate and other impurities. *Gob pile* is the waste heap left on the mine floor. Hence, McBryde's commentary was a form of editorial wisdom sifted out of the copy assembled in presenting a new paper to coal miners.

439

The word *gob* was found in British print as early as 1839; in the United States it was extended to special combinations such as *gob orator*. This usage described the articulate miner "who climbed up on the gob, the heap of dirt and slate, in the corners of the rooms at the dinner hour, and talked for union and against the bosses."[2] Many trades have traditional counterparts of such characters in the form of sea lawyers, spittoon philosophers, and even "Calhouns," named after the loquacious and stereotyped attorney in the Amos and Andy radio series of the 1930's. It is my belief that many folklorists are like miners who separate coal from its waste, with the difference that we continue endlessly to shovel and screen the gob in search of slack or overlooked items of value. Further, we resemble gob orators in our need to pontificate on work site, findings, companions, and compensation. The very convention of ending every scholarly study with a summation or epilogue holding a theoretical overview is itself a kind of rhetorical mounting of the gob pile.

I have endeavored in these studies to set each recorded song in its own contextual network, and to cap each study with a conclusion springing from my views of folklore. My simple definition of folksong, tied to variation over time, is probably unsuited to the total American corpus, but it has helped me and, I trust, my readers to distinguish such items as "Coal Creek Troubles" from "Dark as a Dungeon." Regardless of definition, I have tried to demonstrate that folksongs and non-folksongs are equally important and interesting as objects of exploration.

Although the preceding chapter case studies conclude my formal discussion of recorded coal-mining blues and ballads, a few words remain. Nowhere did I make explicit my methodology except to note that I would draw on three formal disciplines: ballad scholarship, labor history, and popular-culture studies. It must be apparent to anyone who has come this far that I have pulled from these fields only certain elements. Generally I have eschewed classificatory, structural, and esthetic criteria in favor of the consideration of socioeconomic change introduced into folk society by industrialization, urbanization, and the technology of mass media. Also, I have departed from conventional investigations of ballad origin and evolution which are tied to close textual analysis, literary exegesis, and poetics.

440

Vertical and internal studies of this nature are appropriate to such ballad families as "Lady Isabel and the Elf-Knight" or "Barbara Allen," which have lived for centuries in tradition throughout many lands, and hold a near-infinite number of versions. It seems to me that "The Death of Mother Jones," alive for less than four decades and available in but three or four versions, demands horizontal and external treatment. Mother Jones's song entered tradition and was tremendously important to some of her coal-miner "children." I could not have assayed the importance of this song to them without knowing something about philosophic conflicts within the American labor movement, as well as knowing a great many specific details about John L. Lewis' United Mine Workers of America and Frank Keeney's dual union in West Virginia.

In this book I have occasionally referred to personal experience as both a field collector and a library researcher. Nevertheless, this distinction in roles has not seemed to me to be particularly relevant. I began gathering material on recorded coal-mining songs while working as a maritime and building tradesman in San Francisco. From time to time I would be on a job with a former miner who had found his way to California following a period of unemployment at home or, possibly, an intra-union dispute. To name but two such fellow workers: Chet Bartalini made dramatic for me the tragedy of internal union war in the mine fields of Illinois; Merle Croy, a former Oklahoma "fire-boss," exposed me to the beliefs and customs associated with danger underground. I was especially fortunate as a young man to absorb firsthand the traditions of trade unionism as well as the work lore of shipbuilding and construction carpentry. At the same time, mining lore came to me in secondary form from articulate former coal diggers. Meanwhile, I had access to the library of the University of California in Berkeley. In San Francisco I also made good use of the Mechanics Institute and the research library of the International Longshoremen's & Warehousemen's Union, whose librarian, Anne Rand, was a friend.

From the job, I could literally walk many times not only to these excellent libraries but to such other San Francisco "institutions" as Peter Tamony's private archive, rich in examples of American language and culture, and to "Jack's Record Cellar," presided over by Norman Pierce. It was in Pierce's used-record

PORTRAIT OF A MINER

emporium, in a ghetto neighborhood, that I first met friendly collectors like Bob Pinson and Fred Hoeptner, and was encouraged to
undertake correspondence with discographers as distant as Eugene
Earle in Florida, George Tye in England, and John Edwards in
Australia. Discography, as it was presented to me by Earle and his
colleagues, seemed to be a simple, logical extension of bibliography.

Whether or not my avocational-centered, cross-disciplinary,
and horizontal approach is useful in folksong analysis, each reader

442

will have to judge. To me it seemed natural, and therefore correct, to base my method on direct work and union experience, as well as on my pleasure in book and record collecting. While still a tradesman I was exposed to the discipline of folklore at academic meetings in California, learning by listening to papers by Bertrand Bronson, Wayland Hand, and Archer Taylor. As my formal reading deepened, I encountered a model ballad study by Américo Paredes of a Mexican border hero, *"With His Pistol in His Hand,"* and determined to use as much of its technique as I could absorb. During the 1960's I was able to study folklore within classroom walls at the University of Pennsylvania. There MacEdward Leach and Tristram P. Coffin revealed to me two intriguing aspects of ballad scholarship. Despite the fact that my various case studies have dealt with pieces substantially different from the classic ballads to which "Mac" was devoted, I cherish his limitless enthusiasm for the folksong as an expressive form of intense beauty.[3]

In this work I have drawn on one of Coffin's provocative formulations: Anglo-American ballad poems frequently display "a balance attained in oral tradition between stress on plot unification and stress on emotional impact."[4] This latter force, Coffin suggested, cemented together the structural units in balladry: action, characters, setting, theme. However, he noted that over time ballads which begin as narratives may become lyric folksongs, held together by an emotional core. Coffin developed this notion in the course of an examination of "Mary Hamilton," the tragedy of a beautiful girl led astray and subsequently hanged. His study of this ballad's movement over a long time span and of the concomitant breakdown of its story element led me to two additional areas: a search for the heart of a song itself, and the means by which a narrative-become-lyric holds its dual elements in tension.

In my interpretation of coal-mining songs selected for close examination, I have assumed the validity of Coffin's view of balance attained in tradition, without forcing each mining item into a mechanical half-lyric, half-narrative mold. It seemed obvious, for example, that "Only a Miner" was partly ballad, partly lament, and that "Coal Mountain Blues" was fully a lyric song but with a story hidden in Sonny Scott's mind or heart.

Beyond this problem of balance, I have tried to phrase for

443

myself the query: Where does a song's emotional core lie? In seeking to place this element outside the poem — in a mine chamber, a saloon, a company shack, a union hall — I have endeavored to surround each song with evidence of its value to recording artists and to various audiences. Because Coffin has concentrated on textual analysis, primarily of English and Scottish popular ballads showing considerable age and variation, he perceives the emotional core of a folksong as a luminous jewel locked within the poetry of the piece. Because I deal with recent material of less universality than the ballads studied by Francis James Child, I tend to view a song's emotional core not as an inner element but rather as a looking glass reflecting the joys and sorrows, or aspirations and fears, of a community. At best, these contrastive symbols of *jewel* and *glass* are both metaphoric usages whose referents can be understood to lie within ballads and communities, respectively.

My conception of folksong as a mirror of the interplay of emotions within a given community returns me to the perplexing problem of defining the combination *folk society*. We know that over the years "Mary Hamilton" has appealed to separate groups — courtiers and cottagers in Scotland, backwoodsmen and collegians in the United States. This ballad, originally known to the nobility and peasantry alike, in time reached a "folksong revival" public. Sixteen Tons," in its short life, also has had varied listeners: country-music fans and urban "revivalists," TV watchers, some coal miners still close to their folk roots. Despite the fact that this hit — the most widely distributed mining song — reached tens of millions of persons, it is difficult to assert that Merle Travis' number was retained in the memory of as many traditional singers as was "Mary Hamilton."

In contrasting these dissimilar songs, I have merged problems involving both temporal and sociological dimensions. The question of the qualitatively distinct audiences reached by the two pieces is partly one of time, for the girl who became known as Mary Hamilton went to the scaffold nearly four centuries before young Travis could walk to the looming tipples near his Kentucky home. But this question of disparate listeners is also one about the massive changes wrought in American society, in part by the very music industry

444

which brought "Sixteen Tons" to Kentucky miners Bob Garland and Bob Baker — to name but two workers who still might be labeled *folksingers*.

In opening these studies, I suggested that the formal usage *folklore* might well be viewed at three levels: folklore, poplore, and patriotic lore. I have no special feeling that the word *poplore* will take hold, nor do I desire to impose it on others; however, the lore conveyed and accepted from commercial entertainment and advertising media must be gathered and analyzed regardless of how it is viewed or named. *Folk* with Germanic roots and *popular* with Latin roots both ultimately derive from a conception of the people, whether enclaved in a forest cove or spread throughout a great nation. Even after one selects either term as basic, it is still awkward to tag material disseminated largely by mass media to great numbers of people in a relatively short time with the same name used to describe word-of-mouth material slowly spread in small, stable associations.

I do not mean to suggest that this awkwardness concerns only today's scholars caught up by problems in folklore–popular culture analysis. Writing for the *Nation* in 1945, Margaret Marshall stated that *folklore* had already become a meaningless label in the United States. It seemed misleading to her that Joseph Wood Krutch, an astute and intelligent critic, should call "Oklahoma" (a "highly romanticised, sophisticated musical comedy . . . by two Broadway song writers") a "folk opera." Her attempt at naming the "folklore" of mass media and urban living was to call it *folkslore*. However, she had little hope that her new label would find acceptance. Nevertheless, she felt that it "would be useless . . . to try to shrink folklore back to its anthropological meaning." She sagely observed that the necessity to cling to the term came "out of desire for stability and continuity" among our people.[5] Miss Marshall, of course, wrote well before Joan Baez and Bob Dylan were dubbed *folksingers* in common parlance.

During 1967 *Cash Box,* a music-trades journal also troubled by denominative frustration, presented an editorial, "New Pop Music Brew," which offered *contemporary music* as a substitute for such labels as *pop-rock, pop-blues, pop-folk,* and *psychedelic rock.*

445

Cash Box knew that these "convenient phrases" were all inadequate to describe the new popular music of the late 1960's, but this journal, deeply concerned with the shape and sound of American entertainment, was not able to apply beyond its own pages the coinage *contemporary music*.[6] Seemingly, where folk and mass-society exponents come together, abrasive problems in meaning are thrust to the surface faster than lexicographers can apply balm. Late in 1970 a Nashville artist, Kris Kristofferson, was treated to a sympathetic profile in the *New York Times Magazine* precisely because he is in background more establishment than redneck, a Rhodes Scholar rather than a rural school dropout. After Kris's near-underground hit, "Sunday Mornin' Comin' Down," was named the Country Music Association "Song of the Year," Paul Hemphill, author of *The Nashville Sound,* called him "the hottest country songwriter going," and added that "the term 'country' is used advisedly . . . in a period when the distinctions separating all types of popular music are being blurred."[7]

Such writings by Hemphill, Miss Marshall, and the editor of *Cash Box* demonstrate that many observers of modern lore are forced into novel and sometimes painful conceptual or neologistic modes, whether or not their phrases take hold. However treated, the expressive forms spawned by the rotary press, cabaret stage, jukebox, cinema screen, and television camera will continue to raise challenges for many decades, I am certain.

This book has not been conceived as an analysis of folk or mass society as such, or of its nomenclature. I have stated that American coal miners in the twentieth century constitute a folk-like group with some attributes of rural dwellers and some attributes of urbanites. Clearly, miners form neither an agrarian class with a tightly patterned and persistent tradition, nor an amorphous band of hobbyists with but a tenuous hold on a few expressive forms. My model of the mine patch as a folk-like society is not a static one, and it must be adjusted to a time scale.

No special American community, work or otherwise, has ever been completely isolated from large society, except that of Indian tribes prior to contact with Europeans. Colonial ship caulkers in Boston, even while plying an ancient and tradition-bound trade, were abreast of then-current and radical notions of political freedom. Before the Civil War, slaves not far removed in time from their African heritage were exposed to minstrel-stage ditties as well as to elegant concert music. The Molly Maguires, but one step removed from peasantry, thrust tradition-tested notions of survival against the bastions, physical and philosophical, of the most "advanced" industrialists of their era. During the 1880's and 1890's the Irish immigrants in Pennsylvania's hard-coal counties, who had seemed to George Korson almost biblical in their isolation, were learning such music-hall songs as "Down in a Coal Mine" from "Howerth's Hibernica," a traveling magic-lantern and vaudeville show.

This process of a commercial entertainment medium introducing a mine song into a camp continued at least through the 1950's, via Tennessee Ernie Ford's television program. I have already suggested that the intensely popular "Sixteen Tons" did not "catch on" within a folk society as did some previous numbers largely disseminated by radio and records, such as "The Dream of the Miner's Child." This contrast is mainly a statement that tradition itself must have life in the context of special groups.

I am aware that nearly all the separate songs chosen here will present problems in categorization and analysis to a few scholars, by virtue of the fact that these pieces were so intimately associated with the sound-recording industry. Like some folklorists, I have long accepted the notion that individual recorded songs entered tradition and became "folksongs" in much the same manner as did broadsides. However, I have also, in my introduction, advanced the term *poplore* in an attempt to cope with the complexities stemming from the changes wrought in folk society by industrialization. Poplore tells us that expressive forms disseminated by communications technology may enter the traditions of folk-like society, however changed. Each reader-listener will accept, reject, or modify this word in reference to two basic variables: his conception of the sound-recording industry's role in this century, and his conception of the individual's place in modern society.

To touch these points briefly, one's preconception of an individual as a member of folk society may not fit the fact that a contemporary worker in the United States, whether he lives in mountain cabin or ghetto tenement, has access to television and auto-

447

mobile, two of the most powerful tools in breaking the former stability of the folk. Our response may take two forms: a rejection of fact in favor of a preconceived model, or a redefinition of terminology. Just as each folklorist responds quite differently to his assessment of culture and personality interaction, each tends to differ in his judgment of the sound-recording process as a corrosive or creative force. The view of the phonograph as an enemy of tradition, treated in my introductory chapters, need not be restated here. Much of this work has stressed the positive aspects of the recording industry in preserving and extending folksong.

Conceptions of individuality and industrialism must be refashioned in future areas of American Studies. When scholars first encountered "exotic" blues, largely disseminated from the stage and by sound recording, they sought to place this expressive form in a frame of African primitivism or deep-South rurality. It is only recently that some observers have taken a hard look at the intimate connection between blues and industrialization. Anthropologist John Szwed has pointed to a modern view: "Blues arose as a popular music form in the early 1900's, the period of the first great Negro migrations north to the cities. . . . The formal and stylistic elements of the blues seem to symbolize newly emerging social patterns during the crisis period of urbanization. . . . By replacing the functions served by [rural] sacred music, the blues eased a transition from land-based, agrarian society to one based on mobile wage-labor urbanism."[8]

Similarly, Norman Cohen, in a consideration of parallel hillbilly material, has stated strongly the view that the recording's documentary function was itself welded to industry's advance:

> The same processes of industrialization leading to the confrontation of Negroes and whites in the coal camps and roundhouses — and thereby ultimately to the blend of Anglo-American and Afro-American traditions that characterized so much of early hillbilly music — were of course responsible for the development of the advances in mass media that disseminated the music. One could no more regard as fortuitous the rise of broadsides at just the right time to document the social revolution of the late Middle Ages. The broadsides were a part of the social revolution. Hillbilly music was a part of the industrial/social revolution of the late nineteenth and early twentieth century.[9]

MINERS

Until recently many folklorists have been content to talk about mass media's products entering tradition without studying the changed society in which the oral process itself operated. Some folklorists, despairing at the difficulty in redefining formal notions of folk society, have abandoned the folk in favor of the lore. I see no value in collapsing distinctions between the words *folk* and *lore*. Rather, I feel it incumbent upon scholars to attempt to keep definitions abreast of change. In plural America with its fantastic associational network, and with the relative freedom of individuals to play many roles, the task of labeling items as folklore becomes immensely complicated. Nevertheless, it is a task of tremendous challenge and one to which, I trust, this investigation of recorded mining songs has contributed.

I shall be happy if these separate case studies, as well as the concluding examples of some coal songs on 45 rpm discs and LPs, will in any way advance folklore and its related disciplines in the United States. Despite my attempt to use discography as a hu-

449

manistic craft, I am aware that in this book I have not related coal folksong to comparable graphic and literary endeavor. Ideally, we need for each society where men toil underground a survey of work-inspired art. I commend to readers of my studies the beautiful volume *Der Bergbau in der Kunst* (1958) by Heinrich Winkelmann and the parallel portfolio *Les Mines, et les Arts à travers les Âges* (1956) by Marcel Barbier. These breathtaking anthologies depict the miner in world art from ancient stone carvings to recent sketches and paintings by Henry Moore and Ben Shahn.[10] No comparable view of the miner in formal literature — poetry and fiction, short story and drama — is known to me. Obviously, a tremendous challenge lies ahead for all students of that artistic expression which springs from or comments on work.

Perhaps Patrick McBryde's *gob pile* term can now be invoked for a final time. The coal mined by "Uncle Jesse" James, Uncle George Jones, "Uncle Rob" Travis, James Adams, Dock Boggs, Jim Garland, and the many other diggers mentioned in this tome has long been reduced to ashes and cinder. It is itself waste — a form of gob. Even the blood on the coal, whether from mine disaster or labor strife, has been consumed in locomotive firebox, steel-mill blast furnace, and home fireplace, and it, too, is waste. But some of the energy expended by James and his brothers found concrete and lasting expression in "Roll Down the Line," "Nine Pound Hammer," and other pieces which I have treated.

At least for the present these songs are not ash and cinder; nor are they on any gob pile, actual or figurative. Essentially, sound recordings have helped preserve coal miners' energy and emotion — their folklore. Discs holding any songs are artifacts of plural function: capsules of verbal and musical data, marketable objects intended for profit, pleasure-giving devices, commentaries on the society in which records themselves are produced and purchased. Each reader-listener, close to or far from the grime and clatter of the mine, is free to select a wide variety of sound recordings in places as diverse as supermarket or archive. He is also free, according to his needs, to respond to any or all of the multiple roles inherent in sound recordings. In this sense, any particular disc is a tool that both holds and extends American tradition, that speaks on the question of our indivisibility.

450

1. For a portrait of McBryde and data on the start of the *Journal,* see Andrew Roy, *A History of the Coal Miners of the United States,* 3rd ed. (Columbus, Ohio, 1907), 278-280, 293-294.

2. McAlister Coleman and Stephen Raushenbush, *Red Neck* (New York, 1936), 251.

3. For responses by Mac's students, including mine, see John Greenway, ed., MacEdward Leach Memorial Issue," *Journal of American Folklore,* LXXXI (1968).

4. Tristram P. Coffin, "Mary Hamilton and the Anglo-American Ballad as an Art Form," in *The Critics and the Ballad,* ed. Tristram P. Coffin and Mac-Edward Leach (Carbondale, Ill., 1961), 245. See also Coffin's *The British Traditional Ballad in North America,* rev. ed. (Philadelphia, 1963), 114, 164.

5. Margaret Marshall, "Notes by the Way," *Nation,* CLX (Aug. 21, 1945), 447.

6. "New Pop Music Brew," *Cash Box,* XXVIII (June 3, 1967).

7. Paul Hemphill, "Kris Kristofferson Is the New Nashville Sound," *New York Times Magazine* (Dec. 6, 1970), 54.

8. John Szwed, "Musical Adaptation among Afro-Americans," *Journal of American Folklore,* LXXXII (1969), 117, 118.

9. Norman Cohen, "Hillbilly Music: Reissues," *Journal of American Folklore,* LXXXII (1969), 94.

10. In addition to Winkelmann and Barbier, I have cited five books on work-centered art in the bibliography: Baynes, Egbert, Gutman, Klingender, O'Connor.

ABANDONED MINE

Bibliography

Abrahams, Roger D., and George Foss. *Anglo-American Folksong Style*. Englewood Cliffs, N.J.: Prentice-Hall, 1968.

Adams, James Taylor. *Death in the Dark*. Big Laurel, Va.: Adams-Mullins Press, 1941.

Allen, John W. *It Happened in Southern Illinois*. Carbondale: Southern Illinois University Press, 1968.

Amburgey, Don Carlos. "Folk Songs," *Kentucky Folklore Record*, IX (1963), 11.

Ames, Russell. "Implications of Negro Folk Song," *Science and Society*, XV (1951), 171.

———. *The Story of American Folk Song*. New York: Grosset & Dunlap, 1955.

Anderson, E. W. *Choice Selections*. Cleveland, Tenn.: Holiness Church Evangel Office, ca. 1936.

Anderson, Geneva. "A Collection of Ballads and Songs from East Tennessee," master's thesis. Chapel Hill: University of North Carolina, 1932.

Anson, Charles F. "A History of the Labor Movement in West Virginia," thesis. Chapel Hill: University of North Carolina, 1940.

Armes, Ethel. *The Story of Coal and Iron in Alabama*. Birmingham: Chamber of Commerce, 1910.

Barbier, Marcel N. *Les Mines et les Arts à travers les Âges*. Saint-Étienne (Loire): Société de l'Industrie Minérale, 1956.

Barnicle, Mary Elizabeth. "The Story Behind This American Ballad," *People's Songs,* II (July, 1947), 12; reprinted in *Reprints from the People's Songs Bulletin.* New York: Oak Publications, 1961, 85.

Baroni, Monsignor Geno. "I'm a Pig, Too," *Steel Labor* (Sept., 1970), 9.

Barton, William Eleazar. "Recent Negro Melodies," in *The Negro and His Folklore in Nineteenth-Century Periodicals,* ed. Bruce Jackson. Austin: University of Texas Press, 1967, 302.

Bascom, Louise Rand. "Ballads and Songs of Western North Carolina," *Journal of American Folklore,* XXII (1909), 249.

Bastin, S. L., and S. A. Morey. *History of Coal Mining in Laurel County, Kentucky, 1750-1944.* London, Ky.: The Sentinel-Echo, 1944.

Bayard, Samuel Preston. "The British Folk Tradition," in *Pennsylvania Songs and Legends,* ed. George Korson. Philadelphia: University of Pennsylvania Press, 1949.

Baynes, Ken, and Alan Robinson. *Work: Art and Society, Two.* Boston: Boston Book and Art, 1970.

"Beaming Tennessee Ernie Ford Is Presented with a Gold Record . . . ," *Record* (Jan. 9, 1956) [photograph in Capitol Records publicity brochure].

Belden, Henry M. *Ballads and Songs Collected by the Missouri Folk-Lore Society.* Columbia: University of Missouri Studies, 1940.

Belissary, Constantine G. "Behavior Patterns and Aspirations of the Urban Working Classes in Tennessee in the Immediate Post–Civil War Era," *Tennessee Historical Quarterly,* XIV (1955), 24.

Bernstein, Barton J. *Towards a New Past.* New York: Pantheon, 1968.

Bernstein, Irving. *The Lean Years.* Boston: Houghton Mifflin, 1960.

Blackard, Malcolm. "Wilmer Watts and the Lonely Eagles," *JEMF Quarterly,* V (Winter, 1969), 126.

Boatright, Mody C., and William Owen. *Tales from the Derrick Floor.* Garden City, N.Y.: Doubleday, 1970.

Bokelman, Marina. "The Coon Can Game: A Blues Ballad Tradition," master's thesis. Los Angeles: University of California, 1968.

Botkin, Ben. "Dust on the Folklorists," *Journal of American Folklore,* LVII (1944), 139.

———. "George Korson (1899-1967)," *New York Folklore Quarterly,* XXIII (1967), 237.

———. *A Treasury of Southern Folklore.* New York: Crown, 1949.

———. *A Treasury of Western Folklore.* New York: Crown, 1951.

Bowen, Charles G. "Buell Kazee: The Genuine Article," *Sing Out,* XX (Sept., 1970), 13.

Bowen, Eli. *The Pictorial Sketch-Book of Pennsylvania.* Philadelphia: Willis P. Hazard, 1852.

454

Brand, Oscar. *The Ballad Mongers.* New York: Funk & Wagnalls, 1962.

Brodeur, Arthur G. "The Robert Winslow Gordon Collection of American Folksong," *Oregon Folklore Bulletin,* I, no. 4 (1962), 1.

Broehl, Wayne G., Jr. *The Molly Maguires.* Cambridge: Harvard University Press, 1964.

Bronson, Bertrand H. *The Ballad as Song.* Berkeley: University of California Press, 1969.

——. *The Traditional Tunes of the Child Ballads,* 4 vols. Princeton: Princeton University Press, 1959-71.

Broonzy, William. *Big Bill Blues.* New York: Oak Publications, 1964.

Brophy, John. *A Miner's Life.* Madison: University of Wisconsin Press, 1964.

[Brown]. *The Frank C. Brown Collection of North Carolina Folklore,* 7 vols. Durham: Duke University Press, 1952-61.

Brown, Sterling A. *Southern Road.* New York: Harcourt, Brace, 1932.

Bubka, Tony. "The Harlan County Coal Strike of 1931," *Labor History,* XI (1970), 41.

Burlin, Natalie Curtis. *Negro Folk-Songs,* Hampton Series, 4 vols. New York: G. Schirmer, 1918-19.

Burns, Walter Noble. *The Saga of Billy the Kid.* Garden City, N.Y.: Doubleday, 1926.

Burton, Thomas G., and Ambrose N. Manning. *The East Tennessee State University Collection of Folklore: Folksongs.* Johnson City: East Tennessee State University Press, 1967.

Bush, Michael E. *Folk Songs of Central West Virginia.* Glenville: Folk Festival, 1969.

Cable, George Washington. "The Convict Lease System in the Southern States," *Century Magazine,* XXVII (Feb., 1884), 582; reprinted in *The Silent South.* New York: Charles Scribner's, 1885, 113.

——. "The Freedman's Case in Equity," *Century Magazine,* XXIX (Jan., 1885), 409; reprinted in *The Silent South,* 1.

" 'Cajan' Folk Song Recorded by General Phono Corp.," *Talking Machine World,* XXI (July, 1925), 12.

Carnegie Commission on Educational Television. *Public Television.* New York: Harper & Row, 1967.

Catalogue of Copyright Entries: Musical Compositions. Washington: Library of Congress, Copyright Office, various years.

"Catching Convicts," *United Mine Workers Journal* (Apr. 23, 1891), 7.

Caudill, Harry. "The Appalachian Tragedy," *New York Review of Books,* XV (Nov. 19, 1970), 17.

——. *Night Comes to the Cumberlands.* Boston: Little, Brown, 1963.

Chaplin, Ralph. *When the Leaves Come Out*. Cleveland: Ralph Chaplin, 1917.

————. *Wobbly*. Chicago: University of Chicago Press, 1948.

Chappell, Louis W. *John Henry: A Folk-Lore Study*. Jena, Germany: Frommannsche Verlag, 1933.

Chappell, Winifred L. "Embattled Miners," *Christian Century*, XLVIII (Aug. 19, 1931), 1043.

Charters, Samuel. "Abbe Niles: A Pioneer Jazz Critic of the '20s," *Jazz Review* (May, 1959), 25.

————. *The Bluesmen*. New York: Oak Publications, 1967.

————, and Leonard Kunstadt. *Jazz: A History of the New York Scene*. Garden City, N.Y.: Doubleday, 1962.

Chidakel, Adele. "Folklore Smudged with Coal Dust," *Washington Star Magazine* (Feb. 16, 1958), 28.

Clifton, Bill. *150 Old Time Folk and Gospel Songs*. North Wilkesboro, N.C.: Adams Printing, 1956.

The Coal Miner and His Family. Washington: Department of Interior, Coal Mines Administration, 1947.

Coffin, Tristram P. *The British Traditional Ballad in North America*, rev. ed. Philadelphia: American Folklore Society, 1963.

————. "Mary Hamilton and the Anglo-American Ballad as an Art Form," in *The Critics and the Ballad*, ed. Tristram P. Coffin and MacEdward Leach. Carbondale: Southern Illinois University Press, 1961, 245.

Cohen, John, and Mike Seeger. *The New Lost City Ramblers Song Book*. New York: Oak Publications, 1964.

Cohen, Norman. "Railroad Folksongs on Record — a Survey," *New York Folklore Quarterly*, XXVI (1970), 91.

————. "Record Reviews: Hillbilly Music: Reissues," *Journal of American Folklore*, LXXXII (1969), 90.

————. "Tapescript Interview with Welby Toomey," *JEMF Quarterly*, V (Summer, 1969), 63.

————, and others. *The Early Recording Career of Ernest V. "Pop" Stoneman: A Bio-Discography*. Los Angeles: John Edwards Memorial Foundation, 1968.

Cohn, Lawrence. Brochure notes to *Leadbelly: the Library of Congress Recordings* (Elektra EKL 301/2).

Coleman, McAlister, and Stephen Raushenbush. *Red Neck*. New York: Harrison Smith & Robert Haas, 1936.

"Columbia Co. Recording in Chicago," *Talking Machine World*, XX (Sept., 1924), 126.

Combs, Josiah H. *Folk-Songs of the Southern United States*, ed. D. K. Wilgus. Austin: University of Texas Press, 1967.

"A Communist Organizer in Court," *Daily Worker* (Nov. 1, 1935), 5.

Conn, Harry. "Labor Songs . . . ," *RWDSU Record* (Mar. 18, 1956), 13.

Cox, John Harrington. " 'The Yew Pine Mountains,' a 'John Hardy' Ballad," *American Speech*, II (1927), 226.

Crabtree, Lillian G. *"Songs and Ballads Sung in Overton County, Tennessee,"* master's thesis. Nashville: George Peabody College, 1936.

Crabtree, Marean. "The History of Grundy County," five-page typescript, received Jan. 3, 1969. Green files.

Crawford, Captain Jack. *Lariattes.* Sigourney, Iowa: William A. Bell, 1904.

————. *The Poet Scout.* San Francisco: H. Keller, 1879.

Creason, Joe. "One-Ton Honor Given Composer of 'Sixteen Tons,' " *Louisville Courier Journal* (June 30, 1956).

————. "Sixteen Tons — What Do You Get?," *Louisville Courier Journal Magazine* (July 15, 1956), 13.

Creighton, Helen. *Songs and Ballads from Nova Scotia.* Toronto: J. M. Dent, 1933.

Cumberland Chronicle [Huntsville, Scott County, Tenn.] (Apr. 5, 1890).

Dawkins, Jim. "Poster Depicts 'Old Time Kentucky Fiddler,' " *Ashland Daily Independent* (Jan. 22, 1969).

Day, John F. *Bloody Ground.* Garden City, N.Y.: Doubleday, 1941.

Dean, M. C. *The Flying Cloud.* Virginia, Minn.: The Quickprint, 1922.

"Death Takes Bill Day, Fiction's Singin' Fiddler," *Louisville Courier Journal* (May 8, 1942).

Delaunay, Charles. *Hot Discography.* Paris: Hot Jazz, 1936.

Denisoff, R. Serge. *Great Day Coming.* Urbana: University of Illinois Press, 1971.

Dennis, Norman, and others. *Coal Is Our Life: An Analysis of a Yorkshire Mining Community.* London: Eyre & Spottiswoode, 1956.

Dix, Keith. "Mother Jones," *Peoples' Appalachia,* I (June, 1970), 6.

Dixon, Robert M. W., and John Godrich. *Recording the Blues.* London: Studio Vista, 1970.

Doerflinger, William Main. *Shantymen and Shantyboys.* New York: Macmillan, 1951.

Doherty, Herbert J., Jr. "Voices of Protest from the New South, 1875–1910," *Mississippi Valley Historical Review,* XLII (1955), 45.

Dombrowski, James. *The Early Days of Christian Socialism in America.* New York: Columbia University Press, 1936.

————. "Fire in the Hole," unpublished manuscript, ca. 1941. Copies at Tuskegee Institute, Alabama, and in Green files.

"Dombrowski Retires as SCEF Executive," *Southern Patriot,* XXIV (Feb., 1966).

457

Doussard, James. "Appalachian Poverty Is Impressive," *Louisville Courier Journal* (Nov. 27, 1968).

Dreiser, Theodore. *Harlan Miners Speak.* New York: Harcourt, Brace, 1932; reprinted, New York: da Capo Press, 1970.

Drifting Pioneers Song Folio Number One. Portland, Ore.: American music, 1939.

Duncan, Ruby. *"Ballads and Folk Songs Collected in Northern Hamilton County,"* master's thesis. Knoxville: University of Tennessee, 1939.

Eby, James Brian. *The Geology and Coal Resources of the Coal-Bearing Portion of Wise and Scott Counties, Virginia.* Baltimore: J. B. Eby, 1922.

Edwards, John. "Buell Kazee," *Caravan,* no. 17 (June, 1959), 42.

Egbert, Donald Drew. *Socialism and American Art.* Princeton: Princeton University Press, 1967.

Elwood, Philip. "Folk Music Goes on a Rock Basis," *San Francisco Examiner* (July 1, 1967), 10.

Emrich, Duncan. "The Song Prospector," *Mines Magazine,* XXXII (Jan.-Aug., 1942).

————. "Songs of the Western Miners," *California Folklore Quarterly,* I (1942), 213.

"Enigmatic Folksongs of the Southern Underworld," *Current Opinion,* LXVII (Sept., 1919), 165.

"Entertainer Succumbs," *Ashland Daily Independent* (May 7, 1942).

Erskine, Gilbert. "Jazz Books and Comments," in *Down Beat's Music '63: Eighth Yearbook* (1963), 85.

Fahey, John A. "A Textual and Musicological Analysis of the Repertoire of Charley Patton," master's thesis. Los Angeles: Uuiversity of California, 1966.

Fay, Albert H. *A Glossary of the Mining and Mineral Industry,* Bulletin 95. Washington: Department of Interior, Bureau of Mines, 1920.

Federal Music Project. *Folk Songs from East Kentucky.* Work Projects Administration, ca. 1939.

Fife, Austin. "The Prayer Book in Cards," *Western Folklore,* XXVII (1968), 208.

Fishwick, Marshall. "Folklore, Fakelore, and Poplore," *Saturday Review,* L (Aug. 26, 1967), 20.

Foner, Philip S. *History of the Labor Movement in the United States,* II. New York: International Publishers, 1955.

Ford, Ernest J. *This Is My Story — This Is My Song.* Englewood Cliffs, N.J.: Prentice-Hall, 1963.

Ford, George W. *Second Annual Report of the Commissioner of Labor and Inspector of Mines to His Excellency, Governor John P. Buchanan.* Nashville: Marshall & Bruce, 1893.

————. *Special Report of the Commissioner of Labor and the Inspector of Mines to His Excellency John P. Buchanan.* Nashville: Marshall & Bruce, 1891.

Foreman, Ronald C., Jr. "Jazz and Race Records, 1920-32," thesis. Urbana: University of Illinois, 1968.

Foster, George M. "What Is a Peasant?," in *Peasant Society: A Reader,* ed. Jack M. Potter and others. Boston: Little, Brown, 1967, 2.

————. "What Is Folk Culture?," *American Anthropologist,* L (1953), 159.

"Fourth Man Makes the Trio Tick," *Business Week* (Feb. 23, 1963), 57.

Fowke, Edith, and Joe Glazer. *Songs of Work and Freedom.* Chicago: Roosevelt University, 1960.

Frankenstein, Alfred. "Britannic Ballads — and Other Recorded Folk Songs," *San Francisco Chronicle, This World* (Feb. 10, 1957), 20.

————. "George Alley: A Study in Modern Folk Lore," *Musical Courier,* CIV (Apr. 16, 1932), 6.

Franklin, Ben A. "The Scandal of Death and Injury in the Mines," *New York Times Magazine* (Mar. 30, 1969), 25.

Fuller, Justin. "History of the Tennessee Coal, Iron and Railroad Company, 1852-1907," thesis. Chapel Hill: University of North Carolina, 1966.

Fuson, Harvey H. *Ballads of the Kentucky Highlands.* London: Mitre Press, 1931.

Gaisberg, Fred W. *The Music Goes Round.* New York: Macmillan, 1943.

Gelatt, Roland. *The Fabulous Phonograph,* rev. ed. New York: Appleton-Century, 1965.

Gellert, Lawrence. *Negro Songs of Protest.* New York: Carl Fisher, 1936.

"Gennett Records Advance Release: October 15, 1928." Richmond, Ind.: Starr Piano Company [single sheet printed announcement].

"George G. Korson, Folklorist, Dead," *New York Times* (May 25, 1967), 47.

Glassie, Henry. "MacEdward Leach, 1892-1967," *Journal of American Folklore,* LXXXI (1968), 107.

Glazer, Joe. Liner notes to *Songs of Coal* (Sound Studios 12-1137).

Gleason, Ralph J. "The Lively Arts," *San Francisco Chronicle* (Jan. 3, 1956), 19.

Glenn, L. C. *The Northern Tennessee Coal Field,* Bulletin 33 B. Nashville: Department of Conservation, Division of Geology, 1925.

Glusman, Preval. "Harry Simms — a Young Revolutionist," *Daily Worker* (May 8, 1934), 5.

Godbout, Oscar. "On TV from Hollywood," *New York Times* (Jan. 8, 1956), sec. 2, 11.

459

Godrich, John, and Robert M. W. Dixon. *Blues & Gospel Records 1902-1942,* rev. ed. London: Storyville Publications, 1969.

Going, Allen J. "The Agrarian Revolt," in *Writing Southern History,* ed. Arthur S. Link and Rembert W. Patrick. Baton Rouge: Louisiana State University Press, 1965, 362.

Goldstein, Kenneth S. "Bowdlerization and Expurgation: Academic and Folk," *Journal of American Folklore,* LXXX (1967), 374.

Gordon, Robert Winslow. *Folk-Songs of America.* New York: National Service Bureau, 1938.

————. "Folksongs of America: Jail Ballads," *New York Times Magazine* (June 19, 1927), 15.

————. "Old Songs That Men Have Sung," *Adventure,* XLI-LXIV (July 10, 1923–Sept. 15, 1927).

Gould, Jack. "TV: Appalachia Poverty Documented," *New York Times* (Nov. 13, 1968), 22.

Govan, Gilbert E., and James W. Livingood. *The Chattanooga Country: 1540-1951.* New York: E. P. Dutton, 1952.

Grainger, Porter, and Bob Ricketts. *How to Play and Sing the Blues Like the Phonograph and Stage Artists.* New York: Jack Mills, 1926.

Grauman, Lawrence, Jr. " 'That Little Ugly Running Sore,' " *Filson Club Historical Quarterly,* XXXVI (Oct., 1962), 340.

Green, Archie. "American Labor Lore: Its Meanings and Uses," *Industrial Relations,* IV (1965), 51.

————. Brochure notes to *Girl of Constant Sorrow* (Folk-Legacy FSA 26).

————. Brochure notes to *Railroad Songs and Ballads* (Library of Congress AFS L 61).

————. Brochure notes to *Tipple, Loom & Rail* (Folkways FH 5273).

————. "A Carter Family Bibliography," *Sunny Side Sentinel,* no. 2 (Jan., 1963), 3.

————. "The Carter Family's 'Coal Miner's Blues,' " *Southern Folklore Quarterly,* XXV (1961), 226.

————. "The Death of Mother Jones," *Labor History,* I (1960), 68.

————. "A Discography (LP) of American Labor Union Songs," *New York Folklore Quarterly,* XVII (1961), 186.

————. "A Discography of American Coal Miners' Songs," *Labor History,* II (1961), 101.

————. "Folksong on Records," *Western Folklore,* XXVII (1968), 68.

————. "Hillbilly Music: Source and Symbol," *Journal of American Folklore,* LXXVIII (1965), 204.

————. Liner notes to *The Railroad in Folksong* (RCA Victor LPV 532).

———. "Record Review: *Songs and Ballads of the Bituminous Miners* and *Songs and Ballads of the Anthracite Miners*," *Ethnomusicology*, X (1966), 361.

———. "The Workers in the Dawn: Labor Lore," in *Our Living Traditions*, ed. Tristram P. Coffin. New York: Basic Books, 1968, 251.

———, spec. ed. "Aunt Molly Jackson Memorial Issue," *Kentucky Folklore Record*, VII (Oct., 1961).

———, and Eugene Earle. Brochure notes to *The Carolina Tar Heels* (Folk-Legacy FSA 24).

Green, Fletcher Melvin. "Some Aspects of the Convict Lease System in the United States," in *Essays in Southern History*, ed. F. M. Green. Chapel Hill: University of North Carolina Press, 1949, 122.

Greene, Daniel W. " 'Fiddle and I': The Story of Franz Rickaby," *Journal of American Folklore*, LXXXI (1968), 316.

Greenleaf, Elisabeth B. *Ballads and Sea Songs of Newfoundland*. Cambridge: Harvard University Press, 1933.

Greenway, John. *American Folksongs of Protest*. Philadelphia: University of Pennsylvania Press, 1953.

———. "American Folksongs of Social and Economic Protest," thesis. Philadelphia: University of Pennsylvania, 1951.

———. "George Korson (1900-1967)," *Journal of American Folklore*, LXXX (1967), 343.

———, ed. "MacEdward Leach Memorial Issue," *Journal of American Folklore*, LXXXI (1968).

Gregg, Robert. *Origin and Development of the Tennessee Coal, Iron & Railroad Company*. New York: Newcomen Society of England, American Branch, 1948.

Grimm, Karen. "Prolegomenon to a Catalog for the Robert W. Gordon Collection of American Folksong," *Northwest Folklore*, II, no. 1 (1967), 8.

Guthrie, Woody. *American Folksong*. New York: Oak Publications, 1961.

———. "Songs of Woody Guthrie," typescript manuscript, ca. 1941. Original at Library of Congress, Archive of American Folk Song, Washington.

Gutman, Herbert G. "The Negro and the United Mine Workers of America," in *The Negro and the American Labor Movement*, ed. Julius Jacobson. Garden City, N.Y.: Anchor Books, 1968.

Gutman, Judith Mara. *Lewis W. Hine and the American Social Conscience*. New York: Walker, 1967.

Gysel, Dean. "An American Tragedy on TV," *Chicago Daily News, Panorama* (Nov. 9, 1968), 31.

Haden, Walter D. "If I Had Wings Like an Angel: The Life of Vernon Dalhart," in *Country Music Who's Who, 1970*, ed. Thurston Moore. New York: Record World, 1970, Part 7, 3.

Halpert, Herbert. "Some Recorded American Folk Song," *American Music Lover*, II (Nov., 1936), 196.

Hamill, Dorothy. "Bowman Band Recalls 'The Good Old Days,' " *Johnson City* [Tenn.] *Press-Chronicle* (Feb. 5, 1960), 2A.

Hand, Wayland. "American Occupational and Industrial Folklore: The Miner," in *Kontakte und Grenzen: Probleme der Volks-, Kultur- und Sozialforschung*, ed. Hans Foltin. Göttingen: Geburtstag, 1969.

———. "California Miners' Folklore: Above Ground," *California Folklore Quarterly*, I (1942), 25.

———. "George Korson and the Study of American Mining Lore," *Keystone Folklore Quarterly*, forthcoming 1971.

———, and others. "Songs of the Butte Miners," *Western Folklore*, IX (1950), 1.

Handy, William C. *Father of the Blues*. New York: Macmillan, 1941.

———, ed. *Blues: An Anthology*. New York: Albert & Charles Boni, 1926.

Hareven, Tamara K. *Anonymous Americans*. Englewood Cliffs, N.J.: Prentice-Hall, 1971.

Harrington, Stephanie. "Living With It," [New York] *Village Voice* (Nov. 21, 1968).

Harris, Evelyn, and Frank Krebs. *From Humble Beginnings*. Charleston: West Virginia Labor History Publishing Fund, 1960.

Harrison, Robert W. *Levee Districts and Levee Building in Mississippi*. State College: Mississippi Agricultural Experiment Station, 1951.

Heilfurth, Gerhard. *Das Bergmannslied: Wesen, Leben, Funktion*. Kassel: Bärenreiter Verlag, 1954.

———. "George Korson — an Appreciation," *Keystone Folklore Quarterly*, forthcoming 1971.

Hemphill, Paul. "Kris Kristofferson Is the New Nashville Sound," *New York Times Magazine* (Dec. 6, 1970), 54.

———. *The Nashville Sound*. New York: Simon & Schuster, 1970.

Henry, Mellinger E. *Folk-Songs from the Southern Highlands*. New York: J. J. Augustin, 1938.

Herling, John. "Women's Lib — Bah," *John Herling's Labor Letter* [Washington] (Sept. 26, 1970).

"High-Priced Pea Picker," *Time*, LXIX (May 27, 1957), 72.

Hille, Waldemar. *The People's Song Book*. New York: Boni & Gaer, 1948.

Hindley, Charles. *The Life and Times of James Catnach*. London: Reeves & Turner, 1878.

"A Hit on the Double," *Newsweek,* XLVI (Nov. 28, 1955), 110.

"Housewives' Hillbilly," *TV Guide,* IV (Aug. 25, 1956), 17.

Hubler, Richard G. "That Pea-Pickin', Philosophizin' Tennessee Ernie," *Coronet,* XL (Aug., 1956), 115.

Hugill, Stan. *Shanties from the Seven Seas.* London: Routledge & Kegan Paul, 1961.

Humphrey, H. B. *Historical Summary of Coal-Mine Explosions in the United States, 1810-1958,* Bulletin 586. Washington: Department of Interior, Bureau of Mines, 1960.

Hutson, Andrew C., Jr. "The Coal Miners' Insurrections of 1891 in Anderson County, Tennessee," *East Tennessee Historical Society's Publications,* VII (1935), 103.

———. "The Overthrow of the Convict Lease System in Tennessee," *East Tennessee Historical Society's Publications,* VIII (1936), 82.

"The Insurrection in Tennessee," *Harper's Weekly,* XXXVI (Aug. 27, 1892), 834.

"I Reside Wherever . . . ," *New York Times Magazine* (May 10, 1970), 17 [ILGWU advertisement].

Ives, Burl. *Song in America.* New York: Duell, Sloan & Pearce, 1962.

Ives, Edward. *Lawrence Doyle: Farmer-Poet of Prince Edward Island.* Orono: University of Maine Press, 1971.

Jenkin, A. K. Hamilton. *The Cornish Miner.* London: George Allen & Unwin, 1927.

"John Hart Is Held under Bond of $5000," *Pineville* [Ky.] *Sun* (Oct. 31, 1935), 1.

Johnson, Alva. "Tenor on Horseback," *Saturday Evening Post,* CCXII (Sept. 2, 1939), 18.

Johnson, Guy B. *John Henry: Tracking Down a Negro Legend.* Chapel Hill: University of North Carolina Press, 1929.

Jones, Howard Mumford. "Book Review: *American Folksongs of Protest,*" *Midwest Folklore,* IV (1954), 48.

Jones, LeRoi. *Blues People.* New York: William Morrow, 1963.

Jones, Mary Harris. *Autobiography of Mother Jones,* ed. Mary Field Parton. Chicago: Charles H. Kerr, 1925; reprinted, New York: Arno Press, 1969.

Joyce, Patrick Weston. *Old Irish Folk Music and Songs.* New York: Longmans, Green, 1909.

Jydstrup, Doug, and others. "The Paramount 3000 Numerical Listing," *Blue Yodeler,* nos. 7-15 (1967-68).

Kael, Pauline. "The Current Cinema: Duds" ["The Molly Maguires"], *New Yorker,* XLV (Feb. 7, 1970), 91.

Kahn, Ed. "The Carter Family: A Reflection of Changes in Society," thesis. Los Angeles: University of California, 1970.

————. "Hillbilly Music: Source and Resource," *Journal of American Folklore*, LXXVIII (1965), 257.

————. "Merle Travis: Folk Informant," eighteen-page typescript, 1965. Duplicate in Green files.

Kauffmann, Stanley. "Stanley Kauffmann on Films: 'The Molly Maguires,' " *New Republic*, CLXII (Feb. 21, 1970), 20.

Kay, George W. "Those Fabulous Gennetts," *Record Changer* (June, 1953), 4.

Kazee, Buell. "The Wagoner's Lad," unpublished manuscript, ca. 1949. Duplicate in Green files.

Keil, Charles. *Urban Blues*. Chicago: University of Chicago Press, 1966.

Keiser, John H. "The Union Miners Cemetery at Mt. Olive, Illinois," *Journal of the Illinois State Historical Society*, LXII (1969), 229.

Kincaid, Bradley. *My Favorite Mountain Ballads and Old Time Songs, Book 5*. Pittsburgh: Radio Station KDKA, 1932.

Kingsley, Walter. "Miss Gray's Sad Air Cheers Broadway," *New York Herald* (July 12, 1919), sec. 3, 12.

————. "Walter Kingsley Writes . . . ," *New York Sun* (Aug. 3, 1919), sec. 4, 2.

Kirkland, Edwin C. "A Check List of the Titles of Tennessee Folk Songs," *Journal of American Folklore*, LIX (1946), 423.

Klingender, Francis D. *Art and the Industrial Revolution*. London: Noel Carrington, 1947.

Knipe, Edward E. "Change in Mining Technology and Workers Interaction," paper read at International Seminar on Social Change in the Mining Community, Jackson's Mill, W.Va., Oct., 1967. Duplicate in Green files.

————, and Helen M. Lewis. "The Impact of Coal Mining on the Traditional Mountain Sub-Culture," paper read at Southern Anthropological Society, New Orleans, 1969. Duplicate in Green files.

————, and Helen M. Lewis. *Toward a Methodology of Studying Coal Miners' Attitudes*, Open-File Report 8-69. Washington: Department of Interior, Bureau of Mines, 1968.

Kohn, Lucile. "Pioneer Youth and the Labor Movement," *Labor Age*, XXI (Nov., 1932), 20.

————. "Solidarity in Kanawha Valley," *Labor Age*, XX (Sept., 1931), 11.

————. "There Are Classes in the West Virginia Hills," *Labor Age*, XXI (Sept., 1932), 11.

Kornadt, H. J., ed. *Social Change in Mining Communities*. Saarbrücken: University of the Saar, 1970.

Kornbluh, Joyce. *Rebel Voices*. Ann Arbor: University of Michigan Press, 1964.

Korson, George. *Black Rock: Mining Folklore of the Pennsylvania Dutch*. Baltimore: Johns Hopkins Press, 1960.

―――. Brochure notes to *Songs and Ballads of the Anthracite Miners* (Library of Congress AFS L 16).

―――. Brochure notes to *Songs and Ballads of the Bituminous Miners* (Library of Congress AFS L 60).

―――. *Coal Dust on the Fiddle,* 2nd printing. Hatboro, Pa.: Folklore Associates, 1965.

―――. "A Communication from Folklorist George Korson," *United Mine Workers Journal* (Jan. 15, 1965), 18.

―――. "A History of the United Mine Workers of America," *United Mine Workers Journal* (May, 1965–July, 1967).

―――. *Minstrels of the Mine Patch,* 3rd printing. Hatboro, Pa.: Folklore Associates, 1964.

―――. " 'My Sweetheart's the Mule in the Mines': Memories of Tom and Maggie Hill," in *Two Penny Ballads and Four Dollar Whiskey,* ed. Kenneth S. Goldstein and Robert H. Byington. Hatboro, Pa.: Folklore Associates, 1966, 1.

―――. *Songs and Ballads of the Anthracite Miner*. New York: Frederick H. Hitchcock, 1927.

Ladd, Bill. "Beech Creek Coal Miner Gave Son Idea for 'Sixteen Tons' Song Hit," *Louisville Courier Journal* (Nov. 30, 1955).

―――. "The Home Town Smokes Travis Out," *Louisville Courier Journal Magazine* (Nov. 16, 1947), 6.

Langdon, Emma. *The Cripple Creek Strike*. Denver: Great Western Press, 1908; reprinted, New York: Arno Press, 1969.

Lantz, Herman R. *People of Coal Town*. New York: Columbia University Press, 1958.

Larkin, Margaret. "Revolutionary Music," *New Masses,* VIII (Feb., 1933), 27.

―――. *Singing Cowboy*. New York: Knopf, 1931.

Lauck, Rex. *John L. Lewis*. Washington: United Mine Workers of America, 1952.

―――. "Merle Travis Day," *United Mine Workers Journal* (July 15, 1956), 10.

Laws, G. Malcolm, Jr. *American Balladry from British Broadsides*. Philadelphia: American Folklore Society, 1957.

465

————. *Native American Balladry,* rev. ed. Philadelphia: American Folklore Society, 1964.

Leach, MacEdward, and Horace Beck. "Songs from Rappahannock County, Virginia," *Journal of American Folklore,* LXIII (1950), 258.

Leeds, Joseph. "The Miners Called Her Mother," *Masses and Mainstream,* III (Mar., 1950), 38.

Le Mon, Melvin. "Pennsylvania Anthracite Miners' Folk-Songs," thesis. Rochester: Eastman School of Music, 1941.

————, and George Korson. *The Miner Sings.* New York: J. Fischer, 1936.

Levy, Lester S. *Grace Notes in American History.* Norman: University of Oklahoma Press, 1967.

Lewis, Helen M. "The Changing Communities in the Southern Appalachian Coal Fields," paper read at International Seminar on Social Change in the Mining Community, Jackson's Mill, W.Va., Oct., 1967. Duplicate in Green files.

————. "Occupational Roles and Family Roles, a Study of Coal Miners," thesis. Lexington: University of Kentucky, 1970.

————, and Edward E. Knipe. "The Sociological Impact of Mechanization on Coal Miners and Their Families," *Proceedings of the Council of Economics, American Institute of Mining, Metallurgical, and Petroleum Engineers* (1968), 268.

Lewis, Lloyd. "Last of the Troubadours," in *It Takes All Kinds.* New York: Harcourt, Brace, 1947, 73.

————. *Myths after Lincoln.* New York: Blue Ribbon Books, 1929.

Library of Congress, Copyright Office. *Catalogue of Copyright Entries: Musical Compositions.* Washington: Government Printing Office, various years.

————, Music Division. *Check-list of Recorded Songs in the English Language in the Archive of American Folk Song to July, 1940.* Washington: The Archive, 1942.

Lindsley, John Berrien. *On Prison Discipline and Penal Legislation.* Nashville: Robertson Association, 1874.

Lingenfelter, Richard E., and others. *Songs of the American West.* Berkeley: University of California Press, 1968.

Lippard, Lucy R. *The Graphic Work of Philip Evergood.* New York: Crown, 1966.

Lippincott, Martha Shepard. "To Mother Mary Jones," *Federation News* (Jan. 17, 1931), 10.

Lively, Gerald J. "Mother Jones," *Solidarity* (May 10, 1913), 3.

Lloyd, A. L. "Book Review: *Das Bergmannslied,*" *Journal of the International Folk Music Council,* IX (1957), 87.

466

————. *Come All Ye Bold Miners.* London: Lawrence & Wishart, 1952.

————. *Folk Song in England.* New York: International Publishers, 1967.

Lomax, Alan. "The Best of the Ballads," *Vogue,* CVIII (Dec. 15, 1946), 208.

————. *The Folk Songs of North America.* Garden City, N.Y.: Doubleday, 1960.

————. "List of American Folk Songs on Commercial Records," in *Report of the Committee of the Conference on Inter-American Relations in the Field of Music,* ed. William Berrien. Washington: Department of State, 1940, 126.

————, and others. *Hard Hitting Songs for Hard-Hit People.* New York: Oak Publications, 1967.

Lomax, John A. *Adventures of a Ballad Hunter.* New York: Macmillan, 1947.

————. *Cowboy Songs and Other Frontier Ballads.* New York: Sturgis & Walton, 1910.

————, and Alan Lomax. *American Ballads and Folk Songs.* New York: Macmillan, 1934.

————, and Alan Lomax. *Folk Song U.S.A.* New York: Duell, Sloan & Pearce, 1947.

————, and Alan Lomax. *Negro Songs as Sung by Leadbelly.* New York: Macmillan, 1936.

Lumpkin, Ben Gray. "Book Review: *American Folksongs of Protest,*" *Western Folklore,* XIII (1954), 142.

Luther, Edward T. *The Coal Resources of Tennessee,* Bulletin 63. Nashville: Department of Conservation, Division of Geology, 1959.

McBryde, Patrick. " 'Slack' from the Secretary's 'Gob Pile,' " *United Mine Workers Journal* (Apr. 16-30, 1891).

McCarthy, Albert, and others. *Jazz on Record.* London: Hanover House, 1968.

McCormick, Allen. "Development of the Coal Industry of Grundy County, Tennessee," master's thesis. Nashville: George Peabody College, 1934.

McCulloh, Judith. "Hillbilly Records and Tune Transcriptions," *Western Folklore,* XXVI (1967), 225.

————. " 'In the Pines': The Melodic Textual Identity of an American Lyric Folksong Cluster," thesis. Bloomington: Indiana University, 1970.

McDaniel, William R. *Grand Ole Opry.* New York: Greenberg, 1952.

MacKenzie, John. "Herwin," *78 Quarterly,* I (Autumn, 1967–[Winter], 1968).

Mahony, Dan. *The Columbia 13/14000-D Series: A Numerical Listing.* Stanhope, N.J.: Walter C. Allen, 1961.

Malone, Bill C. *Country Music, U.S.A.: A Fifty-Year History.* Austin: University of Texas Press, 1968.

"A Man with Staying Power," *Southern Patriot,* XXI (Nov., 1963).

Marshall, Margaret. "Notes by the Way," *Nation,* CLX (Aug. 21, 1945), 447.

Martin, Pete. "I Call on Tennessee Ernie Ford," *Saturday Evening Post,* CCXXX (Sept. 28, 1957), 124.

Mason, Robert. "Folk Songs and Folk Tales of Cannon County, Tennessee," master's thesis. Nashville: George Peabody College, 1939.

Mathews, Mitford M. *A Dictionary of Americanisms,* 2 vols. Chicago: University of Chicago Press, 1951.

A Medical Survey of the Bituminous-Coal Mining Industry. Washington: Department of Interior, Coal Mines Administration, 1947.

"Merle Travis Biography." Capitol Records Information Bureau (ca. 1946) [two-page mimeographed release].

"Merle Travis Biography." Capitol Records Information Bureau (1949) [two-page mimeographed release].

"Merle Travis' 'Sixteen Tons' Took Eight Years to Become Smash Hit," *Music Views* (Jan., 1956), 4 [Capitol Records publicity magazine].

Merriam, Alan P. *A Bibliography of Jazz.* Philadelphia: American Folklore Society, 1954.

Meyers, Frederic. "The Knights of Labor in the South," *Southern Economic Journal,* VI (1940), 479.

Michaels, Ken. "Wait Up, Gene," *Chicago Tribune Magazine* (May 28, 1967), 18.

Mikeal, Judith. "Mother Mary Jones: The Labor Movement's Impious Joan of Arc," master's thesis. Chapel Hill: University of North Carolina, 1965.

Miller, Charles. "Music: Collection of Folklore," *New Republic,* CXVII (Nov. 17, 1947), 34.

Montell, William Lynwood. *The Saga of Coe Ridge.* Knoxville: University of Tennessee Press, 1970.

Mooney, Fred. *Struggle in the Coal Fields.* Morgantown: West Virginia University Library, 1967.

Morris, Alton C. *Folksongs of Florida.* Gainesville: University of Florida Press, 1950.

Morris, Homer L. *The Plight of the Bituminous Coal Miner.* Philadelphia: University of Pennsylvania Press, 1934.

Morris, James O. *Conflict within the AFL.* Ithaca: New York State School of Industrial and Labor Relations, 1958.

"Mother Jones: An Impression," *New Republic*, II (Feb. 20, 1915), 73.

"Mother Jones' Boys Gather at Bier of Valiant Leader of Labor's Cause," *Federation News* (Dec. 20, 1930), 2.

"Mother Jones, the Industrial Crusader, after a Century of Life, Succumbs to Death," *Federation News* (Dec. 6, 1930), 1.

"Muhlenbergers to Honor 'Sixteen Tons' and 'Admiral' Travis Friday, June 29," [Central City, Ky.] *Times-Argus* (June 28, 1956), 1.

Munn, Robert F. *The Coal Industry in America: A Bibliography and Guide to Studies*. Morgantown: West Virginia University Library, 1965.

Muste, A. J. *The Essays of A. J. Muste,* ed. Nat Hentoff. Indianapolis: Bobbs-Merrill, 1967.

Neal, Willard. "Writing Songs at Five Points," *Atlanta Journal Magazine* (Apr. 8, 1934), 7.

Nelson, Wilbur A. *The Southern Tennessee Coal Field,* Bulletin 33 A. Nashville: Department of Conservation, Division of Geology, 1925.

Nevins, Nathan. "Reviews: *Red Song Book,*" *Worker Musician,* I (Dec., 1932), 13.

"New Pop Music Brew," *Cash Box,* XXVIII (June 3, 1967).

Niles, Abbe. "Ballads, Songs and Snatches," *Bookman,* LXVI-LXVIII (Feb., 1928–Jan., 1929).

———. Introduction, in *Blues: An Anthology,* ed. William C. Handy. New York: Albert & Charles Boni, 1926, 9.

Nolan, Paul T. *Three Plays by J. W. (Capt. Jack) Crawford*. The Hague: Mouton, 1966.

Norton, Helen G. "Feudalism in West Virginia," *Nation,* CXXXIII (Aug. 12, 1931), 154.

Nyden, Paul. "Coal Miners, 'Their' Union, and Capital," *Science and Society,* XXXIV (1970), 194.

O'Connor, Francis V. *Federal Art Patronage 1933 to 1943*. College Park: University of Maryland Art Gallery, 1966.

Odum, Howard W. "Folk-Song and Folk-Poetry as Found in the Secular Songs of the Southern Negroes," *Journal of American Folklore,* XXIV (1911), 386.

———, and Guy B. Johnson. *Negro Workaday Songs*. Chapel Hill: University of North Carolina Press, 1926.

"Officials Fear Renewal of Campus Violence," *Champaign-Urbana Courier* (Sept. 2, 1970), 2.

O'Hanlon, Thomas. "Anarchy Threatens the Kingdom of Coal," *Fortune,* LXXXIII (Jan., 1971), 78.

"Old Time Tune Artists Given Test Recordings," *Talking Machine World,* XXI (Oct., 1925), 71.

469

Oliver, Paul. *Blues Fell This Morning*. London: Cassell, 1960.

———. *Conversation with the Blues*. London: Cassell, 1965.

———. *Screening the Blues*. London: Cassell, 1968.

———. *The Story of the Blues*. London: Cresset Press, 1969.

Oster, Harry. *Living Country Blues*. Detroit: Gale, 1969.

A Paint Creek miner. "Mother Jones," *International Socialist Review*, XIV (Apr., 1914), 604.

Panassie, Hugues. *Le Jazz Hot*. Paris: Correa, 1934.

Pankake, Jon. "Mike Seeger: The Style of Tradition," *Sing Out*, XIV (July, 1964), 6.

Paredes, Américo. *"With His Pistol in His Hand": A Border Ballad and Its Hero*. Austin: University of Texas Press, 1958.

Peabody, Charles. "Notes on Negro Music," *Journal of American Folklore*, XVI (1903), 148.

Perrow, E. C. "Songs and Rhymes from the South," *Journal of American Folklore*, XXVI (1913), 165.

Pew, Marlen. "Shop Talk at Thirty," *Editor & Publisher*, LXIII (Dec. 6, 1930), 56.

Posey, Thomas E. "The Labor Movement in West Virginia," thesis. Madison: University of Wisconsin, 1948.

Potter, Jack M., and others, ed. *Peasant Society: A Reader*. Boston: Little, Brown, 1967.

The Poverty War Is Dead (Dillons Run DLP 103), unsigned liner notes.

Powell, J. C. *The American Siberia*. Chicago: H. J. Smith, 1891; reprinted, New York: Arno Press, 1969.

"Pratt Mines Accident," *United Mine Workers Journal* (June 4, 1891), 4.

Prison and Mountain Songs. New York: Shapiro, Bernstein, 1959.

Ramsey, Frederick, Jr. Brochure notes to *Sonny Terry: Harmonica and Vocal Solos* (Folkways FA 2035).

[Randolph, Vance]. *The Autobiography of a Pimp*. Girard, Kan.: Haldeman-Julius, ca. 1920.

———. *Ozark Folksongs*, 4 vols. Columbia: State Historical Society of Missouri, 1950.

Read, Oliver, and Walter Welch. *From Tin Foil to Stereo*. Indianapolis: Bobbs-Merrill, 1959.

"Recordings Preserve Colorful Anthracite Folk Ballads," *United Mine Workers Journal* (Jan. 15, 1949), 6.

Redfield, Robert. *Papers*, ed. Margaret Park Redfield, I: *Human Nature and the Study of Society*. Chicago: University of Chicago Press, 1962.

Reisner, Robert. *The Literature of Jazz*. New York: New York Public Library, 1954.

Reuss, Richard A. "American Folklore and Left-Wing Politics: 1927-1957," thesis. Bloomington: Indiana University, 1971.

———. "Woody Guthrie and His Folk Tradition," *Journal of American Folklore*, LXXXIII (1970), 273.

Richardson, Ethel Park. *American Mountain Songs*. New York: Greenberg, 1927.

Richmond, W. Edson. "Book Review: *American Folksongs of Protest*," *Journal of American Folklore*, LXVII (1954), 96.

———. "Record Review: *American Industrial Folksongs*," *Journal of American Folklore*, LXXI (1958), 179.

Rickaby, Franz. *Ballads and Songs of the Shanty-Boy*. Cambridge: Harvard University Press, 1926.

Riesman, David. *Individualism Reconsidered, and Other Essays*. Glencoe, Ill.: Free Press, 1954.

Rinzler, Ralph. Brochure notes to *Old Time Music at Clarence Ashley's* (Folkways FA 2355) and *Old Time Music . . . Part Two* (Folkways FA 2359).

———. Liner notes to *Doc Watson and Son* (Vanguard VRS 9170).

———. "Some Considerations Regarding the Musical Style of Dock Boggs," supplementary notes to brochure for *Dock Boggs* (Folkways FA 2351).

———, and Norman Cohen. *Uncle Dave Macon: A Bio-Discography*. Los Angeles: John Edwards Memorial Foundation, 1970.

Ritchie, Jean. Liner notes to *Clear Waters Remembered* (Sire SES 97014).

———. Liner notes to *A Time for Singing* (Warner Brothers W 1592).

———. *Singing Family of the Cumberlands*. New York: Oxford University Press, 1955.

Rooney, Jim. *Bossmen: Bill Monroe and Muddy Waters*. New York: Dial, 1971.

Rosenberg, Bruce. *The Folksongs of Virginia: A Checklist*. Charlottesville: University of Virginia Press, 1969.

Ross, Malcolm. *Machine Age in the Hills*. New York: Macmillan, 1933.

Ross, Mike. "Life Style of the Coal Miner," *United Mine Workers Journal* (July 1, 1970), 12; reprinted in *Papers and Proceedings of the National Conference on Medicine and the Federal Coal Mine Health and Safety Act of 1969*. Washington: The Conference, 1970, 243.

Roy, Andrew. *A History of the Coal Miners of the United States*, 3rd ed. Columbus, Ohio: J. L. Trauger, 1907.

Russell, Oland. "Floyd Collins in the Sand Cave," *American Mercury*, XLII (Nov., 1937), 289.

Russell, Tony. *Blacks, Whites and Blues*. London: Studio Vista, 1970.

Rust, Brian. *Jazz Records A-Z 1897-1931*, 2nd ed. Hatch End, Middlesex, England: Brian Rust, 1962.

Sackheim, Eric. *The Blues Line*. New York: Grossman, 1969.

Sandburg, Carl. *The American Songbag*. New York: Harcourt, Brace, 1927.

Sandburg, Helga. *Sweet Music*. New York: Dial Press, 1963.

Sargent, Helen Child, and George Lyman Kittredge. *The English and Scottish Popular Ballads*. Boston: Houghton Mifflin, 1904.

Scarborough, Dorothy. "The 'Blues' as Folk-Songs," in *Publications of the Texas Folk-Lore Society*, no. II, ed. J. Frank Dobie. Austin: The Society, 1923, 52.

————. *On the Trail of Negro Folk-Songs*. Cambridge: Harvard University Press, 1925.

Schatz, Philip. "Songs of the Negro Worker," *New Masses*, VI (May, 1930), 6.

Seeber, R. Clifford. "A History of Anderson County, Tennessee," master's thesis. Knoxville: University of Tennessee, 1928.

Seeger, Charles. "The Folkness of the Non-Folk vs. the Non-Folkness of the Folk," in *Folklore and Society*, ed. Bruce Jackson. Hatboro, Pa.: Folklore Associates, 1966, 1.

Seeger, Mike. Brochure notes to four LPs: *Excerpts from Interviews with Dock Boggs* (Folkways FH 5458), *Dock Boggs* (Folkways FA 2351), *Dock Boggs: Volume 2* (Folkways FA 2392), *Dock Boggs: Volume 3* (Asch AH 3903).

Seeger, Pete. "The Coal Creek Rebellion," *Sing Out*, V (Summer, 1955), 19.

————. "Record Review: 'Sixteen Tons,'" *Sing Out*, VI (Winter, 1956), 40.

Shaner, Dolph. *The Story of Joplin*. New York: Stratford House, 1948.

Sharp, Cecil. *English Folk-Songs from the Southern Appalachians*, 2 vols. London: Oxford University Press, 1932.

Sharp, James A. "The Entrance of the Farmers' Alliance into Tennessee Politics," *East Tennessee Historical Society's Publications*, IX (1937), 77.

————. "The Farmers' Alliance and the People's Party in Tennessee," *East Tennessee Historical Society's Publications*, X (1938), 91.

Shayon, Robert Lewis. "A 'No' to Question-Begging," *Saturday Review*, LI (Dec. 14, 1968), 53.

Shellans, Herbert. *Folk Songs of the Blue Ridge Mountains*. New York: Oak Publications, 1968.

Shelton, Robert. *The Josh White Song Book*. Chicago: Quadrangle, 1963.

————, and Burt Goldblatt. *The Country Music Story*. Indianapolis: Bobbs-Merrill, 1966.

Shepard, Leslie. *The Broadside Ballad*. London: Herbert Jenkins, 1962.

Sherrill, Robert G. "West Virginia Miracle: The Black Lung Rebellion," *Nation*, CCVIII (Apr. 28, 1969), 531.

Sherwood, John. "Machines Only Music Left in Mines, Folklorist Finds," *Washington Evening Star* (Oct. 19, 1965), sec. B, 1.

Silber, Irwin. *Lift Every Voice.* New York: People's Artists, 1953.

Simon, Morris. "Labor Leader 70 Years, Founder of CLU, George Ford Still Alive at 82," *Knoxville News-Sentinel* (Sept. 6, 1937).

Simonin, Louis Laurent. *Underground Life,* tr. H. W. Bristow. New York: D. Appleton, 1869.

Simpson, Claude M., Jr. "Book Review: *American Folksongs of Protest,*" *Southern Folklore Quarterly,* XVIII (1954), 197.

"Sixteen Tons and Deeper in Debt," *March of Labor,* VII (Dec., 1955), 21.

" 'Sixteen Tons,' Hit Parade Topper, Amazes DU Song Authority," [Denver] *Rocky Mountain News* (Dec. 4, 1955), 17.

Sizemore, Asher. *Fireside Treasures,* 1936 ed. Louisville, Ky.: Asher Sizemore, 1935.

————. *Hearth and Home Songs,* 1935 ed. Louisville, Ky.: Asher Sizemore, 1934.

Smith, Charles Edward. "Collecting Hot," *Esquire,* I (Feb., 1934), 96.

Smith, Harry. Brochure notes to *American Folk Music* (Folkways FA 2953-55).

Smith, Stephen W. "Collecting Hot," in *Jazzmen,* ed. Frederick Ramsey, Jr., and Charles Edward Smith. New York: Harcourt, Brace, 1939, 287.

Smith, Vern. "From an Era That Has Passed: Mother Jones," *Labor Defender,* VI (Jan., 1931), 16.

"Songs of the Homeland," *Talking Machine World,* XX (May, 1924), 57 [advertisement].

Souvenir of Company C, First Regiment of National Guard, State of Tennessee. St. Louis: Woodward & Tiernan Printing Company, 1893.

Sowing on the Mountain. Knoxville: Highlander Research and Education Center, Nov., 1967 [eleven-page mimeographed songbook].

Spaeth, Sigmund. *Weep Some More, My Lady.* New York: Doubleday, Page, 1927.

Spargo, John W. "Book Review: *Coal Dust on the Fiddle,*" *Journal of American Folklore,* LVII (1944), 91.

Spivey, Victoria. "My Porter Grainger," *Record Research,* no. 79 (Oct., 1966), 8.

Spottswood, Richard. "An Interview with Bill Clifton," *Bluegrass Unlimited,* II (Mar.-May, 1968).

Stachel, Jack. "Lessons of Two Recent Strikes," *Communist,* XI (June, 1932), 527.

"Starr Co. Sending Expedition to Make Records of Melodies of Hopi Indians," *Talking Machine World,* XXII (June, 1926), 16.

Stewart-Baxter, Derrick. *Ma Rainey and the Classic Blues Singers.* London: Studio Vista, 1970.

Straube, L. P. "Editor Straube Speaks on Mother Jones," *Federation News* (Dec. 20, 1930), 3.

Stringfield, Lamar. "America and Her Music," *University of North Carolina Extension Bulletin,* X (Mar., 1931), 21.

"Students Teach West Virginia Class," *Brookwood Review,* XI (Dec., 1932), 4.

Szwed, John. "Musical Adaptation among Afro-Americans," *Journal of American Folklore,* LXXXII (1969), 112.

Taft, Phillip. "Mother Jones, Pioneer Woman of Labor," paper read at Springfield, Ill., Nov. 21, 1970. Notes in Green files.

Tamony, Peter. "Bop: The Word," *Jazz,* I (Spring, 1959), 114.

Taubman, Howard. "Records: The Smokies," *New York Times* (Aug. 31, 1941), sec. 9, 6.

"Ten Thousand Attend Merle Travis Day," [Central City, Ky.] *Messenger* (July 5, 1956), 1.

Tennessee Coal, Iron & Railroad Company. *Annual Report for the Fiscal Year Ending January 31, 1890.* Nashville: 1890.

—————. *Annual Report for the Fiscal Year Ending January 31, 1891.* Nashville: 1891.

—————. *Annual Report for the Fiscal Year Ending January 31, 1892.* Nashville: 1892.

—————. *Annual Report for the Fiscal Year Ending January 31, 1893.* Nashville: 1893.

—————. *Tennessee Coal, Iron & Railroad Company.* Birmingham: 1897.

"Theater for Miners," *Dramatic Mirror,* LXXX (Aug. 7, 1919), 1227.

Thomas, Gates. "South Texas Negro Work-Songs," in *Rainbow in the Morning,* Publications of the Texas Folklore Society, no. V, ed. J. Frank Dobie. Hatboro, Pa.: Folklore Associates, 1965, 154.

Thomas, H. Glyn. "The Highlander Folk School," *Tennessee Historical Quarterly,* XXIII (1964), 358.

Thomas, Jean. "The American Folk Song Festival," *Register of the Kentucky Historical Society,* LXV (1967), 20.

—————. *Ballad Makin' in the Mountains of Kentucky.* New York: Henry Holt, 1939.

—————. *The Singin' Fiddler of Lost Hope Hollow.* New York: E. P. Dutton, 1938.

Thomas, Will. "Some Current Folk-Songs of the Negro and Their Economic

Interpretation" (1912), in *Rainbow in the Morning,* Publications of the Texas Folklore Society, no. V, ed. J. Frank Dobie. Hatboro, Pa.: Folklore Associates, 1965.

Thompson, E. P. "English Trade Unionism and Other Labour Movements before 1790," *Bulletin of the Society for the Study of Labour History,* no. 17 (Autumn, 1968), 19.

Thompson, Stith. "Book Review: *American Folksongs of Protest,*" *American Historical Review,* LIX (1954), 454.

Thrush, Paul W. *A Dictionary of Mining, Mineral, and Related Terms.* Washington: Department of Interior, Bureau of Mines, 1968.

Tippett, Tom. "Black Star Mothers," *Labor Age,* XIX (Sept., 1930), 14.

―――. *Horse Shoe Bottoms.* New York: Harper, 1935.

―――. *Mill Shadows.* Katonah, N.Y.: Brookwood Labor College, 1932.

―――. *When Southern Labor Stirs.* New York: Cape & Smith, 1931.

Todd, Alden. "The Horror at Monongah," *United Mine Workers Journal* (Dec. 1, 1957), 14.

Todd, Arthur Cecil. *The Cornish Miner in America.* Truro, Cornwall: D. Bradford Barton, 1967.

Todd, Laurence. "Mother Jones, 100 May 1, Honored by Labor," *Labor's News* (May 10, 1930), 6.

Toffler, Alvin. "Convict Miners in Tennessee: Briceville Saw Them 67 Years Ago," *United Mine Workers Journal* (Aug. 1, 1958), 8.

―――. "Joe Glazer, Union Songster . . . ," *Labor's Daily* (Apr. 27, 1955), 3.

"Top repertoire personnel at Capitol records . . . examine first record and album . . . ," *National Hillbilly News* (Nov.-Dec., 1947), 21 [photograph].

Townsend, Ed. "People at Work: 'Sixteen Tons' Impact," *Christian Science Monitor* (Jan. 7, 1956), 9.

Traum, Happy. *Finger-Picking Styles for Guitar.* New York: Oak Publications, 1966.

Travis, Merle. "I Have a Sick Sister in Texas," in *Country and Western Keepsake,* ed. Larry Moeller. Nashville: Moeller Talent, 1967.

―――. *Merle Travis Hit Parade Folio No. 1.* Hollywood: American Music, 1956.

―――. "The Saga of 'Sixteen Tons,' " *United Mine Workers Journal* (Dec. 1, 1955), 5.

Trillin, Calvin. "U.S. Journal: Jeremiah, Kentucky. A Stranger with a Camera," *New Yorker,* XLV (Apr. 12, 1969), 178.

Turner, Arlin. "George W. Cable as a Social Reformer," in *The Silent South* (reprint). Montclair, N.J.: Patterson Smith, 1969.

"Two Miners Held on Frameup in Kentucky," *Daily Worker* (Oct. 29, 1935), 1.

Vanover, Frederick D. *James Taylor Adams*. Louisville, Ky.: Dixieana Press, 1937.

Vechten, Carl Van. "The Black Blues," *Vanity Fair,* XXIV (Aug., 1925), 57.

———. "The Great American Composer," *Vanity Fair,* VIII (Apr., 1917), 75.

———. " 'Moanin' wid a Sword in Ma Han',' " *Vanity Fair,* XXV (Feb., 1926), 61.

Vernon, Bill. "Country Music News from the U.S.A.," *Country News and Views,* VI (Jan., 1968), 3.

Victor Records of Old Familiar Tunes and Novelties. Camden, N.J.: RCA Victor Company, 1931.

Victor Records Supplement, Dec., 1925. Camden, N.J.: Victor Talking Machine Company, 1925.

Vreede, Max. *The Paramount 12/13000 Series*. London: Storyville Publications, forthcoming.

Wakefield, Dan. *Supernation at Peace and War*. Boston: Little, Brown, 1968.

Wallace, Anthony F. C. *The Death and Rebirth of the Seneca*. New York: Knopf, 1969.

———. "Revitalization Movements," *American Anthropologist,* LVIII (1956), 264.

Walsh, Jim. "Vernon Dalhart," *Hobbies,* LXV (May-Dec., 1960).

Ward, Robert, and William Rogers. *Labor Revolt in Alabama: The Great Strike of 1894*. University: University of Alabama Press, 1965.

Ware, Norman J. *The Labor Movement in the United States 1860-1895*. New York: Appleton, 1929.

Warren, Robert Penn. *The Cave*. New York: Random House, 1959.

Webb, W. C. "Celebration of Convicts' Departure at Briceville," *United Mine Workers Journal* (July 28, 1892), 5.

———. "District 19," *UMWJ* (May 28, 1891), 5.

———. "From the Districts," *UMWJ* (July 30, 1891), 1.

———. "Kentucky and Tennessee," *UMWJ* (July 16, 1891), 5.

———. ". . . Scene of the Late Convict Limbo," *UMWJ* (Nov. 19, 1891), 6.

———. "Strike of Boy Trappers at Coal Creek," *UMWJ* (Sept. 3, 1891), 4.

Welding, Pete. "Mail," *Living Blues,* I (Autumn, 1970), 38.

Werstein, Irving. *Labor's Defiant Lady*. New York: Crowell, 1969.

476

West, Don. "Georgia Wants Me — Dead or Alive," *New Masses,* XI (June, 1934), 15.

————. [Letter on Gilford], in Michael Gold, "Change the World," *Daily Worker* (Nov. 8, 1935), 7.

West, George P. "Correspondence: Mother Jones among the Twelve," *Nation,* CXV (July 19, 1922), 70.

West, Hedy. Brochure notes to *Old Times and Hard Times* (Folk-Legacy FSA 32).

————. *Hedy West Songbook.* Erlangen, West Germany: Rolf Gekeler, 1969.

————. Liner notes to *Hedy West* (Vanguard VRS 9124).

West Virginia State Federation of Labor. *Proceedings of the Thirteenth Annual Convention.* Charleston: The Federation, 1920.

"Whatever Happened to Love? Coal Mining Song No. 1 on Hit Parade . . . ," *News from BMI* (ca. Dec., 1955) [five-page mimeographed release].

"What Made 'Sixteen Tons' a Hit," *Cowboy Songs,* no. 46 (May, 1956), 4.

Whelan, Pete, and Bill Givens. Liner notes to *Really the Country Blues* (Origin Jazz Library OJL 2).

White, Lucien H. "Fifteenth Infantry's First Band Concert and Dance," *New York Age* (Jan. 28, 1922), 1.

White, Newman Ivey. *American Negro Folk-Songs.* Cambridge: Harvard University Press, 1928.

Whitten, Norman E., Jr., and John Szwed. *Afro-American Anthropology.* New York: Free Press, 1970.

Wiebel, Arthur V. *Biography of a Business.* Fairfield, Ala.: Tennessee Coal & Iron Division — U.S. Steel Corporation, 1960.

"The Wild Birds Do Whistle," *Time,* LXVI (Dec. 19, 1955), 78.

Wilgus, D. K. *Anglo-American Folksong Scholarship since 1898.* New Brunswick, N.J.: Rutgers University Press, 1959.

————. "Billy the Kid," *Western Folklore,* forthcoming 1971.

————. "A Catalogue of American Folk-Songs on Commercial Records," master's thesis. Columbus: Ohio State University, 1947.

————. " 'Don't Go Down in the Mine, Dad,' " *Western Folklore,* IX (1950), 266.

————. "Folksong and Folksong Scholarship, Part IV," in *A Good Tale and a Bonnie Tune,* Publications of the Texas Folklore Society, no. XXXII, ed. Mody C. Boatright and others. Dallas: Southern Methodist University Press, 1964, 229.

————. "The Oldest (?) Text of 'Edward,' " *Western Folklore,* XXV (1966), 77.

————. "On the Record," *Kentucky Folklore Record,* VII (1961), 126.

————. "Record Review: *American Industrial Folksongs,*" *Kentucky Folklore Record,* III (1957), 41.

————. "Record Reviews: Revival and Traditional," *Journal of American Folklore,* LXXXI (1968), 173.

Wilkison, Betty. "Gift Recorder Made to Blind Ballad Writer," *Atlanta Constitution* (Dec. 17, 1951), 18.

Wilson, Edmund. *The American Earthquake.* Garden City, N.Y.: Doubleday, 1958.

————. *The American Jitters.* New York: Scribner's, 1932.

Wilson, Walter. "Historical Coal Creek Rebellion Brought an End to Convict Miners in Tennessee," *United Mine Workers Journal* (Nov. 1, 1938), 10.

Winkelmann, Heinrich. *Der Bergbau in der Kunst.* Essen: Verlag Glückauf GmbH, 1958.

Wolf, Eric R. *Peasants.* Englewood Cliffs, N.J.: Prentice-Hall, 1966.

Wolff, Bill. "For Cisco Houston — the End of the Road," *Sing Out,* XI (Oct., 1961), 8.

Workers Music League. *Red Song Book.* New York: Workers Library Publishers, 1932.

Yarborough, Willard. "Miners' Guns Finally Helped End Convict Lease Law," *Knoxville News-Sentinel* (Oct. 30, 1966), sec. F, 3.

Yoder, Don. "Folklife," in *Our Living Traditions,* ed. Tristram P. Coffin. New York: Basic Books, 1968, 47.

————. *Pennsylvania Spirituals.* Lancaster: Pennsylvania Folklife Society, 1961.

Yorke, Dane. "The Rise and Fall of the Phonograph," *American Mercury,* XXVII (Sept., 1932), 1.

Young, Otis E., Jr. *Western Mining.* Norman: University of Oklahoma Press, 1970.

Zimmerman, Jane. "The Penal Reform Movement in the South during the Progressive Era, 1890-1917," *Journal of Southern History,* XVII (1951), 462.

List of Interviews

The symbol (T) indicates that a tape-recorded interview is in my possession; other interviews are represented by field notes, correspondence, and memorabilia in my files.

Luther F. Addington. Wise, Va., Aug. 26, 1961.

E. A. "Tony" Alderman. Washington, D.C., June 3, 1962; Dec. 31, 1962 (T); Jan. 9, 1966 (T); July 5, 1969.

John W. Allen. Carbondale, Ill., Feb. 16, 1960.

Ned C. Arbuckle. Tracy City, Tenn., Oct. 10, 1970 (T).

Moe Asch. New York City, Aug. 6, 1969.

Clarence Tom Ashley. Shouns, Tenn., Aug. 15, 1961.

Green Bailey. Trapp, Ky., May 27, 1969.

Bunnie Baugh. Drakesboro, Ky., Aug. 2, 1961 (T).

Dock Boggs. Urbana, Ill., Dec. 8, 1964; New York City, June 18, 1965.

Bill Bolick. Greensboro, N.C., Mar. 10, 1963; Aug. 16, 1963.

Ben Botkin. Croton-on-Hudson, N.Y., Jan. 3, 1965.

Charles Bowman. Union City, Ga., Aug. 10, 1961 (T).

Elbert Bowman. Johnson City, Tenn., Aug. 8, 1963 (T).

Polk C. Brockman. Atlanta, Ga., Aug. 11, 1961 (T); Aug. 22, 1963.

Monroe Brinson. Charlotte, N.C., Aug. 19, 1963.

John Brophy. Washington, D.C., Mar. 21, 1960.

Fleming Brown. Glen Ellyn, Ill., May 3, 1964.

Dick Burnett. Monticello, Ky., Aug. 17, 1962 (T).

Florence Calaway. Malverne, Pa., June 7, 1959.

479

Cliff Carlisle. Lexington, Ky., Aug. 18, 1962 (T).

Maybelle Carter. Nashville, Tenn., Aug. 31, 1961 (T); Madison, Tenn., Sept. 9, 1962 (T).

Johnny Cash. Urbana, Ill., July 25, 1963.

Ted Chestnut. Chicago, Ill., Feb. 1, 1970; Aug. 31, 1970 (T).

Bill Clifton. Charlottesville, Va., Mar. 12, 1963.

Bernice Coleman. Princeton, W.Va., July 31, 1970.

Dorsey Dixon. East Rockingham, N.C., Aug. 20, 1961 (T); Aug. 8, 1962 (T).

Lonia Doulen. Arjay, Ky., Aug. 27, 1961.

Agnes Martocci Douty. Chicago, Ill., May 16, 1959.

Jimmy Driftwood. Urbana, Ill., Nov. 17, 1961 (T).

Sleepy John Estes. Urbana, Ill., Apr. 12, 1962.

Ike Everly. Nashville, Tenn., Aug. 3, 1963.

Billy Faier. Berkeley, Calif., Jan. 31, 1958.

Harvey Fink. Watertown, Wis., May 7, 1961.

Bob Forrester. La Follette, Tenn., Aug. 28, 1961.

Garley Foster. Taylorsville, N.C., Aug. 12, 1962 (T).

Curly Fox. Nashville, Tenn., Aug. 3, 1963.

Irene Spain Futrelle. Atlanta, Ga., Aug. 8, 1961 (T); Aug. 22, 1963; Mabelton, Ga., Nov. 9, 1969 (T).

Bob Garland. Arjay, Ky., Aug. 27, 1961 (T).

Jim Garland. Washougal, Wash., May 31, 1961 (T).

Joe Glazer. San Francisco, Calif., June 16, 1956; Sept. 29, 1956; Nov. 20, 1957.

Edna Gossage. Crossville, Tenn., Aug. 29, 1961 (T).

Lou Gottlieb. San Francisco, Calif., Apr. 15, 1958.

John Greenway. San Francisco, Calif., Feb. 17, 1956; July 20, 1958.

Sarah Ogan Gunning. Detroit, Mich., Jan. 2, 1964 (T); Mar. 3, 1964 (T).

Hattie Hader. Crumpler, N.C., Aug. 13, 1962; Aug. 9, 1963.

Emory Hamilton. Wise, Va., Aug. 26, 1961.

John Hartford. Nashville, Tenn., June 16, 1967; Reseda, Calif., Nov. 26, 1968.

Mary Harvey. Beckley, W.Va., Aug. 14, 1962 (T).

Will Roy Hearne. Los Angeles, Calif., Dec. 31, 1956.

Sam Hinton. Berkeley, Calif., June 28, 1958.

Bill Hopkins. Boone, N.C., Aug. 9, 1962 (T).

Roy Horton. Nashville, Tenn., Sept. 8, 1962; New York City, Aug. 7, 1969.

Walter Hughes. Cranberry, N.C., Aug. 14, 1963 (T).

Mississippi John Hurt. Berkeley, Calif., June 26, 1964.

Robert Hyland. Springfield, Ohio, Aug. 19, 1962.

Aunt Molly Jackson. Sacramento, Calif., Jan. 12, 1958 (T); Apr. 5, 1958 (T).

Albert M. James. Palmer, Tenn., Oct. 10, 1970.

Janette Carter Jett. Maces Springs, Va., Aug. 25, 1961.

Robert Johnson. Urbana, Ill., Feb. 24, 1963 (T).

Rosa Lee Carson Johnson. Decatur, Ga., Aug. 27, 1963 (T).

Curtis Jones. Urbana, Ill., Oct. 28, 1961.

Grandpa Jones. New York City, June 20, 1965.

Buell Kazee. Urbana, Ill., Mar. 21, 1969 (T); Winchester, Ky., June 14, 1970.

Luis Kemnitzer. El Sobrante, Calif., May 10, 1958; May 29, 1961.

Bradley Kincaid. Springfield, Ohio, Aug. 21, 1962 (T).

Cecil Kinzer. Fries, Va., Aug. 24, 1961 (T).

Freeman Kitchens. Drake, Ky., Aug. 6, 1961.

Lucile Kohn. New York City, Mar. 7, 1960.

George Korson. Brown County State Park, Ind., July 29, 1962.

Thomas R. Levy. New York City, July 22, 1971.

David McCarn. Stanley, N.C., Aug. 19, 1961 (T); Aug. 18, 1963.

Brad McCuen. New York City, June 3, 1963.

Kirk and Sam McGee. Nashville, Tenn., Aug. 5, 1961.

Brownie McGhee. Urbana, Ill., Apr. 26, 1961.

Clayton McMichen. Louisville, Ky., July 31, 1961; Urbana, Ill., May 8, 1965; Battletown, Ky., May 25, 1969.

Dorris Macon. Nashville, Tenn., Aug. 5, 1961.

Charlie Marshall. Berkeley, Calif., June 30, 1967.

Asa Martin. Irvine, Ky., May 26, 1969 (T); Sept. 4, 1969 (T); June 16, 1970.

Gladys Carter Millard. Maces Springs, Va., Aug. 25, 1961.

Bill Monroe. Chicago, Ill., Feb. 3, 1963; New Tripoli, Pa., Aug. 28, 1968.

David Morris. Pipestem, W.Va., Aug. 1, 1970.

Naomi Mullins. Big Laurel, Va., Aug. 26, 1961.

Dick Parman. Corbin, Ky., Sept. 6, 1969 (T).

Callie Payne. Landis, N.C., Aug. 9, 1962.

Charlie Poole, Jr. Johnson City, Tenn., Aug. 13, 1962 (T).

Mose Rager. Central City, Ky., Aug. 2, 1961 (T).

Vance Randolph. Fayetteville, Ark., Oct. 26, 1963.

Arville Reed. Pipestem, W.Va., Aug. 2, 1970.

Lloyd Richardson. Timbo, Ark., Jan. 1, 1962 (T).

Ralph Rinzler. Cambridge, Mass., Nov. 19, 1966.

Doc Roberts. Richmond, Ky., May 26, 1969 (T).

James Roberts. Lexington, Ky., June 13, 1970 (T).

Oda Roberts. Laager, Tenn., Oct. 10, 1970.

Earl Robinson. Chicago, Ill., Jan. 30, 1965 (T).

Earl Scruggs. Scottsville, Ky., Aug. 4, 1961; Madison, Tenn., Sept. 9, 1962; Aug. 4, 1963.

Charles Seeger. Pacific Palisades, Calif., July 26, 1964; Santa Monica, Calif., Nov. 25, 1968.

Mike Seeger. San Francisco, Calif., June 30, 1960; Urbana, Ill., Oct. 29, 1962 (T); Nov. 19, 1963; New Freedom, Pa., Aug. 9, 1970.

Pete Seeger. Palo Alto, Calif., Oct. 5, 1956.

Richard Spottswood. Arlington, Va., Dec. 31, 1962; Jan. 10, 1966 (T).

Carl T. Sprague. Urbana, Ill., Apr. 8, 1964 (T).

Ralph and Carter Stanley. Chicago, Ill., Feb. 5, 1961.

Mr. & Mrs. Mark Starr. Long Island City, N.Y., June 12, 1959.

E. V. "Pop" Stoneman. Carmody Hills, Md., Dec. 29, 1962 (T).

Jimmie Tarlton. Phenix City, Ala., Aug. 25, 1963.

Tom Tippett. San Francisco, Calif., June 16, 1958; Seattle, Wash., June 3, 1961.

Welby Toomey. Lexington, Ky., May 27, 1969 (T); June 13, 1970.

Merle Travis. Van Nuys, Calif., Apr. 20, 1960; Chicago, Ill., Oct. 28, 1966; Nashville, Tenn., June 15, 1967; Washington, D.C., July 6, 1969.

Mr. & Mrs. Tom Troutman. Beckley, W.Va., Aug. 15, 1962 (T).

Alvin H. Vowell. Briceville, Tenn., Aug. 28, 1961 (T).

Dock Walsh. Millers Creek, N.C., Aug. 11, 1962 (T).

Jim Walsh. Vinton, Va., Aug. 5, 1962; Mar. 10, 1963.

Jay Watkins. San Francisco, Calif., Sept. 26, 1957.

Doc Watson. Deep Gap, N.C., Aug. 10, 1962 (T).

Luther Watson. Nashville, Tenn., Aug. 30, 1961.

Don West. Pipestem, W.Va., Aug. 2, 1970.

Hedy West. Urbana, Ill., Nov. 23, 1963.

Booker T. White. Urbana, Ill., Apr. 3, 1968.

John I. White. Westfield, N.J., Dec. 31, 1966.

Paul Whitter. Fries, Va., Aug. 24, 1961.

Big Joe Williams. Urbana, Ill., Mar. 23, 1962.

Robert Pete Williams. Urbana, Ill., Feb. 12, 1965.

List of Illustrations

Illustrative material obtained by me from individuals or institutions is identified by source. Additionally, names of photographers or artists and dates of their works, when known to me, are included. Material from published sources is identified here briefly with full citations in the bibliography. Graphic items such as LP covers and handbills in my collection are not identified beyond title. To the best of my knowledge most of the illustrations used here are not covered by current copyrights. Those that are so covered are used with permission of copyright holders. In cases where I have not learned names of photographers, artists, or publishers I shall appreciate additional credit-line data.

Index

490

499

501